The Trace of God

John D. Caputo, *series editor*

PERSPECTIVES IN
CONTINENTAL
PHILOSOPHY

Edited by EDWARD BARING
and PETER E. GORDON

The Trace of God
Derrida and Religion

FORDHAM UNIVERSITY PRESS
New York ▪ 2015

Fordham University Press has no responsibility for the persistence or accuracy of URLs for external or third-party Internet websites referred to in this publication and does not guarantee that any content on such websites is, or will remain, accurate or appropriate.

Fordham University Press also publishes its books in a variety of electronic formats. Some content that appears in print may not be available in electronic books.

Library of Congress Cataloging-in-Publication Data

The trace of God : Derrida and religion / edited by Edward Baring and Peter E. Gordon. — First edition.
        pages cm. — (Perspectives in Continental philosophy)
    Includes bibliographical references and index.
    ISBN 978-0-8232-6209-0 (cloth : alk. paper) — ISBN 978-0-8232-6210-6 (pbk. : alk. paper)
 1. Derrida, Jacques.   2. Religion.   I. Baring, Edward, 1980– editor.
    B2430.D484T73 2015
    194—dc23
                                                                    2014008413

Printed in the United States of America

17 16 15   5 4 3 2 1

First edition

Contents

The Trace of God

for Helen Tartar, in memoriam

Introduction

For over a quarter of a century, scholars have been interested in a set of questions broadly grouped under the heading "Derrida and Religion." Since the 1980s, when Derrida began to apply deconstructive insights directly to questions of faith and religion, the provocation of this engagement has remained of major concern across the humanities.[1] For this reason, it would be wrong to consider the question of Derrida and religion simply as a partial look at an important thinker, similar to, say, Hegel and aesthetics or Hume and politics, where research is limited to the overlap between the two: the conjunction in the phrase "Derrida and Religion" is not the compound limitation of the Boolean AND. Rather, as we shall see over the course of the volume, one of the merits of studying Derrida's engagement with religion is that it brings to the fore several central debates over the meaning of his work, as well as offering new insights into political and theoretical issues that extend well beyond the boundaries inside which religious questions are often confined.[2]

The greater share of the papers assembled in this volume were first presented, albeit in abbreviated form, at a conference on Derrida and religion that convened at Harvard University in March 2010.[3] The passage of time provided us opportunities to invite other scholars to contribute, and the fruits of our editorial labor are now assembled here in published form. The richness of the topic demands a number of perspectives. For this reason in this volume we bring together established voices in the field—like John Caputo, Hent de Vries, and Richard Kearney—along with younger scholars whose work has begun to make its impact felt. Moreover, we have gathered contributions from a range of different academic fields: religious studies, philosophy, literature, political theory, and history. Forming the core of this collection is a set of investigations about the ways in which Derrida drew upon and worked over resources from a number of religious traditions. The essays ask how Derrida situated his writings within broader debates about religion, how ideas and concepts from Judaism, Christianity, Islam, and atheism function in Derrida's texts. But this should not be seen as an attempt to find an "origin" for deconstruction or to settle some putative debate about Derrida's beliefs. As we will try to show over the course of the Introduction, the question of "Derrida and Religion" is complex in its indeterminacy, resisting easy answers to questions such as whether Derrida harbored any personal commitments of faith, whether he even believed in God, and the no less vexed questions concerning the status of his own identification, practical, institutional, or existential, with Judaism.

Derrida was born to a Sephardic Jewish family in the French colony of Algeria in 1930. He attended secondary school in Algiers, but to fulfill his ambition of being a writer, he responded to the call of the French metropolis. Derrida moved to France in 1949 to attend the Parisian Lycée Louis-le-Grand, and from there the École normale supérieure (ENS), an institute for higher learning in the Latin Quarter that has trained a large majority of the most important French philosophers, historians, and mathematicians, among others, over the last two centuries.

After passing the *agrégation* in philosophy (a state exam qualifying lycée teachers) in 1956, Derrida deferred his obligatory military service and traveled to America to spend a year studying at Harvard, during which time he married Marguerite Aucouturier, the sister of a fellow Normalien. Return from America marked the beginning of his military duties and he spent two years teaching in a military school in Koléa, Algeria. Once this service was over, Derrida accepted first a lycée post in Le Mans, then a year later a position at the Sorbonne. He taught at the Sorbonne as an assistant under Paul Ricoeur, Suzanne Bachelard, and Jean Wahl until 1964, when he was offered the post of agrégé-répétiteur at the ENS, which served as his base for the next twenty years.

Derrida was propelled into the intellectual limelight in the annus mirabilis of 1967, when he published three books: *Voice and Phenomenon*, *Writing and Difference*, and *Of Grammatology*. It was this final text that made Derrida's name, associating him with the dominant structuralism of the time, while introducing readers to a new and powerful way of reading texts: what Derrida called "deconstruction." His prominence in France brought him renown in America. Derrida's introduction to American academia was facilitated by his last minute addition to the 1966 Johns Hopkins structuralism conference that had as its major goal the promotion of French ideas in the United States. Over the next forty years, in addition to his positions in France—at the ENS and then, after 1984, the École des hautes études en sciences sociales (EHESS)—Derrida held a number of visiting appointments in American universities. His presence especially at Johns Hopkins, Yale, and later at UC Irvine, along with a growing group of scholars who drew on his work at these and other institutions, allowed the emergence of deconstruction as a significant school in American literary studies.[4]

The success of Derrida's writings in the English-speaking world elicited a backlash in the 1980s and '90s. Many criticized him for the obscurity of his writing and his seeming failure to follow the traditional rules of academic endeavor. Moreover, several worried that his philosophy was nihilistic, stymied political action, and encouraged quietism. Most famously, several prominent academics initiated a campaign to refuse Derrida an honorary degree at Cambridge University in 1992, which even as it was unable to achieve its immediate goal served as a rallying point for those who feared the impact of Derrida's ideas on academic study.

At about the time these criticisms gained prominence, Derrida's thought seemed to undergo a change, a change that, moreover, provided considerable counterevidence to those criticisms. Though the existence of "political," "ethical," and "religious" turns in Derrida's writing has been called into question, not least in this volume, in the last two decades of his life Derrida did address contemporary issues with greater directness, a development that helped make Derrida's work appealing to scholars in a number of disciplines beyond the literature departments where he had previously found most support.[5] By the time of his death from pancreatic cancer in 2004, Derrida's influence was noteworthy and widespread, reaching into legal studies, architecture, gender and race theory, political science, history, and religious studies, to name but a few.

Derrida's work became influential in a number of different academic disciplines chiefly because his philosophy unlocked new and productive strategies for reading texts. Right from his first published essays up until his last books, Derrida dedicated most of his writing to the close study of the texts of other thinkers: philosophers, playwrights, novelists, social theorists, and theologians, mostly from the Western tradition. Deconstruction is in this way disciplinarily nomadic. Engaging with this archive, Derrida hoped to uncover moments where texts seemed to transgress their own self-imposed limits. For instance, while Husserl had wanted to develop a "philosophy of presence," Derrida sought out those moments in Husserl's works where he was led to rely on an idea of absence.[6] Though Marx promulgated a materialist philosophy, Derrida drew attention to the moments in Marx's thought where he was compelled to draw on ghostly metaphors.[7]

In highlighting such moments of aporia, Derrida did not want to show up the frailties of some of the world's most important philosophers. Rather, it was his contention that these moments demonstrated the rigor of their thinking; here they followed the logic of their arguments even as it contradicted their deepest-held commitments. Further, these small cracks in their putatively coherent philosophical systems spoke against the possibility of such coherence and thus showed the limitations of the philosophical project as traditionally understood.

In his most famous deconstruction, from *Of Grammatology*, Derrida extended this critique to the entire Western metaphysical tradition. Despite the multitude of different philosophical schools, Derrida argued that European philosophy was unified by the privilege it granted the spoken voice over the written word.[8] This, Derrida claimed, pointed toward the deepest presuppositions of the tradition. According to Derrida, the philosophical tradition cleaved to a "logocentric" understanding of the relation between speech and writing: speech was extolled as the phenomenon of immediacy and purified "presence," while writing was condemned or merely tolerated as derivative, a supplement to the pure event of spoken meaning. Whereas the voice was supposed to have a direct intentional connection to what it signified, writing was the "sign of a sign," the written word signifying the spoken one; it enjoyed only a mediated relationship to the signified object.

Despite this asserted priority of the spoken over the written word, Derrida sought to bring attention to several moments in the history of philosophy when scholars had to appeal to metaphors of writing to explain even speech, metaphors that belied their attempts to present writing as derivative. Such moments suggested to Derrida that the instability and assumed secondarity of writing—produced by what he called "différance"—served as a better model for thinking than speech. Moreover, the movement of différance challenged any claims of absolute priority or any absolute foundation for philosophy. For this reason the recognition in literature of the power and limitations of metaphor, and its refusal to make definitive claims about the world, was more justifiable than the constant yearning of the philosopher to get at the world as it really is; hence the famous "deconstruction of literature and philosophy."

"A Determined Moment in the Total Movement of the Trace"

An overview of the connections and meeting points between Derrida's work and religion would be impossible in such a short introduction, even more so in view of Derrida's explicit engagement in his later life with the Western religious tradition, including texts by Kierkegaard, Saint Augustine, and Meister Eckhart. In the following few pages, we will merely present a brief overview of those strands in Derrida's thought that have made this topic so pressing and so complex.

In the classic formulations of deconstruction, Derrida seemed to oppose religion unilaterally. Derrida argued in *Of Grammatology* that the precedence of the voice, even in secular philosophy, was dependent upon the idea of an "infinite understanding" that could reach the signified immediately and declare it to be a stable reality, independent of the structures (and complications) of language.[9] In this way, "the époque of the sign," Derrida assured us, was "essentially theological."[10] Conversely, in one of his first elaborations of grammatology, Derrida urged a type of writing freed from the constraints of "metaphysics and theology." As Derrida noted in an early interview, différance "blocks every relationship to theology."[11] A central injunction of Derrida's thought (if there is such a thing) might be that we must free ourselves from the grip of the infinite, especially in its most canonical formulation: the God of much religious philosophy.

Furthermore, we can only claim to achieve an absolute ground, or assert the theological, to the extent that we are able to deny or efface the movement of différance. But since the movement of différance—or as Derrida sometimes said, the "trace"—is this effacing, the theological could no longer be thought of as an ultimate foundation. In a phrase that has achieved considerable currency in this collection as in others, Derrida stated that the theological was a "determined moment in the total movement of the trace."[12] Such claims have lent considerable support to the assumption that Derrida partook in a Nietzschean and antireligious tradition whose goal was the overthrowing of all religious belief.[13]

"Passing As an Atheist"

The presentation of Derrida's work as antithetical to religious thinking gains support from Derrida's most direct response to the religion question: he wrote in 1991 that he "rightly passed for an atheist."[14] But the words "rightly" and "pass" seem to pull in different directions, and the phrase gains its potency from its refusal to give a simple answer. The ambiguity in Derrida's statement can be heightened if we recall that an atheistic strand is interwoven into much of the religious tradition. Across its history, religious thinkers have concerned themselves with rejecting rival assertions of the divine, at times even more assiduously than denials of it. Indeed, at least to its victims, iconoclasm is often indistinguishable from atheism. For some, Derrida's thought seems to resemble this religious "atheism" more closely than the secular variant. His broader philosophical targets are reminiscent of the traditional antipodes of much religious thought, including humanism, which many religious philosophers see as Man's attempt to take the place of God, and human philosophical certainty, which has been criticized by those arguing for human humility in the face of the divine at least since Pascal. This aspect of Derrida's thought first attracted religious scholars in the early 1980s, including the "Death of God" theologian Thomas Altizer and the religious studies scholar Mark Taylor.[15]

More particularly, and especially during the early part of his reception, religious scholars observed that the strategies of Derrida's readings often seem to repeat, perhaps even mimic, those of the apophatic tradition, or negative theology.[16] Such a comparison suggested itself, in part, because of the ways in which Derrida emphasized the constant failure of language to secure stable meaning. Just as all images of the divine might be declared inadequate, Derrida's thought highlighted the difficulty and incompletion of any intentional relation between a word and its object. Meaning constantly threatened to slip away. Parallels to negative theology can also be seen in Derrida's treatment of this slippage itself. Derrida declared early on that différance was "neither a word nor a concept," and his attempt to refuse the hypostatization of différance by appealing to an open-ended list of non-synonymous substitutions—trace, pharmakon, supplement, hymen, etc.—resembled the representative modes of that tradition.[17] For many religious scholars, Derrida's thought thus can be read, like negative theology, as a reaction against dogmatic forms of the divine and for them it opens up the intriguing possibility of a phenomenon that John Caputo has called "a religion without religion."[18] But this reading of Derrida's thought has also drawn the attention of critics, like John Milbank, who see in the relentless attack on determined religious forms only a liability in deconstruction.[19]

The interpretation of deconstruction as a renewal or postmodern reprise of negative theology runs up against a second difficulty. Derrida seemed to dispense with the very element that has traditionally separated the religious rejection of idolatry from the atheist rejection of God. In the religious tradition, the smashing of idols was often performed in the name of a "true" God.[20] False idols were swept away because they did not live up to the divine. But one of the defining features of deconstruction has been its resistance to such a structuring antithesis of the genuine and the false, the divine and the merely idolatrous. The goal of grammatology is to redeem writing from the secondary status to which it had always been relegated and, more precisely, to complicate the categories of the "fallen," the "derivative," and so forth. In *Voice and Phenomenon* Derrida criticized Husserl for maintaining the structuring *ideal* of pure presence, against which all forms of indication are found wanting, even if he was never able to achieve that presence in his phenomenology.[21] Similarly, in his famous text "Structure, Sign, and Play in the Human Sciences," Derrida did not criticize Lévi-Strauss because he asserted the certainty of science, but rather because, while recognizing the impossibility of such certainty, he continued to measure the failings of actually existing science by it. Deconstructive readings often draw attention to the tension inherent in maintaining the teleological power of a principle whose possibility we refuse.[22]

Transposed onto the religious frame, then, Derrida would criticize the negative theologians for retaining a pristine idea of the divine in comparison to which they could declare the inadequacy of any of its earthly manifestations. Indeed, within his famous discussion of Levinas in "Violence and Metaphysics" (1964), Derrida explicitly rejected negative theology because it opposed a fallen human writing to a divine one, the central error he saw in logocentrism.[23] As he observed apropos the Christian mystic Meister Eckhart, "this negative theology is still a theology and, *in its literality at least*, it is concerned with liberating and acknowledging the ineffable transcendence of an infinite existent, 'Being above Being and superessential negation.' "[24]

"Dieu Déjà Se Contredit"

One way to confront this criticism would be to use Derrida's thought to reevaluate what the word "God" might mean. Unlike negative theology, which can often leave the idea of a transcendent God intact, the advantage of Derrida's thought would be that it changes the terms of the discussion. In many cases Derrida was careful to restrict the God that he opposed: when he challenged ideas of God, it was often the God of the "classical philosophers," of Hegel and Leibniz, or it was an attack on "*infinitist* theologies."[25] Derrida's constant reliance on such modifiers when discussing God or theology suggests that the criticism might not apply without them: what might be true of Hegel's God might not be so for other understandings. We would just have to change the way in which we think about the divine.[26]

Moreover, one can find certain moments in Derrida's early texts where he seems to affirm a particular understanding of God in positive terms: a

God who exhibits an essential "negativity" such that we are never given a divine law in a direct fashion we would be unable to resist.[27] As Derrida wrote, "there is no *simplicity* of God."[28] In a phrase that Hent de Vries chose as the epigraph for his book *Philosophy and the Turn to Religion*, Derrida asserted that "Dieu déjà se contredit" (God contradicts himself already). Derrida seemed to prioritize the notion of a God without simplicity, or later a God without power, in tension with itself.[29] In this line John Caputo has argued for a "weak God" and Richard Kearney has presented a God that "may be."

It is for this reason that, despite Derrida's attempts to assert the distinction, many scholars have seen in Derrida's "différance," which models this self-contradiction and tension, a new figure of the divine.[30] In *Origin of Geometry*, Derrida used the idea of God to model the constant deferring (*différant*) of the infinite idea,[31] and in his first published essay, "Force and Signification," he asked, "what we call God (that which imprints every human course and recourse with secondary) isn't this the passageway, the deferred reciprocity [*réciprocité différée*] between reading and writing?"[32] Because this notion of the divine refuses all hierarchies and opens itself up to the negative, rather than using the negative moment to eliminate all mundane contamination, it would not succumb to Derrida's criticisms of negative theology. But it is worth entertaining the skeptic's rejoinder: If the negative does, in fact, inhere within God, does this God still qualify as divine?[33]

Read in different lights, Derrida's work seems to be a rejection of either all assertions of the divine or all human ones. At times it looks like another contribution to the age-old tradition of iconoclasm; at other times it appears to be a determined attack on the certainty that produces iconoclastic violence. And in this discussion we should be equally wary about drawing too many conclusions from structural parallels between modes of thought, such as between deconstruction and negative theology. After all, just as one constant criticism of post-Enlightenment philosophy has been that it maintains religious concepts and structures in secularized form, so too one can declare, as did Feuerbach, that religious concepts are merely humanist ones estranged from their earthly origins. The fluidity and changing affiliations of philosophical concepts lend valuable support to the scholarly maxim that one should resist making windows into men's souls.

"The Last of the Jews"

This maxim would have been perhaps easier to follow if scholars hadn't been tempted by Derrida to make gestures in this direction. Over the past thirty years, the debate over Derrida's religious affiliations has gained impetus from his own autobiographical writings. Hence the interest when Derrida declared that he was a man of prayers and tears, an Augustinian confession that provided the title for John Caputo's famous 1997 book, which played a significant role in concentrating discussion in the English-speaking world.[34]

Derrida's temptation was a mischievous one. By encouraging the prurient investigation of some inner secret being, Derrida wanted to challenge the notion of an absolute or stable identity. Many of his works in this period resisted the notion that a characteristic or language can ever be fully ours, or that we can make certain claims about who we are. As we have seen this suspicion about identity or proprietary claims holds *a forteriori* for declarations of religious faith.

Derrida's favored vehicle for complicating the concept of identity, especially his own, was reflection on his Jewish heritage. And it is no coincidence that this privileged theme should resonate, albeit in various and conflicting ways, with the discussion of religion. For in the discussion of his Jewish heritage, in particular in his reading of the practice of circumcision, Derrida brought together notions of religion, identity, and community, while challenging the communitarian impulses that these have often implied. In his autobiographical writings from the 1990s, including "Circumfession" and *Monolingualism of the Other*, Derrida emphasized how he resisted the identification first and foremost as a Jew, especially since, in Vichy France and beyond, that identification was often accompanied by anti-Semitic prejudice, and in 1940 the revocation of his French citizenship.

Further, his description of this Judaism shows how difficult it is to define pure identities. As he wrote, in his family circumcision was called "baptism" and the bar mitzvah, "communion." His famous declaration to be the "last of the Jews" served both to highlight a heritage and, in a way, to betray it.[35] Derrida's continued treatment with Jewish themes across the course of his career, from his early essays on Jabès up until his last writings, emphasized the irreducible problem of belonging.

For this reason, rather than seeking to make positive claims about the meaning of Derrida's engagement with religion, several of the essays in this book look at the ways in which that engagement has developed and follow how Derrida redeployed, often in contradictory ways, the tropes and concerns of particular strands of religious thought. Thus the question of Derrida and religion need not simply take the religious as an abstract category, nor must it rely on the simple essentializations at work in questions such as: "Is deconstruction a 'Jewish' science?"[36] If we are to talk about the ways in which deconstruction and religion are intertwined we would have to turn to particular "figures" of the Jew or particular types of Christianity and examine how they function and are transformed in Derrida's texts. It is here that de Vries's discussion of a religious "archive" in his essay "Et Iterum de Deo" is particularly helpful. Ethan Kleinberg, in his "Not Yet Marrano," demonstrates the richness, but also the blind spots, of the "être-Juif" as it functions in Derrida's writing by showing how he inherited and transformed concepts from both Sartre and Levinas. As Sarah Hammerschlag elaborates in her essay "Poetics of the Broken Tablet," the political implications of Derrida's thought can be gleaned from the way in which he poeticizes Levinas's concept of Jewish election, to open it up to the universal without losing sight of its particularity. Edward Baring, in "Theism and Atheism at Play," analyzes Derrida's reading of a particular Christian archive and locates his early thought in proximity to but also at a certain distance from a brand of Christian Heideggerianism that emerged in the early 1960s.

Because this volume tends to focus less on the application of Derrida's ideas to religious study and more on the way in which he engaged with traditions of religious thought (though as the contributions here demonstrate, that distinction is easier to state than maintain), it manifests a serious imbalance, where two branches of the Abrahamic religions all but eclipse the third.[37] This priority stems from contextual and biographical considerations, in addition to the prominence of Jewish and Christian themes in Derrida's work.[38] Derrida was born to a Sephardic Jewish family in Algeria, and he spent much of his life in conversation with both Jewish and Christian thinkers. But such considerations should caution us to see the emphasis on Judaism and Christianity as de facto rather than de jure. Indeed, the need to engage productively and openly with other religions, especially Islam, has never felt so pressing. Deconstruction, if it can indeed be used to inform religious thinking, would provide valuable tools for breaking down exclusionary walls, even if, as Anne Norton suggests in "Called to Bear Witness," this would require us to confront Derrida's own disavowals of Islam.[39]

"Tout Autre Est Tout Autre"

While many of the contributors to this book examine Derrida's engagement with a religious archive, other scholars have used Derrida's ideas to engage with that archive themselves and open it up to the future.[40] In his essay "Derrida and Messianic Atheism," Richard Kearney draws on Derridian ideas in order to develop his own project of an ana-theism, while recognizing the differences between the two. Joseph Cohen and Raphael Zagury-Orly, in "Abraham, the Settling Foreigner," employ Derridian readings of Kierkegaard and Hegel to work out the limitations of a certain religious canon and to imagine a new idea of Europe. In this sense the implications of the study of Derrida and religion cannot be restricted to the scholarly research on a single thinker. Living in what many describe as a "post-secular" world, Derrida's thought seems to offer a way beyond forms of fundamentalism, while allowing the non-religious new means to understand a world where religion remains a powerful force.[41]

The significance of religious concepts for broader political and ethical questions is manifest in Derrida's own texts. Indeed, the texts constituting what has been labeled Derrida's "religious turn" are surprisingly diverse in their subject matter. The functioning of religious themes and concepts in Derrida's work has served to highlight the peripatetic nature of the religious. Derrida's most forceful presentation of the "messianic without messianism" can be found in his *Specters of Marx*, his clearest contribution to political discussions.[42] The messianic has also found one of its most influential formulations in Derrida's "démocratie-à-venir,"[43] a discussion of religion has informed his interventions into the second Algerian War[44] and the philosophy of law,[45] his discussion of hospitality has confronted antipathy toward migrants and *sans papiers*, and Derrida's meditations of forgiveness have found powerful resonance in his discussions of the "Truth and Reconciliation Commissions" in South Africa.[46] Similarly, the comparison with his French-Jewish contemporary, the philosopher Emmanuel Levinas, has informed much debate on Derrida's own relationship to religion and it has encouraged scholars to assign great meaning to his reflections on the complex bonds that may obtain between religious thought and ethics.[47] Further, as Peter E. Gordon shows in his essay "Habermas, Derrida, and the Question of Religion," we can locate and read the long-running philosophical entanglement between those two thinkers at the intersection of religion and politics. In the essays that follow the constant reference to politics and the recurrent question of the ethics of deconstruction demonstrate the significance of the question of Derrida and religion for a broader range of questions than the topic might at first suggest.[48]

"The Undeconstructable"

For all the often-sharp disagreement and debate between the contributors to this volume, a disagreement that reflects debates within the broader intellectual community, it is valuable at the end of this introduction to recall what unites them all. No contributor denies the significance of deconstruction; all are, at least to some degree, convinced of the impor-tance and enduring value of Derrida's work. Indeed, in their debates they formulate different ways to preserve deconstruction—or, at the very least, to pay homage to the philosophical lesson of deconstruction by resisting the fantasy that it must remain immune from criticism. Both in France and America many critics have insisted that deconstruction hews too closely to religion and that this should arouse our concern; the opposition of religion to philosophy has been used by many to reject Derrida's thought, alongside both Heideggerianism and phenomenology, as a new form of mysticism, and hence as profoundly aphilosophical. Thus when Martin Hägglund, in "The Autoimmunity of Religion," sets out to save deconstruc-tion from religion, and challenge the readings provided by scholars like John Caputo, he does so in order to preserve it as a valuable theoretical approach. Radical atheism in this view would be the key to deconstruc-tion's survival.

In contrast, for Caputo in "Unprotected Religion" deconstruction has a future within theology; he challenges the two-worlds Augustinianism that has often led to religious violence and, rather, draws on Derrida to propose an "unprotected religion." For some it is the richness of Derrida's reading of his Jewish heritage and his engagement with the Jewish textual tradition that ensures its continued relevance, for others it is the way in which Derrida was able to breathe new life into various texts of the Chris-tian tradition. Even when the contributors here have reached differing conclusions, the debate over the place of religion in Derrida's work has helped reinvigorate both the theory and practice of deconstruction.

"Et Iterum de Deo"
Jacques Derrida and the Tradition of Divine Names

HENT DE VRIES

> State et nolite iterum iugo servitutis contineri. (Stand fast therefore, and do not submit again to a yoke of slavery.)
> — ***Galatians*** **5:1, the Latin Vulgate, RSV**

Neither traditional philosophical theism nor modern secular humanism nor, for that matter, theoretical or practical humanism and atheism seem adequate designations to capture the simultaneous generalization and trivialization, intensification, and exaggeration to which Derrida subjects the religious and theological—indeed, theologico-political—categories, drawn from the vastest and deepest of archives.[1]

Instead of demonstrating what is wrong with these alternative interpretations of Derrida's projects—I have neither a gift nor much patience for polemics—I would like to give a few examples of what this apparent laboriousness and tediousness, as well as indecisiveness, looks like. I will do so, basing myself on a few fairly recent texts, not least since I have addressed some earlier statements elsewhere and do not feel I need to summarize or significantly restate my view. In sum, I claim that Derrida, as he himself often enough indicated, remains at once near to and far from—indeed, *infinitely close to and at an infinite remove from*—the archive that makes up "religion."

This archive, which is not only an ensemble of words and things, images and sounds, gestures and powers, that reconfigure themselves in both structural and random ways, but also a past whose metaphysical status (as Henri Bergson and Gilles Deleuze knew and insisted throughout their writings) is best described as absolute, pure, and virtual—this archive, then, has lost nothing of its historical and, perhaps, ontological weight, even though in any of its singular and collective instances and instantiations it remains contestable and, indeed, deconstructable through and through.

Let's assume for a moment that the known debates concerning so-called turns in Derrida's work (whether toward ethics and/or religion or to, say, the "literary object," architecture, law, America, perestroika, Europe, animals, learning how to live—and the differences matter little)—in other words, debates concerning any "turning," quasi-Heideggerian *Kehre*, or what have you, all of which assume a before and an after, a linearity of progression, conversion, inventions of the other, and the like—have largely run their course. They are either inconclusive or simply moot (an urgent matter for intellectual historians and biographers at best). For the sake of argument and the attempt to find common ground, we can easily postulate a continuum and coherence of the Derridian project and oeuvre and bury the rhetoric of "turns" once and for all. Yet, this would still leave us with an important question, one for which the reference to Descartes's *Meditations*, at a central point of the argument in *Limited Inc*—notably its invocation of (and need for) the "*iterum*" at the heart of theological proof—could well serve as an emblematic rendering. It is summed up in the following question: What drives the need to repeat—that is to say, recall, reiterate, and change—a tradition, even and especially when it is seemingly over and done with, and to do so without submitting oneself once again (*iterum*) to its most dogmatic assumptions and codifications, pictures and images? As I have sketched elsewhere, there is throughout Derrida's more recent writings a quasi-Pauline stance of belonging without belonging to a tradition, whose legacy one knows to be virtually all-determining in the history of Western thought, from the age-old onto-theological constitution of metaphysics up to the "globalatinization" (to cite Samuel Weber's apt translation of *mondialatinisation*) of our days.[2] Indeed, this legacy casts its shadow over any attempt to say, write, or do something else as well, which is, precisely, why not even the thought by trace or our "learning finally how to live" can ever fully hope to escape it.

"And"

We can, I think, all agree that the title of our symposium—"Derrida and Religion"—neither asks nor allows for a simple answer. In one word, it can hardly mean that the "and" implies a merely disjunctive clause—in logical symbol, indicated by "∨" (suggesting the Latin adverb *vel*)—as if we ought to begin by differentiating and ending up choosing between "Derrida" and "religion" as alternatives, let alone opposites, standing apart from each other, linked negatively, as it were, through disjunction alone. Speaking of "Derrida and Religion," we do, I take it, not imply "Derrida 'or' religion" (say, p ∨ q) intimating that there is "Derrida"—the man, the thought—on the one hand, and "religion"—the historical reference, concept, and practice, name and spirituality or ritual—on the other. The title "Derrida and Religion"—in logical notation, p ∧ q—connotes something else.

Nor, conversely, can our conference title signify that we simply equate or identify these names (more precisely, but here all our difficulties begin, the proper name and the concept or practice), conflating "Derrida" and/or his work (perhaps even just a part of it) with "religion" (or any distinctive part or element of it). Again, in logical notation, "Derrida and Religion" hardly suggests p = q, nor, evidently, its opposite, namely that p does not only not equal q, but is actually the strict negation or exclusion of q, just as q would be the exact opposite of p, without any overlap of the references (values or sets) represented by these symbols.

In other words, there is a conjunction *and* disjunction of and between the two symbols or, rather, "names"—a proper name ("Derrida") and a common name or, rather, noun ("religion")—that merits further reflection. And the unexpected ways in which a singular name may inflect a general or generic concept leads to the very heart of the problem that interests us here.[3]

In fact, taken in isolation, neither the inclusive (weak or connective) use of the adverb "and" in our title, "Derrida and Religion," nor its exclusive disjunctive reading makes much sense in light of the readings and interpretations that Derrida himself proposed, whether speaking of "religion" directly or expressly, or discussing the messianic, the law, its so-called mystical foundation, the shibboleth, circumcision, confession, or, I would venture to add, *just about anything else*. Indeed, precisely the "fact" that a name or term (here: "religion") can come to stand in—or non-synonymously substitute for—just about anything whatsoever, investing it with a value that is absolute or, in any case, absolves itself from easy determination, is what troubles and confounds the question we seek to answer. How and why is it that "religion" invades a territory (a mind, an oeuvre) in which it has, perhaps, no place? Is this yet another example of the way life affects and, perhaps, precedes (*primum vivere deinde philosophari*) thought, illustrating the very "contamination" of the transcendental by the empirical and vice versa that is one of Derrida's earliest and most original and influential insights?[4] Or is the cohabitation of religion and philosophy (literature, psychoanalysis, political analysis, etc.) in Derrida's writings—a curious and enigmatic coexistence and, perhaps, coextensiveness, whose peculiar figure and format interests us here—of an altogether different nature? Could its proper phenomenality obey a logic that is, strictly speaking, indestructible, "indeconstructable," as Derrida (sometimes) says?[5]

That there is an undeniable disjointedness of the proper name and its metonymic use (after all "Derrida" comes to stand here for much more), on the one hand, and the referent or concept and practice (namely "Religion," whose reference is even vaster in scope), on the other, goes without saying. Nonetheless, the relation between these names or terms calls for an interpretation that does justice to the complexity and subtlety of their mutual implication, interrelation, which hints at a rapport that goes further than a mere overlapping of edges, and this *to the point* of confusion.

What should puzzle us is that this holds true, especially, where "Derrida" and "religion" (more than, say, "Derrida" and "literature," "Derrida" and "psychoanalysis," "architecture," and even "politics") are concerned. After all, why is there this doubtful, even dubious privilege and why does it deserve our attention more than anything else? What causes or justifies, in any case, explains this prima facie implausible conjunction of names and terms (or of one name and one term or noun, rather than others)? What accounts for this drawing and pulling of certain meanings and forces that "haunt" our present, preventing it from ever coinciding with itself? What are these

> overwhelming questions of the name and of everything "done in the name of": questions of the name or noun "religion," of the names of God, of whether the proper name belongs to the system of language or not, hence, of its untranslatability but also of its iterability (which is to say, of that which makes it a site of repeatability, of idealization and therefore, already, of *techné*, of technoscience, of tele-technoscience in calling at a distance . . .)[?][6]

Before attempting to answer these questions, let me suggest that if we read our title—"Derrida and Religion"—we need to mobilize all our skills in reading ambiguous titles such as *Being and Time, Truth and Method, Totality and Infinity*, and, perhaps, *Mind and World*, that suggest something else, and something more than, the mere hermeneutic complementariness of the terms (names and nouns) in question. That is to say, we must not cede to yet another temptation, which is to assume contiguity, complementariness, or partial overlap between the references, realities, and realms, for which these "conjugated" words ("Being," "Truth," etc.) stand, where, in fact, there is none. Perhaps the proper name in our title ("Derrida") prevents us from going there? Or is the relationship between an individual thinker and a general subject merely an illustration of the very problem that these modern philosophical classics and their authors (here: Martin Heidegger, Hans-Georg Gadamer, Emmanuel Levinas, John McDowell) evoke?

Things are not that simple and it would seem, at first glance, that, paradoxically, a certain *undecidability* of the "Derrida and/or Religion"—the "and-slash-or" expressing our sense of not quite knowing as to where or how to locate their relative positions vis-à-vis each other—is de rigueur. Instead of any identity or difference, let alone resemblance or analogy, between "Derrida" (the proper name and metonymy, the man, the work), on the one hand, and "religion" (the historical reference, concept, and practice), on the other, there might well be total overlap, congruity, but one that does not exclude or deny the—non-numerical—distinction or distinctiveness of these two poles of analysis or points of attention. The relationship between them, if there is one (*s'il y en a*, as Derrida so often cautions), would be "without relation" or, rather, it would be one (but, one wonders, just one?) of being distinct, distinctive, and indistinguishable at once, not unlike Joseph Jastrow's duck and/or rabbit, which "now you see, now you don't," that Ludwig Wittgenstein uses to great effect in his *Philosophical Investigations* to illustrate the implications of so-called dual aspect seeing. Perhaps, we might even say that they are—in what are often the most indirect, oblique, and occulted of ways—reciprocally, if not symmetrically, constitutive of each other, without yielding one simple and undivided picture, a unique image of oneness, of the One—one of the Divine names—that would, supposedly, stand on its own and be one of a kind, the sole "example" of its kind.

If we steer clear from all biography, from all psychologizing, as indeed we should; if we focus on matters of principle and method or, rather, of axiomatics, theoretical matrix, and interpretive praxis (all of them terms that stem directly from the Derridian idiom)—leaving the proper name (here: Derrida) for what it is—then our topic becomes simply this: "deconstruction and/or religion." The Spinozistic understanding and rhetorical use of the Latin *sive* rather than *vel*—as in the well-known, but still little understood, expression *Deus sive natura*—would thus form a second best alternative to that of taking the "and" as, precisely, undecidable, that is, a relation without relation, without us being able to determine the place (call it the meaning and/or use) of its constitutive terms, once and for all.

But, again, do these terms—"deconstruction" and "religion"—and the unlimited set of concepts and/or practices on which they rely indeed form a pair? Do they represent the dual aspects of one and the same eternal and necessary truth, as in Spinoza's one and only substance, which is named both God and Nature and gives itself to be thought and intuited and loved at once (as the second and third order of knowledge make strikingly clear)? Or is deconstruction—meaning, in part, the disassembling of a "machine" so to transport it elsewhere—for linguistic, epistemological, moral, and political reasons unable to reassemble the elements (and, hence, the One) that it had begun by taking apart?

Be that as it may, the title "Derrida and Religion," we may now see, is much more suggestive and promising than, for example, "Deconstruction and the Possibility of Religion" (to parody an earlier title and, indeed, conference, which took place some twenty years ago in New York and which got the debate about these matters started in the first place).[7]

For we can now suspect that neither the deconstructive argument nor, for that matter, any of its key elements or terms, such as the "trace," the "supplement," "*différance*," can claim to name or designate the place or locality (as Derrida says, the *khora*) of the archi-, quasi-, ultra-, simili-transcendental condition of possibility (and/or of impossibility) for anything whatsoever. To claim as much would mean to assume that any such conditioned thing, for example and a fortiori "religion," would be somehow dependent and parasitical upon this condition, as if it came chronologically and logically "later," so to speak. But, as we will see, it is the condition—at least, our philosophical meditation upon it—which comes later and, paradoxically, follows the conditioned wherever it goes.

Perhaps the proper name in our conference's title—however metonymically it may further be intended, as a stand-in for the deconstructive operation at large—reminds us of this singular footing and nature of the co-implication of "Derrida and Religion" no less than of the curious "fact" that they may always come to be seen and judged as mutually—and simultaneously or eventually—at odds or opposed ("out of joint," as Derrida, citing Hamlet, so often says). Bound and unbound at once.

I would like to follow up on this somewhat abstract preamble by merely declaring and clarifying that what I mean to suggest is, all in all, fairly straightforward, in fact, a truism, of sorts: it is the insight that Derrida intuits and formalizes with great consequence, namely that with respect to tradition—that is to say, under the modern, current regimen of "faith" and "knowledge" in which global markets and media affect and inflect global religion in a variety of ways (just as they are informed and driven by its "two sources" and manifestations, in turn)—we all find ourselves in a continuously shifting position that is both closest to and at an infinite remove from the archive that, for lack of a better term, we call "religion."

Before giving a few concrete examples of the lingering—the living-on (*survivre*), remaining (or remaindering, *restance*), or haunting spectrality (*hantologie*)—of the religious, suggesting that Derrida helps us understand that if *religion outlives or has already outlived itself* it may well come out or have come out stronger, indeed, more viable and alive than ever before, let me clarify the relevant context from which my title's reference to religion's repetition—or, in the jargon: iterability—takes its lead. More important, let me explain why the reference to "the Divine name" is pertinent here at all.

Taking my lead from this context will allow me to avoid repeating—at least, all too explicitly—some of my own earlier tentative attempts to understand and sketch the logic of Derrida's mention and use of Divine names (in the chapter on "Hypertheology," in *Philosophy and the Turn to Religion*, in the chapter on the "mystical postulate," drawing on his borrowings from Michel de Certeau, in *Religion and Violence*, and in the chapter on the "other" or "inverse" theology as well as the appendix on the apophatics of deconstruction, in *Minimal Theologies*).[8] These analyses, for all their inevitable shortcomings, must speak for themselves and, *grosso modo*, contain absolutely nothing that I would not be prepared to *reiterate* today.

I will not revisit the different stages of Derrida's engagement with apophatics, with so-called negative and mystical theology (in Pseudo-Dionysius, Meister Eckhart, and Angelus Silesius, his explicit references) directly; nor will I return to the telling expressions with which Derrida himself tried to capture the subtle dialectics and aporetics of his thinking and operating at once from within and without the tradition that has been (and, perhaps, still is) "our language," namely metaphysics. And, by implication and extension, this would mean also natural, philosophical, or onto-theology.

These expressions are well-established and known and range from the adopted Levinasian figure of the *à Dieu/adieu* (as a simultaneous turn toward and away from God, and whatever comes to substitute for His place, name, and concept) to the *tout autre est tout autre* ("the every other is every bit—or totally—other," which at once infinitizes finite singularities and de-transcendentalizes and pluralizes the one, for example, ethical Other), to Derrida's ironic self-description as the *le dernier des juifs que je suis* ("the last and the least of the Jews that I am or follow") that, likewise, conveys a Blanchotian motif and motivation, which is that one can every so often find oneself to be *at once closest to and at the furthest remove from a certain legacy*.

Derrida's magnificent readings of Heidegger's analytic, in *Being and Time*, of being-toward-death, use this paradoxical, near-aporetic characterization to indicate Blanchot's—and, at greater distance, Levinas's—relation to, at least, this part of Heidegger's thought.[9] But it is fair to say that this relation governs Derrida's own rapport to all of these thinkers as well as that it regulates his approach and more occasional stance on the tradition and contemporary phenomenon or set, indeed sets, of phenomena that interest us here and that go under the heading of "religion."

"Iterum"

As you may recall—and it merits repeating—in his long riposte to John Searle, in *Limited Inc*, Derrida sheds light on the concept of iteration by referring to one of the subtitles of the essay that kicked off the debate around J. L. Austin's *How to Do Things with Words* (the unlikely, confusing, and, at times, somewhat disingenuous debate on Anglo-American speech act theory, the performative, and so-called perlocutionary and passionate utterances to which many, most significantly, Stanley Cavell and Jean-Luc Marion have contributed since in a somewhat more distanced—one might add, serious and sincere—tone and demeanor).[10]

The subtitle in question is taken from Derrida's seminal 1971 essay "Signature Event Context," republished in 1972 as the concluding chapter of *Margins of Philosophy*. It reads: "Parasites. Iter, of Writing: That It Perhaps Does Not Exist." This subtitle cites and parodies, perhaps interprets, a title by Descartes, to be precise the subtitle of the fifth of his *Meditations on Metaphysics*, which reads: *De essendi rerum materialium; et iterum de Deo, quod existat*; in French: *De l'essence des choses matérielles; et derechef de Dieu, qu'il existe*; or, finally, in English: "On the Essence of Material Things: And Likewise of God, That He Exists" (or, in yet another rendering: "The Essence of Material Things, and the Existence of God Considered a Second Time"; "Concerning the Essence of Material Things; and Again Concerning God, that He Exists").[11]

Derrida recalls that the latter part of the title that begins with the adverbial expression "*et iterum*" (meaning "and again," "and afresh," "another time," "once more," "for the second time") and, in the French version of Descartes's *Meditations*, with "*et derechef*" (that is to say, "and likewise" or "a second time")—in the literary and archaic use in French, often used somewhat in jest, for "once again," "once more," "anew," in a more current rendering: "*une seconde fois, de nouveau*"—is a later addition made by Descartes "who thus returned to his original title, repeating and changing it in this way, augmenting and completing it with a supplementary *iterum*."[12]

Derrida also reminds us that this seemingly minute and almost trivial addition inspired a "classical" debate as to "why Descartes deemed it necessary to demonstrate the existence of God for a second time, after the proof had already seemed established according to the order of reasons in the third *Meditation*."[13] He then raises the question that interests me here: What could that curious fact that inspired a long round of discussion among eminent Descartes scholars such as Martial Guéroult, Henri Gouhier, and Léon Brunschvicg, some fifty years ago now, still teach us about the very "structure of iterability"[14] itself or in general?

Furthermore, what would "God," more precisely, the "Divine name" of God have to do with it? Is the Divine name—and the longer, wider, even deeper tradition for which it stands—an illustration or exemplification, an ultimate and enabling condition, or is it an ulterior and merely secondary—however, "special"—effect? If so, it would be an effect without necessary, sufficient, or, in any case, determining—that is, efficient—cause, as an earlier text in *Margins of Philosophy*, namely "*Différance*," had also suggested, in a context that likewise invoked the tradition of Divine names and, more specifically, of negative theology.

Derrida muses about the interest of an investigation for which, he says, the argument of *Limited Inc* leaves no room, but which, in retrospect, may well have found its place in earlier and later writings, whether they deal with "religion" directly, indirectly, obliquely, or not at all. It is the "endeavor to shift the question out of the necessary and rigorous debate" held among the generation of his teachers as to the correct interpretation of Descartes's text and to "draw it towards regions" in which Derrida claimed he had been "navigating,"[15] discussing the relationship between "signature," "event," and "context" and the element and effectuation of an *in principle* infinite repetition and change of and between them.

Now, could one say that such iterability begins with nothing less than—the name and concept, perhaps, revelation and veneration of—God Himself and, hence, with no One less than God, with nothing more than the "One"? Does—for Descartes, for Derrida—everything begin with God, with His being One, the first and the last and everything in-between? In sum, does this—paradoxical, aporetic, in any case, repeated, reiterated—reference to God (and everything—and it is everything—this reference, stands for) find no end anywhere, at any time, in nothing and no one?

Why, as seems the case here, prove things again, or at least twice (afresh, anew, once more), especially if the thing in question is the ultimate Thing, that is, neither the thinking or extended thing, soul or body, but the supreme substance, the un- or self-caused Cause (*causa sui*), which is the metaphysical name of God par excellence?

> What of *use* and *mention* in the case (unique or not?) of the Divine name? What, in such a case, of reference and of citation? What shall we think of the possibility or even of the necessity of repeating the same demonstration several times, or rather of multiplying the demonstrations in view of the same conclusion, concerning the same

object? And this precisely where the object concerned (God) is held to be beyond all doubt and the ultimate guarantee (being unique, irreplaceable, beyond all substitution, both *absolutely repeatable* and *unrepeatable*) of all certitude, all proof, all truth?[16]

"Unique or not?" But also: exemplary or not? These are the questions that are raised here, where the Divine name is mentioned or used in this most unlikely of contexts. Repeatable, although unrepeatable, and both of these "absolutely." I will return to both motifs in a moment, not least since they mark a decisive feature of sovereignty—often in its most outspoken theologico-political formations—namely to conceive of itself in terms of oneness and indivisibility as well as exemplariness, whereas Derrida thinks of iterability, precisely, in terms of a repetition *plus* change, in view of the "1 + at least one more," the "n + 1."

Put differently, while the reference, if not invocation, of God and His Divine Name may well be unavoidable in matters metaphysical *and* political—and this on conceptual no less than historical or, as we might say, *deeply pragmatic* grounds—God, His name and concept, definitely cannot claim to be or speak the last word. As a matter of fact and of principle, "God"—like all "religion"—need neither be first nor last to play a historical and phenomenal role and, hence, remains *an eminently quotable quotation at best.*

But then, that this is so cannot, must not, ought not be ignored, let alone dismissed or disparaged. In this sense, Derrida's writing, almost throughout, insists on the more than merely traditional, let alone documentary, *deep significance* of "the theological" archive and a fortiori of the "Divine Name." Indeed, one is tempted to place this archive in somewhere the vicinity of the "authentic mode of *ideality*"—that is to say, "what may be indefinitely *repeated* in the *identity* of its *presence*, because of the very fact that it *does not exist*, is *not real* or is *irreal*—not in the sense of being a fiction, but in another sense which may have several names . . ."— with which Derrida, in *Speech and Phenomena*, characterizes the "non-worldliness" that Husserl seeks to ascertain in the first of his *Logical Investigations*.[17] This "nonworldliness" of the logical space of reasons, as we would now say, is neither "another worldliness" nor "an existent that has fallen from the sky," but an "ideality" whose sole "origin" lies in the always possible "repetition of a productive act."[18] For this possibility to be radically "open, *ideally* to infinity," requires the assumption of an "ideal form" that assures the "unity of the *indefinite* and *ideal*" and it is this form and unity that Husserl, Derrida claims, implies in the concept of the "*living present*," of "transcendental life."[19] Derrida, however, probes further, even deeper, if one can say so, insisting that this ideality—and, hence, phenomenology's very method and project—remains "tormented, if not contested from within," premised as it must be on a simultaneous and coextensive "nonpresence" and "nonlife," an "ineradicable nonprimordiality" as well.[20] And yet, this observation does little to diminish the first and primary aspiration of so-called first philosophy, of metaphysics, just as, we might add, it does little to demean its onto-theological corollaries, including the anti-philosophical positions that oppose religion and reason, faith and knowledge, pure and simple. As Derrida writes with respect to Husserl:

> This does not impugn the apodicticity of the phenomenological-transcendental description, nor does it diminish the founding value of presence . . . . It is only a question of bringing out that the lack of foundation is basic and nonempirical and that the security of presence in the metaphorical form of ideality arises and is set forth again upon this irreducible void.[21]

Only this perspective, Derrida goes on to claim, would invite an investigation of "language *in general*," of the "transcendental logos," that is to say, of the "inherited" and the "ordinary" language—that is, the language of "traditional metaphysics"—within whose horizon phenomenology operates its reductions and whose determining force is never quite "bracketed."[22] Indeed, Derrida concludes: "Transforming a traditional concept into an indicative or metaphorical concept does not eliminate its heritage."[23] There is, as it were, a larger, wider, and deeper, historical and more than simply historical "a priori" that an analysis that reduces *logos* to logic and reason to epistemology does not "cover" or "exhaust."[24]

Mutatis mutandis, the same would seem to hold true of everything Derrida's own more consequent meditation upon the premises and reaches of phenomenology (or any other philosophical ambition) brings to bear upon the theological tropes and topoi it traverses and, of necessity, only barely transcends. We could extend, therefore, what Derrida concludes into Husserl's own thought and method:

> There is, then, probably no choice to be made between two lines of thought; our task is rather to reflect on the circularity which makes the one pass into the other indefinitely. And, by strictly repeating this *circle* in its own historical possibility, we allow the production of some *elliptical* change of site, within the difference involved in repetition; this displacement is no doubt deficient, but with a deficiency that is not yet, or is already no longer, absence, negativity, nonbeing, lack, silence. Neither matter nor form, it is nothing that

any philosopheme, that is, any dialectic, however determinate, can capture. It is an ellipsis of both meaning and form . . . . More or less, neither more nor less—it is perhaps an entirely different question.[25]

A host of descriptions would seem equally valid here: Derrida speaks of "parallelism," echoing Husserl's "duplication [*Verdopplung*]," that is, the opening up of a realm of "sense" that is situated somehow "alongside, right next to" the data that naturalisms of all stripes mistake for our world, forgetting that the transcendental ego—as opposed to the worldly soul—"incorporates" the latter and vice versa, the one "inhabiting" the other.[26] And yet, the two are irreducible, if supplementary, to each other.

The "Total Movement of the Trace"

But what does Derrida mean by the two references that interest us here ("the theological" and the "Divine Name"), both of which are mentioned and used almost interchangeably?

If "the theological"—the Divine name, God—is a "determined moment" of the "total" movement of the "trace," as Derrida writes in *Of Grammatology*, then it is clear that it neither is nor determines this "movement" *as such*, that is to say, from the start, midway, at the end, or *in toto*. But does this reduce the "moment"—and, we are nowadays tempted to say, momentum—of "the theological" in this "total movement" to something merely partial and derivative, inessential and arbitrary, temporary and doomed to render itself obsolete? Could we even have thought and spoken of the "trace," without ever referring to it?

Here we encounter the problematic, once again, of what *Of Grammatology* calls "paleonymics" and what "Faith and Knowledge" sees as "the grave question of the name." It is a problematic that allows one to see the whole of tradition—including and especially the tradition of Divine names—as a gigantic *non-formal tautology* in which one non-synonymous substitution follows, echoes, haunts, and prophecies another, none of them either first or last.

Further: even or especially if the theological regimen of Divine Names, on the one hand, and the total movement of the trace, on the other, are parallel, yet coextensive, universes—one unimaginable, indeed, impossible without the other, indeed, the one accompanying and somehow "conditioning" the other, each step along the way—each one of them is irreducible to the other.

This much is clear, then. If an existing being—any "entity" and, hence, likewise the highest or super-essential being called "God" or "the other"—

comes into presence or represents absolute presence, then the latter is a priori "determined," that is to say, predetermined or structured (we could even say, fated or *predestined*) by differences and differentiations, temporalizations and spatializations, that *are not quite it* (or even *quite up to it*), that potentially betray and pervert it, and that will, of necessity, never allow it to come fully into its own (let alone be "intact, safe and sound," as "Faith and Knowledge" stipulates a certain definition or "source" of "religion" would seem to require).

Let me recall the full passage from *Of Grammatology* that frames our original citation:

> The "theological" is a determined moment in the total movement of the trace. The field of the entity, before being determined as the field of presence, is structured according to the diverse possibilities— genesis and structure—of the trace. The presentation of the other as such, that is to say, the dissimulation of its "as such," has always already begun, and no structure of the entity escapes it.[27]

But then, we might add—and Derrida does so elsewhere with so many words—that the reverse holds true as well. As with Saussure's *langue*, the system of language, and *parole*, the unique-singular utterance ("passionate" or not), the conditioning or determining, if we maintain this vocabulary, works both ways, is reciprocal, even if not symmetrical. In fact and "historically speaking," then, "the theological," like Saussure's *parole*, comes "first."[28]

True enough, Derrida never equates the determining "movement"— what *Limited Inc* calls the "graphematic drift"—the supplementary substitution in which the "determined moment" of the theological is both produced *and* effaced, with its supposed "effect," which would be, say, the pronunciation of the Divine name and its subsequent negative determination or unsaying.

But, in the logic of *différance*, the effect has no determining or effective cause, *stricto sensu*, and is, therefore, no *mere* effect or effected instance or instant either. That is to say, it is precisely *not* a "moment" (dialectical or other), just as it is hard to imagine what it would mean to say of the "movement of the trace" in whose "drift" the theological is supposedly caught, and whose "graphematic" tracing produces or "determines" the Divine Name's proliferation or dissemination, that it could be somehow and eventually "total" (whether in dialectical terms or not).

In fact, if we keep this terminology, it is only the effected instance that manifests—one might be tempted to say, *reveals*, in any case, *phenomenalizes, historicizes, theologizes,* and *politicizes*—the supposed "drift" in the first place. Like Saussure's "system of language," the graphematic drift of the trace and its determining movement (whether "total" or not) has no existence or meaning in and of itself, outside this repetition or, more precisely, reiteration of instants and instances (of "paroles," as it were), that is, it has no actual life outside of the subsequent and "nonsynonymous" substitutions it "traces" and that, in a sense, follow in its "wake." By the same token, the trace erases not just presence and self-presence but, necessarily, also itself and, hence, paradoxically, yields a certain phenomenality that is now no longer seen as present or present to itself—and, perhaps, never was. As a consequence, the theological, likewise, has no existence, no life, independent of the ("total") movement of the trace, taken now as a radically finitizing drift that is, ultimately, infinite, nothing less.

To use a quasi-Spinozistic vocabulary and general thought: its "substance" is (or is "in") its very "expression" and can claim no conditioning or determining role beyond (i.e., before or without) it.

As Emmanuel Levinas put it aptly in the opening pages of *Totality and Infinity*: "The Infinite does not exist first so as to reveal itself in a second moment." The same, *mutatis mutandis*, holds true for the Divine Name that draws this philosopheme (the "Infinite" or, as Levinas would come to say, "In-finite") into the singular naming that—apophatically—never has the final word.

What's in a Name?

But what names called "Divine" are there? And how many does Derrida use or mention or both? Tradition has it that there are infinitely many, all of them equally expressive or indicative of the existence and essence—and, at times, in-existence and hyper-essentiality—for which "God" (*deus*) remains the proper name, indeed, the most proper name (even if this name is inviting and welcoming of innumerable others, metaphysical and properly divine, that is to say, theological or, rather, mystical ones).

Derrida references a number of Divine Names, notably in his reference to Kabbalah and to Meister Eckhart in *Writing and Difference*; in his reading of Pseudo-Dionysius's *Mystical Theology* and *Celestial Hierarchy*, with yet another reference to Eckhart, in "Denials: How To Avoid Speaking"; in his poetic musings in between the lines of Angelus Silesius's *The Cherubinic Wanderer*; and the list is far from complete. What these names have in common is a certain mystical quality or postulation whose peculiar phrasing and modality is that of an absolute performative, of sorts.[29] It is this motif and motivation—a "passionate utterance" (Stanley Cavell), if ever there was one—that has great relevance for us today and this well beyond the reception of (and tribute to) Derrida's oeuvre.[30]

Whatever one could say further about the phenomenological conception of the "trace" and the deconstructive formalization and radicalization it invites and receives from Derrida's earliest writings on Husserl onward, there is absolutely nothing in these analyses that contradicts the Levinasian schema of the criteriological indiscernibility that the "trace of the other" (as *Autre* and *Autrui*, as metaphysical alterity, human face and divine name, whether the Infinite, Illeity, or God) presents beyond representation. Derrida adopts this reference in "Violence and Metaphysics," his first major essay on Levinas, in *Writing and Difference*, and elsewhere, and nowhere, to my knowledge, does he stress the variation or, rather, alteration this Levinasian conception of the trace—of the ethico-religious Other—might bring to his own earlier elaboration of this (at least nominally identical) theme he shares with this author.

By the same token, Derrida further nowhere denies the consequence that Maurice Blanchot, in *The Infinite Conversation*, draws from Levinas's version of this idea: the fact, namely, that the "trace of the trace" yields not so much a further absence but rather a "presence" of sorts. It is precisely this paradoxical reversal or inversion of the very concept of the trace—in both its Levinasian and Derridian rendering—that makes the link between the negative and positive or apophatic and the kataphatic moment in all mystical theologies, like the relation without relation between the ethico-religious "Saying" and the ontologico-phenomenological "Said," inevitable and irrevocable. Indeed, it is the very same logic that makes the slippage of deconstruction into the apophatic-kataphatic discourse of Divine names not so much necessary, but *unavoidable*, making all its initial "denials"—including those explicitly formulated in the early programmatic essay on "Différance," as "How to Avoid Speaking" explains in abundantly clear terms—vain and vulnerable.

"*Deus*"

In the limited context of *Limited Inc* on which I am focusing here, all this is abundantly clear for several reasons. Let me tease out at least two. Recalling the replacement of the Fifth Meditation's amended and supplemented title "On the Essence of Material Things: And Likewise of God, That He Exists" by "Signature Event Context"'s own subtitle "Parasites. Iter, of Writing: That It Perhaps Does Not Exist," Derrida asks:

What is repetition—or the iteration of the "iterum"—in this exemplary case, if this exemplariness is both that of the unique and that of the repeatable? What does its possibility or its necessity imply, in particular concerning the event of language and, in the narrow sense or not, that of writing? In substituting "of writing" for "of God," *Sec* [i.e., "Signature Event Context"] has not merely replaced one word by another, one meaning or finite being by another which would be its equivalent (or not); *Sec* [as it were, almost dryly] names writing in this place where the iterability of the proof (of God's existence) *produces writing*, drawing the name of God (of the infinite Being) into a graphematic drift (*derive*) that excludes (for instance) any decision as to whether God is more than the name of God, whether the "name of God" refers to God or to the name of God, whether it signifies "normally" or "cites," etc., God being here, *qua* writing, what at the same time renders possible and impossible, probable and improbable oppositions such as that of the "normal" and the citational or the parasitical, the serious and the non-serious, the strict and the non-strict or less strict.[31]

In other words, from the "exemplary" case that God, the Divine name (more precisely, "the Existence of God Considered a Second Time") presents here, already in the fifth of Descartes's *Meditations*, but more significantly even in the adoption and ironic repetition and extension of, at least, part of its title, several things can be gleaned.

First, Derrida ties Descartes's and his own repetition or *iterum* of the supplemental title to a peculiar "event," namely the "event of language" and, more specifically, to "writing" in either the "normal" (i.e., "narrow") or "general" sense of the term. More tellingly, having "writing" or "Writing" (i.e., scripture, with a lower case or capitalized, as in "Holy Scripture"; or "Difference," with a capital "d," that is to say, *différance*) take the place of God is not just any "substitution." It is, I quote, "not merely [replacing] one word by another, one meaning or finite being by another which would be its equivalent (or not)."[32]

But, then, what else or more could it be? What, if anything, outweighs— or deepens, intensifies—the equivalency? And why would God, the Divine name, not to mention the—renewed yet once again failed—proof for His existence (which, moreover, would hardly have been the proof of a being whose existence or meaning could be called "finite"), why would God be the very instance that renders that something else legible, if not visible and tangible, audible and intelligible? What, in other words, is the *surplus* value of "God," the "Divine name," such that "writing"—of all things—and, ultimately, "God *qua* writing," should substitute for it, as its "universal equivalent" (cf. Marx) and truth variable (cf. Wittgenstein), indeed, its "n + 1," of sorts?

Second, Derrida rightly observes that Descartes's repetition of the "proof"—just as his own repetition and variation of Descartes's "*et iterum de Deo quod existat*"—introduces and requires "writing," in both the quotidian or conditioned (or lower case) and the emphatic or conditioning (or capitalized) meaning and use of this term. To prove God's existence demands writing and it is this process or, rather, this "production" that draws "God," His Divine Name and concept and/or Referent, into a slippage or, as Derrida writes, "graphematic drift" that no theology—and notably no onto-theology—could wish for without contradicting its very premise (which is the uniqueness and unity, self-causation and freedom of its One subject, namely God, the "infinite Being").

God knows what will come to be said and predicated and preached of "God"—and "in the name" of religion—where the "event of language" takes place and nothing protects the Divine name from being misspoken, idly used, producing a host of idolatries and blasphemies, parodies and ironies that make up the very history of religion *in toto*. Not even God's own word, speech, or name could stop these derivative mentions, uses, and abuses.

Indeed, "*Dieu déjà se contredit*," "God contradicts Himself already" (as the essay on Edmond Jabès, in *Writing and Difference*, has it). Where God says "I," he is already an "other" (to perversely parody Rimbaud's famous phrase). And we are thus hard-pressed to tell the one (even the "One") from the other (whether a lower case "other" or capitalized "Other" or something, someone, different still).

Again, in Derrida's words, which I quoted earlier (but they merit repeating): the so-called graphematic drift of writing, besides many other things,

> excludes . . . any decision as to whether God is more than the name of God, whether the "name of God" refers to God or to the name of God, whether it signifies "normally" or "cites," etc., God being here, *qua* writing, what at the same time renders possible and impossible, probable and improbable oppositions such as that of the "normal" and the citational or the parasitical, the serious and the non-serious, the strict and the non-strict or less strict . . . . [33]

One can easily suspect why I insist on this point. For, if it has any pertinence—and I firmly believe it does, just as I am convinced that it is maintained and explained, indeed, reiterated throughout virtually all of Derrida's writings—then the whole question concerning his supposed theism (whether Judeo-Christian or not), atheism (whether "radical" or not) or even a-theism (whether *ad majorem Dei gloriam* or not), and anatheism (whether it espouses "not knowing" and the provisos of "maybe" or not) becomes moot.

This question is not what interests Derrida in the proper name or noun "God" and even less in the language—the *encomium*, praise, and prayer, in short: the "passionate utterance"—that the "Divine name" inspires and calls for. The religious and theological archive—epitomized by the Divine name—has a different, more deeply pragmatic, relevance that all attempts to co-opt Derrida's writing and legacy in either confessional God-talk or some quasi secular-materialist thinking of "life" and "finitude" tend to ignore and leave unexploited.

We have no way of answering—indeed, we just and justly find no interest and desire in answering—the question concerning the existence or non- and in-existence of "God" and the very posing of (and posturing around) this question blocks our view of the more challenging engagement with "religion" that is proposed in Derrida's writings. Call this approach "post-theist" and "post-secular," if you like. But, of course, these terms have their respective difficulties as well, and I will not be so foolish to insist all too much on them here.

The matter is not one of skepticism either. After all, the point being made is not so much that just or especially God's existence or inexistence is "undecidable," for so is the existence or inexistence of "writing." And neither one of these indecisions, on Derrida's view, ever yields the "indifference" (moral and other) that characterizes the modern *honnête homme* since Pascal and well beyond.

> The "perhaps" of the "that it perhaps does not exist" [the "Of Writing: That It Perhaps Does Not Exist," again, substituting and, perhaps, parodying the far from original but already supplemented Cartesian "Of God, That He Exists"] does not oppose the status of writing to that of God, who, Himself, should certainly exist. It draws the consequences from what has just been said about God himself and about existence in general, in its relation to the name and to the reference. In leaving the existence of writing undecidable, the "perhaps" marks the fact that the "possibility" of graphematics places writing (and the rest) outside the authority of ontological discourse, outside the alternative of existence and non-existence, which in turn always supposes a simple discourse capable of deciding between presence and/or absence. The rest of the trace, its remains [*restance*] are neither present nor absent. They escape the jurisdiction of all ontotheological discourse even if they render the latter at times possible.[34]

In sum, "writing," taken here in its generalized sense, does not assume a "status" that would "oppose" the one ascribed *here* to the Divine name, since, as the supplemental proof of Descartes's Fifth Meditation demonstrates indirectly, God's existence and being are nothing outside—or before and beyond—their in-principle infinite repetition, which inscribes alteration in their meaning no less than their use. And of this "drift"— which one could call "graphematic" or also "machinal"—the Divine name is historically and systematically the most "exemplary" example (and will probably remain so for, at least, some time still to come).

Why is this so? The answer, I think, is that this name, like the category of religion, and everything it stands for—that is, presupposes and, indeed, names, even as it suggests the insufficiency of all names and every concept, including these ones ("Divine," "name," their conjunction, indeed, "religion")—epitomizes, condenses, and conjures the vastest and deepest of archives, whose virtual existence precedes and pervades, exceeds and inspires, unsettles but also temporally (locally) stabilizes our thoughts and endeavors, and does *exemplarily*. There is no denying that there are many archives that have taken over that function in more limited regions and with partial success. What makes the religious archive—hence, the tradition of Divine names—stand out is its greater depth and global reach, the simple and indisputable fact that, historically and intellectually as well as institutionally and economically speaking, there is no space of reasons and affects that has more power, indeed, power of thinking and imagination, invested in it.

This said, a more interesting question—not least in terms of Derrida's overall philosophical argument, here and elsewhere—remains: Does "writing," in its turn, call for "God," for His "existence" or "inexistence," for both, for the undecidability between this affirmation and negation or for yet another mode of His "remaining" or "haunting" that coincides with neither one of these traditional or modern predicates or attributions that are, admittedly, deeply steeped in ontology, onto-theology, and the conceptions of sovereignty they imply and, inevitably, generate?

Again, the answer is not so much unclear as it is—wisely—left in abeyance, that is to say, neither affirmed nor denied. But that, I think, is a remarkable answer in its own right. It is echoed in Derrida's suggestion, in "Faith and Knowledge," that, *like writing*, "the machinal," the technologies of media (both old and, especially, new) that are its most visible expression in our "universe" may very well "produce" what we could only call "religion" or "gods." Bergson, whom Derrida cites approvingly, had suggested as much in the final words of his 1932 book (which would be his last) *The Two Sources of Religion and Morality*.[35]

"Unique or not," the Divine name allows, invites, and requires both Descartes and Derrida to go back on what has been proven or said already, in both cases with all the necessary detail and rigor. Yet, as the "example" makes abundantly clear—the example that, as Derrida writes, is "an event of parasitism, that of one title by another (which hence is no longer quite a title), the parasitism of the famous title borrowed from *René Descartes*, a title that had already parasited itself"[36]—there is no beginning or end to grafting one thing on another, or further adding one thing (one word, one name) to the next. This will always already have taken place.

Yet there is also a sense in which substituting "writing" for "God," or ontological and theological "non-existence" for existence, even existence *par excellence*, adds *almost or virtually nothing* to the equation as such, that is to say, alters nothing in the infinite series—or, as Derrida says, "*seriature*"—of "non-synonymous" substitutes that make up the history of theological, no less than philosophical, thought.

For the reverse substitution—that is to say, of "God" for "writing," speaking not only of "God *qua* writing," as Derrida does, but of "writing *qua* God"—is, of necessity, possible and, perhaps, unavoidable as well. (Does this make Derrida not so much a traditional or modern theist, but what could only be called a "radical theist"? Nothing could be further from the truth. That there can be nothing "radical"—not even God, even less so his opposites—is precisely the point.)

Further, was it necessary to ascribe to "writing" a theological moment, motif, let alone motivation? It needs no discussion that the answer is no. Was it avoidable that this association—often to the point of identification or confusion—took place? The answer is, again, probably not.

Indeed, it is this substitution that Derrida—in this particular context, citing and, as he says, parasiting Descartes, but also in so many others where very different texts and contexts, occasions and concerns, form his point of departure—invites us to meditate on, traversing and transcending a traditional as well as modern concern for which, again, "God" is the oldest and most proper (as we said, exemplary) of names. It is, in one word, the one—the "One"—that gives and demands us most to think and do. Its exemplarity is that it has extensively and intensively most to offer (philosophically and theologically, semantically and semiotically, pragmatically and, indeed, politically speaking).

One could, of course, object that, in *Limited Inc* and elsewhere, this reverse implication of one thing—name or referent—in another is a fleeting and, hence, non-necessary one; further, one might add that other things—figures or concepts—might have been cited and parasited instead and with equal or, who knows, greater right and effect. But this incontestable fact does not so much undermine as it only reiterates—and, indeed, *once more* (iterum) *proves*—my point, namely that the theological instance (here: the Divine name, but also the supposed "entity" for which it stands) is, for Derrida, not only a "determined moment" in what *Of Grammatology* calls "the total movement of the trace." Conversely, it is a *determining* moment as well and this, if we can say, so where several infinities (of the Divine and its infinite names, of *différance*) are at issue, *in equal measure*. In other words, the determining "movement" and the determined "moment" are mutually constitutive and, in Heidegger's idiom, equiprimordial. How could they be? But also, how could they not be?

Needless to say, to answer these questions we would need to spell out what we mean by "determining" as opposed to "determined" and also what Derrida might have meant by deploying an overly dialectical term such as "moment" to elucidate the "movement," even "total movement," of the "trace."

Further, why invoke the Divine name if what one has demonstrated or proved—the logic of iterability, of the trace, the supplement, of citations and parasites, and the like—would seem to exclude any reliance on transcendental signifiers, and first of all the one—the "Big One"—named "God"?

But also this: Why is it God or the Divine name—indeed, the whole negative-theological or mystical problematic of Divine Names—that is best positioned to make iterability and the like, if not fully intelligible, then at least intuitable as necessary, unavoidable, a genuine chance as well as a fatality (or *Ananke*, as Derrida says)? The answer would have to be that God and, hence, the Divine Names form the alpha and omega of our philosophical and theological discourses, including all the theoretical propositions and practical norms that rely upon them, and do so historically and conceptually—indeed, more than that—steeped as these notions are in a virtual archive (a pure and not always actual, immemorial past) that has no parallel as to its sheer breadth and depth. No concept or name exemplifies this archive more than God or whatever Divine Name substitutes for it.

The common ground of the no-longer and not-yet quite there or here of the presence (i.e., the reality or actuality) for which the Divine name still stands is that they are both immemorial—that is to say, an-archical and virtual—and also that their more than simply historical or future weight weighs upon us in ways we have hardly begun to fathom. In the age of global, ever-expanding markets and media, our social space is *curved* by these idealities—that is to say, irrealities and inactualities—whose phenomenal effects (indeed, effects without causes and, hence, special in more than one respect) are increasingly difficulty to ignore.

A Preliminary Ending

We can all quickly agree: no one should attempt to "accommodate Derrida's thinking to religion."[37] To my knowledge, no serious reader of his work—whether early, middle, or late, dealing directly or obliquely with religious themes and theologoumena in its pages—ever did. Nor should anyone claim that Derrida critiques religion, if critique means engaging in a negative operation or even—in a more Kantian vein—delineating the conditions of its possibility (and, presumably in Derrida's case, impossibility) alone. The reason for this dual rebuttal of two temptations is simple. For both these operations presuppose or require that one keep at a distance a legacy—in Derrida's idiom: an archive—whose limitation one is supposedly able to measure with criteriological, that is to say, linguistic and epistemological, normative and conventional means (or that, at the very least, one can fathom with the intuitive reach of imagination). All this, we now realize, not least thanks to Derrida's decisive insights, is only pretended in vain. Our criteria are too fallible, too "disappointing," Stanley Cavell would say, to warrant any assurance as to their adequacy or aim. They decide nothing, nor can we as long as we follow their lead. Indeed, their decision, like any other, as Kierkegaard knew, is in its very "instant" nothing less, nothing more, than "madness."[38]

In fact, Derrida's engagement with "religion"—with some of its isolated themes as well as with the immensity of its immemorial archive, indeed, with the sum total of its social fact—is far more laborious, at times, tedious, in any case, indecisive, than any sweeping account of its supposed implicit religiosity or its apparent, indeed, "radical atheism," seems to suggest.

For reasons of space, I will end on a different note, in a different tone, taking leave from the letter, if, perhaps, not the spirit, of Derrida's text. Let me offer a preliminary and tentative conclusion that sums up my argument.

What I am suggesting here simply reiterates what one of Derrida's much later writings, *Voyous* (*Rogues*), states very clearly, namely that "secularization is always ambiguous in that it frees itself from the religious, all the while remaining marked in its very concept by it, by the theological, indeed, the ontotheological."[39]

One might, of course, counter that the concept and practice of de-construction—or grammatology, even pragrammatology—should not be confused with that of secularization (indeed, that the former is as much at odds with the latter as it is with, say, secularization's supposed opposites, namely "religion," the political theologies and ideas of sovereignty of all ages).

But to do so would be to miss the point, which is that, for Derrida, the conditioned (here: "the theological"), however paradoxical this may sound, is *conditioning what conditions it, determining what determines it* (namely: "the total movement of the trace"), in turn, as well. The two directions, each of which finds ample evidence and staunch defenders throughout the history of Western religion and philosophy, faith and knowledge, cannot be separated metaphysically or ontologically (to say nothing here of the empirical and psychic life of individuals and societies where they are irrevocably bound up with each other), even though they remain analytically or conceptually distinct and gesture, albeit often in a less than rigorous or strict fashion, to "two sources," each of them integral moments of the religious archive and its cultural, political expressions as a whole.

To be sure, the conditioning in question is anything but empirical, say, causal or even transcendental. And, in earnest, to qualify the latter determination by invoking some "archi-," "quasi-," "ultra-," or "simili-transcendental" function does not do much to clarify things further. Which is another way of saying that there can be no "determining" in any understandable sense of the term, other than the mutual and reciprocal—if not necessarily symmetrical—"impression" of one aspect or element of this relation between "the theological" (the "Divine name") and the "trace." And even "impression," "contamination," "spectralization," and "haunting" are inadequate concepts to express this relation. "*God, What More Do I Have to Say? In What Language to Come?*," Derrida quips in one of the subtitles of *Rogues*.

Indeed, when we realize, once more, that the relation between the Divine name and the "unnamable possibility of the Divine name" remains "without relation" and, hence, has no actuality and presence in itself or for us, other than the one we are able and willing to *attribute* or, rather, *ascribe* to it—*calling it names*, as it were, becoming idolators and blasphemers as we speak—then we must also know that these aspects, elements, or (quite literally) "elliptical" poles of our general experience change places, revert into each other, in ways that elude all criteria and that are, therefore, *indiscernible*. It is no accident that *Of Grammatology* associates "the possibility of the Divine name" not just with Heidegger's later thought of Being, nor only with grammatology's "theoretical matrix" of "graphematic drift," but also—and, in this strategic context, perhaps, first of all—with "Kabbalah." But the series or "seriature [*sériature*]" doesn't stop here.

For example, of the two lectures that make up the body of *Rogues* Derrida says that they are based upon a "common affirmation" that "resembles," as he puts it, "an act of messianic faith—irreligious and without messianism."[40] Not so much a "religion within the limits of reason alone," which would be "still so Christian in its ultimate Kantian foundation," this affirmation, he goes on to say, would "resound through another naming,"[41] namely that of the *khora*. The motif, freely adopted from Plato's *Timaeus*—and arguably the greatest challenge for any interpretation of Derrida's work that would wish to situate him in an unbroken lineage of apophatic discourse, whether of negative theology, mysticism, or both—stands here for what Derrida calls "another *place* without age, another 'taking place' . . . a spacing from 'before' the world, the cosmos, the globe, from 'before' any chronophenomenology, any revelation . . . ."[42]

Thinking "the theological" and, say, the political—hence, engaging oneself morally and pragmatically—thus entails the simultaneous invocation of two heterogeneous, irreducible, yet indissociable aspects and virtualities, whose relationship, Derrida insists, remains non-conclusive—paradoxical, indeed, aporetic—to be decided in an infinite series of singular instances, that is to say, case by case, time and again.

No other tradition, no better figure, *so far*, than that of the saying and unsaying of the Divine name, of the different ways of naming (proving) God—*et iterum de Deo*—can capture this most *ordinary*, if at times tragic, of circumstances, practices, and responses to the "undecidables" that make up our lives. Indeed, there is nothing more—nothing less—to "the theological" as it reveals itself as a "determined moment in the total movement of the trace" and becomes a "determining" moment of it, in turn.

For this remarkable relation to be thought through—but also experienced and experimented with—in all its philosophical and spiritual, practical and aesthetic repercussions, no historical (and, in fact, more than simply historical) *archive* offers more conceptual and argumentative (but also: rhetorical and imaginative, motivational and affective) resources than that of religion and theology, apophatics and mysticism, whose shared legacy constitutes a virtual repository for the expression and articulation of the greatest possible variety of questions and problems, acts and affects that are still ours (or that may well become ours, yet again).

Needless to say, the religious archive also contains the greatest reservoir of—quite literally—dogmatic representations and figurations of what it is that blocks our access to these greater depths and wider dimensions for which the Divine name, in both its backward and forward and sideways oriented perspectives, stands as well. Which is, precisely, why it cannot but keep naming God, the Divine.

To counter that "the infinite *différance* is finite" won't help, because this sentence merely reminds us that the infinitizing operation that this technical term captures has to traverse and transcend the finite differences that are mistaken and dogmatically fixed as limited signposts of the infinite plurality of infinitely differentiated "worlds" that there are.

This, nothing else—and regardless of whatever it is one has (always) already affirmed—dictates whatever there is or still may be that is (a future or forever) "to come." Hence, an important "axiom" that Derrida, in "Faith and Knowledge," formulates as follows, drawing once more on a theological idiom (here: that of the Biblical covenant and of the ecclesial sacrament of confirmation):

> no to-come without heritage and the possibility of *repeating*. No to-come without some sort of *iterability*, at least in the form of a covenant with oneself and *confirmation* of the originary yes. No to-come without some sort of messianic memory and promise, of a messianicity older than all religion, more originary than all messianism.[43]

But, again, messianicity—"older" and "more originary" in a way that contravenes all chronology in terms of the before and the after and every logic of founding and the founded—is contaminated or haunted by the very historical messianism that it makes possible and that it must traverse and transcend *to speak its unspeakable name*. What makes religion possible is made possible by it; what makes religion impossible (to come first, coming into to its own, having the final say) is what is, in turn, made impossible—and, as Derrida says, "occulted"—by it.

More than anyone else of his generation, Derrida has taught us that the distinction and often opposition between tradition and modernity, between the thinking of infinity and of finitude, theism and atheism, orthodoxy and heterodoxy, theology and idolatry, prayer and blasphemy—in short, between our being either on the "inside" or the "outside" of our historical legacy, including its contemporary contestations—is, on closer scrutiny, no longer pertinent. And, perhaps, never was.

There is a remarkable consequence to this observation that we have only begun to slowly realize—namely, that certain habitual patterns of assuming and experiencing temporal and spatial separation, of the now and here, perhaps, even of cause and effect, of the first and after, simply no longer obtain in full rigor, if ever they did. As a consequence, Derrida writes in *Learning to Live Finally*: "One can be the 'anachronistic' contemporary of a past or future 'generation.'"[44]

The Divine name ("God," the *à Dieu*—or, again, the *iterum*: *adieu*/ *a-dieu*—the "toward-and-away-from-God-including-His-nether-side," or everything and every "One" that has come or may still come to take His or its place) draws and pulls our concepts and discourses, acts and affects, both backward and forward, into an *immemorial* past and an unidentifiable, as of yet unrecognizable, *future-for-ever-to-come*. The Divine name is *both* archival in all the archeological, genealogical, genetic, documentary, dated, and outdated senses of the term *and* still further projected, infinitely iterable, yet again to be proved and quoted. *Et iterum de Deo . . . QED.*

Not Yet Marrano

Levinas, Derrida, and the Ontology of Being Jewish

ETHAN KLEINBERG

> If Judaism had only the "Jewish Question" to resolve it would have much
> to do, but it would be a trifling thing.
> **—Emmanuel Levinas, "*Être-Juif*," 1947**

A trifling thing? In 1947, a trifling thing? This is how Emmanuel Levinas
begins his response to Jean-Paul Sartre's *Reflections on the Jewish Question*
and it is here that I would like to begin my reflections on the divergent
though intertwined presentations of Jewish identity in the post–World
War II philosophies of Emmanuel Levinas and Jacques Derrida.[1] To be
sure, there is a temporal, geographical, and cultural gulf that separates
these two thinkers. Levinas, a contemporary of Sartre, was born in 1906
in Kovno, Lithuania, and completed his university training in Strasbourg
before the Second World War. Derrida was born in El Biar, Algeria, in
1930 and attended the École Normale Supérieure in Paris after the war.
Both were brought up in Jewish households though Levinas was of Ash-
kenazi descent, while Derrida was born into a Sephardic milieu. Furthermore, Levinas belonged to the "first generation" of the post-Holocaust
world, having spent the war in a German prisoner-of-war camp while his
family in Lithuania fell victim to the Nazi final solution.[2] Derrida belonged "both by birth and by self-conscious identification to that 'second
generation' of the post-Holocaust world on whose psyche has been indel-
ibly inscribed an event in which it did not participate." He was "marked"
by his expulsion from school in 1942 as a result of the reduction of the
numerus clausus, because of which he attended a Jewish school in Algiers
until the end of the war.[3]

But these temporal, geographic, and cultural distances can be bridged
at the site of Sartre's *Reflections on the Jewish Question* insofar as Levinas's

and Derrida's respective responses to Sartre create a textual intersection between Levinas's "Being-Jewish," published in 1947, and Derrida's "Abraham, the Other," presented in December 2000.[4] The relation and connection between Levinas and Derrida becomes more clear when one considers the way that Derrida's essay, though explicitly written as an engagement with Sartre, is implicitly and more importantly a confrontation with the philosophy of Levinas, a point argued by Sarah Hammerschlag.[5] What's more, the texts by Levinas and Derrida are each predicated on responses to the philosophy of Martin Heidegger as appropriated by Sartre, but also on its own terms. But it is telling that, despite the fifty-year separation between the texts of Levinas and Derrida, both these thinkers chose to replace, evade, or preempt (we will have to determine which) this "Jewish Question" by instead posing the question of "being-Jewish" (*être-Juif*). This is a point to which I will return.

But first a preliminary question is in order: How can one, in 1947, consider the "Jewish Question" to be no more than a trifle? The phrase itself was a product of the mid-nineteenth century as "the crystallization of a series of questions whose modern formulation goes back to the eighteenth century: Should Jews be granted civil and political rights equal to those of Christians? Would civic education make them more like Gentiles? Can they serve as loyal soldiers? Are Jews a distinctive people, race or nation? Is there an inherent dichotomy between Judaism and modernity?"[6] All of these questions revolve around the place of the Jews in a modernizing world. Under Nazi rule, however, this Jewish question was replaced by the "Jewish problem" to which there was ultimately only one final solution. Sartre's own reflection on the Jewish question was authored on the other side of the chasm that was the Holocaust and his treatment of the question bears the historical weight of the event. Whatever its faults, and there are many, Sartre's text was one of the first in France to address the issues of anti-Semitism and the Jewish victims of the Holocaust.[7]

Réflexions sur la question juive was published in 1946 though the work had already caused a stir when Sartre published the first section, "The Portrait of the Anti-Semite," in the December 1945 issue of *Les Temps modernes*.[8] A second printing was issued in February 1947 and soon thereafter Sartre was invited by two French Jewish organizations to present lectures based on that work. The first was held on May 31, 1947, at the request of the French League for a Free Palestine where he lectured on "Kafka, a Jewish Writer."[9] The topic of the lecture is striking given that Derrida's later engagement with Sartre, "Abraham, the Other," is framed by Derrida's own analysis of a Kafka parable on Abraham. This even more so given that the review of Sartre's lecture makes reference to the "motif of

Abraham that haunts Kafka."[10] The second lecture was held on June 3, 1947, under the auspices of the Alliance israélite universelle, where Sartre lectured on "The Jewish Question." Excerpts from this talk were published in the June 27 issue of *Les Cahiers de l'Alliance* with a short introduction, "Anti-Semitism and Existentialism," authored by Emmanuel Levinas.[11] Levinas followed this with a more substantial response to Sartre's writings and lecture on the "Jewish Question" published as "*Être-Juif*" in *Confluences* also in 1947.[12] Here we must remember that the lectures and discussions surrounding Sartre's *Reflections on the Jewish Question* took place at the same time as the first Heidegger Affair in the pages of Sartre's journal *Les Temps modernes*, which focused on the extent of Heidegger's relation to National Socialism and the impact of Heidegger's political choices on existential philosophy.[13] Though Levinas directs his analysis at Sartre's text, it is really Heidegger's thinking that is at issue.

But perhaps most striking, certainly for our purposes, is the way that in his *Reflections on the Jewish Question*, Sartre presents the inauthentic "Jew" as defined by the Other: "the Jew is the one whom other men consider a Jew."[14] When defined from without, the Jew lacks "authenticity," which Sartre defines as consisting "in having a true and lucid consciousness of the situation, in assuming the responsibilities and risks it involves, in accepting in pride or humiliation, sometimes in horror and hate."[15] When placed within the logic of *Being and Nothingness*, this quite simply means that the Jew as defined by others embodies Sartrian inauthenticity. Jonathan Judaken has argued that because Sartre categorized the "Jew" as defined by the Other, for the Jew to achieve "authenticity" he must shed this definition thus becoming what he is not. Following this reasoning we can recognize in Sartre's philosophical presentation of the "Jew" an intractable crystallization of what he had earlier defined in *Being and Nothingness* as the human condition: "The Being of human reality is suffering because it rises as perpetually haunted by a totality which it is without being able to be it. Human reality is therefore by nature an unhappy consciousness with no possibility of surpassing its unhappy state."[16] By contrast, Peter Gordon has argued that Sartre's *Reflections on the Jewish Question* marks a break with *Being and Nothingness* because Sartre allows for the possibility of Jewish authenticity wherein the transcendence of one's transcendence is merely an abject condition to be avoided through self-assertion and the "choice" of an authentic life.[17] But whether one reads Sartre in the light of Judaken or Gordon, the text and Sartre's particular take on the "Jewish Question" must be seen in relation to his larger existential phenomenology and, behind this, the influence of Martin Heidegger.[18]

And yet for Levinas, Sartre's emphasis on the "Jewish Question" was no more than a trifling thing. Levinas certainly credits Sartre, if not for the success of his arguments, for the "new weapons" he deploys to attack anti-Semitism "with existentialist arguments" in order to bring the Jewish Question back from the "outmoded discourses where it is often broached [enlightenment or rationalist arguments] to the very summits where the twentieth century's true, terrible, and gripping history is taking place."[19] But the "Jewish Question," as presented by Sartre or by the thinkers that preceded him, merely scratches the surface because, as Levinas wrote,

> posed in exclusively political and social terms—and this is the rule for public meetings, in the press, and even in literature—the question refers to a right to live, without seeking a reason for being. This rhetoric that invokes the right to existence for an individual or for a people reduces or returns the Jewish event to a purely natural fact. No matter how much one hopes for a cultural and moral contribution to the world from the political independence of Israel, one still does no more than expect one more kind of painting or literature. But to be Jewish is not only to seek a refuge in the world but to feel for oneself a place in the economy of being.[20]

Thus for Levinas, the issue is not equal rights, citizenship, or participation, nor is the issue that of a state or nation of one's own although these are, of course, essential issues in political and social terms. In all of these cases the establishment of such rights or territories simply establishes the Jews as one people among many, which at one level they are . . . simply another kind of "painting or literature." But by phrasing the "Jewish question" in this way the universal has prevailed over the particular and a certain assumption about assimilation is both presumed and fulfilled. If the Jews are simply another people and their ways equivalent to all others, then, in fact, they have been assimilated into the "modern world." What is more, as one people among many Judaism has sought to justify its survival by "rediscovering in the [politics, culture, and religion of the] Christian or liberal world the harvest of ancient sowings."[21] But, Levinas continues, "to claim a message that has already fallen into the public domain is an ambition denied by the whole impulse that for one hundred and fifty years has carried Judaism toward assimilation and in which religion, shrinking more and more, is limited to a colorless ancestor worship." What matters the provenance of Jewish thought, or Judaism for that matter, if its ideas are simply part and parcel of the "common patrimony of humanity"?[22] Being-Jewish must mean something other than this or there is no reason to be Jewish. No reason not to assimilate.

"But toward what kind of existence does assimilation tend?" Levinas asks: "Is it reducible to a general sociological phenomenon in which a minority dissolves into a majority that encompasses it and fascinates it with its force and the very value of its being a majority?"[23] On one level this question and this text are imbued with the fear that assimilation will lead to annihilation. A worry conditioned by the "twentieth century's true, terrible, gripping history." But at another, though related, level, the question provokes an answer concerning two kinds of "being": "the ontological meaning of this existence of the non-Jewish [modern] world toward which assimilation acceded" and the ontological meaning of being Jewish.[24] For Levinas, there is an "affinity among all of the non-religious manifestations of this world, and there is an affinity between these and the Christianity that remains their religion."[25] Thus, according to Levinas, the modern world is essentially Christian at least insofar as the ontological meaning of the non-religious and Christian manifestations are compatible. Levinas describes this meaning as "everyday life" that is "essentially a present: to have to deal with the immediate, to introduce oneself into time not by moving through the entire line of the past, but all at once to ignore history."[26] For Levinas, this emphasis on the present at the expense of the past is the fundamental difference between the ontological meaning of the everyday modern world and the ontological meaning of being-Jewish.

For Levinas, this presentist logic is exemplified by "Alexander's sword, which does not untie knots, which does not redo the knotting motion in reverse, but which slices,"[27] this is to say severs the relation with the past. In Christianity, one is born again in the "power of a new birth promised at each instant."[28] In science, it is the discovery that breaks with our previous understanding of the world "that is, without reference to the origin that was implied, still, by the idea of cause."[29] For the nation-state, it is the revolution where politics are created *ex nihilo* the calendar restarting at the year one. All are predicated on a logic of the now that breaks with the past in pursuit of a perpetual present. In this way the relation with being in everyday life is "action" in the present that the existential philosophy of a Sartre or Heidegger sees as the basis for freedom.

By contrast, Levinas asserts that Jewish existence is not an existence predicated on the present but "refers to a privileged instant of the past and the Jew's absolute position within being [that] is guaranteed him by his filiality."[30] This is the moment of election, the moment when choice itself was bestowed upon the Jewish people but that was not itself chosen.

Now here, it is important to point out the ways that Levinas's presentation of the presentist existence of everyday life in contrast to the privileged instant of the past that conditions Jewish existence can be seen to mirror the structure of Martin Heidegger's analysis of Dasein in his 1927 work *Being and Time*.[31] For Heidegger, the issue is the ways that our everyday existence (what Heidegger refers to as "inauthentic being") has lost track, forgotten, or has fallen from its original or "authentic" relation with being. It is not a stretch to map Levinas's characterization of the everyday existence of the modern and presentist world onto the forgetful and inauthentic mode of being in distinction from the original and originary mode of being that characterizes both Heidegger's authentic existence and Levinas's being-Jewish. Furthermore, Levinas can be said to replicate the distinction between "authentic" and "inauthentic" Jews that he finds so problematic in the text by Sartre insofar as he equates the assimilationist tendencies of the Jewish people with the "everyday" or "inauthentic" mode of being as opposed to the seemingly forgotten model of election that characterizes the essence of being-Jewish, "authentic" being-Jewish.

The symmetry is not entirely unexpected but nevertheless surprising given that at that very moment, in 1947, Levinas was attempting to break with the philosophy of Heidegger. Levinas had begun to distance himself from Heidegger as early as 1933, the year that Heidegger publicly joined the Nazi party. One can see this in the 1934 article, "Reflections on the Philosophy of Hitlerism," where Levinas presented reason, liberalism, and the Judeo-Christian tradition as a counter to the racialist "philosophy of Hitlerians," and we must assume that Heidegger is to be included in this last grouping.[32] In 1935 Levinas's critical edge and distinction from Heidegger became sharper and better defined in his essay "On Escape" where Levinas took issue with what he saw as the limiting and ultimately solipsistic nature of Heidegger's philosophy and advocated the need to think beyond being, beyond traditional concepts of metaphysics, and beyond ontology.[33] But in both of these essays and throughout the thirties, Levinas's interest was primarily philosophical and his confrontation focused on the issue of the limits of ontology. While the possibility of accessing something beyond being (such as in his category of the *il y a*) was present in Levinas's prewar work, the resolution of this confrontation was not realized until *after* the Holocaust and the war. Up until the war, the "need for escape," Levinas tells us, "leads into the heart of philosophy."[34]

But Levinas's emphasis began to shift during his time in a German prisoner-of-war camp. While in captivity, Levinas began to develop his critique and counter to Heidegger's ontological philosophy but now, segregated with the other Jewish soldiers in a special section of the camp and made to wear the yellow star on his uniform, this counter was predicated on Levinas's development of "being-Jewish" as a way to think otherwise than Heidegger.[35] In the seven notebooks written between 1940 and 1947, with the majority of entries written before 1945, Levinas sought to develop "Judaism" or "being-Jewish" as a category distinct from Heidegger's Dasein.[36] "To start from Dasein or to start from Judaism," reads an entry from 1942 just above a note that presents "Judaism as a category."[37] The notebooks are filled with fragments and reflections on the role and place of Judaism in relation to philosophy, and specifically to Heidegger's philosophy, that foreshadow both his later philosophical work and what have come to be known as his confessional writings.[38] In the fifth notebook from 1944 he states that "one essential element of my philosophy—and this is where it is different from the philosophy of Heidegger—is the importance of the Other. Another element is that it follows the rhythm of Judaism."[39]

But in the years following the war, and specifically after the news that his family in Kovno, Lithuania, had been killed in the Nazi final solution, Levinas expanded his target beyond Heideggerian ontology to include a reevaluation of the entire Western metaphysical tradition. Thus, in an entry from 1946, Levinas defines his philosophy in terms of his Judaism: "My philosophy is a philosophy of the face to face. The relation with the other without an intermediary. This is Judaism."[40] In the notebooks and in his immediate postwar writings, we see a double move by Levinas. As he began to break definitively with the philosophy of Heidegger and to question the viability of Western philosophy, we also see an evaluation of what it means to be a Jew under Nazi rule and then after Auschwitz. Both of these questions, one announced and one performed, eventually led Levinas to the study of Talmud, which completed the inversion of his prewar emphasis on the primacy of philosophy in the investigation of religion. This inversion of priority began with the substitution of "being-Jewish" for Dasein. After the war and the Shoah, it is this category of "being-Jewish" that Levinas sees as the necessary precondition for the study of philosophy and that is manifest in the "joy of having Torah" (*Simchas Torah*) that Levinas announces in a note directly below the equation of his own philosophy with Judaism.[41]

The shift in emphasis is presented, albeit in Sartrian or Heideggerian language, in Levinas's essay "being-Jewish": "to do the will of God is in this sense the condition of facticity. The fact is only possible if, beyond its power to choose itself, which cancels out its facticity, it has been chosen, that is elected."[42] But it appears fully formed in his 1964 Talmudic lecture on "The Temptation of Temptation." Here Levinas examined a text from tractate Shabbat (pages 88a and 88b) about the moment in Exodus when Moses brought the Torah to the Jewish people. Rav Abdima bar Hama bar Hasa instructs us that the Lord said: "If you accept the Torah, all is well, if not here will be your grave."[43] The tract is about receiving the Torah at Mount Sinai but the emphasis is again on a seemingly predetermined choice, this time in response to the Lord's statement. The issue gets more interesting for Levinas as he tells us that the "temptation of temptation" of which he speaks "may well describe the condition of the west." This temptation of temptation is the temptation of philosophy, the seduction of reason as a tool by which humans can master and control the world around them. This, too, was a theme in Levinas's prison notebooks where he opposes the "infallibility" that is the subject of "classical philosophy" to the possibility of "being fallible but not feeble, living in a world where many things escape my comprehension." To this end, for Levinas "faith = knowledge without mastery."[44]

We must also be aware that this temptation of temptation is one that seduced Levinas himself in the years before World War II and led him to Martin Heidegger.[45] But if knowledge—philosophical, scientific, or historical—is not the answer, then what is? Here Levinas returns to the text: "The revelation which is at stake in the following text will permit us to discover this order prior to the one in which a thought tempted by temptation is found."[46] This revelation is conditioned by the threat of death but it also is the basis for choice: "The teaching, which the Torah is, cannot come to the human being as a result of a choice. That which must be received in order to make freedom of choice possible cannot have been chosen, unless after the fact."[47] This is the election that Levinas earlier articulated as an essential condition of the ontology of "being-Jewish" in distinction from the mechanisms of "choice" in the philosophy of Sartre and Heidegger. "We must advance a bit further into certain notions that the great talent of Sartre and the genius of Heidegger have substantiated in contemporary philosophy and literature."[48] For Levinas, the "transformation of supreme commitment into a supreme freedom" is indicative of the temptation of temptation insofar as philosophical cunning has supplanted the idea of origin. For Sartre, this leads to the formulation that even "not to commit oneself would still be to commit oneself; not to choose would still be to choose." For Heidegger, it is the resolute choice in the face of one's own death that results in authentic Dasein and that can be achieved at any moment. "To cut loose the fact from its origin in this way," be it via the emphasis on contingency or *Geworfenheit* that undergirds the supreme freedom in both Sartre and Heidegger, "is precisely to dwell in the modern world, which in its science has abandoned the quest for the origin, and in its religion exalts the present."[49] To Levinas's mind, Sartre and Heidegger have made "choice" and "commitment" into empty categories by cutting through the Gordian knot rather than untying it. "The past that creation and election introduce into the economy of being cannot be confused with the fatality of a history without absolute origin."[50] By contrast, it is through reflection on election and revelation that we discover the "order prior to the one in which a thought tempted by temptation is to be found."[51] But here we return to the revelation conditioned by the threat of death.

In Levinas's text from 1947, the "meaning of election, and of revelation understood as election" is not initially pronounced in relation to Moses and Sinai but in relation to the rise of Hitlerism and National Socialism. "The experience of Hitlerism was not sensed by everyone to be one of those periodic returns to barbarism which, all in all, is fundamentally in order, and about which one consoles oneself by recalling the punishment that strikes it. The recourse of Hitlerian anti-Semitism to racial myth reminded the Jew of the irremissibility of his being. Not to be able to flee one's condition. . . ."[52] This is almost immediately followed by a reference to Isaiah Chapter 53 and while Levinas's portrayal of the experience of Hitlerian anti-Semitism is understated, the wider implications are clear when read in concert with a notebook entry from 1945 that contains the same biblical reference: "In persecution I rediscover the original meaning of Judaism, its initial emotion. Not just any persecution—I mean absolute persecution that chases down being to seal it in the bare fact of its existence. But it is also that, {(ch. 53, Isaiah)} in this despair that no one can comprehend, the presence of the divine reveals itself."[53]

In his later Talmudic reading, election is the consent to Torah that is given before the revelation of the laws of Moses, and that is done so when faced with the alternative of death. God chose the Jewish people. But immediately following the war, Levinas presents the signs of this election in the suffering of the Jewish people faced "with the systematic will to extermination that rendered the Geneva Convention nothing more than a piece of paper."[54] In either case, it is this election conditioned by the possibility of death that distinguishes the ontology of being-Jewish from that of everyday or presentist existence and here again Levinas mimics the Heideggerian structure of authentic Dasein, which can only be achieved through Dasein's confrontation with the possibility of its own death. For Heidegger, death is one's ownmost possibility, but it is also the possibility of the impossible as the confrontation with one's own finitude. "In Dasein there is undeniably a constant 'lack of totality' which finds an end with death. This 'not-yet' 'belongs' to *Dasein* as long as it is."[55] *Dasein* does not complete itself until the moment of death, when all possibilities disappear for *Dasein*. After death *Dasein* has no more possibilities; it is completed, which is to say it has finished.[56] Levinas agrees with Heidegger's presentation of

Dasein as a temporal construct but does not agree with Heidegger's understanding of the finitude of being localized in the singular *Dasein* as defined in Being-toward-death and thus the "not yet" that signifies the lack of totality takes on a different significance for Levinas.

As a prisoner of war, faced with the pressing possibility of death at any moment, Levinas came to divine a parallel between his own condition and that of Abraham as he rode out to sacrifice his son. Levinas understood this period of delay before the terrible event to come as a time of reflection and meditation. "It is because of this [Abraham's] journey and the time that it took that the test has meaning. It is because of the misery suffered by the Jewish prisoner that he could become aware of Judaism and the seeds of a future Jewish life that transports him who only knew torture, death and Kiddush-Hashem [a martyr's sanctification of the divine name]."[57] Thus in captivity Levinas came to fashion an understanding of the ontology of being-Jewish as a temporal construct between an elected past and a "future Jewish life" to come. Whereas the Heideggerian structure is predicated on the finite temporal totality of Dasein as a whole, Levinas's presentation of "being-Jewish" eschews completion in that it is always situated in the "not yet" of an "infinite time behind us" and the promise of a messianic future to come.[58] This move also allowed Levinas to differentiate this ontology of "being-Jewish" from the ontologies proffered by Heidegger and Sartre in that the Jewish "fact" of existence "receives the structure of his personhood from election. In fact, there is a contradiction in the notion of 'ego' ['*moi*'] that defines this notion. The ego is posited as a simple part of reality and, at the same time, as endowed with the exceptional privilege of the totality. The ego is equivalent to the whole of being, of which it constitutes nevertheless only one part. This is a contradiction that is overcome in the emotion of election."[59] Thus, for Levinas "being-Jewish" is a privilege and election but only insofar as it announces the ethical imperative of understanding the ego as commencing from a position of a responsibility and not absolute freedom.

But this reconciliation of the finite ego with infinite being is only possible as an alternative to the "presentist" or "everyday" understanding of existence (itself a sort of annihilation by assimilation) where the finite ego retains its dominant position. In turn the move requires that Levinas refute Heidegger's presentation of Dasein's radical finitude as demonstrated in "being-toward-death" via Levinas's own presentation of the infinite time of transcendence and the possibility of an election, which is the ontological condition of being Jewish.[60]

It is this ontology of being-Jewish that Jacques Derrida finds both instructive and obstructive. Derrida phrases this in terms of a question:

How, and by what right, can one distinguish for example between that which, in my experience, touches *in part* my "being-jew" at its most intimate, its most obscure, its most illegible (however one takes "being-jew," and later I will in fact complicate the stakes of this expression—one cannot do everything at once) and *in part* that which, let us say, seems to belong in a more legible fashion to my work, the public work of a good or a bad student, which does not necessarily, nor always, bear visible traces of my "being-jew," whether it concerns itself with writing, teaching, ethics, law or politics, or civic behavior, or whether it concerns itself with philosophy or literature.[61]

At one level, this distinction between a public everyday existence and a private individualized existence evokes the distinctions offered by Levinas to counter Sartre. The everyday public existence of a social, a political, or a professional life bears no obvious mark of "being-Jewish" (they are just another painting or literature) but nonetheless at its most intimate, its most illegible, the ontological category remains.

But on another level, Derrida challenges this distinction when he asks by what right one can distinguish between the two. Derrida brackets this question in order to "act for awhile as if these two orders were distinct, to seek to determine later on [not yet], here or elsewhere, at least as a disputable hypothesis, the rule of what passes [*ce qui passe*] from one to the other, the rule of what occurs [*ce qui se passe*] between the two, and for which I would have, in sum, to respond."[62] It is in this "in between" that Derrida finds his response to the "Jewish Question." "Yes, it is a matter, once again, of responding. And *yes*, of responding 'yes.' "[63] Here, too, the work of Levinas is in play as this statement echoes one Derrida made on the occasion of Levinas's death on December 27, 1995. In *Adieu to Emmanuel Levinas*, Derrida cites Levinas's lecture on "The Temptation of Temptation," expressing his debt to "all the great themes to which the thought of Emmanuel Levinas has awakened us, that of responsibility first of all, but of an 'unlimited' responsibility that exceeds and precedes my freedom, that of an 'unconditional yes.' "[64] In *Adieu*, this unconditional yes is articulated (by both Levinas and Derrida) as a movement stronger than death that in this way "sets out on a path that ran counter to the philosophical tradition extending from Plato to Heidegger."[65] Thus, we must keep the earlier reference to the "Temptation of Temptation" in mind as Derrida continues his response:

Without even naming Abraham, prior to daring to issue a summons toward the immense figure of the patriarch presumed to respond to the calling of his name, "yes, here I am," "I am here," "I am ready," one must know (and this is the first Abrahamic teaching, prior to any other) that if everything begins *for us* with the response, if everything begins with the "yes" implied in all responses ("yes, I respond," "yes, here I am," even if the response is "no"), then any response, even the most modest, the most mundane, of responses remains an acquiescence given to some self-presentation.[66]

Derrida's answer is ambiguous as the "for us" could refer to either the "public" sphere of universalism or the intimate realm of Jewish identity, but both are predicated on the named but disavowed call to Abraham. One might call this the original "Jewish Question" to which Abraham responds, "I am here," and without which there would be no further question about Jews or Judaism. Derrida refers to this as an "acquiescence to some self presentation" and by maintaining the status of the "in between" he conserves its secular/universal utility. Thus, as for Levinas, the response to the call is an election, it is a matter of "answering-*to* (to whom? to someone, always, to a few, to everybody, to you), of answering *before*, therefore, and of answering for (for one's acts and words, for oneself, for one's name; for example, for one's being-jew or not, etc.). In short it would be a matter of taking responsibility, a responsibility that we know, in advance, exceeds all measure."[67] This, of course, puts Derrida in close proximity to Levinas both in terms of the call to responsibility but also in announcing the privileged place of the Other.

But Derrida is uneasy with this call, with this election:

> . . . every time I have had to address seriously, if in a different mode, within the history of philosophy and of onto-theology, for example in Nietzsche, Heidegger, or Levinas [I want to note that Derrida includes Levinas], and in many others as well, this theme of an originary guilt or incrimination, a guilt or a responsibility, the theme of a debt, an indebtedness, a being-indebted, all originary, prior to any contract, prior to contracting anything; well then, every time I have addressed this great philosophical problematic, I would see returning, from the bottomless ground of memory, this dissymmetric assignation of being-Jew, coupled immediately with what has become, for me, the immense and most suspect, the most problematical resource, one before which anyone, therefore the Jew among others, must remain watchful, on guard, precisely: the cunning resource of *exemplarism*.[68]

On the one hand, the call to and from the Other announced in the call to and response from Abraham is the exemplary moment of putting oneself before the Other, of giving oneself over to the hospitality of the other, the revelation of the dissymmetric assignation of "being-Jewish." But on the other hand, it is a moment of separation, of hierarchical elevation, and of the temptation to assume such an election consists of having been "chosen a guardian of a truth, a law, an essence, in truth here of a universal responsibility."[69] This is the paradox and contradiction that Derrida sees inherent in "being-Jewish."

But it is also the basis for Derrida's main critique of Sartre in *Reflections on the Jewish Question*. Derrida states that his principal reproach to the "Sartrian logic" is Sartre's assumption that he has defined and mastered the concept of what it *means* to be a Jew. That he can assign a fixed and stable identity or essence to the Jew (but not only to the Jew). It is on the basis of this initial assumption that Sartre is able to distinguish the positive and negative attributes of authentic and inauthentic Jews. Derrida's preference for the dissymmetric, as opposed to fixed, nature of being-Jewish, leads him to counter Sartre by instructing us that "what *must not* be done is to pretend to know, to dissemble as if one believed one knew what one said, when one does not know."[70] Following Derrida's logic, if the exemplary attribute of "being-Jewish" is the non-coincidence of identity, the answering to the call of an other that puts oneself in question, then Sartre's presumption to know the fixed identity of the Jew is faulty and renders Sartre's further distinction of Jews as either authentic or inauthentic untenable. Furthermore, Derrida tells us, what Sartre "does not recognize is from whence came and toward what the ruin of the distinction is going, wherever it is in use, and in the discourse of the age, first in the Heidegger of *Being and Time*, for whom the question of authenticity was no doubt more originary and more powerful than the question of truth."[71] The allusion to Heidegger and the issue of authenticity in relation to Jews opens an avenue of investigation that Derrida chooses not to pursue. Instead, he returns to the ruin of the distinction and the way this affects "any utterance of self-presentation of the type: 'I affirm that I am Jewish'; or 'here I am, I am a Jew of such and such kind'; or 'there is no possible misunderstanding, here is why I call myself, why I am called, me, Jew.'"[72] But on what grounds does one know if one's self-presentation, one's Jewishness, is authentic or not? Here the register has shifted from the external categorization of the Jew by Sartre, or the more universal designation of authentic and inauthentic by Heidegger, to the "self-presentation" of Jews who designate themselves as such.

The solution, for Derrida, lies embedded in the constitutive dissymmetry imposed by the law of what announces to the Jew his own identity and the perpetually futural nature of this identity that is always to be determined. The "here I am," the "I am Jewish," is itself a response to the order or injunction of the other "to whom the 'I' of the 'I am Jewish' is held hostage" and to whom it must respond. The "I" of the "I am Jewish" is not the first to know that "I am Jewish" and thus the logic of Jewish identity is necessarily predicated on a displacement of the self in relation to the other. It is an identity that does not coincide with itself.[73] Derrida is quick to assert that one should recognize "in this heteronomous dissymmetry of the hostage that I am, the very traits, the universal features that Levinas gives to ethics in general, as metaphysics or first philosophy—against ontology."[74] The work of Levinas thus provides Derrida with a counter to the logic of essentialism and exemplarism that Derrida diagnosed as inherent in Sartre's understanding of what it means to be a Jew. This is so in the way that Derrida's "constitutive dissymmetry" or non-coincidence of identity mirrors Levinas's understanding of election structuring personhood wherein "there is a contradiction in the notion of 'ego' ['*moi*'] that defines this notion." But it is also so in the way that Derrida's temporal construct of "being-Jewish" conserves Levinas's presentation wherein "being-Jewish" eschews completion in that it is always situated in the "not yet" of an "infinite time behind us" and the promise of a messianic future to come.

But here we must be vigilant to the ways that Derrida *includes* Levinas in the lineage of "the most problematical resource" that he begins with Nietzsche and Heidegger. Despite Derrida's laudatory words regarding Levinas's ethics, he concludes his statement by cautioning that here "again is posed the great question of an *exemplarist* temptation."[75] Derrida's work seems to imply that in Levinas's attempt to overcome the temptation of temptation, Levinas himself has given into the *exemplarist* temptation instead. The promise and problem of Levinas's stance in relation to Derrida can be seen in "The Temptation of Temptation." Whereas one can certainly reconcile Levinas's statement that "the world is here so the ethical order has the possibility of being fulfilled" with Derrida's own pronouncements about "messianicity" and the "not yet" of a Judaism/Jewishness to come, there is divergence with the more particular statement that conditions Levinas's remark: "The meaning of being, the meaning of creation, is to realize Torah . . . the question of ontology will thus find its answer in the description of the way Israel receives the Torah."[76] So while Levinas avoids the ego-centered model of fixed identity that Derrida associates with the work of Sartre, he does so by positing a transcendent theological relationship predicated on election. Here the cunning ruse of exemplarism is fulfilled not by the assumption of fixed identity but by the relation between an unknowable God and the specific people He has chosen to fulfill His covenant. And yet, Derrida does not forfeit this category of "being-Jewish" and instead seeks to provide a definition that will not yield to the temptation of exemplarism as manifest in either racial or theological boundaries. This is a presentation of the ontology of being-Jewish that is still reliant on Levinas but not on the theological implications of Levinas's model of transcendence and the related problem of the ways that election still addresses a people chosen by God and thereby elevated above all others.

Derrida commences "Abraham, the Other" by instructing us to think of "another Abraham" and concludes by articulating that this possibility, "that there should be yet another Abraham," is "the most threatened Jewish thought, but also the most vertiginously, the most intimately Jewish one that I know to this day."[77] This is because, for Derrida, this possibility of another Abraham, the possibility of a mistaken election, that "perhaps I have not been called, and that perhaps I will never know it is not me who has been called. Not yet. Perhaps in a future to come, but not yet" threatens the origins and identity of Judaism itself and thus is indicative of the constitutive dissymmetry of being-Jewish.[78] But this suspended identity that perpetually calls itself into question is itself held up, authorized as it were, not by another Abraham (the condition of dissymmetry) but by another Moses to whom this condition has been revealed.

This transposition of Moseses begins with *Moses and Monotheism* when Freud replaces the "Moses" of Jewish religion with an Egyptian Moses to reveal the scientific or psychoanalytic essence of Jewishness.[79] In terms of Derrida's attempt to provide a definition of the essence of Jewishness, we see a "performative repetition" of Freud who himself performed such a repetition of Moses. Just as Freud "opened" and "enriched" the archive of Jewish tradition through his psychoanalytic interpretation of the story of Moses, Derrida likewise "opens" and "enriches" it through his deconstructive reading of Abraham. But, I would argue that this move of inscription is more violent than Derrida allows. In the case of Freud, by revealing the "historical" psychoanalytic truth about Moses and Jewishness he revokes the divine Revelation at Sinai and removes the cloak of religion, leaving only his own revelation and interpretation of what it means to be Jewish. Derrida, in turn, preempts Freud's interpretation of Moses by destabilizing Abraham. In so doing, Derrida inserts himself into the inheritance from Moses and Abraham but also Freud and Levinas by inscribing deconstruction into the heart of Jewish identity. This move absolves the category of "being-Jewish" from both the theological and racial/cultural boundaries (a fixed and stable Jewish identity) that Derrida associates with exemplarism, but it also dictates that whatever quality might found this category remain perpetually hidden or secret and always to be determined.

Derrida presents the ontology of "being-Jewish" as the "experience of appellation and responsible response" where "any certainty regarding the destination, and therefore the election, remains suspended, threatened by doubt, precarious, exposed to the future of a decision of which I am not the masterful and solitary—authentic—subject."[80] For Derrida, the oscillation and undecidability that condition the non-coincidence of Jewish identity and thus permanently resist the temptation of exemplarism are precisely what is revealed as *exemplary* about "being-Jewish." Here "being-Jew would then be something more, something other than a simple lever—strategic or methodological—of a general deconstruction; it would be its very experience, its chance, its threat, its destiny, its seism."[81] For Derrida, "being-Jewish" is the experience of deconstruction.

In this way Derrida is able to maintain the category of "being-Jewish," and even its exemplary nature, by employing the temporal structure inherited from Levinas shorn of its theological implications by way of Freud. But to maintain the futural nature of the dissymmetrical identity, Derrida must provide a mechanism that conserves the Levinasian refutation of Heideggerian finitude without recourse to divine transcendence. Now, we have shown the way that Levinas confronts Heidegger's model of being-toward-death and how this revision is the basis for the opening to transcendence, infinity, and the Other. For Derrida, this move is important but problematic. In Derrida's text *Aporias* from 1993, Derrida cites Levinas to demonstrate the ways that Levinas's attempt to refute Heidegger on the issue of death and "mineness" actually conserves several key aspects of Heidegger's argument:

> when Levinas says and thinks that, against Heidegger, he is saying "I am responsible for the other in so far as he is mortal," these statements either designate the experience that I have of the death of the other in demise or they presuppose, *as Heidegger does*, the co-originarity of *Mitsein* and *Sein zum Tode*. This co-originarity does not contradict but on the contrary, presupposes a mineness of dying or of being-toward-death.[82]

Levinas, like Heidegger, still assumes a certain self-presentation of fixed "mineness" in the positing of an exemplary ego, not in relation to one's own finitude, but in relation to the death of the other. Derrida contests the fixed nature of this election in an attempt to correct the exemplary ontological assumptions of Levinas's reading of "being-Jewish," providing a deconstructive emphasis on the ways that "being-Jewish" is always an "in-between." "Being-Jewish" is exemplary but in the way that it eschews fixed categories by announcing an identity or election to come. Not yet. But as with Levinas, the crucial philosophical move is based on a confrontation with Heidegger and specifically Heidegger's presentation of death.

If we return to *Aporias*, we see the way that this confrontation turns on a critical reading of Heidegger's "death" and specifically the categories of "authentic" and "inauthentic" that he likewise challenges in "Abraham, the Other," and it is here that Derrida introduces the figure of the Marrano. "Death is always the name of a secret, since it signs the irreplaceable singularity. It puts forth the public name, the common name of a secret, the common name of the proper name without name," and "to that which lives without having a name, we will give an added name: Marrano for example. Playing with the relative arbitrariness of every nomination, we determine the added name [*surnom*], which a name always is, in memory of and according to the figure of the Marrano (of the crypto-Judaic, and of the crypto-X in general)."[83] The Marrano is the exemplary "crypto-X in general" but breaks down the logic of essentialism, of "mineness," authenticity, and exemplarity, because the identity of the Marrano, as Marrano, is predicated on the fact that it is not one's own in any way that can be owned or pointed to. Indeed, at the moment one "discovers" that one *is* a Marrano, the secret is revealed and thus one is a Marrano no longer. One is perhaps a Jew, a former Jew, or a converso, or even a former Marrano, but one is no longer a Marrano. Thus, the figure of the Marrano embodies the "not yet" and as such announces a future to come. Here Levinas's portal to the other through recourse to the transcendence announced by election and revelation is replaced by a logic of trace and the non-coincidence of identity:

> In the "not-yet" that bends us toward death, the expecting and waiting is absolutely incalculable; it is without measure, and out of proportion with the time of what is left for us to live. . . . Through an entirely interior path, which Heidegger does not signal, one then necessarily passes from the ontological "not yet," insofar as it says what is, in the indicative, to the "not yet" of prayer and desire, the murmured sigh: that death not come, *not yet!*[84]

This is a complex move because Derrida's "Marrano" conserves the structure of "being-toward-death" inherited from Heidegger in that the completion or totality of the Marrano is only complete at the moment when it no longer exists and thus the Marrano embodies the "not yet." But Derrida's "Marrano" does so by also conserving the category of "being-Jewish" inherited from Levinas in that the call or appellation of Marrano is made from without, thus denying the radical finitude of the Heideggerian model in favor of an opening to the Other.

But the Marrano, the secret Jew whose identity is bound up with the ignorance of that identity, holds weight beyond its use as a counter to the Heideggerian or Levinasian understanding of *Angst* in the face of death. For Derrida's "Marrano" is a category that is ultimately Jewish even if, unlike Levinas's model of election and revelation, Derrida's "Marrano" is predicated on a secret. It is "secretly but visibly, sheltered by a secret he wants manifest, by a secret he is anxious to make public," a secret that Derrida wants to reveal.[85] In "Abraham, the Other," Derrida speaks of himself "both as the least Jewish, the most unworthy Jew, the last to deserve the title of authentic Jew, and at the same time, because of all this . . . the last and therefore the only survivor fated to assume the legacy of generations, to save the response or responsibility before the assignation, or before the election, always at risk of taking himself for another."[86] It is because he sees himself as unworthy of the title that he finds himself as the inheritor of this legacy. Derrida's self-description as "the last and the least of the Jews" is based on the constitutive dissymmetry of identity articulated in his presentation of "another Abraham," one who is never truly sure that it is he who has been called. But it belies the ways that in talking about the "last and least of the Jews," Derrida is actually talking about Moses. For it was Moses who was drawn from the water and raised as an Egyptian, not a Hebrew. It was Moses who quarreled with God in the desert about his unworthiness for the task. And it was also Moses who saw an Egyptian beating a Hebrew and recognizing his kinfolk, his people, his secret identity, killed the Egyptian making his secret public.[87] In this way we might say that Moses is the first Marrano and this could very well make Derrida the last. "The last and therefore the only survivor fated to assume the legacy of generations." But as with Moses, for Derrida there remains something essential and exemplary about the ontology of "being-Jewish." Something violent.[88]

Indeed, despite Derrida's claim that he is "playing with the relative arbitrariness of every nomination," there is nothing arbitrary about his use of the Marrano, the secret Jew who is at his or her core, at his or her most intimate and most illegible somehow *still* a Jew. Even if I do not know it, I am *still* a Jew. It is not only the future that holds a "not yet" but also Derrida's conception of "being-Jewish" that "does not necessarily, nor always, bear visible traces" but announces that assimilation or eradication has not come, *not yet!* And yet, the "Marrano" is no neutral philosophical term. It evokes, and is bound by, a history of persecution and violence, of forced conversion and of the need to hide one's identity. It is haunted by the issue of "*limpieza de sangre*," the cleanliness or the purity of blood, but also the need to maintain this purity, to keep the "authentic" pure Spaniard separate from the impurities of the Jew. For Derrida and for Levinas, these issues of Jewish identity, of authenticity and inauthenticity, of essentialism, nationalism, and purity, all come to bear in their respective responses to the philosophy of Heidegger and the issue of death. But Heidegger is no neutral figure either.

Here the question that is evaded, disavowed, is the question of the place of the Shoah, the Holocaust, the final solution in Levinas's and Derrida's investigation of "being-Jewish." It casts a dreadful light on Sartre's *Reflections* and there is no doubt that it occupies a central place in the responses of Levinas and Derrida and yet it is not allowed to be central. The philosophical issue is Heidegger, not National Socialism; authenticity, not racial purity; death, not the Holocaust. And yet, with very little effort we can see the one at the center of the other. The issue of the Holocaust necessarily provokes a questioning of Jewish existence. This is so for Levinas and Derrida (and perhaps for others, perhaps for us today) and yet it is an issue that cannot be announced as the positive basis by which to articulate such an identity. Like the Marrano, it must necessarily remain a secret, for once it is revealed the fundamental nature of the conversation has changed: it is no longer a question of "being-Jewish" but instead a question of the Holocaust. "It is the murderer who wants to equate death with nothingness"—on this point both Levinas and Derrida agree.[89]

Thus, for Levinas and Derrida, the "Jewish Question" in France after the Holocaust is a question deferred. Not yet answered, and yet there is a response. The Jewish Question is replaced by the question of "being-Jewish." For Levinas, this category of "being-Jewish" creates a blind spot where he conserves aspects of the authentic/inauthentic distinction inherited from the philosophy of Heidegger. It is a retention that cannot be taken lightly because in the aftermath of the Holocaust, Levinas realized all too well the potential and actual danger of this construct. And yet it is precisely because of the Holocaust that Levinas cannot let go of this distinction for fear that the very annihilation assigned to the Jews by the Nazi final solution will come to be fulfilled by assimilation into the "modern" world. Derrida detects this blind spot in the work of Levinas, and thus by all rights one would expect that he discard the category of "being-Jewish" because of the way it is imbued with what he calls "exemplarism." And yet Derrida, too, is compelled to maintain the category even as he strains to decontaminate it from the dangers of the authentic/inauthentic divide by means of what he calls constitutive dissymmetry. But here we must recall that Derrida establishes this category in relation to his own childhood in Algeria under Vichy rule and no matter what else the categories of "being-Jewish" or the Marrano may hold for Derrida, they are still categories that conserve and retain some form of particularly Jewish identity.

On the surface and at its most legible, this response evades the ways that Levinas and Derrida each construct a paradigm of Jewish identity in response to the Holocaust by replacing the Jewish question as articulated by Sartre with the originary Jewish Question that preempts all others: the call from God to Abraham that elicited Abraham's response, "I am here." This is *the* Jewish question and the response dictates the conditions of the ontology of "being-Jewish" that Levinas and Derrida each articulate in a manner to conform with their respective philosophical programs even as it strains the logical consistency of their larger ethical or philosophical statements. In the end, both Levinas's call for responsibility and openness to the Other and Derrida's constitutive dissymmetry designed to avoid essentialism are principally and essentially Jewish qualities. This surely has philosophical and political ramifications.

Thus hidden, at its most intimate, at its most illegible, this "I am here" conceals the secret impulse of a "not yet" that reveals the way both Levinas and Derrida build their philosophical constructs on an unyielding need to conserve an indissoluble kernel of Jewish identity. This is the "not yet" of the Marrano that is the answer to the Jewish Question after the Holocaust. "I am *not yet* assimilated," "I am *not yet* annihilated." Inserted and concealed at the very heart of the response is a temporal mechanism that holds us between an elected past and a future to come through a forceful exclamation of existence: "I am *still* here!" By a logic or a mechanism that Levinas and Derrida are not yet able to confront: Not yet Marrano.

Poetics of the Broken Tablet

SARAH HAMMERSCHLAG

I'd like to begin with two of Derrida's citations of Levinas. The first is from the essay "Avowing," Derrida's 1998 paper given at the Colloque des Intellectuels Juifs de langue Française, a nearly annual meeting of French Jewish intellectuals. From its commencement in 1957 until the end of his career, Levinas was the most frequent contributor to this colloquium, as well as its strongest intellectual force. The year 1998 was Derrida's second appearance at the meeting. His first was in the 1960s at Levinas's behest. Here he is quoting from a Talmudic reading that Levinas himself gave at the Colloque in October 1963 on the topic of the Pardon:

> The respect for the stranger and the sanctification of the name of the Eternal are strangely equivalent. And all the rest is a dead letter. *All the rest is literature.*[1]

The second citation is from *Literature in Secret*, the supplementary essay that Derrida added to the second edition of *Gift of Death*:

> [. . . I remember how one day on the sidelines of a dissertation defense Levinas told me, with a sort of sad humor and ironic protestation, "Nowadays, when one says 'God,' one almost has to ask for forgiveness or excuse oneself: 'God,' if you'll pardon the expression . . . ."][2]

Considered contextually, like so many of Derrida's citations of Levinas, both seem to be offered as a means of solidifying Derrida's alliance with

Levinas. In the first case, Derrida has just finished describing his proximity to Levinas, the closeness of their friendship and indeed his admiration for the teaching. In the second, the comment is proposed as an aside, inside brackets and with the disclaimer that the anecdote is not essential to what Derrida has to say. Yet like so many of Derrida's citations—of Levinas in particular—they should be read at a slant. That is to say, we should consider how Derrida's repetition of his source in a new context alters and indeed undermines the content of the original.

Nonetheless, it is probably Derrida's insistence on the proximity between the two philosophers that has allowed critics to associate the two, an association that has been key in the recent spate of arguments that target the alleged postmodern fetishization of otherness. Each in its own way, the attacks all confirm the move that makes the Jew a metonym for "the other." They represent deconstruction as a Jewish science and invoke the Greek and Christian alternatives with their own anti-Jewish rhetoric to counter. Besides Žižek and Badiou, both of whom we can obviously include in this camp, there is also Jacques Rancière, who laments what he calls the "new reign of ethics," which, he suggests, leads to a depoliticization of the public sphere and replaces politics with "the sheer ethical conflict of good and evil."[3] Rancière goes as far as associating the Bush era rhetoric of "infinite justice" with this turn of thought.[4] In the essay "Should Politics Come? Ethics and Politics in Derrida," Rancière criticizes Derrida, specifically claiming that his dependence on Levinas's ethics leads him to a politics that is predicated on theology.[5] Rancière's concern is to differentiate his own political philosophy from Derrida's, a difference he delineates in the following terms: Where his own political thought is committed to an idea of the political actor "playing the part of anyone," speaking as the uncounted, for the principle of the demos, a principle that demands on the part of the polis "an indifference to difference," Derrida's "democracy to come" is predicated on a commitment to an absolute other, who cannot make a demonstration of the relationship between his or her inclusion or exclusion. What Derrida would reject, Rancière contends, about his own politics, is the principle of substitutability, an indifference to difference as the enactment of politics. More specifically, he argues that Derrida would reject the possibility that inclusion and exclusion can be staged, that anyone can and should take up and represent as "the no one in particular" the wrongs done to another.

Rancière's position is based on a misreading of Derrida's relation to Levinas, one that fails to take into account Derrida's and Levinas's respective relations to Judaism, election, and, above all, literature. We can elucidate this misreading, as well as the political stakes of Derrida's treatment of Judaism, by considering the twin figures of the poet and rabbi in his thought. By analyzing specifically the relation between the poet and the rabbi it becomes clear that at least one strand of Derrida's political thought *is* fundamentally a staging of the political actor's inclusion and exclusion. For both Rancière and Derrida the "as if" or the "*comme si*" are, in fact, key to the enactment of political identity. For both, this implies an active role for a literary/aesthetic procedure, that is to say, for the role of performance in the articulation of the political identity. One could even say that the figure of the Jew is central to the way in which each comes to his political model. What differentiates Rancière and Derrida is not that Derrida cannot accept the democratic play of the *as if*, it is the fact that for Derrida such a performance must take place *with* an acknowledgment of what this performance conceals. It is in this capacity that the figures of the rabbi and the poet are key to his political thought. For in thinking through their relation, he reveals a mode of inclusion that does not elide difference, but rather makes tarrying with it a necessity. For Rancière, the performance of the *as if* is what allows for differences to be overcome on the political scene. For Derrida, it is what puts these differences in play.

The Poet and the Rabbi—Jabès and Celan

Derrida treats the relation between the rabbi and the poet in his essays on Edmond Jabès and Paul Celan. An analogy between the rabbi and the poet is already at work in their poetry, which Derrida is keen to highlight. Ultimately, though, it is thinking about the poet's betrayal of the covenantal relationship that is paradigmatic for him, providing a model for how he relates to Judaism, and to those philosophical structures that are tied for him to Judaism by way of Levinas: responsibility, the secret, and election. By tracing out this path we can follow Derrida's movement from ethics to politics. What we'll see is that Rancière is right to see Levinas as a crucial step in this process. The relation is not one of loyalty or reliance, however, but one of betrayal. A poetics of the broken tablet is one path that leads to politics.

Marina Tsvétaeva's comment that "all poets are Jews," most famously used as an epigram by Paul Celan in the volume *Die Niemandsrose*, gets the analogy up and running. Derrida interprets the metaphor as a commentary on the poet's relation to language, which for Derrida is analogous to the relation between the Jew and circumcision. As he establishes most clearly in *Monolingualism of the Other*, this is, in fact, the universal experience of language. Each of us has a native tongue. We are born into language and that language "precedes us, governs our thought, gives us the names of things."[6] We are each of us in this sense circumcised: subject to an idiom we did not choose. Like the cut of circumcision, language binds us to the specificity of a culture. What then differentiates the Jew from every other person born into a specific language? The same thing that differentiates the poet from every other person circumscribed by language. In the case both of the poet and the Jew, the relationship can be read as something like an intensification of the universal. What they share, Derrida suggests, is the structure of their relationship of attachment, which in "Edmond Jabès and the Question of the Book" he refers to as the response to a *"convocation,"* the giving oneself over to a calling.[7] One can even say that what the poet and the Jew share is the structure of election. That is to say, it is by calling attention to their respective ties to the particular, through the idiom, through circumcision, that they testify to the universal. Each marks out for Derrida a position that is neither a pure particularism nor an attempt to eradicate difference in the name of a homogenous universalism. What Derrida says about the Jew one could equally say about the poet: "The Jew's identification with himself does not exist. The Jew is split, and split first . . . between the two dimensions of the letter: allegory and literality."[8]

Nonetheless, the dynamic of election cuts both ways for Derrida. The figure of the rabbi in Derrida's work signifies not merely as another name for "Jew" but as a name for the procedure of inscription that binds one to a community. As he says in *Schibboleth*, the rabbi is the "guardian and the guarantor." He marks "the place of decision for the right of access to the legitimate community."[9] Edmond Jabès's *The Book of Questions* is filled with imaginary rabbis who make elusive statements about the relationship between writing, God, and the Jew. But, as Derrida points out, it is also haunted by the specter of those very real rabbis who would object to their metaphoric function within the text. Derrida quotes the passage in Jabès when he addresses the relation between his fictional rabbis and those real rabbis whose pact is that of the "blood brother." "To make no difference between a Jew and him who is not Jewish, is this not already to cease being a Jew?" they say.[10] The rabbis appear here as the quintessential sentinels, determining who is on the inside of the community and who is on the outside. The rabbi would then seem to be a figure with which Derrida would resist identification for the rabbi seems to be tied, for Derrida, to the violence that is inevitable in any pact, in any claim to election, in any inscription. Yet he famously signs his essays on Jabès with names that are borrowed from Jabès's volume: Reb Rida and Reb Derissa.

The metaphor of the sentinel is also prominent, of course, in Derrida's essay *"Shibboleth*, on Paul Celan," the title of which references the paradigmatic example of border patrol. One element of this essay is certainly to expose the way in which poetry in general but Celan's poems in particular resist translation and declare *No pasarán*—they shall not pass.

The other element of the essay, however, is to consider the way in which the poem gestures toward the universal. In reading Celan, Derrida focuses on the way Celan's poetry expresses the process by which a singular moment, the unrepeatable, is ciphered in the date, which marks the singularity but also enters the singular into the ring of cyclical time.[11] The date is already here a figure for the poem itself. Despite their crypts, despite the way in which they block access to the moments and experiences that provoke the writing of the poem, "the poem speaks!" writes Derrida, quoting Celan. "Instead of walling up, or reducing to silence the singularity of the date, it gives to it the chance, the chance to speak to the other."[12]

It is the structure of the date as cycle that annuls the singularity of the event, but it is also the date that gives the poem a chance to speak, to speak to another: the date provides the chance for an encounter with the date of another. Celan's poems simultaneously speak of the possibility of opening this space of encounter while at the same time drawing attention to the crypts in language, to the way in which language simultaneously opens itself to the other while guarding its singular secrets. Every act of communication, then, is in some sense a missed encounter. What remains, however, even when the discursive element of the poem is inscrutable, is the call, the pure address of the poet to the reader.

The key, then, for Derrida is the way poetry, like the date, places the event into circulation through repetition while at the same time guarding within itself a crypt. Like all language poetry cannot but mean. What differentiates poetry from philosophy, for Derrida, is not the fact that poetry toggles between the literal and the universal—for it is in the nature of language itself that it both universalizes and particularizes—but rather the way poetry handles both of these features. What in general distinguishes poetry or the self-consciously literary text from the philosophical text is the manner in which each relates to the "thetic" act. It is not that literary texts suspend the thetic act, but that they suspend and thus undermine a "naïve belief in meaning or referent."[13] Literary language, whether by means of verse or the use of tropes, circles or turns around the process of meaning making, like a spectator circling but not approaching its object of interest. It calls attention to the process by the very act of complicating it.

The image of the turn provides the basis for the analogy between the poem and circumcision in *Schibboleth*, bringing us back to the figure of the rabbi (or, better yet here, the Mohel). What is the relation between he who makes the circumcision and he who circumscribes the event of the cut? We must deal here not only with similarities but also with differences and, thus, finally with the act that the poet himself performs on the rabbi.

As Derrida writes in "Edmond Jabès and the Question of the Book":

> Poetry is to prophecy what the idol is to truth . . . . Poetic auton-omy, comparable to none other, presupposes broken tablets . . . . Be-tween the fragments of the broken Tablets the poem grows and the right to speech takes root.[14]

While this analogy is taken up in more direct terms in the essays on Jabès, it is in *Schibboleth* that Derrida theorizes what it means for the poet to turn around, as opposed to what it would mean for the rabbi to cut around.

Rabbi Loew, the Maharal of Prague, appears in Celan's poem "Einem, der vor der Tür Stand." This rabbi, most famous for creating a golem, as-serted a belief in the election of the people Israel on metaphysical grounds, created by God to accept the Torah.[15] In this poem he is the object of a request that would universalize that election: "Beschneide das Wort!" (Circumcise the word!) The cut is displaced onto the word. The request both cements the analogy between the poet and the rabbi and performs a literary operation on the cut itself by making it a trope. On the one hand, the request recalls the fact that language can itself function differentially, like the Shibboleth, but it also turns both the rabbi and the circumcision into literary figures whose drama is performed on language and not on the body. What, then, is the relation between the poem and Rabbi Loew, both a very real person and himself already the object of a legend? The poem emancipates, Derrida suggests. "The transfer," he says, "is beholden to the narrative, but absolved from and having no relation to its literal-ity."[16] This emancipation also makes the poem the site of a welcoming. As the title of the poem indicates, the poem awaits the one who is at the door and is itself a gesture of welcome that resists the move to predetermine *who* comes. The poem, unlike the religious text, is indeed destined for anyone and no one. In the opening pages of *Schibboleth*, Derrida quotes another poem of Celan's, "À la pointe acérée," which includes the line "Tür du Davor einst, Tafel" (Door you in front of it once, tablet). It is a line that encapsulates what takes place in the poem "Einem, das vor der Tür stand": The Tafel has become a Tür. In the poem, the tablets (now broken) have become a door.

One can indeed say the same about Jabès's *Le Livre des Questions*, which parodies the rabbinic texts of the canon. There is no law in the poems on which to comment. It is commentary emancipated from the law. The rab-bis' aphorisms, even when they are about Judaism, are not about Judaism proper but Judaism as metaphor for writing. It is the rabbinic commentary, dependent on the original broken tablets, that creates the possibility for this poetic parody, but the difference between the poet and the rabbi is nonetheless irreducible.

So what is Derrida himself doing when he signs his essay "Reb Derissa"? First of all, he is citing Jabès's text, for the signature itself is a citation from *The Book of Questions*. But the repetition is already a displacement. As Derrida writes in "Ellipsis," the final essay of *Writing and Difference* and the second essay on Jabès, "Once the circle turns, once the volume rolls itself up, once the book is repeated, its identification gathers an imperceptible difference which permits us efficaciously, rigorously, that is, discreetly to exit from closure."[17] Many have commented on the fact that Derrida signs these essays "Reb Rida" and "Reb Derissa," the rabbi of the fold, the laughing rabbi. But rarely is it noted that the signatures are themselves citations, a repetition, and thus not the signature of the rabbi but the signature of the poet, he who emancipates the word and sets it into circulation.

It is worth noting that the signature "Reb Rida" precedes "Violence and Metaphysics," announcing perhaps Derrida's own relation to Levinas: a poet to Levinas's rabbi. Is this a conceit of which Derrida was himself always aware, or does it show itself only in retrospect? We cannot be sure. What is clear is that the relation between the rabbi and the poet, as he lays it out in the early essays on Jabès, is one that develops over his career into a theory about the relation between religion and literature—a conjunction that, for Derrida, is intimately tied to his relationship to Levinas as well as to his own relation to Judaism.

Religion and Literature

Let us turn, then, to the first citation with which I began, taken directly from Levinas's Talmud reading "To the Other": "The respect for the stranger and the sanctification of the name of the Eternal are strangely equivalent. And all the rest is a dead letter. All the rest is literature."[18] Given in the context of the 1963 colloquium on the topic of forgiveness, it is one of Levinas's earliest stabs at this new form. As such, Levinas is anxious to specify his method as philosophical, aimed at exposing the Talmud's underlying universalism. He continues after these lines: "The search for the spirit beyond the letter, that is Judaism itself. We did not wait until the Gospels to know that."[19] For Levinas, literature is what remains idiomatic within the text, what cannot be universalized, what should be left aside by the interpreter. The model of interpretation is one that moves from the outside in. The literary aspects of the text are an empty shell. He suggests that the universalism of the message bursts through its particular manifestation. The task of the interpreter is to discard the literary in order to salvage the philosophical.

In Derrida's hands, however, Levinas's words take on a new sense. Indeed, "the rest is literature." But as we've already seen from Derrida's earliest essays on Jabès, this statement also implies an emancipatory promise. Literature is not merely what is left over once one has extracted the spirit of the text. Literature is what takes place after the tablets have been broken. Literature offers its own gesture toward the universal, but it does so without denying the crypts in language.

By *Schibboleth* (1986), Derrida is already beginning to work out the political dimension of this literary remainder. For Derrida, Celan's poem is paradigmatic of a mode of messianic speech. The request made to Rabbi Loew, "Beschneide das Wort," is a demand for the circumcision of the word, for a word that could open toward the other without overcoming the structure of the idiom, without enforcing homogeneity. This is a plea made possible by the literary transformation of a religious figure: Rabbi Loew has not only become a literary figure in Celan's poem, but the plea itself made to the rabbi can be read as a plea that the rabbi become a poet.

One can say the same of the sentence "the rest is literature" when it is put into Derrida's hands. Indeed, it becomes a plea made to Levinas to open the between-two that marks the dynamic of ethics, the covenant and the pact, to a third. In "Literature au Secret," Derrida theorizes exactly the process by which the pact is opened. The essay, added to the volume *Gift of Death* nine years after the original, returns to the themes of election, the secret, and the covenant, once again by way of the paradigmatic story of Abraham and Isaac. Literature is at issue from the very beginning of *Donner la mort*, insofar as Derrida's retelling of the Abraham and Isaac story is already a retelling of Kierkegaard's retelling. The circle has turned, but the stakes of that turning are not themselves theorized until Derrida appends "Littérature au secret" to the original text and rewrites the conclusion of the original essay to reflect this new point of emphasis. One of the primary payoffs of the original text is the model of the secret as paradigmatic for thinking about the covenantal relationship and thus for thinking about Judaism and Christianity. Derrida's own retelling of the Abraham-Isaac story suggests that the key to the story—particularly Kierkegaard's rendering—is the fact that God's test of Abraham becomes the test of secrecy, where telling is the ultimate betrayal. There is no doubt that Levinas is indeed in the background here, as the section entitled "Tout autre est tout autre" has already established the parallel between

Levinas's model of responsibility and the covenant Abraham makes with God. Derrida is speaking here about the nature of the covenant—the brit or the bris (to recall the theme of circumcision)—and about the call of election that pertains both to ethics and to religion. In critiquing Levinas, Derrida often works simultaneously on both the ethical and religious registers by putting into play Levinas's own blurring of this distinction.[20]

So what is the relation of literature to this dynamic? We have already seen it at play in *Schibboleth*, in Derrida's theorizing about the relation between the poem and the date and between the poet and the rabbi, but he makes the function explicit in "Literature in Secret." In *Schibboleth* Derrida exposes the way in which the alliance of circumcision could be opened to the other, to the reader of the poem, without annulling the singularity of the cut. Here Derrida argues similarly that literature (he speaks particularly of fiction) is able to guard the secret while simultaneously betraying it. Literature is a form of representation and thus always involves the third. When I tell a story, I re-present. I betray the secret of what happened in the face-to-face relation. The telling of the story of Abraham's sacrifice of Isaac in the Bible is already a betrayal of the pact between Abraham and God, for it is the recounting of what Abraham could not himself tell, what he could not tell Sarah or Isaac. Modern fiction is the inheritor of this biblical betrayal. But it includes in its mode of representation, according to Derrida, a request of pardon for the betrayal. By treating what it represents as a fiction, it refuses to offer up the secret as something revealed. In that sense it exposes as betrayal what the Bible conceals. "Pardon de ne pas vouloir dire," or "Pardon for not meaning (to say)," Derrida contends in this essay, is the formula of modern literature.[21] This is the case on two accounts. First, fiction is marked by the suspension of a "vouloir dire" insofar as it disrupts any transparent relation between what is represented and reality. A fictional story recounts, it moves the relation between two to the plane of representation, where it becomes a relationship *for* a third. At the same time, it suspends the status of the relationship. In this sense it inherits the biblical task of revealing the secret, but it alters it by presenting its material under the auspices of fiction.[22] Second, even as it might seem to forge a new relation between two, between an I and a Thou, between the writer and the reader, it leaves this relationship undetermined. For even when I know the author of a story or a novel, I recognize that there is a disguise in play. I do not know from whence the story comes. I do not know from whom arrives the request, "Pardon for not meaning to say." Furthermore, she who sends out this pardon does not know to whom it is destined. The circulation of literature opens up the relationship between two to anyone who can pick up and read. It replaces the pure contentless call with content whose status has itself been called into question by the fact of its context itself having been disrupted. Once again, what is key here is a kind of repetition whose function is to undermine the dynamic of election without at the same time eradicating the fact that the call is between two.

Let us recall now the second citation with which I began. It is itself from "Literature in Secret." Let me quote again the passage: "I remember how one day on the sidelines of a dissertation defense Lévinas told me, with a sort of sad humor and ironic protestation: 'Nowadays, when one says "God" one almost has to ask forgiveness or excuse oneself: "God," if you'll pardon the expression.'"[23] In retelling the story Derrida is himself betraying something of the pact between two. The story is told of a moment when Levinas took Derrida into confidence. The act of its recounting not only enacts a betrayal of this confidence, it also reveals something of the transformative quality of literature. What we have here is a redoubled irony, for Levinas appears to have made the comment in a shared moment with Derrida, a moment in which Derrida as audience would appear to be in collusion with Levinas. Yet when Derrida retells the story in "Littérature au secret," it is in the context of describing literature as that which in relation to the naming of God, says "pardon." When Derrida recounts the anecdote he not only betrays the confidence but he re-signifies the meaning of what was said. Derrida, after all, is arguing for the importance of literature as that which does indeed ask for forgiveness for religion, for the invoking of God's name, particularly for invoking God's name as the origin of a call. "Literature," Derrida writes only a few pages earlier in "Littérature au secret," "would begin there where one does not know any more who writes and who signs the receipt of the call and of the 'me voici' between Father and son."[24]

This is exactly its virtue, Derrida argues again in "Abraham, l'autre," a paper given in 2000 on Derrida's relation to Judaism. This essay itself takes up Kafka's retelling of the Abraham parable—a repetition that very clearly uproots any presumed certainty as to both origin and destiny of the call. The payoff of this retelling, for Derrida, is the way in which it calls into question Levinas's model of election. The point is clear: "a call of the name worthy of this name must not make room for any certitude on the side of the destined one."[25]

Rancière, the Figure of the Jew, Politics

To return, then, to Rancière's reading of Derrida's relation to Levinas: Rancière bases his reading of this relation on *Gift of Death*, interpreting

Derrida's democracy to come as merely a turning of God's radical otherness into the otherness of any other. But what he misses, or at least doesn't address, is the role that literature plays for Derrida in relation to Levinas. Derrida demands that the structure of election—which Rancière suggests that Derrida *maintains* from Levinas—be itself uprooted or called into question. And it is the "pardon for not meaning to say" of literature that can serve this function. What the relation of the poet and the rabbi teaches us is that repetition does not involve loyalty, but rather betrayal, albeit a betrayal that Derrida contends is the ultimate loyalty. If Derrida repeats Levinas it is with the aim of inaugurating the moment "where one does not know any more who writes and who signs the receipt of the call and of the '*me voici*' between Father and son."[26] It is in order to interrogate Levinas's literary remainder.

Now Rancière boils his critique of Derrida down to the claim that Derrida cannot endorse the "idea of substitutability, the indifference to difference or the equivalence of the same and the other." What this means for Rancière is that Derrida cannot accept the democratic play of the "*as if*."[27] Ironically, Derrida himself employs the very same terminology—the *as if/ comme si*—to describe the dynamic of "the poetic and the literary," particularly as it relates to politics, to articulate, in fact, the play between the excluded and the included.[28] Let me then, in conclusion, compare the way each of these thinkers uses the mode of the *as if* not to elide their differences, but to recast these differences in new terms.

For Rancière what is at stake in creating a place for the "democratic play of the *as if*" is the idea that democracy is activated when the people take up the role of those who have no part. He calls this the "aesthetical dimension" of politics.[29] Interestingly enough, one of the iconic moments of this aesthetical dimension, for Rancière, is a moment when the figure of the Jew appeared on the political stage: the moment when the student supporters of Daniel Cohn-Bendit, in May of 1968, chanted, "We are all German Jews." It was a moment when the protestors took on the identity of an outsider to make a demand of the democracy that it live up to its name.[30] What makes this moment "aesthetic" for Rancière is the element of performance in which the discrepancy is revealed between the distribution of powers maintained by the police, which involve the ruling of some by others, and the democratic demand for equality. Rancière's further contention is that the new rule of "ethics"—by this he means not only Levinas, but those whose thought is dependent on Levinas—disenables exactly this kind of performance by claiming, as Alain Finkielkraut did after May 1968, that "the facetiousness of its polemical embodiments is an insult to the victims of absolute wrong."[31] Ethics blocks off a space of sacrality, according to Rancière, which disallows political staging and stops thought in its tracks. But Rancière fails to see that Derrida's politics take place by *staging* the very idea of sacrality, the idea of otherness, to which Rancière objects. The result is not the reification of sacrality or even its universalization; it is, rather, the performance of betrayal. Heteronomy is not denied, its necessary betrayal is enacted.

For Derrida, too, the *as if* is taken up in relation to the figure of the Jew. However, for Derrida the staging takes place in relation to his own identification with Jewishness by way of the figure of the Marrano. It is in this role that he most concretely plays the poet to Levinas's rabbi. In fact, Derrida himself takes up the critique levied by Rancière, Žižek, and others that Levinas's notion of election cannot be untethered from his relation to Judaism and that, indeed, the Levinasian notion of ethics is tied up with the sacralization of the Jew as victim. However, he does so not by opposing the Jewish turn in philosophy, but by poeticizing this turn. As we've seen already, he does so through the act of citation and repetition but also by playing out the dynamic of the *comme si* in relation to his own Jewish identity: "*As if* the one who disavowed the most, and who appeared to betray the dogmas of belonging . . . represented the last demand, the hyperbolic request of the very thing he appears to betray by perjuring himself."[32] The play of disavowal for Derrida—which is emblematic of the Marrano—is a procedure that uproots the dynamic of election by calling into question the act of presumption on the part of the one called. I assert that this has not only ethical but also political consequences, very real consequences for how we are to think of ourselves as actors in a political realm.

For Levinas, the model of election that marks ethical subjectivity is mirrored in his analysis of being-Jewish. Jewish election, for Levinas, is "the prerogative of moral consciousness itself, it knows itself at the center of the world and for it the world is not homogenous, for I am always alone in being able to answer the call. I am irreplaceable in my assumption of responsibility."[33] For Levinas, then, being Jewish exemplifies moral consciousness. The Jewish people are the historical bearers of ethical consciousness. Thus, election applies as a structure to moral consciousness in itself but also to the Jews as the exemplar of that consciousness.

The figure of the Marrano, for Derrida, overlays the idea of being Jewish. It signifies a repetition of this idea that undermines claims to my irreplaceability. It replaces irreplaceability with the act of disavowal. This does not eradicate the structure of responsibility, nor does it disrupt the demand that one respond to the other or to others, but it does uproot the claim of propriety, ownership, or performative mineness that Levinas maintains.

The Marrano, for Derrida, is the one who cannot claim Jewishness as his own. For to be a Marrano is to guard Jewishness as an absolute secret, disruptive of all mineness (*Jemeinigkeit*), such that to know one's self as a Marrano is no longer to be one. For Derrida, the mode of being faithful to the idea of the Marrano is disavowal: not to be a Jew in secret, but to claim oneself simultaneously as the least and the last of the Jews, in a performance that brings the figure of the Marrano into play while simultaneously announcing one's betrayal even of that secret, as well as the limits of performativity in general.[34]

We can see this operation as the inverse of the performance highlighted by Rancière in May of '68. In the case of May '68, according to Rancière, the students made a public display of their identification with the Jew, claiming to be German Jews when they were not, in order to announce that it did not matter *who* they were. The structure of the Marrano implies claiming *not* to be Jewish when one is, out of an allegiance to the secret of what one is, but cannot *claim* to be. For Derrida, this is a gesture that turns that identity into a sign of welcome: circumcises the word, makes the broken tablet into a door. For Rancière, the payoff of this moment of protest, this aesthetical dimension of politics, is the indifference to difference that is instantiated by those who play the part of the demos. The name in which this indifference is deployed is beside the point: the name German Jew could have been any name, the name for anyone. For Derrida, to the contrary, to be indifferent to what inscribes us into a particular covenant, a particular language, a particular people is not politics, it is denial. Inscription takes place. Election takes place. We respond. There are rabbis. But there are also poets.

Theism and Atheism at Play

Jacques Derrida and Christian Heideggerianism

EDWARD BARING

There was no religious turn. Many of the papers in this volume focus on texts from the 1990s. It was at this time that Derrida turned the formidable arsenal of a deconstructive methodology to questions of faith, messianism, and negative theology. The concentration on this period has led to an assumption that what one can loosely call "deconstruction" developed elsewhere for different purposes and was only belatedly applied to religious questions and theology. In this narrative religion was the newfound passion of a middle-aged man.

But later texts like *On the Name*, *The Gift of Death*, or "How to Avoid Speaking: Denials" were not Derrida's first explorations of these questions. In his writings before 1964, mostly unpublished courses he taught at the Sorbonne, Derrida grappled with the problems of evil, theology, and God, and placed the aporias of the infinite and the divine at the heart of his reflections.[1] By working through these early writings, I suggest that Derrida's fascination with religious questions provided a major motivation for his first engagement with the philosophical tradition, and lends new context to the earliest formulations of deconstruction. In particular, by drawing out the parallels between Derrida's ideas and a particular strand of postwar French religious thought, I argue that we can reassess Derrida's reading of two of his most important German sources and shed new light on the fraught relationship between religious and secular philosophy in modern intellectual history.

Heidegger in France

It has long been recognized that Derrida immersed himself from an early stage in the study of German phenomenology, especially the work of Edmund Husserl and Martin Heidegger. Derrida's analysis of Husserl's philosophy and, in particular, his concern for the theme of history as it emerged in Husserl's later writing was of crucial importance for his intellectual development. But often in this early work the reading of Husserl acted as a pretext and an opening for a close engagement with Heidegger's thought. Derrida's treatment of Husserlian phenomenology set the terms of this engagement, to be sure, but otherwise an analysis of the older phenomenologist's work served as a propaedeutic to Derrida's main concerns.[2]

Derrida, of course, was not alone in his fascination with Heidegger; since the 1930s, Heidegger had been a prominent figure in French intellectual life. The reading of Heidegger in France is extraordinarily complex, but it is possible to draw out certain strands of his reception. In the postwar period, it was Sartre's redeployment of certain Heideggerian themes that set the terms of the debate.[3] For Sartre, Heidegger's thought was most valuable for its existential description of the *réalité-humaine*, which, while foreign to most earlier forms of humanism, remained defiantly atheist and human-focused.

But by the early 1950s, this interpretation began to provoke responses from Christian thinkers who were particularly resistant to Sartre's atheism, and when Heidegger wrote his famous letter to Jean Beaufret in 1946 to reject the humanistic reading of his philosophy, a number of Christian thinkers came to embrace Heidegger's thought. For these philosophers, Heidegger's letter provided new resources to attack Sartre's atheism. Not only did it allow them to cast Sartre's humanism as the latest form of ontotheology, it also sketched out a new path toward understanding the relationship between man and the divine. Indeed, so central was Heidegger's letter to this group of Christian philosophers that they organized first its translation—an abridged version in 1946 by the Catholic scholar Joseph Rovan and in 1953 in full by the Jesuit Roger Munier—and then its publication as a book in the Christian existentialist *Philosophie de l'Esprit* collection founded by René Le Senne and Louis Lavalle.[4] Though they have been ignored by most scholars of the period, Christian writers produced a large proportion of all Heidegger scholarship in the 1950s, and the traces of their influence can be found in many of the canonical Heidegger interpretations of the time.

The most eminent of the new Christian interpreters of Heidegger in France was Henri Birault. Birault is important in his own right, often named alongside Jean Beaufret as a man who introduced the second Heidegger into France.[5] But as I will show, he is of particular interest here because his approach to Heidegger lends context to Derrida's own meditations on the German thinker and gives us a basis for rethinking the relationship between Derrida's early Heideggerianism and his stance on religion and theology. We know Birault was important for Derrida because he was one of the very few contemporary authors that Derrida cited positively in his own work at the time.[6] In fact, virtually all of Derrida's courses in the early 1960s, when he was teaching at the Sorbonne, followed the narrative laid out in Birault's most important article, "Heidegger and the Thought of Finitude," from 1960.[7]

In this article Henri Birault follows a line of argumentation that will be familiar to many modern scholars interested in post-structuralist approaches to religion. Birault described the need to move beyond a certain form of theology, found in both naïve religion and dogmatic atheism, to make room for a renewed faith. The occasion for this meditation was a reconstruction of the history of the finite within Western philosophy and its changing articulations with the concept of nothingness (*néant*).

The Greek conception of the finite, labeled by Birault "*finition*," presented it as the complete. In this model, and in contradistinction to modern perspectives, "the limit doesn't bring to an end [*ne met pas fin*], it doesn't enclose, oppress, or wound. On the contrary it inaugurates, liberates." The finite was the perfect. Accordingly, the *in*finite was *im*perfect because it lacked limits; it was "a degraded and inferior form of Being."[8] Indeterminate, the infinite was bereft of the limits that were necessary for existence, and so it participated in non-Being or the *néant*.

This was not, however, the only meaning of non-Being in Greek thought. Non-Being was not simply the opposite of Being—inexistence (a *nihil negativum*)—but was also understood as a form of alterity. In Plato's *Sophist*, Theatetus is led by a stranger in a meditation on the Parmenidian idea of non-Being. The Stranger suggests that the very possibility of speaking of non-Being—of making claims about it: "non-Being *is* . . ."—implies that, in Birault's words, "in a certain manner, it is."[9] But since this non-Being cannot be applied to any actual material being, its Being can only be located in the realm of ideas. As the stranger elaborated, and in direct opposition to the first meaning of non-Being in Greek thought, non-Being was the very condition of definition.[10] In this case then, as Birault summed up, negativity acts as the "essential foundation [*fondement*] of discourse . . . . It appears that Being itself must mix itself with non-Being for philosophy to be possible."[11] This second concept of non-Being and negativity thus added a wrinkle into Plato's system. As we saw earlier, non-Being marked the "bad infinity" in the sensible. But now it was equally the "good negativity" of linguistic determination. Both determination and indetermination, non-Being seemed to play both sides in the game of the finite.[12]

This strange duality of non-Being, according to Birault, reverberated throughout the Western metaphysical tradition and its various and changing conceptions of the finite. The Greek conception of the finite was almost completely reversed by the Judaic. In what Birault named *finité*, the finite could no longer be regarded as primary, because the infinite was the defining quality of the divine. Rather than the infinite being the negation of the finite, it was the finite that was a negation, made up of both "Being" and "nothingness"; the finite *lacked* infinity.[13]

The Judaic notion of the finite as *finité* may have lacked the infinite, but, Birault made clear, this was not to be understood as a privation or a fall, something that one might complain about or mourn as a loss. The human and the divine were just too far apart to allow the former any aspirations to the latter. Rather, *finité* was "a lack [*manque*] without pain [*douleur*], innocent negation."[14] Negativity was simply the opposite of Being, it was a *nihil negativum* without being a *nihil privativum*.

While the Judaic conception of the finite dramatically reversed that of the Greeks, it could not divest itself of the central ambiguity that had marked the concept of non-Being throughout its history. Because God was a positive infinite and the only being to participate fully in Being, it had to precede all other beings. Thus, in the Judeo-Christian tradition, God created the world *ex nihilo*, rather than merely ordering formless matter, as the Platonic demiurge had done. But at the same time, because only finite things participated in nothingness, participation in nothingness (*néant*) implied a "non participation in God." Nothingness thus allowed man a certain independence from the Divine.[15] Again, as with the Greek conception of *finition*, with the Judaic *finité*, nothingness seemed caught between two conflicting purposes and definitions: it both asserted our absolute dependence upon God, who created us *ex nihilo*, and marked our independence from divine power, insofar as his Being necessarily had to mix with the a non-divine nothingness in the act of creation.

Finitude was the third and most modern conception of the finite. Rather than the limit inaugurating Being, as in the Greek *finition*, or harmlessly marking the finite as apart from Being in its infinite fullness, as in the Judaic *finité*, in the modern concept of finitude the limit was presented as a "de-figuring and denaturing mutilation, in a word, an authentic privation."[16] Adopting the hierarchical framework of the Greek (the infinite is a *degraded* form of the finite), but the polarity of the Judaic (it is the finite rather than the infinite that participates in nothingness), the modern conception of finitude considered the finite as a fall (*chute*) from the infinite.

Birault elaborated the distinction between Judaic *finité* and finitude by turning to Descartes. In Cartesian philosophy, the notion of error came to add a new dimension to the finite. Error could no longer be understood merely as a result of the "*finité* of the created understanding," a result of our human limitations, like ignorance. Unlike ignorance, it was something for which we were responsible, something that we *should* be able to avoid. Thus, Cartesian error comprised both the recognition of our human limitations and an injunction to overcome them. As Birault wrote, "error arises [*relève*] . . . from the infinity of human will."[17]

Descartes was able to bring these two aspects together by casting the infinity of the will as the "refusal," or "forgetting of that same *finité*."[18] Finitude was thus a "negation of a negation," a negation of the original negation that was finite being, because it posed our limits as in principle surpassable. In this way the concept of finitude allowed for freedom from all constraints: finitude's freedom was the freedom of negativity.[19] And yet because this infinity of human will still remained infinitely far from the divine, "bit by bit it will be constrained to think itself as a *primitive fact*, as the foundation without foundation of the very humanity of man, now determined no longer as *ens creatum* or *son of God*, but as *subject*."[20]

It was, then, just a small step from the Christian idea of finitude to atheistic thought and the "death of God." Atheism set itself the task of overturning this earlier Christian philosophy, of rejecting the idea of a prior infinite and interpreting finitude as originary. In this atheistic and humanist conception, finitude was the *positive* condition for freedom, a yearning to overcome finite limitations, an opening to the indefinite and the unlimited.

But for Birault, this yearning to overcome limits, so foreign to both the early Greek conception of *finition* and the Judaic *finité*, showed that atheistic thought maintained the same essential structure of the Christian idea of finitude. Because atheistic finitude still experienced the finite as something to be overcome, it maintained the sense of the finite as a *mal*, a pain or evil; the secular idea of human infinite freedom caught within a finite form was merely a secularization of Christian sin and culpability, a development and distortion of the Judeo-Christian idea of the fall.[21] As Birault wrote: "What then is this *infinity of free finitude* if not an irreligious and Promethean infinite of Man who, in making himself God, makes himself man by the *transgression* of sin?"[22]

And if this new atheistic model had not fully released itself from an earlier Christian framework, it raised the question as to "whether the unhappy and properly finite dimension of finitude can be maintained when the inanity of the infinite finds itself denounced."[23] If we fully rid ourselves of the idea of God, can we still, as Sartre thought, explain why the *pour-soi* is impelled to overcome its limits? Without the desire for the divine, human freedom seems to lose its very *raison d'etre*: in the atheistic idea of finitude, the rejected God must still be maintained as an unacknowledged ideal.

It is for this reason that Birault turned to Heidegger, because Heidegger had taken some of the most important steps in separating his thought from traditional understandings of the Absolute or Infinity and from traditional metaphysics that remained so closely intertwined with theology.[24] More particularly, Birault wanted to show that there was no break between the "heroic atheism" of the first Heidegger, and the "religious quietism" of the second, because the themes of the second were already at work in the first.[25]

Thus, though the early Heidegger in *Being and Time* had used the term *Endlichkeit*, this could not be assimilated to or translated by the Sartrian concept of finitude, an assimilation that, according to Birault, had marked the first reading of Heidegger in France. Birault was very keen to show that the seeds of the rejection of this "Judeo-Christian idea of finitude," which ultimately led to Heidegger dropping the word *Endlichkeit*, were already to be found in *Being and Time*. As Birault wrote, "if finitude is, as we have tried to establish, a concept that is fundamentally theological and Christian, even up to its profanation of Christianity [*christianisme*], then *Endlichkeit* is not finitude."[26]

Heidegger's theme of *Endlichkeit* was presented by Birault as a direct rejection of this old metaphysical and theological (even when atheist) framework. For Birault, Heidegger's *Endlichkeit* had attempted to dispense with all onto-theologies, the assertion of any particular being as supreme. It was thus continuous with Heidegger's later conception of *das Strittige*, or "Discord,"[27] which, in refusing the stifling idea of a positive infinite as a structuring principle, emphasized a *Néantir*, not in opposition to, but at the heart of Being. As Heidegger wrote in the *Letter on Humanism*, "das Sein nichtet—als das Sein" (Being nothings—as Being).[28] By bringing nothingness right into the heart of Being, Heidegger attempted to leave the troublesome hierarchies that had disrupted previous thoughts of the finite. In this way, according to Birault, Heidegger's *Endlichkeit* sought to honor two principles. First, because Being is always veiled in beings, it never shows itself qua Being; it remains onto-theological to mistake a particular being or type of being (*Étant*) for Being itself (*Être*). But, second, because there is no Being (*Être*) outside of beings (*Étants*), because

Being is not some infinite transcendent principle, this veiling in the finite is essential to its very unveiling; it is irreducible. Rather than being simply opposed to Being, nothingness (*Néant*) should be understood as the "veil of Being absolutely essential to its unveiling."[29]

So the thought of Being had to recall this veiling, "without it," as Birault argued, "Being would always threaten to collapse into one privileged form of being and the thought of Being would remain a latent [*larvée*] theology . . . . It would still be the thought of some Absolute."[30] In short, to avoid onto-theology, we had to respect the ontological difference, the difference between any being (*étant*) and Being itself, even though this difference did not imply some detached infinite lying outside our grasp.[31] The Heideggerian thought of *Endlichkeit* allowed Birault to reconsider the Absolute without tacitly relying on the idea of a positive infinity, a reliance common to both theological and humanistic thought.

Birault's article may look like a radical rejection of religion and theology—a Nietzschean move of attacking not merely religion but also the vestiges of religion in secular thought—but a cursory glance at his broader project suggests that, in fact, the opposite was the case. In an article he wrote in 1961 entitled "Of Being, the Divine, and the Gods in Heidegger," Birault further developed his thought.[32] To know what the word God means we first have to understand the Being of God, or *Gottheit*. In this Birault followed Heidegger's discussion in the "Letter on Humanism" by suggesting that it was only on the basis of the thought of Being that we could open up "*das Heilige*"—the *Sacré* or Sacred—where we could begin to understand what God actually was.[33]

And because it was necessary to move beyond onto-theology to arrive at the thought of Being, the "destruction" of theology, a godlessness (*Gottlosigkeit*), was a necessary first stage. As Birault wrote, "the thought of the divine, and on the basis of this thought, the thought of deity [*Gottheit*] distances itself from the Christian God as well as the God of the philosophers . . . . He can be neither the God of religion nor that of absolute paradox." Neither Hegel's nor Kierkegaard's God allowed the opening of the Sacred, because they were both caught up in the forgetting of Being. For this reason, both served to de-divinize God.[34]

Heidegger's *Gottlosigkeit* was, then, a response to the *Entgötterung*, or in French *dédivinisation*, at work right at the heart of traditional understandings of God and which explained their essential continuity with atheism.[35] In this way, despite its radicality (or, rather, because of it), Heidegger's godlessness could never simply be equated with the rejection of religion. The thought of Being, in Birault's words, hoped, rather, to find "the truth beyond the uncertain duality of theism or atheism."[36]

Such a view distanced Heidegger's work from what Birault saw as the crass atheism of a Nietzsche or a Sartre and the naïve religion that appealed to an accessible infinite. Birault's analysis of Heidegger's *Endlichkeit*, then, was a rejection of both bad theology and bad atheism, because both worked within the same onto-theological structure. For Birault, as for the other Christian Heideggerians, the combined veiling and unveiling of Being in beings, or the ontological difference, allowed them to approach the divine without positing the theological absolute as present (that would forget the veiling), or absent as in the atheistic idea of finitude (that would forget the unveiling). With a concept of nothingness, an irreducible "discord," at the heart of Being, a new approach to the divine would arise. As Birault had asserted in the finitude article, "when one has seen that only the discriminating power of the Negative can found the discursivity of discourse, then, to save discourse and God, it only remains to carry [*porter*] discourse into God himself, that is to say, to interpret God as the Word or Mediation, in order to build on that collapse [*effondrement*] of substance a new figure of the Absolute."[37]

This last point marks Birault's greatest contribution, because the way in which Birault was able to group together positive theology and atheism makes clear how his argument differed from similar gestures in the apophatic tradition. As commonly understood, negative theology refuses to attribute earthly predicates to the divine, including that of (in)existence, because God transcends all human understanding. Thus, inherent in the project of negative theology is the attempt to remove the mundane garb in which God is normally presented. Birault, in contrast, criticized both traditional Christianity and atheism for the way they articulated the relationship between the finite and infinity, a charge that could be applied equally to negative theology. Consequently, while negative theology had to negate human predicates to point toward the divine, for Birault negativity had to be one with God. The mediation between Man and God was not a desecration of the holy but was rather essential to it. The mistake of negative theology, Birault might say, was that it is unable to recognize the divine within earthly manifestations, because it holds all earthly "Gods" up to a false heavenly standard.

Derrida's Difference

If we look at Derrida's courses from the time, those prepared for his students at the Sorbonne, where he taught under Paul Ricoeur as an Assistant from 1960–1964, we can see the same argument about finitude, often openly citing Birault. Take, for example, the 1962 course Peut-on dire oui à la finitude? (Can One Say Yes to Finitude?). Following Birault's lead,[38] Derrida defined finitude as the combination of a finite being and infinite freedom, a freedom that, in a particular modern tradition, stemmed from the recognition of limitations and the possibility of transcending them. Finitude thus described a finite being structured by a recognition, a "yes" (*oui*) to its limits, but also a practical and ethical "no" to them.[39]

As Derrida argued, this practical "no," which was central to the modern conception of finitude, made a surreptitious appeal to the divine. Descartes could only doubt by entertaining the unflattering comparison between his thought and infinite truth, and thus the infinite was the ground of his freedom to say yes or no to any particular type of knowledge. Like Birault, Derrida suggested that the very possibility of Cartesian doubt, of saying no to limits, was dependent on a primordial, though dissimulated, yes to the infinite. He wrote, "it seems that the consciousness of finitude as a lack [*comme manque*] cannot be originary. It always creates itself on the foundation of an infinite" to which the no would be derivative and secondary. And this yes to the infinite, Derrida assured us, was to all intents and purposes a "yes to God."[40] Moreover, because this yes had priority, in classical philosophy finitude could only be secondary and contingent. For this reason, the "yes to God," (*oui à dieu*) must also be a "yes of God" (*oui de dieu*): what Derrida called "a self-affirmation of God."[41] Even the supposed atheism of the indefinite, the constant surpassing of limits, was reliant on a barely submerged theology.

This, according to Derrida, posed a problem. If the yes to God were the unadulterated ground of philosophy, then we would have no choice. A limited human would not be able to resist a divine command. The yes would be what Derrida called an "obligated *recognition*," which would be both a moral and a philosophical "abdication."[42] However, such an interpretation, according to Derrida, missed a crucial aspect of which classical philosophy, attached as it was to a pure infinite, was unaware. As Derrida wrote, in language that is reminiscent of the final section of his introduction to Husserl's *Origin of Geometry*:

> Philosophy is only the *re*cognition of this originary divine speech [*parole*]. It is a yes to the yes of God . . . (in both the cognitive and ethical sense of this word) I *recognize* God.[43]

The "re-sponse" suggested a "re-doubling" of God: "God divides himself to say *yes*." Such division showed that negativity was inherent in the divine, and it was "this negativity that liberates precisely the space of the human and philosophical yes." Citing Kafka, a phrase of which he was particularly fond in this period (we see it several times in his courses and in "Edmund Jabès et la question du livre"), Derrida asserted that "we are the nihilistic thoughts that arise in God's brain."[44]

To understand this inherence of negativity in the divine, the co-primordiality of the yes and the no, Derrida pursued a form of finiteness that was more radical than human finitude. Such a form would need to rehabilitate the finite from its secondary and derivative position, free it from the "shadow of the Judeo-Christian God."[45] Again the argument directly followed Birault's—indeed, Derrida read four pages from Birault's finitude article to his students at this point in the lecture—and like Birault, Derrida turned to Heidegger.[46] In this reading, Heidegger had rejected the idea of a transcendent Being separate from all beings. Because there was no Being outside of beings, the limitation and determination of Being was essential; it could not be regarded as a fall or a lack. At the same time, Heidegger also claimed that beings dissimulated Being. Both a transcendent infinite and a perfect finite were the constructions of onto-theology. If neither Being nor being, neither infinite nor the finite, God or man, were possible alone, neither could preexist or precede the other, then it must be the ontological difference, the difference between Being and beings, that was primary.[47]

I think that at this stage it is worth noting two things: First, though Derrida would later in *Of Grammatology* charge Heidegger with occasionally presenting Being as a transcendental signified, it is precisely because Heidegger refused to understand Being in this way, refused even to consider it outside of beings, that made him such an attractive figure for Derrida in the early stages of his career.[48] And second, when Derrida turned to Heidegger in the early 1960s his reading was consonant with that of the single largest group of philosophers focusing on Heidegger's ontological difference in France: the Christian Heideggerians, a group of thinkers who used Heidegger to counter Sartre's atheism, and for whom the lengthy treatment of questions of atheism and human finitude served as a means to intervene in debates surrounding existentialism in France. And thus I think that we have in Derrida's reading of Heidegger not only a clue to his relationship to religious ideas, but also of his engagement with, and ultimately rejection of, existentialism. Unlike the structuralist anti-humanists like Althusser, who hoped to move beyond the subjectivism in Sartre's account by emphasizing broader intellectual and social structures, Derrida cleaved closer to the Christians, who charged Sartre with hubris and reasserted the fallibility of human thought.

Betting against Nietzsche

One of the major questions that arose when the Christian Heideggerians (and Derrida, in turn) drew on Heidegger was whether it was possible to identify Being and God. Indeed, Birault had opened his article on the "Being, the Divine, and the Gods in Heidegger" with the assertion that "the thought that exerts itself on the thought of Being necessarily meets on its route one day that massive and formidable question: Is Being or is it not God?"[49] And Jean Beaufret, in part responding to this Christian Heideggerian tradition, made it clear on a number of occasions that Being could never be identified as God.[50] In his early work, Derrida gives this question more or less attention, depending on the period. For instance, in the final section of the *Origin of Geometry*, and courses from the time—where he uses the idea of God to segue between the Husserlian infinite idea and Heidegger's difference—there is no explicit discussion of any problem that might arise from drawing an analogy between Being and God. Later, however—such as in the final section of "Violence and Metaphysics," written about two years later, and in a course written at almost the same time, "Ontology and Theology," his last seminar at the Sorbonne—Derrida provides a more complex understanding of the relationship; he refuses to give either Being or God priority.[51] And this refusal is absolutely crucial to any understanding of Derrida's relationship to religious thought. For while God is necessarily subject to the destabilizing movement of the ontological difference (what we might call the radically atheistic aspect of Derrida's thought), God's infinity is simultaneously and paradoxically the condition for that difference.

On the one hand, theology is a regional science, the science of that being (*étant*) called God, and for this reason it remains dependent upon a general ontology: Being precedes God.[52] This was the argument that Birault had put forward, asserting that the openness to Being was a necessary precondition to an understanding of the Being of God. And because we could only approach Being by working through the implications of Heidegger's *Endlichkeit*, and thus of the ontological difference, we must first reject all onto-theological appeals to a positive infinite, even one posed as absent or impossible.

On the other hand, however, Derrida suggested that God also preceded Being. In classical theology, God was not the object of science, but its source: "God is speech [*la parole*] itself, the very origin of speech."[53] The ability to move beyond onto-theologies to arrive at a general ontology required the transcending of all finite beings, the recognition of the difference between any being and Being itself. And this transcendence was only possible, according to Derrida, through the infinity of the divine.[54] In a way that mirrors Birault's account of finitude, though developing a new line of argument, Derrida asserted that the overcoming of limits even in atheistic thought was dependent upon the idea of the infinite, and this was true above all for the ontic determinations of Being. Derrida raised the question whether "God is the very name of the opening in which Being shows itself as Being, Being as such."[55] The twin arguments thus produced a strange aporia: God simultaneously opened up the ontological difference and was dependent upon Being. As Derrida wrote in "Violence and Metaphysics," "paradoxically, this thought of infinity (what one calls the thought of God) permits the affirmation of the priority of ontology over theology, and the affirmation that the thought of Being is presupposed by the thought of God."[56] Derrida finished his course posing the question whether God was difference or rather that in which difference appeared. A question he left open.[57]

Derrida's hesitation in giving priority to either Being or God lends context to his burgeoning interest in that other iconoclastic German thinker: Friedrich Nietzsche. Though Derrida is often presented simply as a French Nietzschean, it is significant that Nietzsche appears only rarely in Derrida's early essays, and even more rarely as the main author under consideration. The major references can be grouped under two categories: 1. Enigmatic, but positive references to Dionysus, *active Vergesslichkeit* (active forgetting), and dance in "Force and Signification," "Structure, Sign, and Play," and "The Ends of Man";[58] and 2. A resistance to Nietzsche's empiricist etymology of "Being," seen in the Levinas essay and in courses at the time, including "Peut-on dire oui à la finitude?" Here Derrida opposed Nietzsche to Heidegger: while Nietzsche presented language merely as a system of signs designed to serve the needs of life, Heidegger asserted that it was also an "unveiling [*dévoilement*] of Being."[59] Derrida's ambivalence to Nietzsche thus matched his ambivalence toward the divine. He refused to take Being or God at face value, yet remained unwilling see either as simply a product of the will-to-power.

That Derrida should have turned to Nietzsche in the finitude course, a course that most clearly bore the imprint of Birault's thought, was no accident. Birault, too, engaged with Nietzsche in his discussions of onto-theology. For Birault the question as to whether Being was God, especially when given a simple yes or no answer, was a great danger to any authentic form of thought, because the question itself relied on an understanding of Being that remained to be elucidated: "*is* or *is not* Being God?"

And to draw attention to the problem, he presented Nietzsche as a key culprit. According to Birault, Nietzsche accepted a simple identity of

Being and God, and thus hoped to reject the first (Being) along with the second (the death of God).[60] For Nietzsche, both Being and God were invoked as the foundation for what appears, and this, according to his schema, was the classic metaphysical illusion. Once we reject the idea of God, a supreme being, we also have to reject the idea of Being lying behind appearances. Nietzsche's critique of theology expanded into a critique of all metaphysics.

But, according to Birault, it was only at a particular stage in the history of Being that Being was understood as a foundation. As he wrote, "the metaphysics that Nietzsche tried hard to destroy, it was metaphysics as a theory of the supra-sensible, coming finally to corrupt the sensible itself." And yet, at the same time, because the rejection of God and Being was so absolute, as in the classic deconstructive schema, it came to reintroduce precisely what it hoped to reject. Birault continued: "the Being [*Être*] that Nietzsche wanted to save was the *L'Être de l'Étant*, which is to say Being as the will-to-power."[61] By rejecting all forms of foundation, all metaphysics, but without interrogating the idea of foundation or of metaphysics itself, Nietzsche came to a new metaphysics: an onto-theology of the will-to-power.

Now this, of course, was a repetition of Heidegger's famous critique in the *Nietzsche* lectures from 1936–1940: Nietzsche had created yet another humanistic metaphysics because his operative categories, that is the difference between foundation and what is founded upon it, diverged from difference; it forgot the ontological difference by understanding Being as a governing principle, and thus as a being.[62] Instead, Birault urged the embrace of the ontological difference that allowed one to move beyond the simple identification of Being and God, because that identification was constructed upon a metaphysical understanding of both. An emphasis on the ontological difference, a "thought of Being as Difference, as Discord, and consequently as Nihilation [*Néantir*] denies such an assimilation."[63] We never have a definitive idea of what Being is, and so we can never fully grasp the Being of God.

And yet Being remains active in traditional metaphysics: "Being [*L'Être*] *is* still a being [*l'Étant*]." In a parallel fashion, "the Divine lies dormant [*sommeille*], still buried and necessarily masked, in the God of Metaphysics, in the God that '*betrays*' . . . the Divine."[64] Though there was no direct access to a transcendent Divine, God was not absolutely inaccessible. The veiling of Being was never total, and God was never entirely absent from idolatrous forms. Thus, the refusal to identify or rigorously split the two was not the sign of the "impotence or the hesitation of a thought which cannot make up its mind [*se décider*] regarding Being and the Divine."

Rather, in a phrase that is reminiscent of several of Derrida's, Birault asserted that "it is . . . by holding oneself to that very oscillation that the decisive [*décisif*] can be decided."[65]

Nietzsche, then, for all his important work in overcoming metaphysics, had erred in equating the thought of Being with its onto-theological presentation. His rejection of Being, and consequently of God, remained dogmatic: he thought he knew what it was he was rejecting. Birault's criticism of Nietzsche fit further into his broader religious project. In another article from 1960, his "Nietzsche et le pari de Pascal," Birault presented Nietzsche's philosophizing with a hammer as the metaphysical counterpart to Pascal's wager. Pascal too, Birault argued, had presented man as "ex-centric" (*ex-centrique*)[66] and instead placed emphasis on what Birault called the "jeu," game or play, at the heart of philosophy; the game of chance that Pascal set up as his argument for the Christian faith was akin to the dance of Dionysus in Nietzsche's philosophy.[67]

But unlike Nietzsche, Pascal had not thrown the baby out with the bathwater, rejecting the thought of Being alongside onto-theology. Using the language of the "De l'Être . . ." article, we might say that Pascal also realized that the veiling of Being and the Divine was also their unveiling.[68] In the wager we recognize the limitations of the old and dogmatic scholastic philosophy, recognize the limits of human thought, without falling into the dangers of perspectival nihilism. Pascal managed to preserve a form of reason that comprised uncertainty—however demonstrative Pascal's proof, the wager did not stop being a wager—without fully submitting to it: "*reason* and *chance* [*le hazard*] reconciling with each other [*se conciliant*] here in an entirely new manner."[69] Whatever the odds—and this is important, because it could not be a simple game of probability, "the risk remains always total"—it was always reasonable to wager a finite good for an infinite one. In fact, reason demanded that one take the bet.[70] Thus "the wager presupposes . . . that *relative* unreason of the Christian faith, and the mystery of an infinitely incomprehensible God"; it allowed a place for the uncertainty of faith within reason. Pascal's *jeu*, then, marked the rise of a new "playful" (*joueuse*) and "joyful" (*joyeuse*) reason, that, according to Birault, "dances on the summits of contingency."[71]

I would like to finish with another moment, where Derrida, this time, evokes a joyful and playful reason. At the end of "Structure, Sign, and Play," Derrida presents two interpretations of interpretation, two readings of the *jeu* at the heart of philosophy: a Nietzschean affirmation that revels in active forgetting, and a Rousseauian nostalgia that hopes for some ultimate ground. In traditional accounts, Derrida is supposed to lean toward the former. After all, Rousseauian nostalgia seems to be his main target in the article as a whole, where he criticizes Lévi-Strauss for limiting the play of his structuralism with the idea of an unobtainable but desirable stable science. But rather than picking the Nietzschean forgetting, Derrida suggested that one could not choose between the two. Nietzsche's active forgetting, as Birault had asserted and Derrida would affirm on several occasions, sometimes tends toward a new foundation in the will-to-power, and yet it provides a productive counterbalance to the "philosophies of presence" that seek an ultimate ground. Instead of deciding for one or the other, Nietzsche or Rousseau, Derrida urged us to think the "différance" between the two: "*le sol commun*" of the thought of a lost origin and the attempt to forget it.[72] And I would like to suggest that in this différance we can perhaps see the trace of Pascal's wager, a game that embraces absolute risk, unlike Rousseau, even as it refuses the nihilistic consequences of the Nietzschean moment.

As I close a caveat is necessary. Though I have spent this chapter elucidating the parallels between Derrida's thought and Christian Heideggerianism (in the guise of Henri Birault), I don't want to suggest that this makes Derrida's work itself *Christian*. Even as Birault himself yearned for a renewed faith, his strand of Christian thought was itself resistant to dogmatism and urged the rejection of all determined theologies; it emerged from a tradition that privileged atheism as a path to the divine.[73] This is, of course, familiar to us. We might see in Derrida's early work a hint of his later "religion without religion," and it would be a mistake to tie Derrida down to any denominational or religious form.

Indeed, those moments when Birault's work does hew more closely to traditional *Christian* theology appeal only to that realm of faith—more specifically the "faith in Jesus Christ"—whose comprehension is allowed but whose grace is not assured by an appeal to the ontological difference. Indeed, for Birault, faith as a gift from God remains independent of the thought of Being: "The thought of Being allows us to understand what 'God' might mean, but it in no way assures us that God would come to us." For Birault the man in prayer was "infinitely closer to God" than the thinker.[74]

Derrida did not follow Birault down this path; in his early work this space of faith is never broached.[75] Indeed from a Derridian perspective, Birault's appeal to faith seems to follow the familiar logic of supplementarity: while Birault's Heideggerianism helped him recognize a dormant divinity even in the metaphysical God of the philosophers, and thereby formulate a "new figure of the Absolute" comprising negativity, his notion of faith tried to rescue the idea of God from all earthly contamination, all limitations, and purify it once again.[76]

From this perspective, we can understand why Derrida was less concerned than Birault to mark an absolute distinction between the thought of God and the thought of Being. Indeed, we might suggest that by seeing a role for God in opening up the ontological difference that in turn opens up the holy—"opening *of* the horizon, and not *in* the horizon"[77]—Derrida also set his work apart from the residual negative theology in Birault's texts. Derrida's atheism here is strategic. Rather than overturning earthly religions in the name of a higher, purer faith, as Birault at times seems to want to do, Derrida suggests that it allows us to appreciate transcendence *in* immanence. And because transcendence and immanence could never be satisfactorily separated out, iconoclasm would reveal itself to be just as violent as dogmatic belief.

It is equally important to recognize that Derrida's thought was not fixed at this early stage. We remain here, in 1964, at the threshold of a new period in Derrida's thought, the "grammatological opening," that would lead him to reassess his appeal to infinity and finitude.[78] Before this opening, Derrida analyzed the mutually conditioning relationship between Being and God: a thought of the infinite to challenge the totalizing aspirations of any onto-theology, and a thought of Being (approached through the ontological difference) to discipline that very appeal. After the grammatological opening, Derrida relied instead on the movement of différance to undercut the pretensions of a limited structure, and no longer had to refer to an infinite, no matter how aporetic; God was effaced in Derrida's philosophy. But the traces of this early history remain visible across the mutations of Derrida's thought.[79] Indeed, one might be tempted to suggest that religion continued to haunt Derrida throughout his career. And though Derrida might, as he said later, "rightly pass as an atheist,"[80] it is significant that this atheism was first expressed in close engagement with a strand of French religious thought. The supposed skepticism of deconstruction was, at least initially, consonant with a Christian discourse on human limits that had as its goal the overthrow not of religion but of the human hubris that made true religion impossible.

Called to Bear Witness

Derrida, Muslims, and Islam

ANNE NORTON

Derrida meets Islam in a magic, ghostly, *geistliche* place. This is a place where the desert meets the ocean, a place of "intimate immensity."[1] This is a place of returning without departing, a place of memory. This is a timeless place belonging to the past and the future—and to a past that might have been but was not and a future that is not yet. One might also name these, as Derrida did in "Faith and Knowledge," "the island, the Promised land, the desert. Three aporetic places: with no way out or any assured path, without itinerary or point of arrival, without an exterior with a predictable map."[2] This is a place inhabited by specters and *revenants*, certainly, and perhaps by *djinn*, demons, and a *daimon* or two.

Derrida also met Islam in the historical demands of politics, in a Mediterranean geography, and in the most mundane of places. He met Islam on the streets of El Biar and Algiers, and later on the streets of Paris. The first set of meetings is punctuated by the call to prayer and sound of a football hitting a dusty street, the second by the averted gaze, the sound of riot, and the smell of burning.

Each of these places calls for more exploration than I have given here. All are inadequately mapped. All are full of promise and danger. I begin in the darkest of these places, where Derrida marks Islam as "the Other of Democracy."

Derrida's *Rogues* was written in the shadow of death. The book was composed in the midst of wars against "rogue states" by states (especially the United States) that had gone rogue themselves. The book was haunted by the dead. There were the dead of the "coalition of the willing," dead partisans, dead soldiers, and the dead civilians of the invaded states. The wars were haunted by the dead of 9/11. Derrida himself labored under the knowledge of a new imminence of death. He would die between the book's publication in French and its translation into English.

If *Rogues* was a critique of the "war on terror," it was not a work open to solidarity with Islam or Muslims. Derrida titles chapter three "The Other of Democracy." In that chapter he argues that "the only and very few regimes that *do not present themselves* as democratic are those with a theocratic Muslim government."[3] The acclamations of democracy are, Derrida acknowledges, often mere pretense, yet he takes them as evidence of values held even as they are neglected or betrayed. Islam is unique, Derrida argues, in its refusal of democracy.[4]

This book, aimed at contemporary politics, nevertheless shares several of the characteristic concerns—and gestures—of Derrida's more evidently philosophic works. This too is a work bearing witness. This too is a book about authority. This too is a work in and on language, on naming, on the word and the *logos*. In this work Derrida exiles Ishmael from the covenant, names Islam the enemy of democracy, philosophy, and reason, and then gestures toward defects, inadequacies, and reversals in his refusal of Islam.

Derrida's first assertion of the "Arabic and Islamic" antipathy to democracy is, despite its bluntness, qualified. There are, as Derrida notes, "very few" such governments. He does not name the governments he has in mind. The most likely candidates appear to be Saudi Arabia and Iran.[5] Yet even in these cases, the assertion is on uncertain ground. Saudi Arabia is a monarchy and, as the Iranian Khomeini pointed out, monarchy is an alien and imported—imperialist—institution, opposed explicitly by the prophet and the martyred Hussain. It has a marked tendency to wasteful and decadent extravagance. Most important, its hereditary character and tendency to give rise to imitative aristocracy violate the Islamic imperative to "place all on an equal footing."[6] Iran, by contrast, has an elected parliament and calls itself an Islamic republic. The denial of democracy must therefore rest on the subordination of legislation to the limits of the *shari'ah.*[7] There are several problems here. If taking fundamental religious precepts as a limit to democratic legislation is at issue, then Israel would present (at best) a difficult case for Derrida. Once again, however, it is Derrida who points us to the greater problem in his argument.

Derrida writes:

the democratic, having become consubstantially political in this Græco-Christian and globalatinizing tradition, appears inseparable in the modernity following the Enlightenment from an ambiguous secularization (and secularization is always ambiguous in that it frees itself from the religious, all the while remaining marked in its very concept by it, by the theological, indeed the onto-theological).[8]

If the theological and onto-theological foundations of the state mark Islam as hostile to democracy, so, it appears, do those of the Græco-Christian and globalatinized West. If Islam is *obéissant* to the theological (and onto-theological), so too is that secularism presented by some theorists of modernity as the ally (if not the precondition) of democracy.[9]

Derrida's understanding of the "Græco-Christian" and "globalatinized" world as committed to democracy and as only ambiguously secularized seems to affirm the openness not only of the Greek but of the Christian lineage to democracy. The European commitment to democracy is not diminished by its only ambiguous secularization. Yet we are not given an account of what in Christian theology opens it to the democratic. There are several possibilities in play here. Perhaps Christian theology opens to secularism (and hence democracy) only as it is overcome. Perhaps the European commitment to democracy is to the word and not the thing. Perhaps democracy is not yet. Perhaps democracy belongs not to Europe or the Middle East, but to Derrida's elsewhere. Perhaps Derrida's understanding of democracy is confounded with his commitment to the concept of sovereignty—and that of the political—given by Carl Schmitt.

Throughout Derrida's work there are visible traces of his debt to Schmitt. "All significant concepts of the modern state are secularized theological concepts," Schmitt wrote.[10] This was, for Schmitt, particularly true of the concept of sovereignty. Schmitt understands sovereignty as a secularized concept of the second person of the Trinity, the incarnate god. Schmitt's famously laconic statement "sovereign is he who decides on the exception" captures his insistence on the incarnation of sovereign power in a single, corporeal person.[11] Derrida assumes this concept of sovereignty. In doing so, he rejects the model of democratic sovereignty Schmitt recognized as an alternative.[12] Schmitt is quite conscious of the specific theological concepts that animate European conceptions of sovereignty. The figure of the sovereign is an instance of "Roman Catholicism as political form."[13] In the sovereign, the word is made flesh and dwells among us. The person who embodies sovereignty, who decides on the exception, who holds the power of life and death, the power to draw boundaries, the power to make and unmake law, is acting after the model of the divine. For Schmitt, dictatorship is properly an *imitatio Christi*.

Derrida is quite correct in seeing this conception of sovereignty as radically alien to Islam. Islam, honoring Jesus as a prophet, abjures the idea of what Leo Strauss called "the godman."[14] Islam refuses the idea of an incarnate or corporeal God, as does Judaism, regarding it as a species of *shirk* (idolatry). For those who accept Schmitt's view that all political concepts are, at bottom, secularized theology, the resistance of Judaism and Islam to a conception of embodied divinity opens the door to alternative ambiguously secularized conceptions of sovereignty. Given their form, these might be particularly resistant to dictatorship. Schmitt's recognition that "in democratic thought the people hover above the entire life of the state, just as God does above the world" offers a point of entry for an ambiguously secularized Islamic political theology as it does for a Christian democratic sovereignty.[15] The *hadith*, or tradition of the Prophet, which holds that "my people will never be agreed upon an error" is only one of the openings to democratic sovereignty that Islam provides. For those who read the Greek as at odds with the Christian in "Græco-Christian," there may be other resources. With regard to sovereignty, as well as democracy in Islam, Derrida points to an opening even as he closes off another.[16]

Derrida's treatment of the relation of Islam to democracy in *Rogues* is also remarkably concrete. He takes us to two historically specific sites: the abridged Algerian elections of 1991–1992, and Muslim philosophy of the classical period.

Derrida knew that Islamist parties had been in the forefront of the campaign for democracy in his native Algeria. In 1991, in a hesitant but significant opening to democracy, the ruling Algerian regime permitted elections. The Islamic Salvation Front (*Front Islamique du Salut*, the FIS) won the first round. The army stepped in and cancelled the second round of elections. In his account of these events, Derrida is silent about the role of the military, calling the coup an "interruption" by "the state and the leading party."[17] More remarkably, he characterizes the intervention as one that saved democracy—from itself. Democratic victory by the FIS would have led "democratically to the end of democracy" so "they decided to put an end to it themselves." They decided "to suspend, at least provisionally, democracy *for its own good*, so as to take care of it, so as to immunize it against a much worse and very likely assault."[18] They were not democrats themselves, these friends—they preferred military rule.

Commentators have been generous in their readings of this action. Martin Hägglund argues that "Derrida's discussion is not concerned with judging whether it was right or wrong to suspend the elections in Algeria" but simply with the phenomenon of autoimmunity.[19] Hägglund is concerned, as he frankly states, with autoimmunity as a philosophic text, which may account for his dismissal of the political effects—and political genesis—of Derrida's work on democratic autoimmunity. That reading, however, ignores the consonance of Derrida's writing in *Rogues* with the political context and aims of the statement Derrida delivered under the aegis of the *International Committee of Solidarity with Algerian Intellectuals*. Derrida's statement, "Taking a Stand for Algeria," was delivered at a political event, under the aegis of a political organization, endorsing a political position. The statement affirms the suspension of elections, justifying it in the name of democracy.

Derrida calls this a decision made "in a sovereign fashion."[20] This nod to Schmitt acknowledges the personal, decisionistic character of the suspension. This was no democratic sovereign, for those who decided were not the Algerian people, not even their elected representatives. Some of them were Algerian, Derrida writes, "although not a majority of the Algerian people."[21] They were also French and other Western governments and intellectuals—primarily French intellectuals like Derrida. Derrida names these with the anodyne phrase "people outside Algeria."[22] In short, the Algerian military, the ruling oligarchy, with the backing of Western governments and other "people outside Algeria" thought it best to put an end to Algerian democracy. Rarely has the postcolonial continuance of colonial authoritarianism shown itself so clearly. It is curious indeed to see this episode of the military suppression of democracy presented as evidence of Islam's hostility to democracy.

Derrida takes "three lessons" from this event. The first lesson is the resistance of Islam to a "European" process "of secularization, and so of democratization."[23] Derrida's analysis thus assumes that democracy either entails or is dependent upon secularization and that this is a European process. Certainly the world beyond Europe has been less receptive to the view that democracy requires secularism. It has very little currency in the Americas, where people have long been persuaded that they could retain their faiths and govern themselves. Derrida does not take up the familiar questions concerning the possibility of a secular Islam. Nor does he examine, in this context, the *laiklik* of Kemalist Turkey, which rivals French *laïcité* in severity. The more compelling questions might concern the implications of ambiguous secularism for the possibility of European democracy. Do the commitments of secularists to secularism make them, in some times and places, the enemies of democracy?

Derrida wrote in *Rogues* that he had based his affirmation of the hostility of Islam to democracy on "the little I know."[24] This admission of limited and possibly errant knowledge seems to invite a response, if not a refutation. This sense is enhanced by his subsequent characterization of Muslim philosophy. Derrida asserts as "fact" that Aristotle's *Politics* was "absent in the Islamic importation" and that al Farabi had incorporated "only the theme of the philosopher king" into his political philosophy.[25] That transmission of Aristotle went through not from Europe to Islam but from Islam to Europe is well known (though one might debate the journeying of particular texts). There are clear references to the *Politics* in classical Muslim philosophy. Finally (though this may be less widely known) al Farabi not only takes more than the philosopher king from Plato, he moves Plato in a democratic direction.[26] The substance of the errors here is less interesting than Derrida's willingness to construct Islam as antidemocratic based on what he himself calls his own ignorance, and his deliberate marking of that ignorance in the text.

The first lesson that Derrida marks as a lesson founded in ignorance is the hostility of Islam to democracy. A careful examination of that lesson offers another lesson subversive of the first: that the argument that Islam is hostile to democracy is dependent on two things we might choose against— willful ignorance and taking secularism as consubstantial with democracy.

The second lesson is what Derrida variously calls the autoimmune vulnerability of democracy, or democracy's tendency to suicide. This lesson depends on a refusal to acknowledge that the abridgment of Algerian elections was not the work of democracy (or even democrats) but of the Algerian military. It requires the acceptance of a familiar liberal logic: that the possibility of murder (or, as in this case, suicide) in the future licenses a preemptive murder in the present.[27] Democracy's enemies, Derrida argued, are those who claim to be "staunch democrats," who work for, call for, and participate in popular elections. Democracy must be killed, as Derrida wrote, "*for its own good*, so as to take care of it." This is not suicide, this is murder.

The third lesson, so closely resembling the second that it might be taken for its twin, is that of democracy as constantly deferred, subject to the forces of autoimmunity. Derrida draws attention in this passage to something in which many democrats take particular pride, that though a democracy belongs to a particular people, a particular *demos*,

> the force of demo*cracy* commits it, in the name of universal equality, to representing not only the greatest force of the greatest number, the majority of citizens considered of age, but also the weakness of the weak, minors, minorities, the poor and all those throughout the world who call out in suffering for a legitimately infinite extension of what are called *human* rights.[28]

Each of Derrida's "lessons" concerning democracy is linked to Islam: to Islam as the other of democracy, to the democratic victory of the Algerian Islamists, and finally to a constitutive ambiguity in Islam (though not only in Islam) between the people and all people. Each of these is presented as a problem, perhaps an insoluble problem. All link democracy with difference, deferral, and death. Yet this democracy, fugitive, deferred, troubled by an inner uncertainty about those who are or are not its own, nevertheless has a place and partisans in the world. They are the rogues.

For all his doubts about democracy, Derrida will not disavow his solidarity with the democratic rogues. In the chapter entitled "Rogue That I Am," Derrida looks to "the weak, minors, minorities, the poor" among his own people, "excluded or wayward, outcast or displaced, left to roam the streets, especially those of the suburbs."[29] Derrida gives us coordinates by which to navigate: first, the suburbs, or *banlieues*—called the "*banlieues d'Islam*" by Gilles Kepel (and thereafter by nearly everybody else)—and second, 1830, "the date of the conquest of Algeria." It is there, among those "pointed out as actual or virtual delinquents," "roaming the streets" jobless and alienated and setting cars on fire, that one finds the rogue, the *voyou*, brothers, "others of brothers, the non-brothers." They are deviants "actual and virtual delinquents," "unemployed" young men who wander the streets. They are the unemployed Muslims who riot in France. "It is always a question of suspicious or mixed origin."[30] It is among these that one can find democracy.

The rogue, Derrida writes, "belongs to what is most common or popular in the people" and the "*demos* is thus never very far away when one speaks of a *voyou*."[31] The rogue is a familiar figure for us, more attractive perhaps to Americans than Europeans. The rogue is an outlaw, roaming the streets, a gangster or a punk, a rebel (often, a rebel without a cause). These rebels, belonging to the people and the street, to "what is most common or popular in the people" are counterposed to law, to civilized citizens, and to the police. They are close to democracy in no small part because democracy is before and against the law. The people must rule the law before the law can rule the people, for democrats. This, as Derrida recognized, sets democracy against liberalism.

Derrida's evocation of the *banlieues d'Islam*, the Muslim suburbs of Paris and (for that matter) Toulouse, Marseilles, and Lyon, as the site of the democratic rogue offers another reading of the democracy. It is in these places, among these people (and some others) that democracy is being born.

The construction of Islam as "the Other of Democracy" is questioned at the margins: by Derrida in the margins of his text, by Derrida in commenting on the rogues in the margins of French society. Islam is named as the other of democracy, but Muslims, the *shebab*, the Muslim youth of Paris and Algiers (and, one might add, Tahrir Square) are rogues and democrats. Derrida marks his own kinship—or friendship—with them.

The disavowal of Islam does not remain, for Derrida, at the level of politics—or indeed, of philosophy—if any question can be so isolated. The question of Islam, the question of the Arab, is the question of the brother and the friend, a question of belonging. Derrida's writing on the Marrano echoes his writing on the rogue, "Marrano that we are." He writes in *Aporias*, "let us figuratively call Marrano anyone who remains faithful to a secret that he has not chosen."[32] The Marrano, John Caputo writes, is an apt figure for the "atheist Arab Jew" who knows that he is not quite: not quite Jewish, not quite Christian, not quite Arab. Mindful of the religious sensibility of his work, one might well add not quite atheist either.[33]

Derrida sees himself, as others have seen him, in the figure of the Marrano, one of the pretended converts hidden in the open after the *Reconquista*. The route his family travelled, from Spain to North Africa, was the route of many Marranos. So too was the route Derrida took later, from North Africa to Europe. Yet it is not the route travelled, not the experience of exile, but the experience of a solitary interiority that marks the Marrano. The Marrano shelters a secret within, a secret that is at once the danger of death and the promise of salvation.

The Marrano is marked not only by a secret, but by a denial: the secret "I am a Jew" is sheltered by the denial "I am not a Jew." So it is with Derrida. In Derrida, however, it is not the Jew but the Arab who is denied; not the heritage of Judaism that is refused but that of Islam. Derrida's citation of the Marrano holds a history of ambivalence within it. After the *Reconquista*, both Muslims and Jews were hidden as Marranos.

As Gil Anidjar has recognized, it is not easy to separate the Arab from the Jew, the Arab from the Muslim.[34] The name "Jew" defines both a religion and a people. Jewishness is at once a faith and an ethnicity. The same oscillation between religious and political identity is present in Muslims and in relation to Muslims in a slightly altered form. The Arab is read as Muslim, the Muslim as Arab. The Arab Jew, the Arab Christian, the Arab atheist, and Arab secularist disappear. Capturing two forms of belonging under a single name enabled the oscillation of Jewish identity and of anti-Semitism. Though the name "Islam" only errantly captures an ethnic with a religious identity, insistence on the absence of a divide between the religious and the political has had similar effects in exposing Muslims to the coupling of religious and political persecution.

The description Derrida gives of himself as a Marrano marks him as a traveler, an Algerian, a Muslim as well as a Jew, a man formed in the history of the Maghreb. The name "Arab" marks these, for it means "traveler." Derrida is many times a traveler: as a Jew, as an Arab, as a theorist. Travel is central to the heritage of Islam. Muhammad took the Muslims from Mecca to Medina, in the *hijra*. The charter of Medina is a covenant between the new Muslims, the followers of the prophet Muhammad, and the Jewish tribes living in that land. The Qu'ran records another journey: "Glory to Him who took his votary to a wide and open land."[35] Islam inscribes the practice of travel in the yearly pilgrimage, the *hajj*. All Muslims should strive to make the *hajj* at least once, to protect the travelers and to support their pilgrimage. Those who have made the *hajj* are honored. Travel, willing and unwilling, is central to the Jewish experience as well. Jews remember the great journey of Exodus and, like Muslims, commemorate that journey every year. The experience of the Babylonian Exile is held in Jewish memory, along with the many moments of escape and exile that mark the diaspora. The figure of the Wandering Jew is inscribed in European myth. In legend and practice as well as scripture, travel is an experience that Judaism and Islam mark as constitutive. The practice of travel is also inscribed in the language of theory. Roxanne Euben writes of the complex pattern of linguistic connections knitting the *Arab*, the traveler, to theory. She observes that the Greek *theoria* refers not only to sight but to travel. The word binds theory both to travel and to theology. *Theoros* "has multiple meanings, including a spectator, a state delegate to a festival in another city, someone who travels to consult an oracle."[36] In travel, the Arab, the Muslim, the Jew, and the theorist meet.

In Derrida's time and ours, as in its Andalusian past, Algeria is a place of travel and travelers. Romans and Arabs, Berbers and Phoenicians travelled there and traveled from there. Arabs and Jews from Spain traveled there, from the great expulsion of the *Reconquista* onward. The great traveler Tocqueville travelled there and, after him, French soldiers and settlers. From the time of the Romans to the time of the French, Algeria has been a place of colonists and pirates. In Derrida's time, Algeria saw Jewish refugees from Northern Europe, Axis soldiers, Allied soldiers, French soldiers fighting to maintain colonialism traveling to North Africa. Algerians saw the *pieds noirs*, the *harkis*, many Jews, and the poor leave Algeria for France after the war.[37] Now young Algerians, jobless and desperate, travel in small boats across the Mediterranean. These are called *haragas*, "burners" because they burn the identity papers that might identify them as illegal immigrants in France. They are part of what Paul Silverstein has called "Algeria in France," part of the Muslim youth that Sarkozy called "*canaille*," scum, and Derrida "*voyous*," rogues.[38]

Derrida bears more than a passing resemblance to these young men. Like them, he was not born to wealth or privilege. Like many of them, he had a spell of leaving school for football. Like them, he left Algeria for opportunity in France. These are the Muslims Derrida disavowed when he left behind his being as an Arab. This is the space in which he grew up.

Jackie Derrida spent the first nineteen years of his life in Algeria.[39] He was born to a family of Arab Jews. In our time, where the Jew and the Arab are given to us as primordial enemies, such people may be seen as the most vulnerable, as the first objects of Muslim hate. More often, they are not seen at all. Derrida's insistent presentation of himself as a Jew, not an Arab, not *Maghrebi*, reinforced this construction of Arab and Jewish identities as mutually exclusive.[40] Derrida's denial of his Arab heritage alters as it enacts the idea of the Marrano. Once the secret Jew became the apparent Christian; now the secret Arab becomes the apparent Jew. The name taken openly conceals the persecuted identity. The denial of an Arab family, an Arab heritage, and his own Arab past may well have been the price of entry (paid under the table, a bribe at the border) into the French academy.

Perhaps French colonization had been so severe that it eradicated Arabic not only from the school but from the household. Perhaps the centuries-old ties to a predominately Muslim world were severed by colonialism. Certainly the French colonial administration insisted on French as the language of the state and civilization, in the accomplishment of the *mission civilisatrice*. Whatever the cause, Derrida insisted that he knew no Arabic. "I have only one language. I don't know any other. So, I was raised in a monolingual milieu—absolutely monolingual." That cannot have been true, even under the heavy hand of the French, and Derrida goes on to say, "around me, although not in my family, I naturally heard Arabic spoken, but I do not speak—except for a few words—Arabic. I tried to learn it later but I didn't get very far. Moreover, one could say in a general way, without exaggerating, that learning Arabic was something that was virtually forbidden at school. Not prohibited by law, but practically impossible. So, French is my only language."[41] Arabic, Derrida tells us, is the forbidden tongue, the speech of the other, not of his family.

The ear, however, is not an orifice that can be closed. Perhaps the young Derrida played only with footballers who spoke French. Perhaps he learned no Arabic in the shops and on the streets of el Biar. In any case, the French authorities did not forbid the sounding of the *adhan*. Five times a day the call to prayer echoes though the city. Five times a day the calls travel from one muezzin to the next. Five times a day the call to bear witness goes out *"ashadu-ana,"* I testify, I bear witness. Five times a day, for nineteen years, Derrida would have heard the call to prayer, the call to bear witness. Though he did not acknowledge hearing it, that is the call Derrida's work answers.

Islam is at the heart of Derrida's work. In her introduction to Derrida's *Of Grammatology*, Gayatri Spivak writes of how Rousseau is set "dreaming of Derrida."[42] Derrida, asleep and in the sleep of death, dreams of Islam.

In looking for the Arab, the Muslim hidden in Derrida, one is only following his directions. It is Derrida who calls himself a Marrano and in so doing tells us to look for the hidden identity, the secret faith. It is Derrida who echoes the call to bear witness. It is Derrida who tells us that the written is already present in the spoken. It is Derrida who direct us to the mystery of the *khora* and tells us that it belongs to the desert. It is Derrida, too, who tells us what is at stake in the taking of the friend, the brother, as the enemy. It is Derrida who links the democracy to come to the figure of the Muslim rogue.

The complex of rejection and belonging entailed in the unchosen secret of the Marrano is evident at the site—intimate, embodied, political, linguistic, and religious—of circumcision, a practice shared by Jews and Muslims. Derrida's account of his own circumcision speaks to his relation to Islam as well as Judaism and Christianity. Circumcision is an Abrahamic ritual, and a marking of the body that binds Jew and Muslim as it has historically set them apart from Christians. Though the mark and the act of circumcision are profoundly personal (for Derrida, as for all), the practice is political and religious and unites three elements of Derrida's work: the linguistic, the theological, and the political. With regard to circumcision and the Abrahamic, Derrida's relation to Islam is seen as imbricated with the other Abrahamic faiths, and the question of Islam with the political, philosophic, and the linguistic.

"Circumfession" is cast in a confessional mode but marks itself as an evasion. In Catholicism, confession is a formal and formally dialogic enterprise. The one who confesses repeats an initiating formula, the priest responds. The variation arises in the sins and in the penance prescribed by the priest—though these too tend to have a ritualistic quality about them. The dialogic structure of the work by (or between) Derrida and Bennington reflects this. The popular and scholarly meanings of "confession" are also on display in "Circumfession." Derrida's scandalous account of his mother staunching his wounded penis with her mouth is at once Biblical and tabloidesque. Is the referent the dramas of incestuous love that play out on television or the Mosaic? Does the reference to the confessional ally this text to Foucault's work on sexuality, on deviance, on the confessional impulse? These questions are themselves a distraction and evasion. Casting circumcision as a drama of sex and violence seems to reveal as it more effectively conceals. The apparent overcoming of the distinction between Jew and Catholic hides the rooted likeness of Jew and Muslim, Judaism and Islam.

In "Circumfession" Derrida places the account of his circumcision in Algeria.[43] This is a place of loss, a lost place. Something is lost here. That which is excised, that which is lost, was Derrida's and is so no longer. Perhaps this is "what the sexed being loses in sexuality."[44] Perhaps it is what the political being loses in belonging to a polity. Derrida enters the covenant as he is separated from that which once belonged to him. The circumcision is the site at which the word and the flesh, writing and the body, meet. In this place, at this site, bandages are stained, texts written, the mouth and the pen, the author of the body and the author of the text meet. The circumcision is the site at which speech and silence, frankness and concealment meet. For all the revelations, Derrida shows us that something is hidden.

The text layers one time upon another. The time of writing and recollection gives way to the time of circumcision, the instant when Abraham raises his knife over Isaac, once in sacrifice, once in circumcision. The account is out of place, improper, inappropriate; it does not belong where it is. The text is out of place: displaced, timeless, separated from the material world, outside Algeria. The wound binds one time to another: the time of the text to the time of circumcision, to all the times of circumcision, and to that time when Abraham raised his knife over Isaac, not to mark but to annihilate him. "As Montaigne said 'I constantly disavow myself.'"[45]

What is held in the mouth? What is concealed here? Another writing, another language, perhaps another phallus, another logos, another center are hidden here. Even as we are told that this is a story of the phallus, of Derrida's phallus, of the Jew and the Frenchman, the all too frank narratives gesture toward the silent and the hidden. The text purports to reveal the author, the phallus, that which is inscribed, but it shows us a phallus and an inscription concealed: a hidden male member. The hidden male member is Derrida's, but there is, in this story, another hidden male member: Ishmael. In his account of circumcision Derrida occupies the place of Isaac, but he gestures toward the hidden Ishmael, from whom all Arabs are said to descend. He marks Ishmael as that which he has lost.

"Circumfession" circles around the question of circumcision. Casting circumcision in a confessional mode allies it to Catholicism, but it evades the recognition of circumcision as a ritual marking shared by Islam. Looking to this ritual reveals it as a hinge, linking and separating Judaism and Islam. Jews and Muslims mark the male body in circumcision. Jews have understood circumcision as a ritual requirement. Muslims locate the imperative to circumcision in the *hadith*, the practices of the Prophet, and in tradition.

The drama of circumcision appears in "Circumfession" as a passion play: the father sacrificing his own body; the mourning mother; the suffering son. Hélène Cixous enhances this effect in *Portrait of Derrida as a Young Jewish Saint*. Cixous begins with the question "Was I Jewish?" ascribed to Derrida, and ends with Derrida as Isaac divided, wresting with himself "vanquished and vanquisher." Derrida is saint and "lamb-child" and in circumcision "the child, then, cries Jewish as Christian, cries Judeo-Christian."[46] Circumcision becomes a sacrifice and, as a sacrifice, can be employed (as Cixous does) to cast the aging Derrida as a "Young Jewish Saint." Islam is excised from this account, cut out of Derrida's past, in order to ensure his belonging, his ability to "cry Jewish as Christian." Something is lost here, not only a bit of Derrida himself but a link between Judaism and Islam.[47]

For Jews and Muslims, the act is understood as a ritual of belonging, marking the body as part of the community. For both Jews and Muslims, the event is a joyful one, celebrated by family and friends. In both Judaism and Islam, circumcision is a link to Abraham.

Though he returns again and again to the story of the sacrifice of Isaac—though he preserves and relies on those children of Abraham, Isaac, and Ishmael—Derrida does not often refer, directly or indirectly, to the three monotheistic religions called by some the Abrahamic faiths.[48] Perhaps Abraham is for Derrida the father of dissemination. His seed becomes first two children, then a posterity as numberless as the stars, seeded across time and space. His seed is the dissemination of writing, too, for each male body is marked with the sign of the covenant, the sign of belonging, the name of the father. Abraham is the icon and incarnation, if not the originary moment, of phallogocentrism.

Abraham is also the site of sacrifice, the site of the holocaust. Abraham is not only the father of two brothers and a numberless posterity, he is also the father of three faiths. He is, perhaps above all, the father of the holocaust. Abraham is the father who puts his son on the pyre, to give him to God as a burnt offering. As the father of Christianity and Judaism, he is the father of another holocaust, the Shoah. Kierkegaard's reading of Abraham as the knight of faith, opposed to ethics and to reason, takes on a still darker meaning here. Abraham is the night of faith as well, the man in whom faith becomes dark and threatening, the place where ethics, reason, and the son are lost. As the father of the Holocaust, Abraham is the icon of the place where faith fails. Jews are burned and Christians, by their own judgment, condemn themselves to burning. Abraham's sacrifice of his own son, "his own family, friends, neighbors, nation, at the outside, humanity as a whole, his own kind" remains "an absolute source of pain."[49]

The sacrifice of Abraham's son on Mount Moriah provides a site for Derrida to depart from Schmitt, at least for a moment.[50]

Derrida's understanding of the political accepts and elaborates the primacy of enmity in the foundation of the political. This is especially evident in *The Politics of Friendship*. That work offers a long meditation on the friend-enemy distinction, one in which the distinction grows ever more uncertain and friendship is subsumed in enmity. The repeated refrain is taken from an apocryphal exclamation of Aristotle: "Oh friends, there is no friend!" In Schmitt, the friend-enemy distinction determines both the boundaries of the polity and the site of sovereignty. "Sovereign is he who decides on the exception."[51] In Schmitt's work, as in that of Agamben and others who have followed him in the wake of the Holocaust, the site of the exception is the site of death. The sovereign, human and divine, who decides the exception, gives life and takes it away. The decisions that belong to sovereignty concern mortality.

In his account of the sacrifice of Isaac, Derrida points toward another, opposing, reading of the exception. The exception is not the occasion for violence but the moment when violence is arrested. Isaac is not sacrificed. In this reading, the sacrifice that faith demands never has to be made. One might argue that here Derrida opens the way to a manifold refutation of Schmitt. The sacrifice of the son who is not the Son, but nevertheless the body of the people to come, does not need to be made. One might call this a Jewish reading, a reading of messianism without messianicity. This is also a historical reading, a reading of triumph in the wake of the Holocaust, reminding us that the Jews continue. Derrida is, however, conscious of what is lost in that reading: the six million and the *Muselmänner* of our time, Ishmael.

The story of Isaac and Ishmael is not a single story for Derrida, even an emblematic, iconic, story. In *The Gift of Death* the story of the sacrifice of Isaac conveys a truth of politics altogether, confronted "in this land of Moriah that is our habitat every second of every day."[52] There, Derrida reads the sacrifice of Abraham as an account of the inevitable betrayals that belong to belonging. "Day and night," Derrida writes, "at every instant, on all the Mount Moriahs of this world, I am doing that, raising my knife over what I love."[53] In this passage, Derrida testifies to the sacrifices that politics, religion, and philosophy demand. What is lost here? Ethics and reason, faith in faith, perhaps. What is sacrificed? Ethics and reason, certainly. Perhaps a son and a brother. Who is sacrificed? Perhaps Isaac, perhaps Ishmael.

The sacrifice of Isaac, as it is given to us in the Judeo-Christian scriptures, is a story with a happy ending. For Derrida, the "bloody, holocaustic sacrifice" is Isaac's, and so a story of redemption.[54] Isaac is staked, put in play, pawned, and then redeemed. Isaac is the laughing one. In him Sarah's laughter is incarnate. He is the sacrifice that need not be made. He is the joyous reversal of Agamben's *homo sacer*. If the *homo sacer* is the one who be killed but not sacrificed, Isaac is the one who can be sacrificed but not killed.

But is Isaac the sacrifice? In Muslim tradition, it is not Isaac but Ishmael who is sacrificed.[55] The Quranic account echoes the Judaic one: the son is spared. If we read not the Biblical but the modern Holocaust, there is no redemption. The Jew Isaac becomes the *Muselmann* of the camps, the man reduced to bare life, given a death. Isaac and Ishmael meet in the figure of the *Muselmann*. There is no redemption.[56]

The figure of the *Muselmann* reminds us of the Jew and the Muslim as marked bodies, then and now. Circumcision still marks bodies as outside the Christian—and now secular—communities. As the body of the Jew was read under Vichy as a marked body, carrying the signs of Judaism, the body of the Arab, the Muslim, is read as marked in racial profiling (whether it goes by that name or not).[57] Under the policies of surveillance adopted in the United States and Europe after 9/11, signifiers of piety also mark the body.[58]

Derrida's Abraham is a timeless figure and so bound not only to his time but ours. Derrida draws attention in *The Gift of Death* to the violence and the sacrifice of the Abrahamic present. Jerusalem, he writes, is

> a holy place but also a place that is in dispute, radically and rabidly, fought over by all the monotheisms, by all the religions of the unique and transcendent God, of the absolute other. . . . They make war with fire and blood. . . . Isaac's sacrifice continues every day. Countless machines of death wage a war that has no front.[59]

Gil Anidjar has noted Derrida's frequent quotation of Joyce, "Hear, O Ishmael."[60] The substitution of Ishmael for Israel faces us once again with the iridescent, oscillating figure of the Jew, the Muslim. This ejaculation collapses Isaac and Ishmael in the imperative of the *Shema*, "Hear, O Israel." Perhaps the two sons of Abraham are one, or perhaps they have one origin that diverges into innumerable posterity. Perhaps they incarnate that oscillation between friend and enemy that is at the center of the *Politics of Friendship*. Perhaps it is a question of the calling. Perhaps it is being toward death.

Both the *Shema* and the *shahada*, the testimony of faith that comes in the call to prayer, testify to the singularity of God. Both are acts of witness that call others to witness. Both are bound in the daily life of the community. The call to prayer is a performance of the imperative "Hear, O Ishmael." Both are allied to being toward death. The *Shema* is traditionally recited when death is imminent, and is linked to stories of martyrdom, ancient and contemporary.[61] The word for martyr in Arabic, and in Muslim tradition more generally, is *shahid* and comes from the same root as *shahada*. The martyr is one who bears witness.

Derrida belongs to that generation of philosophers, writers, and artists who found themselves confronted by the Holocaust. They oriented their thinking to an event they saw as unthinkable and incalculable. The Holocaust is, in the most mundane and most profound sense, the presence of an absence.

The Holocaust was also calculated, ordered, rationalized, mechanized, bureaucratic, and, above all, modern. Martyrdom is bound with bureaucratic rationality, with mechanism as well as messianism, mechanicity as well as messianicity. Hegel's *Abendland* is no longer West of Europe but a dead presence in the European West. Hegel made the Land of the Dead the place of the future, the site of that which is unknowable and waits for all. The *Abendland* as a place of death reveals itself as not outside Europe but within it. Death belongs not to the future but to the past that remains in the present, not to the living but to the dead. The promise of the unknown future has burned away. Bearing witness is at once imperative and impossible.[62]

Derrida recognizes that the "machines of death wage a war that has no front" in the desert of the Promised Land. Who lives there? Who is the hunted now? Ishmael.

Ishmael is the abandoned son, the exiled son, the son who disappears. Abraham abandons Ishmael to Sarah's will. Ishmael goes into exile with his mother, Hagar. The Qu'ran tells of the wanderings of Hagar and Ishmael and of divine intervention on their behalf. They wander, God gives them water, they survive. Ishmael fathers a nation of wanderers, of Arabs. These children of Abraham were also to be "strangers in a land not theirs."[63] Ishmael goes into exile, in time and space. He is sent out of the house of Abraham to wander in the desert. He and his people are sent out of history, out of time. They are sent out of the text.

Ishmael is the name of an absence, the name of the child who is not Sarah's, the child who is not the heir. He will not be given land or property.

He is exiled from the text. Ishmael is *sous rature*, the one who is erased, the sign of a disavowal.

The figure of Ishmael wanders throughout Derrida's work. Ishmael is the lost brother who is and is not (or is no longer) one's own. Ishmael is the *revenant*, the one who returns in the dark hours, the specter, whose spiritual and intellectual, *geistliche* presence marks a loss, a sacrifice, a sin. Ishmael is the undead, that which might be thought to be done, finished, dead, which nevertheless returns to haunt one. Above all, Ishmael stands as the lost friend.

Derrida makes a passage from Nietzsche the epigraph to "The Phantom Friend Returning (in the Name of Democracy)":

> "If we greatly transform ourselves, those friends of ours who have not been transformed become ghosts of our past: their voice comes across to us like the voice of a shade (in a frightfully spectral manner [*schattenhaft-schauerlich*])—as though we were hearing ourself, only younger, more severe, less mature."[64]

Derrida links the phantom friend to his own lost past. The phantom friend is spectral, belonging to a past that has been left behind but which nevertheless remains one's own. The phantom friend is like and unlike the self. The phantom friend is heard. Friendship and loss are bound together with democracy or "the Name of Democracy." This qualification seems to preserve the doubts about democracy that Derrida expresses throughout his work, nevertheless it is Derrida who insists on the importance of the name. Those less suspicious of the possibility of democracy might dispense with the caveat and argue that the possibility of democracy is linked to the reclaiming of the phantom friend, the other who can be one's own.

"Circumfession" suggested that the loss of the other was great, perhaps disempowering: the price of entry into the covenant, an obligatory exclusion exacted with violence. In *The Politics of Friendship* the loss is like shedding a skin: done without violence, accomplished as a maturing, improvement, overcoming. The lost other lingers as a shadow of a self, present only as one dead or left behind. For Derrida, as for Schmitt and Hegel, democracy belongs to the *Abendland*, to a world of shadows. If Derrida departs from Schmitt in his reading of the holocaust, covenant, and exception, he follows Schmitt in seeing the political as dependent upon the presence of enmity and on the centrality of the distinction of friend and enemy to politics. He affirms (where Schmitt does not) the absence of democracy. Schmitt disavows democracy. Derrida defers it and increasingly appears to mark it as an impossibility in this world.

In accordance with Derrida's citation of the spectral and the association of the spectral with friendship (the phantom friend) and democracy, perhaps Derrida is suggesting that democracy belongs in the *Abendland*, in an aporetic future in the West. Derrida seems, however, to worry (or perhaps to hope) that democracy comes bearing its death within it, in the form of a suicidal autoimmunity. This anticipation of the end of democracy enables Derrida to suggest that democracy is always already dead and appears to us only as a shadow, a revenant, as something we once knew, returning.

The lectures of *The Politics of Friendship* are built around the ejaculation, attributed to Aristotle, "Oh Friends there is no friend!" and with reference to Schmitt's assertion that politics is founded on the friend-enemy distinction. The enemy and the friend are confounded in *The Politics of Friendship*: born at the same moment and conceptually inseparable.[65] The line between friendship and enmity is blurred and crossed. Friendship is linked to death.[66] Hospitality is shown to shelter enmity, hostility.[67] The politics of friendship presented as fraternity, in the canonical French fashion, is rejected (and that on the best Nietzschean authority).[68] This is not merely a recognition of possible oscillations between friendship and enmity. Friendship is rendered suspect at every point—except, perhaps, in the closing words that look toward democracy. At that moment Derrida asks, "When will we be ready for an experience of freedom and equality that is capable of respectfully experiencing that friendship, which would at last be just, just beyond the law and measured up against its measurelessness?" Following that question, for the first time, Derrida amends the invocation, eliding if he does not excise, the rejection of friendship. He writes in closing, "O my democratic friends . . . ."[69]

Derrida's privileging of the apocryphal affirmation of enmity—"Oh Friends, there is no friend!"—over the canonical *Politics* in which Aristotle grounds democratic politics on friendship, points toward the rejected alternative of friendship and democracy that emerges only at the closing of his work. This seeming impossibility "would therefore be a matter of thinking an alterity without hierarchical difference at the root of democracy."[70] If one looks back to the canonical rather than the apocryphal Aristotle and to al Farabi, that is what democracy (indeed politics) is.

That Derrida has a particular phantom friend (and enemy or other) in mind is evident here. Derrida makes it clear that the question of the political, as Schmitt construes it, is dependent not only on the relation of friend and enemy but (in this time as in others) on a particular enemy, Islam. "It was imperative not 'to deliver Europe over to Islam' . . . . The stakes would be saving the political as such, ensuring its survival in the face of another who would no longer even be a political enemy but an enemy of the political," one who "shares nothing of the juridical and the political called European."[71] There are now many Muslims in Europe. They are native-born as well as immigrants. Many of them speak French or German or English or Dutch as their first language. They are, as Tariq Ramadan has affirmed, Western. They live under "the juridical and political called European."[72] They vote. Some of them have run for office, some of them have won. This living testimony to a more capacious Europe is put in question twice in this passage from Derrida. The "imperative not to deliver Europe over to Islam" fears a future cast in the image of the past, a future prophesied in the sound of Roland's horn. The disavowal of the Muslim in Europe stands in an uneasy relation to Derrida's disavowal of Algeria for Europe: in leaving, in disavowing himself as an Arab Jew, and in abandoning Algerian democracy. "Oh Friends, there is no friend!" may be a reproach directed not at others but at himself.

As elsewhere, Derrida does not leave the partisans of friendship and democracy without hope. If one listens to the whispers of the *revenant*, one can hear "the critique of the nymph Echo."[73] If one listens to Derrida with an Arab ear, one can hear more than the Greek, the French. If one hears "khora" with an Arab ear, one hears echoes of "*qara'a.*" This is the command that opens the Qu'ran, the command "recite!" The command prefigures Derrida's affirmation that the written precedes the spoken. The text of the Qu'ran is written before it is recited, is already written in the moment of its first recitation. This is the text read in *Of Grammatology.*[74]

Qara'a, the command "recite," carries a constellation of commands within it. This is the command to prophecy. This is the command that Muhammad obeys in bringing the Qu'ran to the people. This is the command Muslims obey in the *shahada*, the testimony that answers the command to bear witness. Five times a day the muezzin calls out to the city, in the voice of the people, "I testify that there is no God but God. I testify that Muhammad is the messenger of God." Tariq Ramadan, in rejecting the distinction between the *dar al harb* (the abode of war) and the *dar al Islam* (the abode of Islam), writes that Western Muslims belong not to either (or to both) of these but to another understanding of place and time, another understanding of their relation to politics and the divine. They are called, he writes, to be the people of the *dar ash-shahada*, the people who bear witness.[75]

Derrida writes of *khora* as something that is at once present and absent, alien and one's own. He writes of "some *khora* (body without body, absent body but unique body and place [*lieu*] of everything, in the place of everything, interval, place, [*place*], spacing). . . . *Khora* is over there but more here than any here." *Khora* is the place of the secret: "Everything secret is played out here."[76] *Khora* is the place of revelation. This place is kept secret. This is the place of Ishmael, the absent but unique body (for, as Derrida tells us, the sacrifice must be unique) who stands for, in lieu of, the other. *Khora* is Derrida's elsewhere, across the Mediterranean, in one sense, across a more fortified boundary, but also the elsewhere carried in the heart and mind, another time, another place, a time past. Between that place and this, between one sound and another, there is the interval, and that, Heidegger tells us, is where thought arises.[77]

The interval is also the place of the echo, the partial repetition produced over an interval of space and time. In the echo, one calls to oneself, one is called by an earlier self. In *khora*, one can hear echoes of the place of revelation, of Derrida's elsewhere. You will see, Derrida writes, "why it is that we left the name *khora* sheltered from any translation. A translation, admittedly, seems to be always at work, both *in* the Greek language, and from the Greek language into some other."[78] One can hear in the Greek the echoes of the *qara'a* with which Islam begins.

One need not hear *qara'a* echoing in *khora* to recognize an evocation of the core of Islam in Derrida's complex of concerns: responsibility, bearing witness, the carrying of the written in the spoken word. One need not hear *qara'a* echoing in *khora* to see the Maghreb as the "over there" that, in France is "more 'here' than any 'here.' "[79] One need not hear *qara'a* echoing in *khora* to see Ishmael as the absent body. Still, I would remind the reader of Derrida's interest in the "otobiographical."[80]

Derrida's writing on the *khora* takes up a series of themes that echo through his work on Islam and Muslims. *Khora* is that which is set against, before, beneath, and perhaps after reason. This is the place where the certainties of the Enlightenment come into question.

Any reading of Derrida on Islam is troubled by the ambiguities in the French *raison* and *droit*. When reason seems to carry right, correctness, within itself, and law and right are entangled in one another, it may be more difficult to maintain or convey a critique of the Enlightenment or a commitment to democracy. This is particularly evident in *Rogues*, which is subtitled "Two Essays on Reason." Reason does not appear much in these essays. The first "essay" (perhaps the French, or archaic English, is more apt here) comprises ten essays under the title "Reason of the Strongest." The second comprises two under the title "The 'World' of the Enlightenment to Come." This points us toward a series of questions, and to that fable of La Fontaine in which a wolf presents to a lamb his justification for eating him. The first line reads "la raison du plus fort est toujours la meilleure." The reason (and the right) of the strongest is always the best.[81]

Derrida writes of the *khora* as "the place of bifurcation between two approaches to the desert."[82] This manifold divide (for it is far more complex than a simple "bifurcation") points toward the divide between reason and revelation, between the Greek and the Abrahamic, between the "techno-scientific" and some other, between a hegemonic political, economic, and juridical regime, which is also a state system, "the sovereignty of states" and some other, between the universal and the particular. Throughout "Faith and Knowledge" (but less certainly elsewhere) Derrida identifies democracy with a universalism that rejects particularity.[83] The virtue (and the danger) of democracy is its ability to be at once universal and particular.

In those writings that deal with Islam, as elsewhere, Derrida is most open in closing. The aporetic form accompanies an openness toward the Muslim other. Derrida is preoccupied with closings, with their form and with the words we use in parting. These, too, can be heard and read otherwise, mindful of the other.

Derrida hears salvation in the "latinity" of *salut*. *Salut* is more than a greeting, it belongs to the name of the party whose anticipated democratic victory seemed to Derrida (and the Algerian military) to put democracy at risk: the *Front Islamique du Salut*. In his attention to echoes, above all to Nietzsche's "critique of the Nymph Echo," Derrida critiques his own judgment. *Front Islamique du Salut* echoes *salut, salut, salut*. Perhaps this forestalled victory, achieved elsewhere in the wake of the Arab Spring, is not a hazard to democracy but democracy's health and salvation. Perhaps we should salute it.

Derrida's *adieu* to Ishmael and to democracy reminds us of the theology inscribed in what we cast out. It recalls the ambiguity of our secularization: the presence of theology inscribed in the everyday. *Adieu* is an easy greeting for a Muslim, even an Islamist, to master. Need we say *adieu*? Derrida's attention to salutations, to greetings and farewells, reminds us that these do not exhaust the vocabulary of Derrida's elsewhere—or the France of the present. If we take Derrida's approach to the *banlieues* where, he told us, we are closer to democracy, we hear other greetings. We hear *ahlan wa sahlan* and *marhaba*. *Marhaba* carries within it the idea that the one greeted is welcome, that there is plenty of room. The root *r-h-b* gives us *rahb*, which means spacious or roomy but also "unconfined" and "open-minded, broad-minded, frank, liberal."[84] This is also the root of *rahaba*, the word for the public square.

The Egyptian poet and scholar Farouk Mustafa translated *Ahlan wa sahlan* to his students as "you are among your people and your keep is easy." This greeting speaks directly to the complex of concerns in "hostipitality"—

and sets it aside. Here the presumption is not enmity but friendship. The other is read and taken as one's own. At a conference at Cerisy-la-Salle, Derrida greeted his hosts in a manner that played, in the same generous spirit, on the ambiguity between host (*hôte*) and guest (*hôte*).[85] *Ahlan wa sahlan* is not said simply to one's own, to family and friends and fellow citizens. Like "welcome" it can be said to foreigners, to travelers, to people who are not, in the ordinary sense, one's own. This greeting marks the possibility that the other, the alien, the wanderer, and the refugee might be met with a welcome rather than with fear. It enacts the commitment to take the other not as an enemy but as a friend, setting aside the intimations of hostility in "hostipitality."

Islam appears in Derrida's writing as his exiled brother, his disavowed friend, and, perhaps, his phantom friend, returning. It is this last relation, the relation to the *revenant*, that links the question to the possibility of becoming democratic, of the democracy to come. At this untimely place, where that which has not been can come into being, where that which once was but is no more can return, there the rogue in Derrida can, perhaps, make common cause with the roguish Muslims of Western Islam. It is this possibility, allusive and uncertain, that opens the possibility of a redemptive, fraternal reading of Derrida and Islam.

Habermas, Derrida, and the Question of Religion

PETER E. GORDON

"Knock, knock! Who's there, in th' other devil's name?"
—*Macbeth* Act 2, scene 3, 1–8

In the history of religion the arrival of the millennium is often imagined as the ἔσχατον, an end of history or "end-time" that brings an apocalyptic and ultimate answer to all human questions. But the perennial quarrel between religion and philosophy can hardly be illustrated with greater force than by recalling that for Socrates the practice of philosophy remains forever marked by ἀπορεία. It is a mode of critical interrogation or *maieutics* that is always incomplete, and that must forever exceed or undo any ideal of plenitude. In this sense, although its detractors consign philosophy to the ostensibly unworldly realm of mere *theoria*, its argumentative history suggests a character of ongoing *praxis* rather than a dogma. To be sure, philosophy may orient itself by means of eschatological hope, the ideal of an argument so compelling and complete that it will put an end to all further dissent. The very logic of argumentation itself may seem to presuppose its annulment. If this philosophical ideal (of fulfillment without remainder, or truth without contestation) were to actually allow for a genuine realization then we might conclude that philosophy and religion do not stand locked in eternal opposition like the two cities, Athens and Jerusalem, that serve as their allegorical representatives. But philosophy in its practice—as long as this practice consists precisely in *questioning*—contradicts this ideal insofar as it always conspires to unravel the fabric of a temporary consensus. It is therefore unsurprising that Hegel's ideal of a *Versöhnung* turned out to be little more than a mirage. The very idea of an eschaton is the negation of philosophy, not its fulfillment.

In this essay I offer a reconsideration of the philosophical debate between Jacques Derrida and Jürgen Habermas. More precisely, my aim in what follows will be to suggest that in the history of their exchanges we can identify a discrete and enduring point of disagreement—a disagreement that should not be minimized or dismissed in the name of some illusory ideal of philosophical consensus. My discussion will conclude with the year 2000, which in this case hardly signifies a millenarian reconciliation, though it might nonetheless serve as a helpful point of reference for identifying the moment at which these two equally celebrated but notably dissimilar theorists began to move, after many years of pronounced disagreement, toward what has struck many observers as a rapprochement in philosophical understanding. The occasion for this renewal of contact was the international conference, Judéités: Questions pour Jacques Derrida, which convened at the Jewish Community Center in Paris in early December, 2000.[1] The conference had a broad purpose of affording Derrida the opportunity to expound at some length about his conceptions of Judaism (or "Judeity"), but it also served as an occasion for Habermas to modify some of his earlier and more negative verdicts concerning Derrida's philosophy. His public presentation was soon thereafter published under the title "How to Answer the Ethical Question" (with a further subtitle in the German edition: "Derrida und die Religion"). In retrospect, one is tempted to entertain the thought that the essay might have inaugurated a phase of intellectual collaboration, had this promise not been cut short by Derrida's death in 2004.

As I will explain below, Habermas's lecture merits our attention not merely as a political and biographical document but as a theoretical interrogation of certain religious themes that came to the fore in Derrida's later years. But it can also serve as a reminder of persistent doubts or questions that might be raised concerning the merits of these themes. The longer story of intellectual exchanges and debate between Habermas and Derrida has been told in great detail and with great acuity in a recent book by Pierre Bouretz, who traces out the dramas of their exchange from beginning to end.[2] In what follows I want to suggest that we should not exaggerate the depth of the philosophical reconciliation between the two protagonists. I will propose instead that we consider Habermas's lecture as a reprisal of fundamental concerns—or, more precisely, questions—that have not ceased to animate critical theory over the course of its long career. These are questions that retain their urgency even today, and not only for Habermas or Derrida. As I will explain, they are questions that, in the ongoing encounter of religion and recent Continental philosophy, continue both to trouble and inspire, and they are likely to persist at least as long as religion itself.

Habermas's Early Critique of Derrida

In one of the twelve lectures included in *The Philosophical Discourse of Modernity* (originally published in German in 1985), Habermas first laid out a vigorous (some would say polemical) assessment of Derrida's theoretical work.[3] According to the book's general argument, the philosophical parameters of modernity first gained conceptual precision when Nietzsche announced an abolition of all traditional limits and celebrated the emancipation of the human individual as a normatively unbounded subjectivity. For Nietzsche, "the death of God" was not merely an event in the secularization of religion since it also spelled the death of traditional ideals of reason, such that the individual subject was now oriented toward nothing besides its own temporalized and aestheticized efforts of self-overcoming. The Nietzschean ideal dispensed with any quasi-transcendental ideals of normative consensus even while it reimagined the horizon of human achievement in purely temporal and this-worldly terms. According to Habermas, this ideal continued to exert a profound influence on the post-Nietzschean critique of reason insofar as its negative verdict on the role of reason in modernity took off from Nietzsche's own "subject-centered" definition of human consciousness.

Within this broad narrative, Habermas scrutinized the succession of post-Nietzschean philosophers—from Heidegger to Adorno and Horkheimer to Foucault and Derrida—as a series of repeated *failures* to overcome the subject-centered model of consciousness that furnished the epistemo-political groundwork for philosophical modernity. Although Habermas was unsparing in his overall criticism of this post-Nietzschean groundwork, his treatment of Derrida is distinguished by the sharpness of his tone. His critique of Derrida fixes its attention primarily on the persistence of an "inverted foundationalism" that has its origins in Heidegger, whose authoritarian and mythopoetic philosophy apparently lurked in Derrida's own work.

Habermas's early critique of Derrida first takes shape as a critique of Heidegger. For Heidegger's *Seinsfrage* is still, according to Habermas, an exercise in "first philosophy" (a phrase he uses polemically to mark the unwanted affinity between Heidegger and Descartes). That is, even while the question of Being is supposed to inaugurate a *non-metaphysical* inquiry into temporality as the only possible ground of understanding, it nonetheless functions as a metaphysics insofar as ontology sends us in search of the formal-metaphysical principle that illumines the what and how of all entities. Now, according to Habermas, Heidegger's ontological efforts are still afflicted with the very same formalist ambitions of a *prima philosophia*, and this same formalist commitment marks the philosophy of Derrida as well. This formalism disables Derrida's attempt to pass beyond a foundationalist metaphysics:

> Derrida's deconstructions faithfully follow the movement of Heidegger's thought. Against his will, he lays bare the inverted foundationalism of this thought by once again going beyond the ontological difference and Being to the *différance* proper to writing, which puts an origin already set in motion yet one level deeper. . . . As a participant in the philosophical discourse of modernity, Derrida inherits the weaknesses of a critique of metaphysics that does not shake loose of the intentions of first philosophy.[4]

For Habermas, Derrida's *différance* is on the one hand the name for a formalistic principle that serves as the analogue to Heidegger's *Sinn des Seins*: Although its temporal character is supposed to exempt it from any complicity with traditional foundationalism, it ultimately recapitulates the obscurantist pathos of Heidegger's own "inverted foundationalism." Derrida styles himself as a philosophical radical who intends to surpass Heidegger. But according to Habermas, it is a radicalism whose indifference to the requirement of social intelligibility ultimately marks its complicity with Heideggerian authoritarianism: "Despite his transformed gestures, in the end [Derrida], too, promotes only a mystification of palpable social pathologies; he, too, disconnects essential (namely, deconstructive) thinking from scientific analysis; and he, too, lands at an empty, formulalike avowal of some indeterminate authority."[5]

This interpretation is admittedly harsh, and it invites serious qualifications. But even while Habermas attempts to document the persistent strain of Heideggerian affiliation in Derrida's philosophy, he also acknowledges a strong dissimilarity, traceable in the last instance to the Jewish themes of an indecipherable text and an exile from metaphysical plenitude. On Habermas's interpretation *différance* works like an absent foundationalism to set in motion a deferral or wandering without any hope for the recovery of what has been lost: "It is, however, not the authority of a Being that has been distorted by beings, but the authority of a no longer holy scripture, of a scripture that is in exile, wandering about, estranged from its own meaning, a scripture that testimonially documents the absence of the holy."[6] But somehow (Habermas does not make this point clear) notwithstanding this obvious allusion to the Jewish theme of exile and the always-already absent divine writing, Derrida is *still not a theologian*:

> *By the same token, Derrida does not want to think theologically; as an orthodox Heideggerian* he is forbidden any thought about a supreme entity. Instead, similarly to Heidegger, Derrida sees the modern condition as constituted by phenomena of deprival that are not comprehensible within the horizon of the history of reason and of divine revelation. As he assures us at the start of his essay on "différance," he does not want to do any theology, not even negative theology.[7]

What is most striking in Habermas's critique is not its polemical character but its disunity. For Habermas first criticizes Derrida as a loyal or "orthodox" Heideggerian whose orthodoxy obviates any commitments to the concepts of traditional religion. But Habermas then praises Derrida for dismantling the authoritarianism of the Heideggerian problematic with instruments that are distinctively *theological*. It is unclear how these two characterizations are compatible. But according to Habermas, this anti-authoritarian or *anarchistic* gesture proves decisive: "Derrida stands closer to the anarchist wish to explode the continuum of history than to the authoritarian admonition to bend before destiny."[8] The difference between Heidegger and Derrida, Habermas explains, is ultimately traceable to the difference between neo-paganism and Judaism. Unlike Heidegger, Derrida "is not interested in going back, in the fashion of the New Paganism, beyond the beginnings of monotheism, beyond the concept of a tradition that sticks to the traces of the lost divine scripture and keeps itself going through heretical exegesis of the scripture."[9] Instead, Habermas sees that Derrida seeks instruction from Levinas and to the pathos of an infinite Torah associated with Rabbi Eliezer (as cited by Levinas): "If all the seas were of ink, and all the ponds planted with reeds, if the sky and the earth were parchments and if all human beings practiced the art of writing—they would not exhaust the Torah that I have learned, just as the Torah itself would not be diminished any more than is the sea by the water removed by the paint brush dipped in it."[10] From this idea of an *infinite* and *indefinite* revelation, Derrida's grammatology (according to Habermas) "renews the mystical concept of tradition as an ever *delayed* event of revelation."[11] There is no final disclosure or primordial *Ereignis* of ontological authenticity because the play of signification appeals to a God whose transcendence cannot be overcome: "The labor of deconstruction lets the refuse heap of interpretations, which it wants to clear away in order to get at the buried foundations, mount ever higher."[12]

For Habermas it is this distinction alone that redeems the monotheistic Derrida from the authoritarian taint of the Heideggerian *Seinsgeschick*. The irony of this distinction is that it qualifies Derrida's prestige as a truly post-foundationalist philosopher insofar as the *critique* of Heidegger gains its energy from a barely acknowledged wellspring of religion. "Mystical experiences were able to unfold their explosive force, their power of liquefying institutions and dogmas, in Jewish and Christian traditions, because they remained related in these contexts to a hidden, world-transcendent God."[13] The light of monotheism sustains its corrosive power of breaking through myth and therefore clears the path to Enlightenment. Derrida, in other words, may *appear* to disavow the monotheistic God (since any such God would stand as a paradigm of an impermissible metaphysics), but Derrida nonetheless retains the *critical* and *anti-mythical* light refracted by the monotheistic tradition.

This is a light Heidegger condemns as metaphysical error, although paradoxically there are religious "illuminations" that still radiate Heidegger's own philosophy. But such illuminations are set free from the transcendental anchors of traditional monotheism and therefore lose all determinacy to become merely anonymous or "diffuse." According to Habermas, if the illumination becomes entirely detached from the notion of a *source*, it may very well nourish an ethic of absolute self-assertion and aesthetic play (Nietzsche). But if one abjures monotheism while holding fast to its paradigmatic idea of a primordial light this may also result in the peculiarly half-secularized religion of anonymous revelation (Heidegger). Neither of these two options promises a way out from the normative aporias of philosophical modernity:

> The path of their consistent secularization points into the domain of radical experiences that avant-garde art has opened up. Nietzsche had taken his orientations from the purely aesthetic rapture of ecstatic subjectivity, gone out from itself. Heidegger took his stand halfway down this path; he wanted to retain the force of an *illumination without direction* and yet not pay the price of its secularization.[14]

Derrida's open-ended practice of textually-oriented criticism undoes the authoritarianism of this neo-pagan illumination, but only because it appeals to the model of an always-already *discursive* revelation (i.e., revelation for Derrida is *textual*, mediated by language, never a pure or sublime *theophany* of the divine face). But the substantive meaning of this revelation is deferred such that its content never has the chance to solidify into anti-critical dogma. Derrida thereby develops under the name of deconstruction a critique of Heidegger's philosophy (notwithstanding the kinship between *deconstruction* and *Destruktion*), but this is only because his critique borrows its power from the monotheistic tradition Heidegger disavows: "Derrida means to go beyond Heidegger," Habermas averred, "fortunately, he goes back behind him."[15]

Although the above remarks may at first glance suggest that Habermas saw Derrida in a favorable light, we should not neglect the noticeably more negative verdict that appears in the ensuing "Excursus," where Habermas laid down a critique of what he considers Derrida's attempt at "leveling the genre distinction" between philosophy and literature.[16] Habermas saw in Derrida, and also in Adorno, a robust affirmation of the critical potentialities of modernist art. The comparison is noteworthy for both the similarity and dissimilarities that come to light. Both Adorno and Derrida contest the ideological immediacy that underwrites the notion of an "authentic" work of art. But they launch their assault along different paths: Adorno does so by criticizing the sham-idealism of aesthetic transcendence and its ideal of aesthetic totality, whereas Derrida criticizes the ideology of the proper and the "original" in favor of the logic of supplementarity (where the marginal and the excluded dismantles the mythological integrity of any absolute origin). This difference of orientation ultimately points to a certain divergence of commitments: Although Adorno contests the false "organicism" and "idealism" of the artwork, he nonetheless wants to affirm an "aesthetically certified . . . faith in a de-ranged reason that has . . . become utopian."[17] Adorno, in other words, deploys the aesthetic as a cipher of critical reason.

But Derrida cannot tolerate this crypto-rationalist commitment to aesthetics as a vehicle for critique, since this would imply a continued belief in the subordination of rhetoric to reason (a subordination that recapitulates the metaphysical priority assigned to voice, presence, and *logos* over and against textuality, supplementarity, and the play of metaphor). Because the "rebellious labor" of deconstruction works against any such hierarchy, Derrida effaces the last boundaries separating literature from philosophy. For Habermas (at least in 1985) this stubborn refusal to differentiate between two logically separate domains demonstrated the fruitlessness of deconstruction: "If, following Derrida's recommendation, philosophical thinking were to be relieved of the duty of solving problems and shifted over to the function of literary criticism, it would be robbed not merely of its seriousness, but of its productivity."[18] It is worth noting that Habermas was ready to grant that aesthetic appraisal obeys its own logic and imposes its own standards of validity, hence, for example, the standard of "sincerity" as applied to expressive utterances in *The Theory of Communicative Action*. But he saw little critical value in the deconstructive practice of treating philosophical texts in the same manner as literary texts. The distinctive argumentative criteria of the philosophical domain was not to be confused with the aesthetic criteria of the literary: "The false assimilation of one enterprise to the other," warned Habermas, "robs both of their substance."[19]

This early verdict on Derrida's leveling of the genre distinction between literature and philosophy reflected Habermas's own principled effort to defend the ideal of philosophy as a rational-communicative practice. Habermas may have appreciated Derrida's turn against Heideggerian "neo-paganism," but he had little patience for Derrida's post-Nietzschean confusion between literature and philosophy. Derrida's more creative and even playful engagement with the philosophical tradition could only appear, from Habermas's perspective, as a dangerous retreat into aestheticism. The historical and political grounds for this aversion are self-evident: It reflects Habermas's own self-conception as a philosopher-critic in the postwar German public sphere, a role whose burdens Habermas found especially pressing in the early 1980s, when, alongside his philosophical work on communicative reason and his critique of post-Nietzschean modernity, he was combating what he considered a resurgence of nationalist nostalgia and historical apologetics.[20] From Habermas's perspective as a public intellectual dedicated to the practice of rational social debate, a society that had in the recent past succumbed to a devastating species of mythopoetic collectivism could hardly afford to blur the boundary line between social rationality and aesthetic experience. In analogous philosophical terms, we can also read Habermas's critique as a repetition of his polemic against the later Heidegger's mythopoetic conception of philosophy as a non-rational mode of "thinking" (*Denken*) or "gratitude" (*Danken*). Whereas Heidegger wished to restore philosophy to an archaic experience of sheer attunement or responsiveness before the self-unconcealment of Being (*Seinsereignis*), Habermas wished to push beyond this aesthetico-contemplative model toward the fully social experience of critical argumentation. According to the theory of communicative action, social experience could not appeal to the truth of an anonymous unconcealment, since truth emerges through the process of rational scrutiny and can never enjoy more than the merely-pragmatic stability of a communicatively achieved consensus. Such a post-traditional understanding of philosophy necessarily kept its distance from any conception of philosophy that conflated rational communication with the merely aesthetic experience of truth as the unconcealment (or *Aletheia*) of Being. Indeed, such a confusion, from Habermas's perspective, would carry the further risk of strengthening what Benjamin (in reference to fascism) had called "the aestheticization of politics."[21]

To be sure, Derrida's own post-Nietzschean unmasking of the philosophical tradition as an infinite deferral of textual metaphor was also meant as a critical practice, powered by its own distinctive spirit of antiauthoritarianism. According to Derrida, both textual and political authority gain their ideological stability *via* the metaphysics of immediacy (conceived in various ways as the proper, the origin, the voice, etc.). For Derrida, the deconstruction of immediacy could be pursued *simultaneously* as a practice of literary *and* philosophical criticism without vitiating its destabilizing and antiauthoritarian energies. From Habermas's perspective, however, this antiauthoritarian critique of "logo-centrism" came at too high a price: It vitiated the only criteria (of socially-generated principles of rational validity) by which acts of communication could sustain their legitimacy. For the early Habermas, then, Derrida's deconstructive practice remained caught in an unworkable self-contradiction: Its anti-Heideggerian gestures of critique were disabled by its own skeptical interlacing of reason and *aesthesis*.

The early phase of philosophical antagonism between Habermas and Derrida was no doubt determined and overdetermined by multiple lines of intellectual and symbolic affiliation: It was almost inevitable that Derrida (especially in his early deconstructive readings of the tradition, such as *Voice and Phenomenon*, *Margins of Philosophy*, and "Différance") would appear as a belated inheritor of the post-Heideggerian mythico-political legacy Habermas wished to combat. A complicating factor for Habermas was that his own training in the left-Hegelian school of critical theory had primed him to reject not only Heidegger but also most remnants of the philosophical countermovements associated with the nineteenth century rebellion against Hegel, especially the religiously-inflected proto-existentialism of Kierkegaard. (It is relevant to note that Habermas confessed to having "read *Being and Time* through Kierkegaard's eyes.")[22] It was therefore unsurprising that for Habermas the existential thematics of the early Heidegger seemed to replicate the irrationalist *subjectivism* of his Danish predecessor. This factor in the history of Heidegger's reception may help to explain the otherwise surprising claim, in *The Philosophical Discourse of Modernity*, that even Heidegger, the arch-critic of modern subjectivist metaphysics, had not escaped the basic template of subject-centered philosophy.[23]

Nor should we forget that Derrida was only one among the many postwar French philosophers who felt drawn to Heidegger's work.[24] Beginning with the early translations of Heidegger's essays by scholars such as Henry Corbin ("Qu'est-ce que c'est la métaphysique" appeared in 1931, for example) and more introductory texts by philosophers such as Jean Wahl, this very stream of Heideggerian phenomenology enjoyed a pronounced philosophical-institutional prestige in postwar France.[25] Derrida's persistent, if conflicted, investments in this philosophical lineage might have sufficed to construct a wall of misunderstanding between Derrida and Habermas. To this philosophical disagreement, however, we must add the surfeit of political meanings that assured the virtual *impossibility* of mutual understanding. From the perspective of a postwar German social theorist who felt he must remain vigilant against the native resurgence of right-wing and nationalist sentiment in his native Germany, the contemporary enthusiasm of philosophers on the French left for a past philosopher on the German right could only seem naïve at best.[26] Although the young Habermas himself had been drawn to Heidegger's philosophy, his own admiration came to an end with the republication in 1953 of the *Introduction to Metaphysics*, originally published in 1935 (a work that Heidegger republished without commentary or criticism, notwithstanding the notorious allusion to "the inner truth and greatness of National Socialism").[27] From this point forward, Habermas understood that one could learn from Heidegger only to better surpass him.[28]

In fairness to Derrida, it is crucial to realize that Habermas severely underestimated the extent to which Derrida, too, read Heidegger in a highly transformative and critical fashion. Habermas acknowledged this critique but deemed it insufficient: "To be sure," Habermas averred, "Derrida distances himself from Heidegger's later philosophy, especially from its network of metaphors" such as those of "proximity" and the associated figurative terms ("dwelling," "listening," and so forth) that are intended to invoke a meditative experience of holistic meaning set apart from a fragmented and technological modernity.[29] But notwithstanding Derrida's deconstructive criticism of Heidegger (and Husserl, and the broader tradition of phenomenology), Habermas still claimed to discern in Derrida's own philosophy a subject-centered and potentially asocial orientation that vitiated the strength of its critical efforts. Habermas's early assessment in *The Philosophical Discourse of Modernity* concludes with this muscular verdict: "Derrida passes beyond Heidegger's inverted foundationalism, but remains in its path."[30]

From Phenomenology to Messianicity

It is well known that in the years following *The Philosophical Discourse of Modernity*, Habermas and Derrida reached a certain rapprochement in political-philosophical understanding. The earlier phase of discord that had risked devolving into near-caricature was succeeded by a late phase of deepened admiration and political agreement, as evidenced by the May 2003 statement in opposition to unilateral military action by the United States.[31]

The discovery of a common cause, in defense of Europe and against the bellicose imperialism of the Bush administration, may have partially submerged the earlier disagreement over Derrida's post-Heideggerian legacy. But it would be wrong to imagine that a sense of *political* solidarity and a revivified identification as Europeans could wholly dissipate the philosophical disagreement that underlay Habermas's earlier critique. The irony of this persistent disagreement is only magnified, however, once we recognize that beginning in the early 1980s Derrida had begun to move considerably *away* from the Heideggerian problematic that had once aroused Habermas's suspicion. The general shift in Derrida's philosophical orientation, which has been both mapped and interrogated with great precision as a "turn to religion," gains its intelligibility if we imagine a chronological arc that stretches from the "Heidegger affair" of the later 1980s to the death of Emmanuel Levinas in 1995: For convenience, the transformation moves from the publication of Derrida's *De l'Esprit: Heidegger et la question* (1987) to his eulogy, "Adieu á Emmanuel Lévinas" (first published in *Libération* in 1995, the same title serving for a book two years later).[32]

We should not underestimate the drama of this transformation. If we recall the critical reading of Levinas as developed in the early essay "Violence and Metaphysics" (originally from 1964), we might have mapped Derrida onto a space of intellectual possibilities that was, at the very least, *resistant* to Levinas's arguments.[33] In fact, the entirety of that essay might be characterized as an exercise in skepticism: Levinas would claim that Heidegger's ontology is "totalizing" and conspires in an eclipse of the other; but Derrida responds that Heidegger's own thinking already articulates this problem insofar as "Being" (*l'être*) is *always other than* "beings" (*l'étant*). Levinas prefers a study in contrasts: He objects to Heidegger's philosophical labors as an essentially "Greek" Odyssey where what is other always returns homeward and its alterity is effaced, restored, and sublated within the domesticity of the same. Against this entire concatenation of Hellenistic themes (unity, neutrality, sameness, an illumination without an outside) Levinas wishes to thematize a relation *beyond* the neutral—an infinity rather than a totality—that sets in motion a powerful discourse of ethical obligation that can only be described as "religion." Because Levinas discovers the relation to infinity in Judaism (and even though Plato, too, recognizes a Good that is "otherwise than Being"), the attempt to recall this metaphysical relation against the "violence" of the West is constantly thematized in his philosophy as a contest between Athens and Jerusalem, Hellenism and Hebraism, Greek and Jew.

In "Violence and Metaphysics" Derrida hastens to observe that "alterity" is not quite as unknown to the philosophical tradition as Levinas would claim. "Kierkegaard had a sense of the relationship to the irreducibility of the totally other," Derrida avers, and it is perhaps unfair when Levinas discerns in Kierkegaardian existentialism an "egoism" that remains implicated in the "violence" of the Western tradition.[34] For Kierkegaard, too, thematized an alterity that was not merely the alterity of the *self* but also the alterity of a religious *beyond*. The curious difference is that whereas for Kierkegaard the totality is precisely "the ethical" that every irreducible "I" must exceed for the sake of religious obligation, for Levinas "totality" is the name for ethical indifference, while the ethical obligation that bursts the bounds of any possible totality is *ipso facto* religion. The difference between Kierkegaard and Levinas, then, is the difference between ethics conceived as intelligible law and an ethics that is conceived as the unintelligible event *prior to* all thematic obligation: "an Ethics without law and without concept, which maintains its non-violent purity only before being determined as concepts and laws."[35]

There is an irony here—which Derrida does not pause to consider—that the Kierkegaardian idea of ethics conforms far more to the "Jewish" image of ethics as a social code (even while Kierkegaard the Christian recapitulates the Pauline desire to break God's law for the sake of God himself), whereas the Levinasian idea of the ethical stands in starkest contradiction with the primordial image of Jewish revelation as revealed (and therefore rationally intelligible) law. This irony notwithstanding, we can already detect in Derrida's early analysis a readiness to dismantle the oppositions that structure Levinas's philosophy, between what is Greek and what is *other-than*-Greek, between totality and infinity, intelligibility and religion.[36]

Against this play of philosophical contrasts, Derrida does not offer a different or superior philosophy; he merely observes that the attempt to thematize alterity must always already have recognized and therefore tainted the purity of its object. In other words, there can be no alterity without a conceptual language that simultaneously identifies that otherness and betrays it:

We are not denouncing, here, an incoherence of language or a contradiction in the system. We are wondering about the meaning of a necessity: the necessity of lodging oneself within traditional conceptuality in order to destroy it.[37]

It may seem that Derrida merely remarks on this paradox without impugning the larger coherence of Levinas's enterprise. He appears to content himself with the task of raising a series of questions (though we might ask ourselves if this sort of questioning does not actually dismantle Levinas's argumentation even more effectively than a more systematic attempt at "refutation"). But the questions are not without direction; they culminate at the end of the essay with the startling claim that Levinas has committed himself to a species of *empiricism*, a term that (as Derrida acknowledges) has always served as the name for the *other of philosophy* or, more precisely, a *"non-philosophy*,*"* and, even more precisely, "the philosophical pretension to non-philosophy, the inability to justify oneself, to come to one's own aid as speech."[38] The relation to what is *other-than-the-logos*, to exteriority, can only enter philosophy as an idea, but it is precisely as an idea that it is no longer the relation it wishes to commemorate. What is "Greek" about philosophy is that it refuses to treat its themes as "sages of the outside" (a phrase Derrida credits to Saint John Chrysostom).[39] But this means that Levinas's study in hyperbolic contrast ("infinity" naming the very paradigm of logical hyperbole) must be tempered by the deconstructive awareness that the difference between Greek and Jew is unstable and each has always already compromised the other: "Jewgreek is Greekjew. Extremes meet."[40]

In 1995, almost thirty years later, Derrida bid adieu to Levinas in an essay that serves as a summary of Derrida's own transformation. Although criticism may conflict with eulogy, the difference in tonality should not be ascribed merely to the obligations of genre. The skepticism articulated against Levinas in "Violence and Metaphysics" falls away in Derrida's later writing, chiefly because it has itself absorbed so many of the themes that distinguished Levinas's own thought: alterity, messianicity, hospitality, and so forth. But the change is not only one of themes. The very idea of an "alterity" sets up an opposition that deconstructive analysis (at least in its earlier phase) could not have left untouched insofar as the logic of the *supplement* demands we mark for exploration any sign of ambivalence: The supplement calls into question any symptomatic antinomies, between same and other, totality and exteriority, social violence and metaphysical purity. In Derrida's later work, however, the language of alterity is no longer subjected to this kind of rigorous dismantling but is instead *welcomed*.

In the "Adieu" Derrida recalls how Levinas could only read Heidegger, could only incorporate Heideggerian insights, in a state of ethical ambivalence. But in Derrida's own homage to Levinas we can find little trace of ambivalence:

> One day, speaking of his research on death and of what it owed to Heidegger at the very moment when it was moving away from him, Levinas wrote: "It distinguishes itself from Heidegger's thought, and it does so in spite of the debt that every contemporary thinker owes to Heidegger—a debt that one often regrets." The good fortune of our debt to Levinas is that we can, thanks to him, assume it and affirm it without regret, in a joyous innocence of admiration. It is of the order of an unconditional *yes* of which I spoke earlier, and to which it responds, "Yes."[41]

In the writings of a theorist who was typically so alive to ambivalence and comprehended the risks (indeed, the *impossibility*) of absolute fidelity, the unqualified confession of "innocent" admiration and an "unconditional" affirmation may strike us as astonishing. To be sure, elsewhere in Derrida's late work (and perhaps when he was not inhibited by the work of mourning) he expressed himself with greater candor and critical complexity regarding the Levinasian thematics of radical alterity and infinite obligation. But we are still permitted to wonder if Derrida's late appropriation of such thematics was perhaps *too* innocent.

Whatever one's views on this matter, the trace of Levinasian problems and insights in the later Derrida is not my topic here. But it is worth pondering the question as to whether this Levinasian démarche in Derrida's later thought permitted Habermas to develop a more favorable assessment of his French colleague. If we were to entertain a counterfactual scenario for philosophical alliances, we *might* have predicted that the turning toward Levinasian themes of hospitality (or "hostipitality") and "messianicity" would have inoculated Derrida against the suspicion that Habermas had once harbored about his insufficiently-critical proximity to Heidegger. For in the entire history of twentieth-century philosophy it would be difficult to name a more stringent gesture of philosophical "departure" than the Levinasian critique of Heidegger, a departure that drew inspiration from Judaism's thematic of divine alterity and thereby broke free of ontological totality for the sake of a "transcendence toward the other." The counterfactual thought is instructive: *Might we have expected Habermas to greet Derrida's ethico-religious and Levinasian turn as a possible overture to Habermas's own more intersubjective and social-communicative philosophy?* If a certain answer to this question strikes us as impossible, it is only because we know that philosophical agreement and disagreement do not obey the crude logic of friend and enemy.

It is worth reminding ourselves that philosophy is not politics. Heidegger's political genealogy alone does not determine how this narrative plays out. (Nor could it determine the philosophical poetics of Paul Celan, who upon his departure from the famous meeting with Heidegger at Todtnauberg wrote: "Now that the prayer stools are burning, / I eat the book / with all its / insignia.")[42] If we are permitted to draw a philosophical-interpretative lesson from a poet's words it would only be the lesson that politics does not lie behind philosophical argumentation like an encrypted but decipherable sign. In the case of French Heideggerianism this lesson seems to demand constant repetition if the error of reductionist reading (committed by polemicists such as Victor Farías and Emmanuel Faye) is not to be repeated again.[43] The loss of a recognizable "insignia" associated with the fascist past cannot suffice to mark a philosophy as a possible ally. Habermas may have regretted (and exaggerated) the imprint of Derrida's early "Heideggerianism." But the mere fact of Derrida's ethico-religious turn and the fading of the earlier imprint did not succeed in redeeming his philosophy from new aporias, which were, in a way, the same aporias that had troubled Habermas since the beginning.

We will see below that the transformation in Derrida's late work only served to introduce different grounds for disagreement: Ironically, the reasons for Habermas's early critique remained essentially the same. But it is only *because* Derrida travelled this later arc of philosophical development and assumed a greater proximity to Levinas, and a fortified (or, at least, more legible) alliance to problems of religion, that Habermas came to recognize how this shift—from the "pagan" to the "messianic"—had *not* dissolved the persistent difficulty in Derrida's philosophy.

That Habermas still harbored powerful reservations even about the later Derrida's ethico-religious reflections is not immediately evident, especially given the respectful tonality of their exchanges and the circumstances in which they occurred. In the December 2000 conference on "Judéités" at the Jewish Community Center in Paris, a formidable assembly entertained "Questions for Jacques Derrida" and among the many speakers Habermas distinguished himself with an opening confession: an "incapacity" that (in his words) "excludes me from most of this philosophical exchange." He added that he was "in no way an expert in the field of Judaism" and that "in view of this distinguished circle I am certainly the one with the poorest knowledge of Derrida's oeuvre."[44]

But outsidership is not always a liability. "Derrida would . . . be the first to explain," notes Habermas, "why a marginal position is not necessarily a disadvantage."[45] A confession of ignorance or incapacity can also serve as a license to raise questions that may otherwise seem impertinent. Habermas's presentation to Derrida also contains an implicit critique, but the challenge differs from the early remarks on Derrida's persistent allegiance to Heidegger. Instead, the new critique calls into question the very Levinasian thematics of alterity by which Derrida effected his departure from Heidegger.

According to Habermas, Derrida's philosophy still bears the imprint of certain Heideggerian philosophemes and, most especially, the notion of an "event" (*Ereignis, événement*) whose arrival is evoked especially in the lecture on the status of the university from the summer of 2000.[46] But in contrast to Heidegger's original thematics of the "event" (as developed in the notoriously difficult text from the 1930s, *Beiträge zur Philosophie: Vom Ereignis*), along with the stringent critique of humanist self-assertion (in the 1946 "Letter on 'Humanism'"), Derrida habitually invoked various ideals that seemed to align him with the discourse of human rights and post-national democracy. Such ideals, in other words, did not so much contest as *revivify* the language of humanism, and it is therefore not surprising that Habermas interpreted such gestures as a "slap in the face" against Heidegger. To explain this apparent contradiction Habermas suggests that we read the division between Heidegger and Derrida as "a division between a neo-pagan betrayal of, and an ethical loyalty to, the monotheistic heritage."[47] Whereas Heidegger wished to disrupt the idealization of ethical-subjective agency, Derrida takes over from religion precisely the language of moral responsibility that has found its secularized expression in humanism. This monotheistic inheritance is due chiefly to the fact that Derrida exhibits in his later work a "loyalty to Levinas" that marks his readiness to articulate ethical problems in the modality of "the self-reflective relation of the self to an Other 'who' speaks in each case through a second person."[48]

Behind Levinas, however, Habermas detects the Kierkegaardian paradigm of a relation between the isolated ipseity and the transcendent Other.[49] "Kierkegaard's ethical subject survives its hopeless despair only in the shape of a religious self that, in its relation to itself, receives its own freedom by *devoting* itself to an 'absolute Other,' to whom 'it owes everything.'"[50] The difficulty, from Habermas's perspective, is that this hyperbolic image of radical dependence recapitulates a certain kind of potentially authoritarian absolutism, since it admits of no qualification or amendment. The God who commands Abraham commands him absolutely, even to the point of irrational sacrifice: This is the very structure of "teleological suspension." To call into question the commandment is to deny one's bond to the Absolute such that the very meaning of one's free-dom, one's very subjectivity itself, is utterly vitiated. But if the religious bond (the binding that constitutes *religio* itself) cannot be questioned, then faith and reason remain separated by a chasm. But this means, on Haber-mas's reading, that Kierkegaard can only experience the bond between self and other as forged in submission; he cannot conceive of it as the fragile but cooperative work of mundane reason. For Kierkegaard, in other words, the event of redemption has no social index. The relation among social beings is degraded precisely in the same measure as the relation to God becomes so transcendent that it exceeds any humanly accessible norms of rationality or adjudication: Abraham (or, to be more precise, Kierkegaard's version of Abraham) cannot argue with God without ceasing to be Abra-ham. The Kierkegaardian paradigm of a bond between self and Other therefore cannot serve as an instructive model for our conception of society as an ongoing and rational achievement.

In his own social theory, Habermas wants to insist that the intersubjec-tive bond remains intelligible *within* the space of human reasons. This permits him to see the "other" as a social being *on whom* I remain depen-dent but only for the *mutual* construction of a self-critical society. The notion that normativity is born with an absolutistic command fails to take on board the full significance of a post-metaphysical world where ethical obligation is neither "revealed" nor "given" from a realm *outside of the social itself.* Although we are indeed dependent on others, this depen-dency is an *inter*dependency and ideally it must exhibit a thoroughgoing *symmetry* (*contra* the Kierkegaardian-Levinasian model of radical asym-metry). Indeed, it is precisely the socially *immanent* and fallibilistic char-acter of social obligation that distinguishes ethical responsibility from metaphysically-solidified submission:

> This reading of dependence on an "Other" saves the fallibilist but anti-skeptical meaning of "unconditionality" in a weak or procedur-alist sense. We know how to learn what we owe to one another. And each of us—taken respectively as members of a community—can self-critically appropriate, in light of such moral obligations, our past histories with a view to articulating a proper ethical self-understanding. Yet the communication remains "ours," even though it is ruled by a logos that escapes our control. The unconditionality of truth and freedom is a necessary presupposition of our practices and lacks an ontological guarantee beyond the cultural constituents of our forms of life. The right ethical understanding is neither revealed nor "given" to us in any other way; it is achieved through joint effort.[51]

Kierkegaard was right, in other words, to locate normativity only in an intersubjective relation between self and other (a paradigm that also informs Levinas's philosophy). But a stringently religious interpretation misreads this relation as a finalistic rather than fallible bond of merely human agents. Habermas rejects the Kierkegaardian paradigm because, in his view, "the enabling power built into language is that of *a trans-subjective rather than an absolute quality*."[52]

Habermas articulates this critique primarily as an objection to Kierkegaard. But it demands little effort to see that it is also directed implicitly against the later Derrida, whose understanding of religion takes on board (via Levinas) the religious conception of the self-other dyad as a radical asymmetry. Normativity begins as an "event" or an injunction from outside the horizon of humanly intelligible discursivity, and no capacity for self-assertion can redress the radical alterity of what is first given. Although the early Derrida might have responded with skepticism that such a conception of sheer exteriority is an empiricist illusion, the later Derrida embraces this model without sufficient criticism insofar as he articulates the democratic future as an unanticipated event or as a "messianicity without messianism." The danger is that this reprisal of Kierkegaardian motifs leaves unanswered the same question that the Dane considered unanswerable: Does humanity possess any criteria of its own by which it can submit to rational scrutiny whatever it is given? Even Abraham, after all, argued with God.

Habermas articulates this objection to Derrida by noting that, already in *Of Spirit: Heidegger and the Question*, Derrida wished to show that Heidegger's conception of the "event" is not wholly alien to the monotheistic tradition. The imaginary dialogue that ends the book offers a conciliatory scenario where Heidegger is welcomed by Jewish and Christian theologians, who discern in his philosophy a (perhaps unintended) vision of their own respective faiths. But Habermas finds this conclusion perplexing insofar as it obscures a salient difference between Heidegger's neopagan appeals to the *Ereignis* and the monotheists' appeal to a redeeming God. The difference is precisely that the normative contents of monotheistic religion remain available for *critical appropriation*: The ideal of eschatological judgment bears within it a seed-concept for moral assessment within the bounds of profane experience. This is an ideal that Adorno captured in his famous dictum concerning the this-worldly significance of the messianic idea, whose redemptive light serves negatively to reveal the injustice and irrationality of our present condition.[53]

Derrida's false reconciliation between Heidegger and the theologians obscures precisely this difference. It is a welcome sign, Habermas grants, that "Derrida's own appropriation of Heidegger's later philosophy rests on a ground that is theological rather than pre-Socratic, and Jewish rather than Greek."[54] But this is merely a restatement of the qualified praise already evident in *The Philosophical Discourse of Modernity*. Now Habermas poses a new and rather different question: Given the later Derrida's "loyalty" to Levinas, what actually distinguishes the radical dispossession of the Levinasian subject when confronted with an infinitely demanding other from Heidegger's experience of neo-pagan gratitude before the "event of Being"? The question is potentially fatal not only to Derrida but also for the Levinasian philosophy he invokes. For, if that philosophy cannot explain the *criteria* by which a messianic "event" can be rationally scrutinized, then we have no reason to believe it has truly abandoned the Heideggerian atmosphere it condemns. Habermas poses this challenge in a more diplomatic fashion, but his meaning is clear:

> Can Derrida leave the normative connotations of the uncertain "arrival" of an indefinite "event" as vague and indeterminate as Heidegger does? And, moreover, what burden of justifications would follow from our accepting the demand to make those normative connotations more explicit, whatever they happen to be?[55]

In this question we can discern a poignant historical-philosophical irony: In his earlier assessments, Habermas had criticized Derrida for the latter's apparent failure to break free from the magic circle of Heideggerian ontology. But in his *Judéités* address Habermas criticizes precisely the conceptual apparatus by which Derrida effects this departure. According to Habermas, Derrida's later meditations on religion are replete with gestures of quasi-transcendence ("messianicity," "alterity") that derive from a tradition of Kierkegaardian-Levinasian theology in which Derrida claims to discern the traces of his own Judaism. But such gestures must always appear in the indeterminate guise of an unanticipated "event" (*Ereignis*). Derrida, in other words, has gained critical distance from Heidegger only because he now invokes the quasi-religious appearance of the second-person singular, whose unanticipated revelation from beyond the ontological horizon awakens the subject to normative responsibility.

From Habermas's perspective, however, this turn against Heidegger via a quasi-monotheistic revelation remains highly unsatisfactory. Indeed, the very indeterminacy of such an arrival is cause for grave concern and may even disqualify this event as a foundation for normativity. The ironic consequence of Derrida's philosophical trajectory—which Habermas characterizes as a broad and increasingly self-conscious movement *away* from the mythopoetic irrationalism of Heideggerian ontology—is that at the end of his career Derrida embraced an affiliation with Levinas that disrupts ontology only to impose in its stead a monotheism of the "event" that is no more accessible to rational criticism. The chief difficulty, from Habermas's point of view, would seem to be that such a quasi-theological event cannot be "made explicit" (a reference, apparently, to Robert Brandom's neo-Wittgensteinian theory of meaning as social use). In other words, the Derridean theme of obligation as an "event" resists the requirement that any and all norms, if they are to be deemed legitimate, must be accessible for scrutiny and debate to all social participants notwithstanding their traditional identification or allegiance. No theophany or quasi-theophanic event can be held to oblige if the grounds of its obligation remain opaque. To violate this requirement is to lapse into a religiously-derived authoritarianism that is no more defensible than the neo-pagan piety it was supposed to disrupt.

But Habermas's critique of the later Derrida remains vulnerable to a serious objection: Derrida (in this respect remarkably *unlike* Levinas, and *unlike* Kierkegaard) forbids himself the thought of a transcendent *source* of obligation whose authority would remain uncontaminated by the meanings it puts into play. Already in *Of Grammatology* Derrida insisted that the theological was a "determined moment in the total movement of the trace."[56] Indeed, the *impossibility* of theology conceived as a pure and uncontaminated event *prior* to human language is arguably the very *meaning* of "différance," along with the various patterns (dissemination, deferral, and so forth) that instantiate it as temporal-linguistic phenomenon. To make any such quasi-revelatory event "explicit" for Derrida would require both obedience *and* betrayal, as it were, in the same breath.

This objection may reveal a deeper disagreement as to how Habermas and Derrida have understood messianism: For Habermas, the "messianic" can serve as a regulative ideal of thoroughgoing consensus, but it retains this prestige *only* if it never intrudes as a metaphysical reality into the ongoing practice of social argumentation. For Derrida, however, the "messianic" is another name for the pattern of deferral that forever contests the authority of a metaphysical ground; paradoxically, the messianic for Derrida also works to undo the authoritarian purity of *messianism*.[57] For Habermas, however, this messianic deferral looks suspiciously like an appeal to a higher principle that would compromise the unforced force of social reasoning. Habermas's "messianism" regulates without supplanting the authority of the social; Derrida's "messianic" relativizes its supremacy, without, however, installing another messiah in its stead.

Conclusion: Habermas's "Last Farewell"

In his "Last Farewell" (published shortly after Derrida's death in October 2004) Habermas restricted himself to the rituals of eulogy by praising the "enlightening impact" of Derrida's work in Germany. The late philosopher had "appropriated the themes of the later Heidegger without committing any neo-pagan betrayal of his own Mosaic roots."[58] But such praise only rehearses the qualified esteem Habermas had expressed in the mid-1980s; it does little to blunt the force of Habermas's final "question" as to how Derrida could sustain a critical stance vis-à-vis the "Mosaic" roots themselves. There is also an intriguing textual variation that has passed without notice in the critical literature: In the German version of Habermas's *Judéités* lecture he remarks on the "determinate [*bestimmten*] religious inheritance" that informs Derrida's work.[59] He does not name this inheritance, but it is clear from the context that Habermas means Judaism. The German version thus underscores Habermas's apprehension in the face of a particularistic cultural-religious tradition when the viability of translating its contents into the criticizable language of public reason remains in doubt.[60]

If philosophy consists in questions rather than answers, aporia rather than eschatology, it should not surprise us that the disagreement between these two philosophers failed to reach a perfect resolution. The religious bid for eternity long ago bequeathed at least a share of its energies to philosophy in the guise of a metaphysics that both Derrida and Habermas inherited but then subjected to vigorous criticism. It is significant that Habermas claimed for himself the task of a "post-metaphysical thinking."[61]

It is here, however, that the true disagreement between the two philosophers comes clearly into view. The Habermasian ideal of a thought genuinely *beyond* or *emancipated from* metaphysics does not conform to Derrida's more conflicted philosophical orientation, according to which deconstructive thought itself remains forever haunted by metaphysics and can never inhabit a space of purity that would come after its certain death.[62] This may explain why Habermas could not cease to ask the "ethical question" in response to Derrida's transformation: Although he welcomed Derrida's movement beyond the problematics of Heideggerian ontology, Habermas nevertheless harbored grave doubts as to whether the messianic patterns of this movement offered a genuine solution to the authoritarianism of the unnamed "event."

From Derrida's point of view, however, this betrayed a serious misunderstanding, insofar as "the messianic" served not as the sign of authoritarianism but as a talisman *against* it. If Derrida had lived just a few years more, we might have wished for his rejoinder: The Habermasian ideal of a rational consensus only escapes the allure of metaphysical finality because it, too, relies on a *messianic* hope that must always be deferred. Argumentation without a metaphysical ground therefore remains oriented toward a messianic event whose actual arrival would destroy the process of argumentation itself. If this rejoinder has any merit, then the distance between Habermas and Derrida would not be as broad as one might have supposed.

But such a conclusion would be premature. Any attempt to characterize Habermas's thinking itself as a messianic adventure runs into serious difficulties once we consider the idea of *post-metaphysical* thinking from Derrida's own perspective: "After all" (we can imagine Derrida saying to Habermas) "your dream of a *post*-metaphysical thinking locates modernity in a purified world that knows itself to be untroubled by tradition, set free of metaphysical illusion, finally arrived, in other words, at the 'enlightened age.' This has always been the rationalist's own eschaton. But isn't this utopia *itself* a species of metaphysical illusion, and couldn't one object that a confidence in *post*-metaphysics itself contradicts the idea of a messianicity without messianism? Kant himself, your great predecessor, took care to distinguish between the enlightened age and the age of enlightenment, between the endpoint achieved and the endless task. So if I am troubled by the idea of a *post*-metaphysical thinking, one might say I am troubled not only for the sake of the messianic, but also in Kant's name."

This is a rejoinder we can only imagine, and at great risk of imputing words to a critic who can no longer speak for himself. Even such a response, however, would only mark out the possible terms of the dispute without bringing it to an end. Questions are eternal; answers are not.

Abraham, the Settling Foreigner

JOSEPH COHEN

AND RAPHAEL ZAGURY-ORLY

The proper name *Abraham* will mark the starting point for the reflections below. For inscribed in this name is at least one transformation, the movement from *Avram* to *Abraham*. This transformation—from the figure of the Father (*Avram* meaning "High Father") to the meaning of the alliance in which God reveals to the "High Father" that he shall become the "Father of a multitude of Nations"—implies a promise. Hence our question: What does this promise promise? And, furthermore: According to which Law has the history of European philosophy heard and interpreted this promise? And, finally: Could there also be in this promise another calling toward an entirely other thought, entirely other than the thought that has structured the European tradition of philosophical thinking?

By posing these questions, we open toward the possibility of reflecting on the relation between the history of philosophical thought and the figure of Abraham. According to which modality has this relation, between the history of philosophy and the figure of Abraham, been thought? What has this relation opened in and for thinking? How has this alliance projected philosophical thinking and to which future has it been promised?

Before entering into the analysis of the figure of Abraham—which will involve the writings of two philosophers for whom this figure remains a persistent signifier, namely Hegel and Kierkegaard—we should first remark that the Abrahamic figure has persistently fascinated and haunted the entire deployment of the history of philosophy. In effect—and we are simply proposing this idea, since it would be too lengthy to explicate adequately here—no other Judaic figure has played such a central and, indeed, radical role in the history of philosophy. Why is this so? Because Abraham provokes philosophical thinking to a constantly reiterated task: to comprehend this Biblical figure whose essential characteristic is to retract incessantly from any conceptual grasp and any fixed identity. As though Abraham already signified a philosophical ambiguity from which the history of philosophy could only emit multiple, often contradictory, readings of this biblical figure. Certainly this is the case for all biblical, but also mythological and historical, figures who have made their appearance in the development of the history of philosophy. However, with the Abrahamic figure, we are facing what one might call a paradigmatic case. For the very identity of the figure of Abraham is, in the biblical text itself, always differentiated and even paradoxical.[1] This "identity" reveals, for philosophical thought, an unceasing questioning of the category of self-identity. Furthermore, where the history of philosophical thought has perpetually sought to interpret and determine the Abrahamic figure, this figure, inversely, incessantly displaces and reverses, overturns and undoes all conceptual determinations that could be made of it. We have already mentioned one of these transformations, marked by the shift in names from *Avram* to *Abraham*, that is from the role of the Father to the role of the witness of the promise. But there are countless others. One of these transformations is marked by the biblical phrase that describes Abraham as a "settling foreigner."[2] We will develop this phrase in the following essay. Another, for example, was revealed by Levinas, who, by his interpretation of the Abrahamic phrase "Here I am" (translation of the Hebraic *Hineni*) opened the possibility of interpreting the "identity" of Abraham as that movement preceding autonomy and thus as a radically exposed *response of responsibility for the Other*. This incessant play of difference at work in the Abrahamic figure displays an "identity" that is persistently distancing itself from any static appropriation. Or again, it reveals in Abraham *more than one* Abraham—a perpetual resistance toward any and all identification. Perhaps it is just this impossible categorization or identification that constantly engages the will and the desire in the history of philosophy to grasp, to comprehend, to come to terms with, the figure of Abraham. This situation, whose effect produces the distinction and the division referred to by the phrase "Athens and Jerusalem," opens what we might call the *unthought* figure of Abraham—unthought, that is, by philosophical thought. For what remains *un*-thought in this tradition is the Abrahamic revelation itself—a revelation that is irreducible to, and irreconcilable with, the un-covering, un-veiling, or dis-covering movement of truth as *a-letheia*.[3]

This unthought otherness, however, ought not to mean that philosophy remains incapable of thinking Abraham, or that it does not attempt to approach the figure of Abraham. On the contrary, we know that philosophy has, throughout its history, advanced various insightful interpretations of the figure of Abraham. More profoundly, these interpretations have often—and, in particular, those of Hegel and Kierkegaard—performed a sort of conversion. As these philosophers have sought to comprehend and reappropriate the essence of Christianity, they have integrated the figure of Abraham into this project as a moment capable of serving and advancing it, an integration that is always accompanied by the exercise of a certain violence. It is almost as if the unthought otherness of Abraham required a translation into an identifiable concept, from which the very history of philosophical thought could deploy itself. The figure of Abraham would reveal itself thus as a *translatable unthought* whose very translation engages the proliferation of philosophical conceptuality. In this sense, our first task will be to note in which manner the figure of Abraham has been subjected to this translation and, furthermore, point to what remains of Abraham in its philosophical appropriation and reduction. In other words, we will seek to grasp according to which Law the figure of Abraham has been integrated in the deployment of philosophical conceptuality and, at the same time, search for what is left of this figure in this integration, in order to suggest, beyond and before philosophical thought, a persistently unconditioned, untranslatable, and unrepresentable *other Abraham*.

For now this suggestion will remain enigmatic. We shall explicate its modality and deploy precisely—or as precisely as possible—what it conceals and secretly keeps. For now it must suffice to say that the negative characterizations (unconditioned, untranslatable, unrepresentable) that we are here obliged to voice about this other figure of Abraham ought not to be understood as a simple denegation of philosophical conceptuality—as if we were setting off to think Abraham *against* philosophy, or, and to put it in broader terms, to think the other *against* the same, difference *against* identity, Jerusalem *against* Athens, or Abraham *against* Ulysses. Rather, we will attempt to reveal, through the figure of Abraham, another understanding of this name that both projects and suspends the course and the permanence of philosophical discourse. We will think in this way a certain "irreducibility" that both presents and exhausts the movement and the onto-theological proliferation of metaphysics. Anticipating our conclusion, we shall attempt to indicate not only in which manner the history of philosophy has compelled and subdued the figure of Abraham to its own conceptuality but also propose a radical distinctiveness of the figure of

Abraham as that which both engages and suspends the very deployment of philosophical thought.

Our task will be to mark in which manner Abraham can be thought, not only in its onto-theological *Aufhebung* but also as that figure which at once renders this very deployment suspect, that is, interrupts its self-accomplishment while committing the necessity of this very history incessantly to deploy itself otherwise and alternately. As if the precedence of the figure of Abraham could here be thought as a "pre-cedency" that a-chronologically engages and suspends, puts forth and subjects the deployment of philosophical thinking, meaning, conceptuality. That is, advances and questions the deployment of philosophical thinking toward an entirely other modality than the one it performed in regard to the figure of Abraham. An entirely other modality reserving possibilities yet unthought by the history of European thought and that maintain the very efficacy of philosophical thought. Hence, perhaps we could here think the figure of Abraham possessing a secret resource that, far from simply inverting the relation to the history of philosophy, in truth forces this very history to activate itself as that which cannot and does not identify itself with itself. Urging philosophical conceptuality to be incessantly subjected to *an-other* that, far from being comprehended in its essence, opens to other performatives irreducible to those signifiers that have formed the ground of the history of philosophy.

But let us firstly ask: Which history is here at stake? In this question, we are already seeking to grasp how the figure of Abraham relates to the place from which the event of philosophy has sprung and the possibility of envisaging for this very event *other* performatives where the history of philosophy would not constitute its ownmost meaning but project itself always beyond the possibility of appropriating a meaning and calling it its own. It is also perhaps the question posed by Derrida on Europe in *The Other Heading: Reflections on Today's Europe*[4] before displacing it toward another formulation in search of other topologies, and perhaps other names, in *Abraham, the Other*.[5] Could there be more than one history of philosophy? Or is philosophy always and already constituted by the Greco-Christian genealogy of European ideals? And from where are we to begin thinking, rethinking, remembering, or projecting the idea of Europe? There would perhaps be an Abrahamic Law capable of subjecting the very deployment of Greece and Christianity. If the history of philosophy does little else but confirm the reappropriation of Hebraism by the Greco-Christian signifier of philosophical thought, it is perhaps here our task to rethink this relation and to suggest—not simply to inverse or reverse—another status for Hebraism. This other status would certainly have an affinity with a novel questioning of the Greco-Christian horizon of European philosophical thought, harboring also a radically irreducible idea of justice at once capable of opening and keeping in check this very horizon named philosophy.

Abraham represents the *other than philosophy* (which already means: the *other of philosophy in philosophy*). This otherness is a primary definition of Abraham. We know that this otherness is textually inscribed in the Hebraic appellation *Abraham ha-ivri*. *Abraham ha-ivri* means Abraham the Hebrew, but it also signifies the *one who comes from the other bank*. Abraham the Hebrew is the figure who comes from the other side or the other frontier. That is, he is other to the determinate, identifiable place. He thinks and speaks otherwise than the teleological reconciliation of thought and speech that always presupposes the very place of its enunciation. Abraham is the foreigner and remains always estranged to the spatial deployment of onto-theology. This foreignness provokes the following: The history of philosophy does not, properly said, form a concept of the figure of Abraham *per se*. This figure remains only that which is not inscribed in the deployment, the formation, the construction of a conceptual schema. The history of philosophy does not "comprehend" this figure. It "deals" with this figure, "treats" it, leaving it nevertheless without figure, other to the figure, and foreign to or estranged from its subsumption in a logical comprehension. As if the figure of Abraham represented a certain untouchable sublime (a sublime greater than Kant's) that remains irreducible to philosophical discourse. Which provokes the following: This figure enters and invites itself in philosophical discourse always as an "other," a "stranger," a "foreigner" whose very advent provokes a disruption or disorder of traditional onto-theological concepts. In this sense, the figure of Abraham is always an "event" in the history of philosophy turning the very rationality of its discourse outside of itself and exposing it radically and entirely to the question: *What is this otherness? What is its essence? Its substance? Its Spirit and its Fate?*

The question "What is this otherness? What is its essence? Its substance? Its Spirit and its Fate?" evokes the title of Hegel's early theological writings. By evoking these texts, it ought to be remarked that the question here posed calls upon the entire language, structure, grammar, that is, the totality of the signified movement of the Hegelian dialectic. It marks the speculative presupposition of reconciliation between substance and subject, between identity and difference, between faith and knowledge.

Hegel's text *The Spirit of Judaism* forms the first part of *The Spirit of Christianity and Its Fate*,[6] and it was written in Frankfurt between 1797 and 1800. The essay was never intended for publication but always remained with the author; the text was found in 1831, after the philosopher's death—in the top drawer of his desk at the Humboldt University of Berlin. It offers an interpretation of all the central concepts of Judaism[7] and examines the manner in which the religion of the Law needs to be accomplished and appropriated by the religion of Love, the "natural speculative religion," Christianity. This interpretation of Judaism is marked by a profound, radical, even violent "anti-Judaism." We will not go into the details of Hegel's anti-Judaism—to grasp properly all the ramifications and effects of this position would require an extensive study all its own. It ought, however, to be noted that, for Hegel, the Judaic figure, as "*odium generis humani*," is the "particularity" that cannot and, *a fortiori*, does not, comprehend the movement of History as Concept and thus resists the effective reconciliation of God and Man. The Judaic figure refuses thus the very modality of Spirit. Hence, it remains attached to the simple "naturality" of a concrete existence and, refusing to elevate itself beyond this condition toward the effective reconciliation of Spirit, is condemned to "be dashed to pieces on his faith itself."[8] The Judaic figure is destined to be always irreconcilable with the deployment of History and, according to Hegel, remains thrown in a condition where, subjected to an abstract and dominating Law proclaimed by an invisible and unrepresentable God, it is cut and separated from the "commonality" of the community, exiled in a "no-man's-land." It also categorically rejects all forms of reconciliation: with God firstly, but then also with other men and with nature. In this sense, the Judaic figure is, for Hegel, always the bearer of the irreconcilable and the unrepresentable. Which means that since it cannot recognize the effective deployment of Spirit, it cannot elevate or relieve its limited and finite condition to the infinite resolution of Absolute knowledge. Consequently, for Hegel, the Judaic figure remains purely subjected to an exterior "positivistic" Law and, by "being-subjected" to this unrepresentable commandment, only seeks to dominate and control others. Hence, the Judaic figure is nothing more than a "dominated dominator," or, moreover, a purely egoistic, self-severing being whose sole project is to exercise its particularity over and above others. It lives only through judgment, since it is always and already both judged and subjected to an invisible, unnameable, and infinitely superior Being.

Hegel never ceases to radicalize the purely negative condition of the Judaic figure. Even the identity of the Judaic figure is problematic. Its identity is structured as pure separation and thus becomes, according to Hegel's logic, the very model of contradiction. Furthermore, the contradiction it incessantly marks cannot elevate itself out of itself. In other words, the Judaic "identity" cannot even affirm itself without falling back into a further contradictory stance, that of affirming an identity as separation or difference. The Judaic figure is thus *absolutely* contradictory. It contradicts the deployment of history as reconciliation, contradicts the universality of reason as human community, and contradicts the speculative ideal of love as effective and concrete reunification of opposites. This means that the Judaic figure always and already empties out and excavates history, community, love, forgiveness, recognition, and reconciliation into an abyss of incomprehension. Fundamentally, it voids the very deployment of philosophical comprehension. Its own Law, structurally incomprehensible and irreconcilable, is infinitely elevated into the purity of an abstract and intangible essence. And consequently, the Judaic figure remains attached to this intangible Law. This implies that his faith, for Hegel, is not a faith, for it remains absolutely foreign to its reconciliation with knowledge. It is thus a purely blind faith which believes that which is without reality, without concreteness, without manifestation, and thus without truth. The Judaic figure remains attached—such is its fate, which is nothing other than a structured decadence—to an incomprehensible heteronomy, chained to an invisible and unperceivable God (who is, as such, not even a God—since, for Hegel, a God that does not manifest itself is not). The Judaic figure is thus condemned to rejecting the all-encompassing totality in which differences (and to name those important to Hegel at the time of this essay: between God and Man, between Man and Nature, between Men and other Men) are brought to reconciliation.

In this philosophical anti-Judaism we must note that Hegel is hardly ignorant of Judaism. On the contrary, Hegel recognizes several of Judaism's central themes—the unrepresentable essence of God, the heteronomic Law, the proscription of images, the Judaic election, the severance with nature, other human communities and God, etc. But he turns them against Judaism, interpreting it as the "religion of separation" and asserting its difference from the Absolute reconciliation of philosophy with itself as reconciliation of faith and knowledge, of identity and difference, of Man and God, Nature and other men. And in order to mark this reversal of Judaism against itself, Hegel calls upon the figure of Abraham. *Why Abraham?* Because he is, in Hegel's words, the "true progenitor of the Jews," and Abraham is therefore the figure that constitutes the Spirit of Judaism.[9] In this sense, the figure of Abraham bears the secret of the Judaic identity: that of not being able to compose itself as an authentic identity and thus being forever structured by separation.

At the outset of the interpretation, Hegel marks the thesis that will determine the entirety of his reading of Judaism: *Abraham's identity is not an authentic identity.* This ought not to mean that Abraham, and consequently that Judaism, has *no* identity. But rather, that his identity is entirely constituted by the partition of identity. The Judaic "identity," if it can be called as such, is but a separation from all that can furnish the possibility of identity. The figure of Abraham is thus identified with the figure of a "passerby" whose being is not includable in the dialectic by which identity defines itself through the movement of its own alienation. Which means that the divided identity of Abraham has no place. He marks a radical separation between himself and place—being always a stranger to place. He is exilic and persistently non-identifiable with any type of characterization or determination, be it national, linguistic, or communal. In this sense, Abraham's divided identity, although it presents itself as a radical "elitism," is in truth but a profound depravity, corruption, and altered form of non-being. His identity is a non-identity and persistently voids all forms of identification. The passages claiming this Judaic non-identity, this absence or voiding of Spirit as Spirit of this "nation," the estrangement to all place, are numerous in Hegel's early theological writings. Indeed, the philosopher constantly revisits the same thesis, fastening his attention on key moments and characters in biblical history where the Judaic figure constitutes itself: Abraham, Isaac, Joseph, Moses, David, and so forth.

The passages are numerous and the explications multiple. But the thesis remains the same: *The Spirit of Judaism cannot love, it does not know how to love, and it does not want to love.* And thus the Judaic figure continuously and incessantly extracts itself from the very possibility of willing, of knowing, of being, by cutting itself from all relations—with God, with nature, with other men. To the point where this figure becomes radically a-historical, a-meaningful, a-intentional and stands always outside, refusing and rejecting, the deployment of history as incarnation of the identity of Spirit reconciling itself with the different moments of its manifestation. In this sense, the Judaic figure does not and cannot even pretend to embrace a faith. It is radically removed from the very essence of faith as it is continuously retracting itself from the meaning of faith, incessantly removed from the reconciliation, always inscribed and present, always maintained and kept in faith, with knowledge. And since, for the young Hegel, knowledge is always reconciled with faith—faith and knowledge being mutually signified one by the other—the Judaic figure—that figure which cannot know anything other than absence and void—can only believe in the absence and the void. According to Hegel, the sky, for the Judaic figure, is empty. The Judaic figure cannot thus believe in anything as it cannot know anything. It is therefore lost, without faith and without knowledge in a world without God, that is, without the effective manifestation of God.

We will focus on one of the most telling of Hegel's passages marking precisely the Spirit *without* Spirit of the Judaic figure. The passage, although brief, is in fact crucial to Hegel's interpretation of the Judaism. It revolves again around Abraham, and most particularly on the sacrifice of Isaac (Genesis 22). The passage marks the incapacity, the inability, the impossibility for the Judaic figure *to love*. And the testimony of this incapacity, this inability, this impossibility, is signified by the non-sacrifice of Isaac, the bearer of the Promise and the beloved son of Abraham. The passage reads as follows:

> Love alone was beyond his power; even the one love he had, his love for his son, even his hope of posterity—the one mode of extending his being, the one mode of immortality he knew and hoped for—could depress him, trouble his all-exclusive heart and disquiet it to such an extent that even this love he once wished to destroy; and his heart was quieted only through the certainty of the feeling that this love was not so strong as to render him unable to slay his beloved son with his own hand.[10]

We ought to notice firstly the manner in which Hegel wholly revises Genesis 22. No mention here of the divine commandment ordering Abraham to sacrifice his only son on Mount Moriah. No mention, thus, of the relation between God and man. On the contrary, Hegel here interprets the entire sequence as a testimony of the purely egoist and egoistical subjectivity of Abraham. This focus places the entire reading on the character of Abraham, soon to be understood as one of the defining traits, if not *the* defining trait, of the "Spirit" of Judaism: the incapacity *to love*. In this sense, the sequence by which Abraham sets his beloved son, Isaac, on the altar of sacrifice is here interpreted as a proof of the capacity for Abraham to master and to measure his love for the other, and thus is read as a confirmation that his only love is a self-motivated love. A love for himself and consequently a measured love for the other. Hegel here reduces the entire sequence of the sacrifice of Isaac to nothing but a test Abraham took upon himself in order to show that the only love that animated his heart was a love of himself. The sacrifice is thus but a simulacrum of sacrifice. Isaac will have remained living, but his life is but the receptacle of an egoist posture and thus an evidence of non-love. In this sense, the sacrifice of Isaac is interrupted not because Abraham loves his only son but rather—as the text suggests—because Abraham does not and indeed *cannot* love him. He loves only his own self-motivated ego. Hence, if the sacrifice of

Isaac is interrupted, it is not in the name of love but rather because this interruption is the testimony of a mastered and controlled, and thus false, love. In truth, there will have never been here an experience of a sacrifice. Only the experience of a preservation of the self for the self. A testimony, thus, of egoism. And the reason that informs this entire interpretation is always the same, as we said: *The Judaic figure does not and cannot love*. It does not know how to love nor does it comprehend the meaning or the truth of love. And hence, the Judaic figure entirely ignores the speculative principle in love, the necessary modality of love, that is, ignores the *essentiality of sacrifice*.[11] In truth, the figure of Abraham, for Hegel, reduces the speculative signification of sacrifice to a merely economical and self-preserving modality of the subject. Abraham thus ignores what Hegel sees as the *truth of sacrifice*: that which renders effective the deployment of the resolution of truth as Spirit. That is, he ignores the speculative movement reconciling meaning, sacrifice, and love as resolution of Spirit in and as History. He ignores the truth of sacrifice and thus conceives of sacrifice and the possibility of sacrificing his son, the bearer of the promise, as that which only reassures him in the domination of his own personhood over and above the other. In stark contrast to this non-knowledge, of this economy of sacrifice performed only for the assurance of his egoism, Hegel presents the figure who grasps and comprehends the speculative reconciliation signified by the experience of sacrifice. For Hegel, this figure is the one who resolves, exposes, and gives himself entirely to the *truth* of sacrifice, that is, to the accomplishment and resolution of sacrifice: the figure of Christ.

The difference between Abraham and Christ could hardly be more pronounced. The Judaic figure ignores all of sacrifice, reducing it to a mere experience of self-preservation, whereas the figure of Christ grasps the essentiality of this modality by comprehending that through it is marked and rendered effective the very presence of Spirit in and as History. For sacrifice is the modality that relieves and elevates the finite, the profane, the difference to the infinite, to the sacred, to the identification of differences. Sacrifice is that which elevates the finitude of death to the infinity of life. And this is precisely what Christ grasps—contrarily to Abraham—in (his) sacrifice. To attain the Absolute, to comprehend and seize the modality of Spirit as and in History, one must sacrifice the limit, the finitude, the difference of the Self. One must negate the marked and stark separation between finitude and infinity, between ideality and reality, between Father and Son. And, thus, reveal in which manner the sacrifice of finitude, deploys, through its negation, its elevation toward its own infinity. In truth, to sacrifice is to recognize that all limits contain in themselves and by their negation the movement of the infinite that Hegel calls "Absolute Life." And this "Absolute Life" requires and commands that all life, all finite and limited life, as all finite and limited thought, must pass through the experience of its own sacrifice, of its own negation, of its own annihilation, and in doing so negate its own limit and reveal by this negation its infinity. In this sense, because Abraham's sacrifice does not correspond to this model, Isaac will have had his life saved, but this salvation is without redemption, without meaning, simply finite and fixed, and thus his life remains without life. Already dead, claims Hegel. In order to grasp the infinity of Life, its Absoluteness, one has to endure and pass through the experience of a sacrifice, of the negation of the finitude of life.

We have just encountered the thought that History might be characterized for Hegel as the place of Spirit. History is the place in which Spirit inscribes itself as process of reconciliation through the moments and singular events that make up the historical development of man. But what is here heard in the word *place*? The place of Spirit? One hears, firstly, the place where Spirit recognizes itself as its own deployment. Which means that Spirit is always in and with itself present as place. Its place is always its own and always recognized as its own. In other words, there is no difference between place and Spirit. Secondly, one hears the modality by which this recognition, and thus this co-belonging of place and Spirit, reveals itself. This modality is, as we have marked it, sacrificial. It is through sacrifice that Spirit recognizes all places as its place. In other words, Hegel is here conceptually rewriting the originary character of all possible human action in history. He is inscribing in a place and instituting as a place the very deployment of Spirit as that movement essentially signified by and as the perpetual sacrifice of finitude. In this sense, this conceptual rewriting always presupposes the negation of Abraham's non-relation to place. It calls for the sacrifice of the differentiation inscribed by Abraham within place. That is, it commands the sacrifice of Abraham's alienation—an alienation that defines the "spirit" of Judaism—in order to mark the place where Spirit and Man recognize themselves mutually and absolutely. We ought here to remark that Hegel could never understand the non-belonging and, consequently, the extraction or the withdrawal from place as a possibility for freedom. The absence of a determined place could have been understood by Hegel as the opening of a space for humanism. But far from this possibility, Hegel will define freedom as the reflection of the presence of Spirit in the affirmation of its concrete and determined place. And the absence of place, which also means the absence of Spirit, or the very stance of Judaism, is always a synonym for violence and terror.

The word "violence" ought here to put us on the way toward another thinker in the history of philosophy, one who has made of Abraham a central and unsubstitutable figure: Kierkegaard.[12] For Kierkegaard, unlike Hegel, the figure of Abraham marks a positive and sublime stance. This positivity and sublimity of the figure of Abraham is not simply that he announces Christianity but, more profoundly, that he is radically exposed to the *truth* of Christianity. In this sense, for Kierkegaard, the figure of Abraham announces the absolute Law of sacrifice. And, furthermore, Kierkegaard grasps that this Law is the defining element of Christianity. Which means that the event of the interruption of sacrifice is, for Kierkegaard, but an empirical accident. What remains important is the absolute paradoxicality that is both lived and existentially marked in the figure of Abraham. This paradoxicality is the paradox between *ethics* and *faith*.

Ethics, for Kierkegaard, is assimilated to the subject capable of marking the universality of its autonomy, that is, capable of translating the subjective moral duty into the objective generality of the community. In this sense, ethics remains that which is attached to the communicable, to the common, to the universality, to the translatable. It marks the ground and the place of symmetry and commonality. Ethics is thus *the proper*, the authentic mark, of all men. Its dictate is clear and transparent: *Thou shalt not kill*. Which means that the figure of Abraham confronted with the divine commandment of transgressing the ethical order is thus exposed to the radical paradox of his subjectivity. To obey the commandment of faith is to betray all other ethical obligations. In this sense, to remain faithful to the divine call is to perjure immediately the ethical order and that which defines the very commonality and community of men. This is the reason for Abraham's solitude. His solitude is radical, and also monstrous, since he is alone in subjecting the ethical order to faith and thus betrays all others in their uniqueness, singularity, particularity, his fellow men and his most beloved son, Isaac. And it is important to note that the suspension of the ethical for the sake of a commandment of faith must here remain radically mysterious. It is kept in a most obscure and incomprehensible secrecy, a secrecy that mirrors the transcendence of God and the profound, unbridgeable difference between God and the common sphere, space, place of man.

And the violence of sacrifice is here a central element in Kierkegaard's analysis of the figure of Abraham. For the violence of sacrifice marks precisely and is, in fact, a synonym for the violence of the subjection of the ethical order to faith. In this sense, the ethical order is sacrificed to faith. And this sacrificial subjection is intrinsically violent as it is tremendously violent. It marks the necessity of breaking off with the ethical, not only to leave room for faith but to overpower, override, overmaster the ethical by faith. The consequence for Kierkegaard here is radical. It stipulates that the figure of Abraham, his responsibility, is entirely riveted to an ethical irresponsibility. Abraham, subjecting himself to the calling of the divine, is entirely imprisoned in the necessity of betraying, of sacrificing, of entirely breaking from the sociality of the ethical order. The paradoxicality of the figure of Abraham is here clearly signified: To attain the highest stance of man, the religious, man must endure the betrayal of man. And thus he must be entirely exposed to ethical irresponsibility in his absolute and authentic responsibility toward God. To be responsible toward God is to be ethically irresponsible, and to be ethically responsible is to be irresponsible toward God. The paradoxical "dialectic" is here perfectly tuned and in tune with the existential situation of Abraham, an existential situation that marks the complete reversal of Hegel's dialectical concept of sacrifice. Since, for Kierkegaard, the figure of Abraham, far from reducing sacrifice to a simple economy of self-preservation, in fact embodies the very sublimity of sacrifice. This sublimity is not grasped as the speculative accomplishment of elevating the finitude of Man to the infinity of God in the presence and manifestation as Spirit, but rather is already and always riveted to the paradoxicality of subjecting, of crushing, of subordinating, the ethical order of man to a dissimulated and hidden divine call that is always infinitely absent and secret. The relation here between God and Man is not one of mutual recognition in the reconciliatory movement of presence, but rather engages the non-symmetric movement between the translatable and universal order of the ethical sphere and the untranslatable, transcendent, and enigmatic sphere of God. Which means that the untranslatable, the transcendent, and the enigmatic sphere radically calls for the sacrifice of the domain proper to man.

This non-symmetric relation or rapport signifies nothing less than Abraham's engagement in the secret calling of a divine order or command. Abraham is here entirely determined by the secrecy of this call, sacrificing thus the entire ethical order. We could then say that, and again in opposition to Hegel's depiction, the figure of Abraham is kept in and is the keeper of an absolute secret as he maintains a singular rapport to the divine calling. Abraham is kept in the secret and is always keeping the secrecy of the divine calling, which renders him the absolute servant of God capable of sacrificing everything to remain faithful to the singularity of the secret. The "knight of faith" is not even comparable to the tragic hero, who cries, laments, speaks, and shares his or her downfall. The figure of Abraham, however, dons entirely the absolute secret of the divine calling in absolute silence, removed from any possible comprehension, which makes him, in return, radically singular and singularized—solitary.

We have already alluded to Abraham's solitude. This solitude is marked and marking Abraham's very language. This language, for Kierkegaard, is entirely *ironic*. That is, Abraham's language always keeps for itself and in itself the secret of the divine calling. For irony is the possibility of saying something even while at the same time not revealing what is said. It is thus the possibility of keeping oneself outside the sphere of the communicable, the general, the shared intentionality of the community. And it is precisely this irony that best translates the untranslatable responsibility of Abraham: to keep the secret secret. Abraham does not speak in fables or through figures, enigmas, or ellipses. His irony is, in fact, meta-rhetorical. For Abraham is entirely—Kierkegaard underlines it—unaware of the resolution. He is entirely riveted to not knowing what God will require of him. But this non-knowledge, far from instilling in him a doubt or a hesitation, marks his resolute decision in favor of an absolute beyond all knowledge or non-knowledge. The decision to which Abraham here responds is and remains entirely secret: This is precisely what makes his decision absolute. And absolutely responsible. For Abraham is here responding to, and conforming his responsibility to, the call of the Absolute Other. Abraham responds of himself before the commandment emanating from the Absolute Other. Paradoxically, Abraham responds for himself, of himself, and by himself, by being responsible in regard to the Absolute Other. Furthermore, and as to aggravate the paradox, this decision and responsibility is also radically irresponsible since it is guided neither by ethics nor justice. As if one could never be at once and at the same time responsible toward the Other and toward the others.

Abraham thus sacrifices the place of generality, of the ethical, of the common, and of community, the place of the others, in order to remain faithful to the sacrificial call of the Absolute Other. This call from the Absolute Other presupposes and implies, at the same time, the sacrifice of the space or place of the others to the point where the call from the Absolute Other is not only a call to sacrifice but, more profoundly, a call to *sacrifice the others*. Through the sacrifice of his beloved son, Isaac, Abraham is, in truth, sacrificing all the others. He is sacrificing place itself in order to remain faithful to that which is beyond place. The sacrifice of Isaac is, in truth, the sacrifice of the place of the ethical and the universal for the absolute beyond, the absolute transcendent secret of singularity. For the place beyond all places cannot be reduced to the generality of place. A place beyond economy and beyond the economy of sacrifice. To think the call of sacrifice as that which projects the entirety of the ethical into its own sacrifice and thus liberates the place of that which always and already exceeds the generality of man. The horizon beyond all horizons that Kierkegaard here identifies with Christianity is entirely centered on Abraham. The Judaic figure is here called to serve the actualization of the event of Christianity. Why? Since it is through Abraham's non-knowledge and thus through his sacrifice of the ethical order in the name of the Absolute Other that is liberated the *event of salvation*. As if God, the Absolute Other, did not yet know what the non-knowing Abraham would do with and by this non-knowledge: Will he sacrifice the generality of the ethical, and thus be responsible to the beyond, the transcendent, the Absolute Other, or will he sacrifice the Absolute Other, and thus be responsible to the generality, the commonality, the community of the ethical order? At the moment when God is assured and reassured of Abraham's absolute fidelity over and beyond the ethical order of man, the event of salvation, of mercy, and clemency arrives. That is, the event by which anxiety and sacrifice are interrupted. In other words, it is by and through the absolute faith of Abraham, absolute in the sense that it repudiates even the ethical and the general, that the event of salvation comes and descends, reveals itself out of its secrecy and reestablishes the place, the lieu of the generality and commonality, the community of man.

In this sense, Kierkegaard opens what we could call a "messianism of the event": of the pure event capable of restoring the negation that permitted it. In other words, Kierkegaard fixes the event by marking the paradoxicality of the decision to negate the common generality of the ethical in being responsible for the divine call. This messianism of the event, in the very difference it marks with Hegel's absoluteness of presence, nonetheless, and through the sacrifice of the economical, restores that very economy. It is thus a messianism of the event that marks a very determined and defined role for the event it is engaging. In this sense, the event here is precisely and can only be the restoration of that which is sacrificed. As Derrida observes in *The Gift of Death*, Kierkegaard reveals this idea when, in the conclusion of *Fear and Trembling*, he quotes Matthew (but without naming him): "but by your Father who is in secret; and your Father who sees what is done in secret will reward you."[13] The messianism of the event is here entirely structured by the restoration, the reestablishment, the reinstitution as restitution, of that which was sacrificed in order to liberate its possibility. In this sense, Kierkegaard inscribes the event in the deployment of Christianity. The event is precisely that which accomplishes the meaning of sacrifice within Abraham's exposition to the paradoxicality between ethics and faith.

We are, therefore, confronted with the following question: What fundamentally distinguishes Hegel and Kierkegaard? That is, what differentiates the messianism of presence and the messianism of the event? Certainly, everything separates and differentiates these two messianisms.

1. The question of *sacrifice*. For Hegel, sacrifice is the modality by which Spirit reveals itself as presence of reconciliation. And, furthermore, Abraham here is already excluded from this revelation—since his exposition to sacrifice revealed itself to be but a simple act of self-preservation and of egoism. For Kierkegaard, sacrifice is the paradoxicality that imbalances and projects the entire relation between ethics and faith in a movement of perpetual and mutual exclusion—the necessity thus to sacrifice the Ethical sphere if one is faithful to the call of the Absolute Other, and conversely—creating thus a situation of perpetual imbalance, ambiguity, and anxiety tearing man himself in the impossibility to maintain both orders at once. And, furthermore, Abraham here is precisely the figure who, in anxiety and solitude, grasps the paradoxicality of this relation.

2. The orientation of each *messianism*. For Hegel, messianism is entirely to be grasped in the revelation of presence, of Spirit as History and History as Spirit, the already and always effective reconciliation between all opposites and differences (between man and God, man and nature, man and the other man) in and within the infinity of the movement that incarnates their mutual recognition and signification. For Kierkegaard, messianism is entirely riveted and exposed to the event abandoning man in the impossibility of reconciling in presence the ethical and faith, the commonality of the ethical community and the faith toward the Absolute Other—leaving man entirely exposed to the paradoxicality of this messianism: being responsible to the Absolute Other is being irresponsible to the ethical order.

3. The question of *place*. For Hegel, place is the place of the effective reconciliation of difference. In this sense, place is the identified identity of Spirit. As we said, place is never to be distinguished from the actual and effective manifestation of Spirit as reconciliation in presence. Place is thus the place of sacrifice accomplishing itself as reconciliation. For Kierkegaard, place is entirely and absolutely riveted to the paradoxicality of a situation in which the ethical order and the order of Faith cannot be reconciled but are constantly mutually excluding each other. It is thus that the place of existence as existentiality is defined as that which perpetually comes out of itself, expropriates itself out of itself and into the paradoxicality that is translated into a radical reception toward the event.

But here again is the same question, rephrased: According to which law can the difference between sacrifice as reconciliation, the messianism of presence, the place as Spirit *and* sacrifice as paradoxicality, the messianism of the event, the place as existential reception, be maintained, sustained, and affirmed?

The law that differentiates Hegel and Kierkegaard is Christianity. Both these Christian thinkers are differentiated by Christianity. But it also forms that which unites them, that which brings them together, that which incessantly forms the indestructible passage between them. Christianity marks both Hegel and Kierkegaard, at once and simultaneously, as *different* and as *complementary*.

Christianity is marked for Hegel as reconciliation. Christianity is symbolized by Kierkegaard as paradoxicality. This difference is radical and constantly reaffirmed between Hegel and Kierkegaard. As we saw, for Hegel, reconciliation is the very deployment of meaning, that is, the essential modality in which, beyond and before Judaism, Spirit appropriates itself in and through the separation, the distinction, the division installed and inscribed by the Judaic heteronomic Law. Conversely, as we saw, for Kierkegaard, paradoxicality marks the existentiality of our divided and irreconcilable situation between ethics and faith. But in and through both these different concepts is elaborated, for Hegel and Kierkegaard, the very possibility of Christianity. That is, the very modality by which Christianity acquires its ultimate meaning, its grounding essence, and fundamental intentionality. For Hegel, reconciliation is the modality by which Christianity is always and already effective in history. For Kierkegaard, paradoxicality is the modality by which Christianity is maintained in its historical effectivity. Which means that Hegel and Kierkegaard persistently maintain, the first for reconciliation and the second for paradoxicality, a *Christian resolution*. The teleological horizon here remains complementary. Which means that Christianity *conjoins* both concepts, reconciliation and paradoxicality, to a midpoint where they incessantly call on to each other. Moreover, reconciliation and paradoxicality are indissociably linked and allied, unthinkable one without the other, and constantly holding in one the trace of the other.

It is in Christianity, retaining Hegel and Kierkegaard in the complementary movement of their resolution, that the place is defined, that the space is identified, that the site of thinking is determined as *Europe*. Europe is the place, the site where the very "plasticity" of Christian resolution is deployed. In this sense, the Christian resolution we have just explicated forms the place of Europe. And the defining element of this movement where Christianity stretches across Europe as that which forms the space of Europe is precisely comprehended from the already-Christian reading of the sacrifice of Isaac and of the figure of Abraham. That is, from the reading that makes Abraham and the experience of the sacrifice of Isaac a *means* toward the *end* as resolution in the "reconciliation" and "event" of Christ. In a certain manner, the resolution both Hegel and Kierkegaard furnish to the sacrifice of Isaac is, for the first, the "reconciliation," for the second the "event," symbolized by the figure of Christ. And it is this figure that will now harbor the name and the place "Europe." For Europe is— returning here to the etymological source of the name—not so much the place of a philosophical universality nor the space of a geographical singularity, but the *advent of a certain gaze*. This gaze is turned upon resolution. It is the gaze that sees "reconciliation" and "event" co-informing and resolving one another. And the place of this co-informing and resolve is named *Europe*. This depiction of Europe, however, ought not to mean that it constitutes a permanent idea of fusion. Rather, it ought to mean the movement of a resolved tension between "reconciliation" and "event." As if both Hegel and Kierkegaard were here forming the concept of Europe from the resolute plasticity of identity and difference, of self and other, of "reconciliation" and "event."

But in this gaze, *where does Abraham stand*? And furthermore, *toward what or where is the gaze of Abraham turned*? For Hegel and Kierkegaard this question is *not* a question. It is as if Abraham were at once blind to Europe and blinded by Europe. Why? Since Abraham is already informing the modality of a Christian resolution. The place of Abraham constitutes thus a blind spot in the resolute gaze that characterizes Europe. This is not to say, however, that Abraham does not have his place in Europe, but rather that his place is precisely that which stands outside, foreign, estranged to the resolution Europe is gazing upon, the resolution that, beyond Abraham, thinks "reconciliation" and "eventuality" as co-informing each other. Which means that Abraham is, in Europe, *the foreigner settled in his being foreign*. But what does this phrase imply? Far from Hegel and Kierkegaard but in and within their very characterization, this phrase perhaps keeps and conceals a resource yet unthought by both Hegel and Kierkegaard. Which means that perhaps Abraham is the bearer of yet unthought and hidden hypotheses outside and within Europe.

Abrahamic hypothesis: to suspend the gaze of the resolution between "reconciliation" and "event" while proliferating its philosophical foundation. This hypothesis, torn between suspension and proliferation, leads us to imagine *an-other place in the place of Europe*. But we must proceed here with care and be careful not to hear in this phrase *a place replacing the place of Europe*. Proceed with care by attempting to think *an-other* place continuously displacing Europe in and within the deployment of its place. As if Abraham were the bearer or the witness of *an-other* gaze capable of thinking a place that at once and simultaneously suspends, brackets, defers the place of Europe in and within the constitution and institution of Europe itself. *A place other than Europe in Europe. An-other gaze retracted from Europe in Europe's own gaze.* An-other place, *an-other* gaze, we could imagine here Abraham continuously wandering between the *other than Europe* and the *place of Europe.*

As if Abraham was both *foreign* and *settled* in and outside Europe. And this also means that Europe is but one possible instantiation of Abraham. Not exactly an effect but more profoundly a determination of what the proper name Abraham could perhaps mean. But *not* its exhaustion. Here must be thought, continuously, shall we say, infinitely, *an-other Abraham.* An undetermined Abraham leaving the space and the place of determination entirely open and de-multiplied in yet unthought meanings, significations, futures, and histories. *An-other Abraham* . . . Jacques Derrida, recalling Kafka's intriguing dream, once thought of *an-other Abraham.*[14] What name could it have? Is it the name Israel? Or the name Europe? And if it does bear any of these names, could there also be, in these names, other yet unnamed potentialities than the one determined under them?

Unprotected Religion
Radical Theology, Radical Atheism, and the Return of Anti-Religion

JOHN D. CAPUTO

Postmodern theology has come of age.[1] It now has its own countermovement, philosophers marching under the flag of materialism, realism, and anti-religion and complaining that the theologians are back at their old trick of appropriating critiques of religion in order to make religion stronger. So this is an occasion to clear the air and see just how hard and fast the borders are between religion and anti-religion, realism and anti-realism, materialism and anti-materialism, especially given that deconstruction is an exercise in anxiety about rigorous borders. Martin Hägglund's *Radical Atheism* is a closely argued contribution to the recent debate that fits hand in glove with this countermovement, although Hägglund does not mention it.[2] His book is a welcome refutation of any attempt to reduce Derrida to an anti-realist or anti-materialist, especially in the light of Meillassoux's caricature of "correlationism," which treats continental philosophers from Kant on as creationists.[3] Given the historical violence religion has provoked and the reactionary meanness of the religious right in American politics today, I am no less nervous about "religion." That makes it all the more important to sort out what I am saying and what I am not, since my own work on Derrida and religion, as Michael Naas points out clearly, is no less informed by protecting Derrida's *laïceté*.[4]

Unprotected Religion

Deploying Derrida's analyses of "auto-immunity," Hägglund isolates the logic of time in Derrida, which is, at it were, the skeletal basis of everything that goes on in deconstruction. Time, he argues, is a process of coming to be and passing away such that its "radical finitude" (RA, 1) is intrinsic to its constitution and not merely a passing defect from which we can or should seek protection (immunity). The very condition under which time is given ensures that what is given will be taken away. Whatever is present is never "absolutely present" (RA, 1); it is always "divided by time," by the "spacing" of time. Its very coming to presence is constituted by its passing away or loss of presence, its passing presence requiring the "trace" to be retained. "Pure" presence—absolute immunity (non-contamination) from passing away—is meaningless and contradictory, since nothing pure could ever be present in the first place. Pure presence is pure death. Presence immunized from spacing and passing away implies the absence of coming to be altogether. Accordingly, desiring a good in a pure or immune condition is a desire divided against itself, desiring a condition under which it would be impossible for that good to be the good that it is. If we remove the condition that consigns a good to perish, we also remove the condition that enables it to be a good. The very condition under which a good is possible—the spacing of time—is also the condition that makes it impossible for that good to be pure. Hence the desire for a pure good would not be idealistic but nihilistic. Purity of presence is not an ideal forever out of reach where reality dictates we must be willing to settle for less. Purity of presence is impossible, nothing at all, and nothing to be desired. Not only are we denied such goods, we cannot and should not desire them. The desire for life is the desire for more life, more time, more mortal time, which Derrida calls "living on" (*sur-vivre*). Survival trades in a time that may, that will, erase the survivor. Survival is not the desire for infinite or immortal life, since immortal life is death. The time of life is "auto-immune," intrinsically exposed and vulnerable, its immunity from perishing disarmed, its desire for immunity broken down.

From this line of argument, to which I think no careful reader of Derrida would take exception, Hägglund takes up Derrida's analyses of phenomenology, ethics, religion, and politics, reaching the conclusion that not only is deconstruction atheistic, it represents a "radical atheism." Garden variety or standard-form atheism admits that we all desire the immortality promised by religion, but it concedes that such a hope is denied to us. This is what Christopher Watkin calls "ascetic" atheism; we deny ourselves the consolations of religion on the grounds of reason and realism, without denying that it would be rather nice to have what religion promises (living forever in a kingdom of pure goodness).[5] Radical atheism, on the other hand, denies that we should or even could have such a desire. We can only desire mortal goods and believe in mortal beings; were there such an entity as God, God must also be mortal. Contrary to the "theological turn," deconstruction is "radically"—constitutively and unequivocally—at odds with religion. To this conclusion, any careful reader of Derrida should take exception, as I most certainly do, especially since I am singled out in *Radical Atheism* as the prime culprit responsible for drawing Derrida down the dark corridors where religion does its shady work in this vale of tears.

The exception I take is this. Time and the trace imply no less what Derrida calls "iterability," the constitutive repeatability and recontextualizability—time and time again—of the trace. That means that "religion" is more than one. Religion, "if there is such a thing," just one thing, undivided against itself, "*la*" *religion*, in the singular, the same all the time—that is exactly what deconstruction deconstructs. What we call in "Christian Latin French"[6] *la religion* is a massive globalatinization that splinters in the face of the real multiplicity of actually existing beliefs and practices colonized by this risky word. Is *that* not the first and most obvious result of taking up religion in terms of time and the trace (which accords perfectly with virtually every important study of religion today)? The point of a deconstruction is to de-sediment our most sedimented concepts, to redeploy and reinvent them and so release their inherent play, not to consign them to oblivion with a reductionistic argument. If that is so, as I think any careful reader of Derrida would agree, then the upshot of every analysis from the "dangerous supplement" to auto-immunity is not the radical extermination of religion, as of a dreaded disease or pure evil, but the invention of a contaminated religion, like Damian among the lepers, one that hails (*Salut!*) the coming of a religion to come (*viens*) rather than take sides in the binary war between theism and atheism. Derrida sketches in the dark a certain religion, a religion *without* religion, which turns precisely on this impure, radically finite, and constitutively contaminated condition predicted by the logic of auto-immunity. For Hägglund, "the logic of auto-immunity is radically atheist" (RA, 9); for Derrida, it presages a contaminated religion that unhinges a religion of purity, that displaces the *puritas essendi* of the good old God of classical metaphysics and negative theology, that disrupts "a positive infinity that is absolutely in itself" (RA, 3) and the corresponding desire for immortal life. But the dualism of Augustinian religion is unfortunately the only "religion" to make an appearance in *Radical Atheism*, a "religion" at whose desedimentation and deconstruction Derrida and I, along with a good many contemporary theologians, have for a long time now been in attendance.

As Clayton Crockett argues in an incisive essay, Hägglund misinterprets my interest in religion, which is not to defend a traditional religion (or confessional theology) in deconstructive terms, but precisely to advance a religion without religion (and hence a radical theology) and has confused me with Jean-Luc Marion.[7] Cast in terms of Derrida's "Faith and Knowledge" essay, a religion without religion turns on a primordial faith (*foi*) in an open-ended but risky promise, not on a confessional belief (*croyance*) in a determinate and assured creedal object, and so draws upon the first of the two sources of religion discussed by Derrida while contaminating the second. Such a faith is deserted and despairing, naked and unsheltered—not unscathed, not safe and sound, not immune from the depths of doubt, error, evil, violence, or death. Unlike Paul, who felt immunized by the blood of the crucified Christ, it does not boast "O death, where is your victory?" On the contrary, the faith to which Derrida and I subscribe is an impossible faith, arising from the abyss of unfaith, uncertainty, and insecurity, from a prayer that is left without a prayer, sustained by what this same Paul calls a hope against hope in an unforeseeable future. That is why, in "Circumfession," instead of denouncing Augustinian dualism, Derrida engages in an *iteration* of the prayers and tears of Augustine's *Confessions*, subtly inflecting its very title and so boldly engaging in unprotected religion, if I may adapt an expression from those who warn us against sexually transmitted diseases.[8] Such unarmed and vulnerable faith affirms a promise that is not merely fraught with risk but is constituted internally by risk. The risk is intrinsic and structural, not provisional and accidental, not a fault that could in principle be removed at a later point, not a matter of seeing now in part, in a glass darkly, but later on in full (Paul again!). This faith is not a compromise with an ideal faith free from doubt that we just cannot achieve given the weakness of the flesh. This faith is made possible by the very condition that makes it impossible, as Derrida says about all the famous operations of deconstruction. The contamination described by the logic of auto-immunity does not obliterate religion but reinvents it, writing the prescription for an unprotected religion.

Deconstruction has always been the critique of such unscathed immunized purity.[9] It has never changed. "Auto-immunity" was just the last trope Derrida came up with before he died. That is what interests me about deconstruction. That is the point I have defended ever since I first described the project of "radical hermeneutics" some thirty years ago in terms of facing up squarely to the "difficulty" of factical life, that is, of dealing with the fact that we never make contact with anything safe and secure, pure and unmediated, immune and unscathed.[10] My work with religion is to bring this confession or circumfession to bear upon religion and to show how deconstruction reopens and reinvents religion in a new way—to the considerable displeasure both of secularizing deconstructors and of confessional theology. Radical theology does not deny finitude and contamination, it begins with them.

But Crockett is too generous to say that, while Hägglund misinterprets me, he does not misinterpret Derrida. While it is true that iterability allows Derrida to be read in the selective way undertaken by Hägglund, this iteration is not nearly as interesting or fruitful as Derrida. It is a torso, a truncated form of deconstruction, not Derrida's doing but Hägglund's, who proceeds at times as if Derrida has nothing to teach him about deconstruction. Hägglund claims (a) that deconstruction reaches an unambiguous result, a decisive refutation of religion (in the singular), and (b) that deconstruction proceeds on a level of neutral, value-free descriptive analysis of the logic of time. These claims, entirely of Hägglund's own devising, are both philologically and philosophically mistaken. They are creatures of everything about modernity that deconstruction sets out to deconstruct, and they are separated by an abyss from both the style and the substance of what Derrida calls deconstruction. Deconstruction is a way of rereading and reinventing religion—or anything else—not of eradicating religion by means of a radical atheism. The atheism attributed to Derrida by Hägglund would be described by Derrida as "absolutely ridiculous."[11] *Radical Atheism* may be a way to philosophize with a hammer (RA, ix). Deconstruction is not.

In what follows I first contest what I find contestable in *Radical Atheism* and then I set out my own interpretation of what deconstruction can do for religion.

Radical Atheism

Let me be clear that I welcome Hägglund's timely presentation of a certain realist-materialist Derrida ("materialist theology" is the order of the day!). He shows that *différance* is not an immaterial spirit but requires a material substance, that the "play of traces" is spacing-timing, and that is all to the good. His mistake is to suppress Derrida's axiomatics of the beyond, of the *super, epekeina, hyper, über, au-delà*,[12] for fear of contamination by Augustinian immaterialism. Derrida himself says that deconstruction has "always come forward in the name of the real, of the irreducible reality of the real—not the real as an attribute of the thing [*res*], objective, present, sense-able or intelligible, but the real as coming or event of the other. . . . In this sense, nothing is more 'realist' than deconstruction."[13] I describe deconstruction not as anti-realism but as "hyper-realism,"[14] let us say an ultra-materialism, an open-ended materialism, just as Žižek thinks that matter is all, but the all is a non-all, and, as Malabou describes, a "reasonable materialism" that does not turn life into a cybernetic or neurological program.[15] Derrida, Žižek, Malabou, and I are all "materialists" in the sense that we do not think there are two worlds, one in space and time, the other transcending space and time. So I speak of a "poetics," not a logic; Malabou emphasizes a transformational "plastics"; and Žižek introduces "parallax shifts." But Hägglund mistakenly thinks that defending a certain realism and materialism comes at the cost of Derrida's religion. This conclusion is reached by systematically abridging and/or altering several crucial notions in deconstruction, which I sketch here and develop at greater length elsewhere (see note 1).

1. *Torsos.* I begin with several elemental concepts in deconstruction that appear only in a truncated form in RA.

a. *The unconditional.* Hägglund identifies the "unconditional" with "the spacing of time" (RA, 25), the "coming of time" (RA, 42), the "exposure to what happens" (RA, 43), the vulnerability of the moment to the unforeseeable future—all irreducibly important—but he omits the unconditional claim of the future upon the moment. This claim (appeal, call), which opens up the axiological space that Hägglund wants to close down, is what Derrida calls the "*unconditionals*," nominalized, in italics and in the plural, like the gift, forgiveness, hospitality "—and by definition the list is not exhaustive; it is that of all *the unconditionals*,"[16] or "the unconditional injunction,"[17] "the desire and the thought, the exigency of unconditionality, the very reason and justice of unconditionality," "the demand, the desire, the imperative exigency of unconditionality," "the exigency of an unconditional justice,"[18] "unconditional ethical obligation,"[19] what elicits from us a "desire beyond desire"—for the unconditional gift, or justice, or democracy to come, etc. Of course, the future is indeed constituted by its unconditional unforeseeability, just as Hägglund says. But it is no less constituted by the promise that the future holds out (and holds back) from us, by the unconditional call that it visits upon us, and that calls for our response.

The difference between the two senses of unconditionality is the difference between existence and non-existence, being and beyond being, or perhaps better, between being and "perhaps," *être* and *peut-être, il y a* and *s'il y en a*. The unconditional exposure to the future is real; it exists; it always exists, always and everywhere, at every moment, whether we like it or not, whether we know it or not. It does not ask for our consent or even, since it can come like a thief in the night (Paul), that we be awake! But (to take but one example) "the unconditional university, the university without condition," which means the unconditional right to ask any question, is irreal; it "*should* be *without condition*," it *should* exist, but it "does not, in fact, exist, as we know only too well."[20] If the unconditional university does not exist, it does insist, that is, it calls in vocative space and awaits our response. It is but a weak and irreal force in a purely vocative and spectral space that is menaced on every side by the all too real "powers" of the "sovereign" nation-state, of market capitalism, of the media, religion, and culture at large.[21] The unconditional university is a weak but unconditional force without sovereignty, a weak force without force, without the wherewithal to enforce itself. "If this unconditionality, in principle and *de jure*, constitutes the invincible force of the university, it has never been in effect. By reason of this abstract and hyperbolic invincibility, by reason of its very impossibility, this unconditionally exposes the weakness or the vulnerability of the university . . . its impotence . . . it is a stranger to power . . . ." It is, like justice in itself, *de jure*, an "invincible force" but it has never existed—which is why its invincibility is "hyperbolic," "impossible," and "weak"—that is the very model of the weakness of God as unconditional without force, invincible without being an agent, of which I make use in *The Weakness of God*.[22]

b. *The "undeconstructible."* This concept undergoes a parallel abridgement (RA, 25, 40–42, 105). What is deconstructible for Derrida is what is constructed in space and time. That means *différance* is not deconstructible for Derrida because, as spacing-timing, it is the condition under which construction takes place, which is the side of this idea that interests Hägglund (RA, 143–44). But Derrida first introduced the word "undeconstructible" in reference not to *différance* but to justice in "The Force of Law": "Justice in itself, if such a thing exists, outside or beyond law, is not deconstructible."[23] He said this not because justice is synonymous with *différance*, which it is not, but because justice is never constructed and hence is always calling for construction (in laws) and therefore at the same time for the *de*construction of any law that is, in fact, constructed. Of course, the historical words for justice in the several natural languages are historical constructions and therefore deconstructible, but "justice in itself, if there is such a thing," does not exist and so cannot be deconstructed. It is a promise of an event, a call for an event. Hägglund keeps a good distance from this side of Derrida, because he thinks it makes the undeconstructible into a Kantian ideal or a pure good. But the undeconstructible is not a pure ideal or a pure good. If the difference between the unconditional claim and the conditional is the difference between *peut-être* and *être*, it is not the difference between the ideal and the real. The unconditional is not an ideal essence. Then what is it? An unconditional call or injunction, an unconditional but dangerous demand, a pure promise that cannot be insulated from a pure threat, where "pure" does not means "ideal" but *peut-être*, a pure promise/threat.[24] The undeconstructible is neither a regulative ideal that monitors empirical words in natural languages, nor an essential meaning that animates the body of corporeal words, but a dangerous injunction—like "give" or "go" or "come"—and a dream set off by language, by what is getting itself promised in words like "justice" ("gift," etc.). It is not an "inaccessible Idea" (RA, 43) but it is an incessant injunction that gives us no peace.

c. *Desire*. For Derrida, desire is the desire of the impossible. The impossible is precisely what we desire with a "desire beyond desire,"[25] the only thing we can truly love and desire, just because it is impossible.[26] "And deconstruction is mad about and from such justice, mad about and from this desire for justice."[27] Even if democracy does not and never will exist, it is necessary to keep the "democratic desire" alive, "with all one's heart."[28] Desiring the possible is the desire of the future-present and less worthy of the name *desire*. A real desire for Derrida, the event of desire, the desire for the event, always turns on the impossible. But according to Hägglund, the logic of the double bind means "a pure gift is neither thinkable nor desirable as such" (RA, 37). Maintaining this view causes Hägglund some difficulty since it is the direct opposite of Derrida's, who says that "one can think, desire, and say *only* the impossible."[29] So Hägglund feels called upon to warn us that Derrida is being "misleading" when he says things like that. Hägglund wants to avoid treating the "pure gift" as a regulative ideal we can never realize and actual gifts as contaminated compromises with our ideals (RA, 38). For Derrida, the pure gift means the gift that does not exist because the conditions under which it could exist have been removed. Derrida analyzes the gift in its unconditional and irreal purity in order to isolate its character as a pure demand or pure call (as in his analysis of hospitality and forgiveness), not to construct a transcendental ideal. Derrida is not complaining that he wished he lived in world where we did not have to compromise our ideals. He is trying to explicate the force or dynamics of the gift as driven "by the impossible," *par l'impossible*, the way the gift shatters the circle of exchange.[30] The impossible is not an ideal but an operator, a function, an injunction; it is not an ideal but an ordeal. Gifts are interruptions of economies that give economies a chance, leading up to ever more generous and open-ended economies and ever more open-ended and hospitable narcissisms. The logic of the double bind belongs to the larger poetics of the dynamics of the impossible.

In fact, then, what is misleading is not Derrida's text, which as usual is quite careful, but what Hägglund makes of it, which is to insist that, since Derrida is not making a distinction between a pure transcendental ideal and a contaminated empirical shortfall, there is no gap, no axiological distance, at all between the impossible gift that we desire and actual gifts. For Derrida the pure gift is not pure because it is a pure good or a pure ideal; it is "pure" because it does not exist but calls for existence, as "justice" calls for laws that it also calls to account. It is a pure call, a pure promise, a pure perhaps, a pure demand, a pure injunction, and hence a pure risk. Actual gifts, on the other hand, which are the only things that exist, are responses made and risks taken. The distance between the two is irreducible, as irreducible as the distance between *peut-être* and *être*, a call and a response. The distance between "give" (*donne*) and our response is never closed—that would shut the future down!—but only momentarily crossed. The two touch only in the madness of the moment, in the event that tears up the circle of time. The pure irreal gift is a measureless measure of the measurable real gifts given. For Derrida it is precisely the irreducible axiological gap that separates the immeasurable from the measured, the impossible from the possible, that elicits desire and the gift in the first place. So the issue turns on determining exactly the nature of this gap, which Hägglund denies is there at all and Derrida makes the centerpiece of his analysis and carefully explicates in the so-called misleading text. Proceeding on the fiction that deconstruction takes place in a purely descriptive space, that Derrida is simply describing double binds, Hägglund wants to make sure that there would never be a gap or shortfall between the desire for the gift, if there is such a thing, and actual gifts given. That contradicts the central purpose of Derrida's analysis. But Hägglund's duty, as he sees it, is to protect (immunize) Derrida from himself, to "fortify" him with occasional booster shots (RA, 11).

The reason Hägglund thinks the text misleading is that in it Derrida invokes Kant's distinction between thinking (ideas of reason) and knowledge (categorical determination of the manifold of intuition). Derrida writes:

> For finally, if the gift is another name of the impossible, we still think it, we name it, we desire it. . . . In this sense one can think, desire, and say only the impossible, according to the measureless measure of the impossible. . . . If one wants to recapture the proper

element of thinking, naming, desiring, it is perhaps according to the measureless measure of this limit that it is possible, possible as relation without relation to the impossible.[31]

The gift occurs in a gap between our "knowledge" of the possible and our "thought" or "desire" of the impossible:

> This *gap* between, on the one hand, thought, language, and desire and, on the other hand, knowledge, philosophy, science and the order of presence is also a gap between gift and economy.[32]

Crossing this gap has the appearance of a transcendental illusion in Kant's sense, where the cognitive faculty strays beyond the limits of experience lured by an illusory *ens realissimum*, and indeed, Derrida says, it is something like that. The aporia of the gift poses a sort of "quasi-transcendental illusion," where it "is a matter—desire beyond desire—of responding faithfully but also as rigorously as possible both to the injunction or the order of the gift (give [*donne*]), as well as to the injunction or the order of meaning (presence, science, knowledge)."[33]

So Derrida is clear that the gift is not an *ideal* but an *injunction*, and we are caught in the middle of a double injunction, of demands coming at us from both directions—from the impossible and the possible, from a thinking, naming, desiring of the impossible, on the one hand, and from what we know and experience of the possible, of the circle of economy.[34] The response (not the resolution or "compromise") to the aporia is to take a risk, to enter its destructive circle, expose oneself to the danger, tear up the circle of time—by *giving*, by *going* where you *know* you cannot go, *facere veritatem*, doing the truth rather than knowing it, for the gift is not finally a matter of knowledge:

> Know still what giving wants to say, know how to give, know what you want and want to say when you give, know what you intend to give, know how the gift annuls itself, commit yourself [*engage-toi*] even if commitment is the destruction of the gift by the gift, give economy its chance.[35]

There is no simple outside of the circle, no "transcendental illusion" in the strong sense. There is only the interruption of the circle and generation of new more ample circles.

d. *The ultra-transcendental.* In this case Hägglund does not truncate the concept but he baldly alters it to his own purposes. He uses the word to mean the ultimacy of the "space-time of the trace," a *ne plus ultra* spatio-temporality, the inescapable horizon "from which nothing can be exempt" (RA, 10). Derrida, on the other hand, does no such thing. For Derrida it is precisely the name of an exemption. Derrida introduces it against Hjelmslev's notion of pure linguistic form to stress that *différance* enjoys an ultra-transcendental exemption, that it "cannot, as the condition of all linguistic systems, form a part of the linguistic system and be situated as an object in its field,"[36] and hence arises from a movement "beyond" the transcendental lest it fall "short-of" it. The target of Hägglund's analysis is the transcendentality of space and time in Kant, which makes them appearances and leaves room for faith in things in themselves; that opens the door to what Meillassoux calls "fideism." So Hägglund uses Derrida's notion of the "ultratranscendental" to close that door, to say that space and time are "ultimate," go all the way down. Derrida has nothing of the sort in mind. For Derrida "ultra-transcendental" has more to do with Mallarmé than any such "materialism."[37] The word does not refer to the ultra-reality of coming to be and passing away in space and time as things in themselves and not mere appearance. It refers to the unformalizable play of linguistic effects we find in writers like Joyce and Mallarmé, just as the figure of the sister/Antigone in *Glas* represents a quasi-transcendental exception to a rigorous dialectical logic.[38] Hägglund simply alters the sense of "ultra" as "beyond" the formal, as the "exception" to the transcendental rule, and redefines the word ultratranscendental to mean ultra-transcendent, the ultimate, unbroken ultra-rule of space and time. Hägglund's ultratranscendental means reality is lodged without remission in spatio-temporal being; the quasi-transcendental condition of experience becomes an ultra-transcendent principle that "being is essentially temporal (to be = to happen)" (RA, 32). Derrida's "ultratranscendental," on the other hand, means the event cannot be contained or subsumed under the universal or transcendental; it is always an excess, a "beyond" (ultra-).[39]

2. *Descriptive and Prescriptive.* The alterations introduced by Hägglund go hand in hand with a decision to treat deconstruction as a strictly descriptive and not prescriptive undertaking, as simply describing the ultra-real, ultratranscendental, ultra-empirical, and unconditional, but never venturing "beyond." This claim is made throughout the text mainly to undercut the ethical and religious (RA, 31), which always mean "beyond" in the sense of Augustinian dualism. Deconstruction is an "ultratranscendental description" of our inescapable vulnerability to an unpredictable future, which means "there must be finitude and vulnerability, there must be openness to whatever or whoever comes" (RA, 31), and there cannot be any normativity or prescriptiveness about it, no need for an injunction to stay "open" or go "beyond," as we have no other choice anyway. We are

open to the coming of the future whether we like it or not, held fast in an unconditional (spatio-temporal) fix.

This is deconstruction *ad usum dauphini*, cut to fit the logic that is driving *Radical Atheism*, and it is at odds with Derrida. Hägglund's radical atheism only requires so much Derrida and no more, after which it cups its ears. What Hägglund leaves out is that, beyond our unavoidable exposure to the future, there lies our "responsibility" to and for the future (and the past), which we *certainly may avoid*. But should we say, then, we "ought" to be responsible to and for the future, and that Derrida's "ethics" is to "prescribe" just that—always and everywhere to stay open to the future? Hägglund thinks not, and again that is correct as far as it goes, for it would be a sad outcome for deconstruction to end up coming up with a new rule. But everything that is interesting about deconstruction turns on the next step, the one Hägglund leaves out, which is the way that Derrida eludes standard form ethical normativity or prescriptiveness. Derrida does not do this the way Hägglund does, by retreating to the descriptive-factual-empirical, but rather by making use of his *own* notion of the ultra-transcendental described in *Of Grammatology*, by going-beyond and by passing-through the transcendental, by passing through the universal-prescriptive (ethical) to an ultra-prescriptive, an "ultra-responsibility" or "hyper-responsibility" beyond prescriptive universality. Otherwise, Derrida says, if you drop the "passage-through," you will fall "short-of" the transcendental into the empirical or descriptive.[40] That Humean, empiricist shortfall, exactly what Derrida is warning against, is exactly what Hägglund embraces.

If this all sounds familiar, it should, since it repeats according to a dynamics of its own the path to Moriah depicted by Johannes de Silentio: through ethical universality to religious singularity (*hyperbole*, beyond) instead of retreating to the aesthetic (*ellipsis*, shortfall). That famous story was the subject of *The Gift of Death*, one of Derrida's most interesting books, where deconstruction emerges from the inclination of Kierkegaard and Levinas toward each other, about which Hägglund observes Abrahamic silence. While Derrida's topics of choice have changed over the years, the basic structure of his thought has not, which is the passage through the universal to the singular, which is why, *pace* Hägglund, I have never said there is a "religious turn" in any deep or structural sense, just a change of topics.[41]

Hägglund either does not see or simply rejects the way that in Derrida deconstruction is driven by a hyperbolic, open-ended, albeit dangerous, injunction that is structured like a religion, and certainly cannot be accommodated by resurrecting a modernist and empiricist distinction between prescriptive and descriptive. Hägglund makes much of the fact that whether the *tout autre* unexpectedly knocking at my door is "good" or "bad," an orphan in need or an axe murderer, is structurally unforeseeable and undecidable.[42] From this, Hägglund concludes that the *tout autre* is not the "good" as such, has no claim on us as such.[43] From the *tout autre* "no norms or rules can be derived" (RA, 232n4). The *tout autre* is the object of an ethically neutral and purely "descriptive" account. "Hospitality" is a pure descriptor meaning we never know who is knocking on the door (RA, 105). That is a half-truth, another torso effect, which serves Hägglund's point but blunts Derrida's. Of course the *tout autre* is not the good as such. Deconstruction is not a theory of the "good" but a theory of "responsibility," of infinite, hyperbolic responsibility. This point could not be more central. The *tout autre* is not good as such but the event as such. Good and bad are the categories of ethics, not of the "hyper-ethics" of responsibility, or the ultra-ethics "beyond" the ethics, which "passes through" the transcendental or ethical universal.[44]

So of course the other is not the good as such. If it were, everything would be programmed and we would have a rule to live by. But that does not mean the *tout autre* is something neutral but rather that, as the event as such, the *tout autre* is the occasion of a heightened responsibility, the "beginning of ethics, of the Law as such," "a principle of ethics or more radically of justice." The ultra-transcendental constitutes the hyper-ethical, ethics beyond ethics, the ethicity of ethics, "hyperbolic" ethics, an "increase of responsibility,"[45] which is an ethics beyond duty. Without the *tout autre*, without "the priceless dignity of otherness," "ethics is dormant," in a "dogmatic slumber."[46] When Derrida says such things, Hägglund remarks, we should not be misled by such "positively valorized terms" (RA, 105)—which is like Heidegger saying that nothing pejorative is intended in speaking of the leveled off inauthentic idle gossip of fallen Dasein. As happens often in this book, when Derrida gets to his point, he is chided by Hägglund for straying from Hägglund's point. It is ironic that a notion upon which Hägglund leans so heavily in *Radical Atheism* (ultra-transcendental) in fact—when we look at what Derrida actually says—exposes the bare-fisted empiricism that Hägglund embraces and Derrida is criticizing.

The account of the *tout autre* is indeed not "normative," not because it is less than normative (*ellipsis*), but because it is more than normative (*hyperbole*). The point of the analysis of the *tout autre* is not to "neutralize" the *tout autre* but to pass through its normative or ethical features, allowing them to break under the pressure of the aporia, in order to intensify the impossible, the passion, the claim, the call, the responsibility, all of which are charges set off upon entering the "beyond" (*ultra, hyper,* etc.). Derrida does not neutralize ethics but destabilizes its transcendental pretensions so as make room for ultra-transcendental responsibility to the singularity of the other. The "suspension" of the ethical is not neutralization but Kierkegaardian fear and trembling and Levinasian irrecusability; it suspends the universal-normative under the intensity of the singular responsibility.

From the fact that the future may bring disaster, Hägglund concludes that we cannot think it is "better to be more open than less open to the future" (RA, 232n4). Once again, Derrida expressly denies the position Hägglund is advancing. Sometimes, to prevent things from happening is not to prevent the event but the only way to keep the future open. We block those things that would themselves block the future:

> *The openness of the future is worth more*; that is *the axiom* of deconstruction, that on the basis of which it has always set itself in motion and which links it, as with the future itself, to otherness, to *the priceless dignity of otherness*, that is to say, to justice . . . . One can imagine the objection. Someone [let's say, the author of *Radical Atheism*] might say to you: "Sometimes it is better for this or that not to arrive. Justice demands that one prevent certain events (certain '*arrivants*') from arriving. The event is not good in itself, and the future is not unconditionally preferable." Certainly, but one can always show that what one is opposing, when one conditionally prefers that this or that not happen, is something one takes, rightly or wrongly, as blocking the horizon or simply forming the horizon (the word that means limit) for the absolute coming of the altogether other, for the future.[47]

> The coming of the event is what cannot and should not be prevented; it is another name for the future itself. This does not mean that it is good—good in itself—for everything and anything to arrive; it is not that one should give up trying to prevent certain things from coming to pass (without which there would be no decision, no responsibility, ethics or politics). But one should only ever oppose events that one thinks will block the future or that bring death with them: events that would put an end to the possibility of the event, to the affirmative opening to the coming of the other.[48]

At this point Hägglund's position is so much at odds with Derrida's that he simply admits it and chides Derrida for "giving in" to a bad argument precisely when Derrida should have stuck with the argument Hägglund is making, which reduces deconstruction to the description of double binds

(RA, 231n4). To the long list of distinguished commentators who have misunderstood deconstruction, according to *Radical Atheism*, it seems we have to add Jacques Derrida himself. Derrida has nothing to teach Hägglund. So just whose radical atheism is this?

3. *L'à venir*. Derrida does not speak of *le futur*, nor even *l'avenir*, but of *l'à venir*. *L'à venir* is not a space of time near or far off in the future; it is not the future present. It is not the descriptive-factual not-yet, even an unpredictable not-yet, which is the abridged form it takes in *Radical Atheism*. *L'à venir* is not a stretch of time at all; it is the very structure of the "to-come," which is the structure of a call or claim made upon us and of a certain hope or prayer or promise *sous rature*. It does not and will never "exist"; it insists, calls, claims, solicits. Deconstruction originates in and belongs to the order of the *viens, oui, oui*, which opens up a scene of risk, of faith and expectation, of what we hope and pray will come, of what could come, what might come, with all the might of the "might be," which means it might be a disaster. The event (*événement*) comes from the "to come" (*à venir*) and the "to come" comes from the *viens!*:

> The event of the "Come" [*viens*] precedes and calls the event. It would be that starting from which there is [*il y a*] any event, the *venir*, the *à venir* of the event [*événement*] that cannot be thought under the given category of the event.[49]

The event takes place in a scene (time-space, *Zeitspielraum*) opened up by a call, by an invocation (*viens!*), and not the reverse. Deconstruction transpires not in a neutral descriptive space but in the sphere of the future active participle, the *ventura*, what is to come, what promises to come, what we call upon to come, which by coming calls upon us like a thief in the night. The call announces "the desire, the order, the prayer, or the demand" that opens the vocative space of deconstruction.[50] That is why I say deconstruction is structured like a prayer. Derrida has isolated the quasi-phenomenological structure of a certain elemental prayer and loosened it from the God of strong theology and confessional religion. He analyzes a circum-fessional prayer of a heart more cut than confessional theology can concede, reinscribing prayer in a desert khoral space that is outside religion even while religion cannot get outside it. That means the cut is inside religion too, striking it through, marking it with its *sans*, and these marks show up inside religious scrolls from which he tries to "extract" a certain philosophical "function."

The "come" belongs not to an empirical descriptive future but to the time of the promise, what I called in *The Prayers and Tears of Jacques Derrida* a "messianic" time, or what Derrida once called an "apocalyptic" time.[51] The "Come" has already come as a famous prayer, as the last word of the New Testament (*erkhou*, *veni*, *viens*). In saying "Come" Derrida was already citing the New Testament, but without realizing it, citationality being a structural feature of every discourse, whether you realize you are citing or not.[52] "Come" calls up what we cannot simply call the "place" but "the advent of what in the apocalyptic in general no longer lets itself be contained simply by philosophy, metaphysics, onto-eschatology." Why not?

> First of all, because "Come," opening the scene, could not become an object, a theme, a representation, or indeed a citation in the current sense, and subsumable under a category, even were it that of coming or event . . . . Nevertheless, I am trying to extract from this, at the risk of essentially deforming it, the demonstrative function in terms of philosophical discourse.[53]

"Come" is not an object you can describe. You can no more "arraign" (*arraisonner*) "Come" before an "onto-theo-eschatology" (strong theology) than before a "logic of the event"—for example, *Radical Atheism*—"however new they may be and whatever politics they announce." "Come" is "neither a desire nor an order, neither a prayer nor a request," because all the standard-form "grammatical, linguistic, or semantic categories"[54] that would determine "Come" are themselves always already traversed by "Come." The "Come" opens the scene in which these categories—like the distinction in *Radical Atheism* between prescriptive and descriptive—are inscribed.

"This 'Come'—I do not know what it is . . . because the question 'what is' belongs to a space . . . opened up by 'come' come from the other."[55] It does not fit into the grammatical category of a standard form prayer, imperative, or a performative; it is not a constative—let alone a descriptive!—because it opens the scene to which all such categories belong. Come is like a prayer—it is neither true nor false, but optative or jussive—but it is a kind of archi-prayer or quasi-prayer before any determinate prayer. Only if we pass through the given category of prayer can we pray this prayer. Still it is not an origin but derivable, or a divided origin, because Come comes from the other, to which it comes in response. Come comes second, after the first Come comes calling. Perhaps one might call this calling a "tonal" difference, a new tone.[56] It does not belong to a descriptive space but opens a vocative space of calling, re-calling, being called upon, calling in response. But this quasi-prayerful tone is left hanging without a prayer, belonging to an "apocalypse without apocalypse, *sans vision*, *sans verité*, *sans révelation*,"[57] as much a threat as a promise, a hope against hope, unveiling the apocalypse as such, which for Derrida means the structure of the "chance." The charged scene opened by the "Come" is not that of "good or evil" or of "truth." It is "older" than good or evil or truth and "beyond Being," not to mention being a good deal older than the descriptive and the prescriptive. It belongs to the domain of chance itself, that is, of a promise that is entirely lacking in assurance and destination, traversed throughout by the strange (il)logic of the *sans*. Indeed, that very *destinerrance*—and here is the so-called philosophy of religion I love in Derrida—is even inscribed inside the scroll of Revelation, in the last lines of the last book of the New Testament, when it says "do not seal" these words (Rev. 22:10), that is, do not close this book; the future is open, quasi-transcendentally.

4. *Negative Ontological Argument. Différance* is a condition of experience, not a metaphysical principle. But Hägglund says that Derrida "repeatedly argues" (no citations) that *différance* "not only applies to language or experience or any other delimited region of *being* [emphasis added]. Rather it is an *absolutely general condition*, which means there cannot even in principle *be* [emphasis added] anything that is *exempt* [emphasis added] from temporal finitude" (RA, 2–3), that "*being is essentially temporal* (*to be* = to happen)" (RA, 32, emphasis added). But if there is a text in which Derrida says he offers an account of absolute, essential being beyond experience, it must have been lost in the mail. The term *différance* is introduced to explain how "language, or any code, any system of referral in general is constituted 'historically' as a weave of differences."[58] What Derrida does "repeatedly say" is that deconstruction is an experience of the impossible, which means that *différance* is an "absolutely general condition"—of *experience*! The very "unpredictability" upon which Hägglund lays all his emphasis is a feature of experience, requiring an experiential horizon of predictability. Deconstruction is not a theory of absolute being. The ultratranscendental does not mean ultratranscendent.

When Derrida warns us against the "theological prejudices" (dogmatic claims) essential to metaphysics "even when it is a theology of atheism" he is warning us against *Radical Atheism avant la lettre*.[59] Hägglund inflates *différance* into a negative ontological argument, an a priori proof of the non-existence of God, thereby turning deconstruction into a metaphysics of becoming. Like Derrida, I have no sympathy for Augustinian metaphysical dualism, but Hägglund is overreaching. He presents *no noncircular arguments against the God of classical metaphysics or the metaphysical idea of eternity*. He simply stipulates everything in advance by "defining" life as "essentially mortal" (RA, 1) and being as "essentially temporal" (RA, 32), from which it merely follows by definition that "desire" is the desire of perishable goods. Nothing is settled by such decisions other than to stipulate how one is using these words. To say that nothing "happens" in eternity (RA, 32, 45, 122) is analytically true, trivially true, since to happen is defined as to happen in time. Similarly, to say that the desire to "survive" would be ruined by "immortality," or that someone who wants to "survive" does not desire "immortality," is simply true by the definition of the terms. It does not settle anything to define desire as the desire of the imperishable—as does Augustine—or to define it as the desire of the perishable—as does Hägglund—and then to insist that reality heed one's definitions. Within the framework of immortality, mere survival is of only passing worth; within the framework of survival, immortality is pure death. Those who desire immortality cannot imagine that anyone would be content with survival, and those who desire surviving cannot imagine that immortality would satisfy anyone. Each side thinks that the very terms in which desire is framed by the other destroy what desire "means." To say that "God is death" simply defines the borders of the binary dispute between Augustinian eschatology and radical atheists. Both sides are agreed about this assertion but they interpret it differently. No one can see God and live, say the Augustinians, but they would rather see God and not live (a merely mortal life) because they think seeing God represents a higher life. Radical atheists would rather live a mortal life and not die any sooner than need be because they think seeing God in another life is an illusion and no life at all. But such completely circular arguments are the hallmark of metaphysics. They accomplish nothing more than to successfully immunize each side against the other, each side treating the other side as a nihilism that denies what is real.

Derrida certainly never claimed, as does Hägglund, that there is an a priori argument against the existence of the God of metaphysics. While Derrida has no faith in such a God, he says that *différance* has "no lever," has "nothing to say," on anything that transcends experience—like saying there is absolutely no such thing.[60] Hägglund, on the other hand, agrees with Anselm and Descartes that the existence of God can be settled on a priori grounds, albeit negatively. He simply uses *différance* to stipulate that life is mortal and that being is spatio-temporal but he offers no noncircular argument that there is no life or being outside space and time. His objection to eternity is that it does not abide by the conditions of space and time. But that is not an objection to eternity; it is the definition of eternity.

Hägglund creates some confusion on this point because occasionally he speaks not of being in general but of being that can be "cognized and experienced . . . thought and desired" (RA, 10, 19, 29). If so, then radical atheism is weaker than traditional atheism, not more radical. For classical atheism maintains that God does not exist, regardless of what we desire, whereas radical atheism is defined by our desire, almost as if, by not desiring it, it will go away. But the real does not depend upon our desire. Furthermore, such a view succumbs to the intractable difficulty of *dénegation*, this time in terms of desire: *Comment ne pas désirer?* How not to desire God, how to not desire God, how to desire not-God without ending up desiring God after all, without being in denial? To deny we desire God would require that we be sure that we are not by some trick of the unconscious desiring God all the more, that desire be transparent to itself, which, as Hägglund points out, Derrida rejects (RA, 57). Hägglund thinks our desire of the imperishable dissimulates a desire of the perishable. Augustine thinks that our desire of perishable things dissimulates a desire of the imperishable. Both claims require an un-dissimulated understanding of desire, immune to self-deception. The positions are perfectly symmetric and caught in an irresoluble metaphysical antinomy, just as Kant predicts. Derrida avoids every such interminable argument over the "final word." The logic of radical atheism requires stable and transparent concepts of desire, God and *la religion*, undisturbed by other voices, unhaunted by specters, everything from which Derrida dissociates himself when he says he only "rightly passes for" an atheist and that the multiplicity of voices within him give him no peace.[61] For Derrida, desire is desire when it is fired by the very thing that makes it impossible—not knowing what we desire. We begin, we desire, *par l'impossible*.

In short, Hägglund's stated aim is to "fortify" Derrida's resistance to religion—in the name of auto-immunity! He mines the works of Derrida for a certain logic that supports his own argument, sweeping aside a great deal of careful work on deconstruction that Derrida himself valued as a new way of thinking about ethics and religion. He uses Derrida where he can, corrects Derrida when he cannot, and ignores what he does not need. However one might judge that strategy, at least it makes clear that when push comes to shove this is not a book about Derrida but about Hägglund's independent orchestration of the logic of auto-immunity in the name of his own radical atheism, which is not to be confused with the work of Jacques Derrida.

The Point of View of My Work as an Author

When I wrote *The Prayers and Tears of Jacques Derrida* I steered around the two prevailing ways to think about Derrida and religion. I loved Mark Taylor's impious deconstruction of classical theology in *Erring*[62] but I thought Taylor failed to remain on the slash of his "a/theology" and made it look like deconstruction dances gaily on the grave of the dead God, is not responsible to anything, and has no faith.[63] I also loved the pious path of negative theology that followed Derrida wherever he went, which Derrida too admired—its "detours, locutions and syntax"[64]—but I emphasized with him that deconstruction is not negative theology, not even the most negative of negative theologies, which turns on an absolute and silent center.[65] I had made the same point in 1978: when Heidegger uses Meister Eckhart's word *Gelassenheit*, Heidegger is talking about the historico-linguistic happening of *Ereignis* whereas Eckhart has in mind the wordless, timeless unity of the soul with God.[66] That applies *a fortiori* to *différance*. Both Heidegger and Derrida repeat certain structures found in negative theology, but both deploy them in order to think radically temporal and mundane operations. So I proposed a third path, both pious and impious, laughing through my tears: neither the death of God nor Christian apophaticism, but the circumfessional path inspired by the impudent figure of an atheistic Jewish Augustine. Deconstruction is structured like a prayer, belongs to the vocative and invocative space and time of prayer, an odd archi-prayer (*viens!*). Deconstruction is praying for the impossible, with a prayer without (*sans*) a prayer, singularly lost and adrift, *destinerrant*. Unlike Taylor's a/theology, this is structured like a *religion*, and unlike negative theology is only *structured* like a religion, a religion without the God of classical religion, a khoral or an-khoral religion without religion.

Derrida famously said that the "least bad" definition of deconstruction is the "experience of the impossible,"[67] which I used as a way to read what he said about this religion *without* religion. I was not speaking about a being called God, but about what is being called (what's happening) in the "name of God." Like Žižek I agree the therapy is over when you see there is no big Other. The possibility of the impossible is not about a Big Being coming to save us by doing the impossible things that we could not possibly do—this central misunderstanding informs everything Hägglund says about my work (RA, 120)—it is about responsibility. Once you "have" a Big Being like that, once you "know" it, you have undermined the experiential structure (the possible/impossible). That is why, like Derrida, I deny that the impossible *is* God, which would collapse the possibility of the impossible into something proper and identifiable. As Derrida said in his commentary on *The Prayers and Tears of Jacques Derrida*:

> If there is a transparent translatability [between "God" and "the impossible"] "the faith" is safe, that is, it becomes a non-faith. At that point, it becomes possible to name [the impossible] . . . because

there is some*one* whom you can name and call because you know who it is that you are calling . . . . If I were sure that it was possible for me to replace "the impossible" by "God" then everything would become possible. Faith would become possible, and when faith becomes simply possible, it is not faith anymore.[68]

When Derrida points out the two sources of religion as faith and the desire to keep safe, he proposes an auto-deconstructive formula that brews a religion *without* religion—because faith cannot be what he calls faith if it desires to be safe. Religion without religion is unprotected religion, faith without safety, a mad risk of everything on the impossible. But in classical metaphysical theology God is precisely the possibility of the impossible in a straightforward sense, for whom nothing is impossible (Marion's "impossibility of impossibility"). Classical omnipotence effectively ruins the deconstructive idea of "*the* impossible" and also of Derrida's "God"—which is why I criticize Peter Damian's God who can change past time (WG, ch. 9). I argue that "God" in Derrida, like justice, can only be a weak force (*force faible*), a dream.[69] But, as Hent de Vries has shown, this is an "exemplary" dream. The becoming possible of the impossible in Derrida is not the name of an Über-being but of an event that goes to the heart of the structure of experience. This structure intensifies the possible to the point of the impossible, constituting the desire, passion, existence, and temporality that are at work *in* religion, *as* a certain religion that deconstruction exposes in all its unsafe, unprotected anarchic energy, with all the "might" of the "might be," not the might of omnipotence. The axiomatics of deconstruction are organized around a poetics of the impossible, of the "becoming possible of the impossible."

I am not arguing that there is a being called "God" somewhere who does or mysteriously declines to do impossible things. Nor do I argue or think that God is the Being of beings, or a hyper-Being beyond Being in the tradition of mystical theology, the "God without Being" of Jean-Luc Marion, a point I have been making ever since I cautioned about confusing *Ereignis* with God.[70] Nor do I, God forbid, attribute any such views to Jacques Derrida, nor, thank God, did Derrida think I was doing any such thing.[71] I am not theologizing deconstruction but deconstructing theology, Christian theology, causing a scandal to the pious and a stumbling block to the theologians, reimagining, reinventing "God," which is why my radical theology is considered radical atheism and a "death of God" by my evangelical friends. In the place of what I call "strong theology," I offer a certain "poetics" of the human condition, not a theo-logic but a "theo-poetics," just as Derrida stresses the necessity of his "grafts of poetry upon philosophy, which are anything but confused."[72] I compare religious beliefs and practices with Wittgenstein's "forms of life," Heideggerian modes of "being-in-the-world," Merleau-Ponty's ways of "singing the world," transpiring on what Deleuze (and Laruelle) would call the "plane of immanence." They have to do with the passion, the intensity, the temporality, and, yes, the mortality of the human condition. Cosmic mercilessness itself (Meillassoux and Brassier owe a footnote to Pascal) only intensifies the religious condition, just as mortality intensifies the preciousness of life, which is the starting point of my own *Against Ethics*[73] and *Radical Hermeneutics*, where I argued that we make no gains by concealing the "difficulty of life."

In this spirit, Derrida has been my coconspirator, a conspiracy occurring in two stages.

In the first stage—*The Prayers and Tears of Jacques Derrida*—I mingled the gorgeous prayers and tears of Augustine's *Confessions* with those of a certain "little black and Arab Jew," producing an atheistic Jewish Augustine, who surprises us by saying he has been praying all his life, kissing his prayer shawl every night, and that nobody, not even his mother or Geoffrey Bennington, knows about his religion, as a result of which, he says, he has been "read less and less well over almost twenty years."[74] He prays to an unknown, even nonexistent God, practices an ironic irreligious religion growing out of rightly passing for an atheist.[75] The religious pulse vibrates precisely in the "rightly passing for"—in the passion of undecidability—in the destabilization of both theism and atheism, launching the work of inventing new parergonal, para-theological post-theistic categories, where not believing in God does not disqualify the religion.[76] Deconstruction, like religion, is "brewed from a devilish mix of 'faith and atheism,' 'radical doubt and faith.'"[77] Everything interesting about deconstruction and religion lies in the way it opens the structure of experience by rendering the binary war between theism and atheism obsolete.

From the point of view of the local rabbi or pastor, Derrida is an atheist, and that atheism has always been irreducibly important to me. Without his atheism, he and I would be lost. I would lose my faith in a religion without religion. If Derrida had at some time been "converted" like Augustine, returned to the religion of his mother, *The Prayers and Tears of Jacques Derrida* would have been ruined. Without this atheism we have to do without the without and we would be immured within the walls of religion, unable to repeat the form of life that religion is, the multiple forms that the several religious traditions take, without being drawn into their doctrines and the dogmas, unable to break open their closed confessional circles, unable to put them at risk as so many precarious ways to "do the truth" (Augustine).[78] Derrida's atheism reopens the books of religion, making texts like the Scriptures and Augustine's *Confessions* available for reading, no longer under either secular censure or ecclesiastical protection (two alternative forms of excommunication, immunization and dogma). Like Derrida, I feel around for the cluster of events that stir within a text like the *Confessions*, repeating religion without its dualist two worlds transcendence-operators—body and soul, time and eternity, this world and the next, etc.—feeling for the pulse or rhythm of the immanence of life, for the life of immanence, for life/death.[79]

I proposed that the "religion without religion" that in *The Gift of Death* Derrida attributed to others is performed in the flesh, scarred on the body, inscribed in the texts of Jacques Derrida himself. *Prayers and Tears* constructs the categories and the images, the tropes and the strategies, of such an ir/religion. I do not assimilate Derrida to Augustine, or conversely, but I read religious texts as a meditation upon our mortal lives, as a certain poetics of the human condition. When I examined the baffling commentary Hägglund made on my work in *Radical Atheism*, I realized that he had confused me with an orthodox two-worlds Augustinian who thinks that a Hyperbeing called God can do impossible things while we humans, alas, cannot. That is, as Hägglund says of me in an excellent phrase, the matrix of a systematic misreading of everything I say (RA, 120). Like Derrida, I think we have "never loved anything but the impossible,"[80] but that has nothing to do with positing the existence of a higher agent who does things impossible for human beings.

The second stage is *The Weakness of God: A Theology of the Event*. That is a book not about Jacques Derrida but about God, about the "event" that stirs within the name of God, inspired by Derrida's remarks on a coming God who would lack sovereignty.[81] The argument that this book makes against divine omnipotence can be extended analogously against any other divine name, including "goodness," which is the one that Hägglund turns to in his contribution to this volume. If I had set out from the point of view of "goodness," I could have named my book *The Radical Evil of God*, meaning the structural possibility of evil inscribed in the name of God (something Boehme and Schelling were pondering on a metaphysical level).[82] I singled out "weakness" because I am interested in the political critique of sovereignty and because the "weakness" of God has a literally crucial purchase in the Christian tradition, in the crucified body of Jesus, in what Johann Baptist Metz calls the "dangerous memory of suffering."[83]

In this book I spoke with undisguised irony of a "weak theology"—like a "minor literature" in the Deleuzean sense, where mystics and heretics snipe at the heels of the majority voices. But I did so with two hands, with a right hand writing a genuine but immanent theology, and with a left-handed Socratic irony, Derridian impishness, and Kierkegaardian humor. I opposed it to Kierkegaard's hilarious riff on a theology all powdered and rouged sitting in the window waiting for a Hegelian to stroll by. In *Radical Atheism*, Hägglund missed the irony and misread *The Prayers and Tears of Jacques Derrida* as if I were staking out an orthodox theological position, while not reading *The Weakness of God* at all.[84] Had he done so he would have found a creation story without omnipotence and a Lazarus read in terms of "living on," *sur-vive* (to which *Radical Atheism* is dedicated). I read the Resurrection against itself, took the moral of the narrative to be "more life," life-death, and Jesus to be someone who talks the sisters of Lazarus through their grief and helps them find a way of "living on," bringing them *salut* as salutation not as eternal salvation, consoling Mary and Martha who say they are not interested in eternal life for their brother but more time (see RA, 225n39).

Having now consulted this book, Hägglund has reorganized his argument around the divine name of goodness but he continues to assimilate me to some form of classical transcendence. After all, if Caputo is speaking about "religion"—*la religion!* always in the singular—then he must be a two-worlds Augustinian, which is what "religion" "essentially" "is" in *Radical Atheism*. Conceding now that I bid adieu to divine omnipotence he turns me into an apologue of the "pure good." So my God is "good" but too weak to do any good. I repeat: I am not saying that God is an innocent but weak being, or a good being who means well even if his means are limited. I am not making ontic, ontological, or me-ontological claims about a hyperbeing or hyper-person called God. I take leave of the order of presence, of being and Beings, weak or strong, good or bad, transcendent or immanent, providential or blind, in favor of the *event* of *peut-être*. I am not debating about a being and which predicates the being takes (omnipotence, omniscience, etc.) but about an im/probable, im/possible promise/threat, about the experience of the impossible, for which the name of God is one of our best and favorite names, which is my view and the express view of Jacques Derrida.[85]

My question is, what is happening in the enormous provocation of that name, what is getting itself said and done there, in the middle voice? Taking up Derrida's suggestive notion of a weak force, of an event without sovereignty, I say this event lays claim to us unconditionally but without force, soliciting us, addressing us, haunting us, like a specter. That does not make the event a pure good but a pure risk, a risky injunction, because such solicitations may lead us into the worst evils, as the history of "God" testifies. The event is no more "pure good" than "pure evil," no more "strong" than "weak," because it is nothing entitative or ontological, is neither a being nor an agent, neither a substance nor a subject, does not subsist and does not "do" things (or fail to do them) for which it could be praised or blamed. As I argue in my most recent book, God does not exist; God insists.[86] So no matter which of the divine names Hägglund settles on, I have, in fact, the same view. If "omniscience," I will defend the cause of the "blindness of God," or if "necessity," the contingency of God. In fact, my precise proposal is that the event harbored in the name of God is the *peut-être*, "perhaps," not the contingency of God but the name of God harboring the force of contingency, not the might of omnipotence but the subjunctive "might" of might-be. As there is an infinity of divine names, this debate could go for some time!

As opposed to Hägglund's essay in this volume, *The Weakness of God* was an argument that the "good, good" of Genesis is to be glossed as "perhaps, let's hope so." The pure good is a pure risk. In my line of work I am frequently glossing Scriptural texts where the notion of the pure good is in play, which I however repeat and redescribe as the pure risk (RA, 120–21; 223–24n21). In my unprotected religion I recklessly expose myself to texts Hägglund seeks to quarantine (the Scriptures), which are dreaming of paradise and the Kingdom of God. But my repetition and redescription of them is obvious, as when I entitle a chapter "The Beautiful *Risk* of Creation," where I redescribe the benevolence of God in strong theology as the chance for the good that is menaced by evil not only on all sides but even from within. I frame the story of creation within a Talmudic gloss that serves as the epigraph of the chapter (epigraphs are important in deconstruction). God attempted and failed to make the world twenty-six times (so much for omnipotence). But on the next attempt he succeeded and then exclaimed not "good, good," as in Genesis, but "let's hope it works," which signifies, the rabbi says, that "history is branded with the mark of radical uncertainty" (WG, 55). God could not foresee what was coming, had no power over it, and realized that everything was at the mercy of chance, so he was keeping the divine fingers crossed. Hägglund reads my citation of the literal words of Genesis[87]—good, good, very good—and then ignores my gloss, my point—which is the "perhaps," *peut-être*.[88] God rolled the dice and took a chance on the good—and by the sixth chapter of Genesis God regrets (not a familiar divine name) the mess he has created and wipes the world out with a flood and starts all over again. Everything in this chapter, and in *The Weakness of God* as a whole, presupposes the structural inhabitation of the good by its constitutive exposure to evil, and the structural chance for good in the most risky situations.[89] Creation launches the promise/threat, the beautiful risk, which landed straightaway in Cain's murder of Abel. I am talking about the chance of an event, not the adventures of a superhero named God.[90]

Radical or structural evil, atheism, or blindness are not objections to my radical theology but constitutive elements within it. That is why I could include Hägglund's own very sensitive account of "Circumfession" in an anthology of what I call radical or weak theology, perhaps polemically the best response to his criticisms. To conclude that in deconstruction the case for atheism is a case against religion is to absolutize the binarity of theism and atheism and to miss the point of deconstruction. The prayers and tears of this religion offer no protection, keep no one safe, but remind the faithful that faith is structured from within by un-faith. There are stretches of *Radical Atheism* that I admire and with which I agree, although I think its logocentric and self-certain presentation are contrary to the style and the stylus of deconstruction, which cannot be isolated from its substance. For any possible "logic" in deconstruction is but one of its styles—it can be called a logic, Derrida says, "up to a certain point"[91]—which is written more *in* fear and trembling than as an attempt to inspire fear and trembling in everyone else.

Like Derrida, and unlike Hägglund, I do not trust any discourse not "contaminated with negative theology,"[92] and like Derrida I heed the non-ousiological voices in mystical theology, voices of errancy, of being lost.[93] If strong theology is a handbook for being saved, weak theology is a circum-fession of being lost—"without salvation, resurrection or redemption—neither for oneself nor for the other"[94]—of something salutary without salvation. I am not seeking to be saved by God, but to save God, to save the name of God, *sauf le nom*, "God, for example," praying more for God than to God, praying for the world in a religion without religion. In deconstruction, we are saved from being saved, just as being lost is the only way to start searching. The unavoidability of being lost, the impossibility of being saved, is the condition of possibility of an aporetic soteriology, which meditates the mercilessness and mortality of our condition. If prayer is a wounded word, as Chrétien argues, there is no more radically wounded word than the prayers and tears of one for whom the very possibility of prayer is lodged in its impossibility.[95]

The atheism of Jacques Derrida is a precious elixir and an irreducible lemma in the dilemma of a religion without religion, without otherworldly transcendence and supernatural dogma. The mortality of our lives clears our head of ethereal otherworldly bodies, exposing the fleshly bodies of an immanent religion, the religiousness of our mortal flesh, of which the crucified flesh of Jesus is emblematic in Christian life. One would be hard put to find a more ardent and profoundly religious dialogue than the haunting conversation between Derrida and Cixous, two Jewish-Algerian atheists, musing over their mortality (more poignant than ever after Derrida's death), started over forty years ago when he commented on the manuscript of her first book entitled nothing less than *Le Prénom de Dieu*. Theirs is a meditation on faith inhabited by un-faith, on life inhabited by death, a faith in life made more intense by death and un-faith, he believing, on his side, that in the end we die too soon, while she, on her side, had more faith in life. Would that he might believe her, where that subjunctive might (*puissé je*) is all the "might" (*pouvoir*) available, the might of the powerless power of might-be, the being of may-being, the possibility of the impossible:

> As for me, I keep forever reminding her each time, on my side, that we die in the end, too quickly. And I always have to begin again.
>
> For she "because she loves to live" does not believe me. She, on her side, knows well that one dies in the end, too quickly; she knows it and writes about it better than anyone, she has the knowledge of it but she believes none of it. . . .
>
> And I say to myself, on my side: "Would that I might [*puissé-je*] believe her, I wish I might [*puisse*], yes, I wish I might believe her . . . ."[96]

The Autoimmunity of Religion

MARTIN HÄGGLUND

> It makes violence of itself, does violence to itself, and keeps itself from the other. The autoimmunity of religion can only indemnify itself without assignable end.
>
> —Derrida, "Faith and Knowledge"[1]

In contemporary debates the most common charge made against religion—whether by those who seek to abolish or to renew religious faith—is that it tends to generate violence and intolerance.[2] While religious teachings often emphasize love and tolerance, it is easy enough to recite a litany of genocides, persecutions, and wars pursued in the name of one religion or another. For the new atheists, such as Richard Dawkins and Christopher Hitchens, this violent track record is the clearest example of how religion poisons everything and corrupts a humanity that otherwise would stand a better chance of being peaceful. For those who seek to renew the sense of religious faith, such as John Caputo and Richard Kearney, the violence of religion is, rather, an effect of a "metaphysical" conception of God, which needs to be relinquished in favor of a "post-metaphysical" theology that would retrieve the goodness and love that is supposedly at the heart of true religious experience.

Thus, in his recent book *Anatheism: Returning to God after God*, Kearney approvingly quotes a passage from *The God Delusion*—where Dawkins produces a long list of atrocities undertaken in the name of religion—while maintaining that such violence is an effect of the belief in an omniscient and omnipresent God. "This is the God rightly dismissed, in our day, by Richard Dawkins."[3] In contrast, Kearney advocates a conception of God as a principle of goodness that has no power to prevent evil but is actualized whenever good is done. The "kingdom of God" is not an eschatological state at the end of history but rather actualized in every good deed. Hence, while the presence of the good is the presence of God, "evil is the absence of God. God has no power over what God is not—namely evil. God can only be good—unconditionally good in a gifting, loving, creating way."[4]

A similar conception of God—and the kingdom of God—emerges in Caputo's "weak" theology. Caputo too highlights the violent history of religious rule ("What has been more violent than theocracy? What more patriarchal, more hierarchical? What more authoritarian, inquisitorial, misogynistic, colonialist, militaristic, terroristic?"), but he goes on to emphasize that "all this power mongering is just rouged and powdered theology," which is "human, all too human, and not to be confused with God."[5] In contrast to the violence of power, the kingdom of God "is found whenever war and aggression are met with an offer of peace. The kingdom is a way of living, not in eternity, but in time, a way of living without why, living for the day, like the lilies of the field—figures of weak forces—as opposed to mastering and programming time, calculating the future, containing and managing risk."[6]

The opposition between two ways of relating to the future—one that generates "war" by seeking to master or calculate time, the other that brings "peace" by renouncing the attempt to program what will happen—is crucial for Caputo's reading of Jacques Derrida. According to Caputo, "deconstruction is a blessing for religion, its positive salvation" since it "discourages religion from its own worst instincts" and "helps religion examine its conscience, counseling and chastening religion about its tendency to confuse its faith with knowledge, which results in the dangerous and absolutizing triumphalism of religion, which is what spills blood."[7] Much of Caputo's work on deconstruction and religion is structured around this opposition between a "good" religion that welcomes others and a "bad" religion that excludes others. The religion *without* religion that Caputo ascribes to Derrida would be a religion that repeats "the apocalyptic call for the impossible, but without calling for the apocalypse that would consume its enemies in fire" and "repeats the passion for the messianic promise and messianic expectation, *sans* the concrete messianisms of the positive religions that wage endless war and spill the blood of the other."[8]

The logic of Caputo's argument runs counter to the logic I pursue in my book *Radical Atheism*, which seeks to provide a new framework for understanding Derrida's engagement with religious concepts.[9] Specifically, the proliferation of apparently religious terms in Derrida's late works—which engage with notions such as the messianic, faith, and God—does not signal a religious "turn" in his thinking. Rather, Derrida analyzes these concepts in accordance with a logic of radical atheism that I trace throughout his writings. Radical atheism does not subscribe to the binary of theism and atheism but seeks to demonstrate that there is a commitment to the persistence of finite life at the "root" of desire, faith, and responsibility. Far from allowing anyone or anything to be exempt from violence, the commitment to finite life accounts for a constitutive violence that is at work even in the most peaceful approach to the world and undermines the religious notion of the good from within.

In his contribution to the present volume, Caputo responds at length to *Radical Atheism*, but he misconstrues both my critique of his work and my reading of Derrida. According to Caputo, my critique is limited to the orthodox two-worlds theology of classical theism. Thus, Caputo defends himself at length against my supposed charge that he believes in the idea of immortality or in the existence of another world that would allow us to escape from time into eternity. I have allegedly taken him to be a defender of divine omnipotence, a "two-worlds Augustinian who thinks that a Hyperbeing called God can do impossible things."[10] In fact, however, I never charge Caputo with making ontological statements about God or believing in the existence of omnipotence, immortality, or another world. Rather, my critique is aimed at Caputo's conception of the *desire* for the impossible in Derrida.[11] In articulating this critique, I also take issue with Caputo's readings of the messianic, the unconditional, and a number of other terms in Derrida. These criticisms are not addressed in Caputo's response and if it were simply a matter of setting the record straight I would not insist on them here. However, given that Caputo's reading is the most influential attempt to make sense of Derrida's treatment of religious concepts—and that our debate speaks to the general question of the relation between deconstruction and religion—I will seek to elucidate the stakes of our differences in the course of elaborating my reading of Derrida.

Following Derrida, I define religion as premised on the idea of something that would be good in itself—regardless of whether the good is posited as transcendent or immanent and regardless of whether it is called God or something else. According to Derrida, all religions are founded on the idea of "the unscathed" (*l'indemne*), which he glosses as the pure and the untouched, the sacred and the holy, the safe and sound. As Derrida puts it, "every religion" holds out a "horizon of redemption, of the restoration of the unscathed, of indemnification."[12] Accordingly, the religious promise of the good is the promise of something that is unscathed by evil. The good may be threatened from the outside—by corruption, idolatry, misunderstanding, and so on—but in itself it is exempt from evil.

Deconstructing the religious conception of the good, Derrida develops a notion of "radical evil." The term is taken from Immanuel Kant's treatise *Religion within the Limits of Reason Alone*, but it receives a quite different meaning in Derrida's work. Schematically, the notion of radical evil can be seen as an intervention in one of the most fundamental theological debates, which concerns the origin of evil. The classic theological problem is how the omnipotence of God can be compatible with the existence of evil. If God created evil he is not absolutely good, but if he did not create evil he is not almighty. Augustine formulated the most influential solution to the problem by arguing that evil does not belong to being as such. Only the good has being and evil is nothing but the privation of goodness; a corruption that supervenes from the outside and does not affect the supreme good of being in itself. Thus, God can be the creator of everything that is (since all that has being is good) without being responsible for evil. The source of evil, rather, resides in the free will of human beings, which makes them liable to turn away from the good.

While prudently avoiding the theological assertions of Augustine, Kant pursues a formally similar argument by treating evil as an effect of the free will, which may lead one to follow the incentives of one's sensuous nature rather than the moral law. Evil is thus "radical" in the sense that the possibility of evil is at the root of our human nature and cannot be finally eliminated from the way we are constituted. For Kant, however, the ever-present possibility of evil does not call into question the Idea of a good that is exempt from evil. Even though we as finite beings can never attain something that is good in itself, we can strive toward it as an ideal that in principle is thinkable and desirable. In contrast, Derrida argues that the possibility of evil is intrinsic to the good that we desire. Evil is thus "radical" in the sense that it is at the root of the good as such; without bearing evil within itself the good would not be what it is.

While this may seem like an abstract argument, Derrida makes it concrete through his notion of hospitality. Derrida argues that even if I invite a good friend and we have a wonderful time it is an irreducible condition that "the experience might have been terrible. Not only that it *might* have been terrible, but the threat remains. That this good friend may become the devil, may be perverse. The perversity is not an accident which could once and for all be excluded, the perversity is part of the experience."[13] Far from restricting this argument to the sphere of friendship, Derrida generalizes it in accordance with the logic of radical evil. As he puts it: "for an event, even a good event to happen the possibility of radical evil must remain inscribed as a possibility," since "if we exclude the mere possibility of such a radical evil, then there will be no event at all. When we are exposed to what is coming, even in the most generous intention of hospitality, we must not exclude the possibility that the one who is coming is coming to kill us, is a figure of evil."[14] Accordingly, Derrida emphasizes that even the other who is identified as good may always *become* evil and that "this is true even in the most peaceful experiences of joy and happiness."[15] The point is not only that evil is a necessary possibility but also that *nothing would be desirable* without it, since it is intrinsic to the experience of the good itself. Following his example of the friend, Derrida thus maintains that "when I experience something good, the coming of a friend for example, if I am happy with a good surprise, then in this experience of happiness, within it, the memory of or the lateral reference to the possible perversion of it must remain present, in the wings let's say, otherwise I could not enjoy it."[16]

We can thus understand why Derrida insists on a distinction between *faith*, on the one hand, and the religious ideal of *the unscathed* on the other. The two are usually conflated in the notion of religious faith, which is understood as the faith in an absolute good that is immune from the corruption of evil. Drawing on his logic of radical evil, however, Derrida reads the religious ideal of absolute immunity against itself. To have faith in the good is not to have faith in something that can be trusted once and for all. On the contrary, the good is *autoimmune* because evil is inherent in its own constitution. As Derrida emphasizes, there is "nothing immune, safe and sound, *heilig* and holy, nothing unscathed in the most autonomous living present without a risk of autoimmunity."[17] The argument here—articulated in Derrida's main essay on religion, "Faith and Knowledge"—is that the very movement of sacralization is contradicted from within by a constitutive autoimmunity. To hold something to be sacred is to seek to immunize it, to protect it from being violated or corrupted. Yet one cannot protect anything without committing it to a future that allows it to live on and by the same token exposes it to loss and destruction. The immunization of the good must therefore "take in trust"—as Derrida puts it—"that radical evil without which good would be for nothing."[18] This condition of radical evil cannot be removed, Derrida goes on to argue, since removing it would amount to the "annulment of the future."[19]

Derrida thus highlights the logic of radical evil through the notion of faith. Derrida argues that faith—taking in trust—is constitutive of experience in general. In order to do anything, we must have faith in the future and in those on whom we depend, since we cannot *know* what will happen or what others will do to us. Consequently, the faith that sustains us, the trust that allows us to act, is necessarily open to being deceived and the credit granted to the other open to being ruinous. As Derrida argues, "this break with calculable reliability and with the assurance of certainty—in truth, with knowledge—is ordained by the very structure of confidence or of credence as faith."[20] Whatever we do, then, we place our faith in a future that may shatter our hopes and lay to waste what we desire. This necessity of faith is not due to a cognitive limitation but to the undecidability of the future, which opens both chance and threat at every moment. As Derrida underscores, "this ex-position to the incalculable event" is "the irreducible spacing of the very faith, credit, or belief without which there would be no social bond, no address to the other."[21] It follows that one cannot maintain a strict opposition between good and evil, or between sworn faith and perjury. Rather, Derrida argues that "only the infinite possibility of the worst and of perjury can grant the possibility of the Good, of veracity and sworn faith. This possibility remains infinite but as the very possibility of an autoimmune finitude."[22]

Derrida's notion of radical evil thus undermines the religious conception of the good. To recall, Derrida maintains that the common denominator for religions is that they promote *absolute immunity* as the supremely desirable. The good may be threatened from the outside, but in itself it is immune from evil. Derrida's argument is, on the contrary, that the good in itself is not a state of absolute immunity but rather autoimmune. To establish this argument, it is not enough simply to insist on the ever-present *possibility* of evil. Rather, one must show that the good in its *actuality* is already violated by evil, already involved in its own destruction. To be sure, Derrida's formulations often emphasize the *structural possibility* of evil, but in his thinking a structural possibility also entails an *actual necessity*.[23] As I will demonstrate in this essay, the latter argument depends on Derrida's conception of time. Given that the present ceases to be as soon as it comes to be, it attacks its own integrity from the beginning and makes it impossible for anything to be unscathed. This is why Derrida maintains that autoimmunity is located "in the very structure of the present and of life."[24] In order to survive—even for a moment—a life cannot have any integrity as such but is already marked by the alteration of time. Even if all external threats are evaded, the good still bears its own destruction within itself. The vulnerability of the good is thus *without limit*, since the source of attack is also located within what is defended.

What needs to be clarified, then, is why and how autoimmunity follows from the constitution of time. Derrida's notion of "the trace" here provides the answer. Derrida defines the structure of the trace as the becoming-space of time and the becoming-time of space, which he abbreviates as spacing (*espacement*). This structure should not itself be understood as a *temporal* process, where time becomes space and space becomes time, but rather designates a *logical* co-implication of time and space.[25] For one moment to be succeeded by another it cannot *first* be present in itself and *then* cease to be. Rather, every temporal moment negates itself—it ceases to be as soon as it comes to be—and must therefore be inscribed as a trace in order to be at all. The trace is necessarily spatial, since spatiality is characterized by the ability to persist in spite of temporal succession. The spatiality of the trace is thus the condition for the duration of time, since it enables the past to be retained for the future. The very concept of duration presupposes that something remains across time and only that which is spatial can remain. The spatiality of the trace, however, is itself temporal. Without temporalization it would be impossible for a trace to remain across time and retain the past for the future. Accordingly, the duration of the trace cannot be exempt from the negativity of time. The trace enables the past to survive, but it can do so only through the exposure to a future that gives it both the chance to remain and to be effaced.

The structure of the trace thereby accounts for the autoimmunity of survival. As the condition of possibility for retaining the past, the trace is also the condition of possibility for life to resist death in a movement of survival. The trace can only live on, however, through a process of erasure and thus breaches the integrity of any immune system from the beginning. The tracing of time that makes it *possible* for life to survive at the same time makes it *impossible* for life to be given or protected in itself. The autoimmunity that follows from the tracing of time is what Derrida calls the structure of the event. It is this structure that, according to Derrida, is *unconditional*, in the sense that it is the condition for anything to happen. As he puts it: "Without autoimmunity, with absolute immunity, nothing would ever happen."[26]

Following the logic of autoimmunity, Derrida argues that life is necessarily open to death, good necessarily open to evil, peace necessarily open to violence. Inversely, an absolute life that is immune to death, an absolute peace that is immune to violence, or an absolute goodness that is immune to evil, is for Derrida the same as an absolute death, an absolute violence, or an absolute evil.[27] Derrida thus calls into question the very *desirability* of the religious ideal of the unscathed. An absolute immunity would close all openness to alterity, all openness to the unpredictable coming of time, and thereby close the possibility of living on.

The above logic is at the heart of what I call Derrida's radical atheism. In short, radical atheism seeks to demonstrate that the temporal finitude of living on is not a lack of being that it would be desirable to overcome. Rather, temporal finitude is integral to why one cares about life in the first place. Without the exposure to loss, there would be no reason to care for something—and no need to sustain a given existence—since there would be no risk that could motivate the act of taking care. Furthermore, the precarious experience of time (of ceasing to be) is not only the negative condition of loss but also the *positive* condition of coming into being and living on. Inversely, an eternal state of being would terminate the possibility of generation, sustenance, and care, since it would eliminate the condition of time.

Accordingly, I distinguish between the desire for *immortality* (an eternal state of being) and the desire for *survival* (a temporal process of living on). To be clear, the desire for survival is *not* reducible to a biological drive for self-preservation. Rather, it includes even the most altruistic commitments to living on in time. If I give my life for someone else, it is because I value his or her life and want it to continue. Similarly, if I sacrifice my life for a cause or an idea, it is because I believe in its importance and want the cause or the idea to be carried on—to be sustained—in history. The desire for survival is thus the condition not only for concern with one's own existence but also for concern with questions of existence that transcend oneself, such as the question of justice. It is because one is invested in the survival of someone or something that one is compelled to fight for the memory of the past or for a better future. Indeed, without the desire for survival one would never be engaged or committed, since one would not care about anything that has happened or anything that may happen.

The desire for survival, then, is at the root of the care for life and the fear of death. This desire for the continuation of temporal life is incompatible with the desire for an eternal state of being. If I seek to prolong my life or the life of another, I seek to transcend the limits of a particular time—to live on—but I do not seek to transcend the condition of time altogether. Far from fulfilling the desire to live on, a timeless state of eternity would eliminate the temporal life I want to maintain. Thus, if one is invested in the survival of temporal life, the eternal state of immortality is not only unattainable but also *undesirable*, since it would terminate the possibility for anything to happen and anyone to live on.

Caputo responds that the above argument does not deliver "an *a priori* argument *against* the existence of God" and does not disprove the existence of eternity, since the fact that nothing happens and nothing survives in eternity "is not an objection to eternity; it is the definition of eternity."[28] This would indeed be a problem for radical atheism if the latter sought to refute the *existence* of God and eternity along the lines of the "negative ontological argument" that Caputo ascribes to me. Radical atheism, however, does not dispute the existence but rather the *desirability* of God and eternity. The state of eternity that traditional theology holds out as "the best" (absolute life, absolute peace) is on Derrida's account "the worst" (absolute death, absolute violence). Whether or not such a state can exist is not decided by radical atheism and nothing in the argument depends on deciding it. The point is rather to show that being in a state of eternity would require that one renounce all care and become completely indifferent to the fate of survival. That is why it is consistent to emphasize (as many religious sages do) that *detachment* from temporal life is the condition for attaining the state of eternity. Only by ultimately detaching oneself from the care for temporal life can one embrace the timelessness of eternity. The radical atheist argument, however, is that such an ideal of detachment dissimulates a preceding *attachment* to temporal life: an attachment that is the source of all care for oneself, for others, and for the world.

Now, Caputo too recognizes that Derrida "describes the irreducible condition of our lives, the inescapable circumstance of living always already under these conditions of archi-spacing."[29] Yet for Caputo there is another type of unconditional that is held out as a "promise" or a "dream."[30] "Derrida is dreaming of something unconditional," he writes, "something for which the current conditions of being are no match, something that belongs to another order."[31] The conditional and the unconditional would thus belong to two different "orders." This is the matrix for what I consider Caputo's misreading of Derrida. Far from being a relation between two different orders, the relation between the conditional and the unconditional is for Derrida an autoimmune relation. Inscribed within the conditions for any given X is the unconditional spacing of time that compromises the integrity of X and undermines the very ideal of absolute immunity. Accordingly, Derrida emphasizes that the unconditional spacing of time "will never have entered religion and will never permit itself to be sacralized, sanctified, humanized, theologized. . . . Radically heterogeneous to the safe and sound, the holy and the sacred, it never admits of any *indemnification*" and is "neither Being, nor the Good, nor God."[32]

In contrast, Caputo aligns Derrida's notion of the unconditional with the name of God, which he glosses as the name of "unconditional love . . . the name of everything we hope for in the future, the name of the one who is coming, or coming again, to save us, to establish a reign of messianic peace, the name of the kingdom to come, of the justice that is coming to lift us up in its arms and embrace us like a mother holding her child."[33] To be sure, Caputo does not claim that such unconditional love, messianic peace, or absolute justice actually exists; they are rather a "promise" and a "dream" that we can never actualize. Yet it is precisely the dream of something beyond the condition of autoimmunity that Derrida calls into question. Atheism has traditionally focused on denying the existence of absolute immunity, without questioning that we desire and dream of it. In contrast, radical atheism seeks to elucidate that what we desire and dream of is itself inhabited by autoimmunity. Whatever I "invite" into my life—whatever I welcome or desire—opens me to the visitation of an other who can destroy my life and turn my dream into a nightmare. But without the possibility of such visitation there would be no one to invite and nothing to desire. No one could come and nothing could happen, since life only can live on through the exposure to a future that opens the chance of survival and the threat of termination in the same stroke. As Derrida emphasizes, "threat is chance, chance is threat—this law is absolutely undeniable and irreducible."[34]

It is thus instructive to consider what Derrida means by the desire for the impossible, which Caputo holds to be the common denominator between deconstruction and religion, whereas I argue that it is the core of Derrida's radical atheism. According to Caputo, "the impossible, being impassioned by the impossible, is the religious, is religious passion," since "our hearts are burning with the desire to go where we cannot go, to the impossible."[35] It is easy to see how misleading this argument is once we realize that the impossible for Derrida is not somewhere we can never go—or something we can never reach—but rather where we always find ourselves to be. The impossible is what happens all the time, since it designates *the impossibility of being in itself* that is the condition of temporality. As Derrida explains, the impossible is "the exposure to what comes or happens. It is the exposure (the desire, the openness, but also the fear) that opens, that opens itself, that opens us to time, to what comes upon us, to what arrives or happens, to the event."[36] That we desire the impossible, then, does not mean that we desire something above or beyond the possible. On the contrary, it means that what we desire is constituted by temporal finitude, which makes it impossible for it to be in itself. This impossibility of being in itself has traditionally been regarded as a negative predicament that we desire to overcome. Derrida's argument, however, is that the impossibility of being in itself is *not* a negative predicament. Rather, the impossibility of being in itself opens *the chance*—the positive possibility—of the desirable. As Derrida puts it in a compact formula: "What makes possible makes impossible the very thing that it makes possible and introduces—as its chance—a non-negative chance, a principle of ruin into the very thing it promises or promotes."[37] Hence, there is no opposition between the possible and the impossible. The impossibility of being in itself makes it possible for anything to happen. Inversely, if the impossible were to become possible everything would become impossible, since nothing could happen.

For Caputo, on the contrary, that we desire the impossible means that we desire or "dream" of the kingdom of God, where the impossible would become possible. Over and over again in his writings on Derrida, Caputo invokes the claim from the New Testament that "for God all things are possible." Or as Caputo himself explains: "To the way things happen when God rules, where with God nothing is impossible, I link what Derrida calls 'the impossible.'"[38] The fact that Caputo is not making a claim about the existence of God or the properties of God—that he is writing a "poetics" and not a metaphysics of the impossible, as he stresses in response to my critique—does not make any essential difference, since his poetics and the conception of the good that informs it is incompatible with what Derrida means by the impossible. Thus, Caputo claims that "deconstruction means the rule of the gift, of the good, of justice, of hospitality."[39] Caputo here inserts "the good" as a term equivalent to Derrida's notions of the gift, justice, and hospitality—despite the fact that Derrida never aligns any of these terms with the good. Indeed, the exposure to alterity that Derrida analyzes as constitutive of the gift, justice, and hospitality is not characterized by goodness but rather by what he describes as radical evil.

Nevertheless, in responding to my work, Caputo claims that his arguments are compatible with a deconstruction of the notion of the good and that his book *The Weakness of God* could even have been named *The Radical Evil of God*, "meaning the structural possibility of evil inscribed in the name of God."[40] Yet, if we examine how Caputo articulates the logic of radical evil, we can see that it continues to privilege a notion of the good that is aligned with God. While Caputo relinquishes the idea of God as omnipotent and as the creator of the world, he retains God as the name of the good. Thus, on Caputo's reading, the act of God's creation is not a movement *ex nihilo* from nonbeing to being; it is rather a movement from being to the good. As Caputo puts it, God is not the reason that things exist but "the reason that things are *good*," since it is God who "calls them *to* the good, when he breathes the life of the good over them . . . beckoning us beyond being to the good."[41] To be clear, I do not assume that Caputo literally believes in the *existence* of a God who created the good; what is important is rather the priority of the good that informs the fable of God in his theological "poetics." Given that Caputo's God is not a "strong" one, he is powerless to prevent his call for goodness from being corrupted by humans and nature, but the "weakness" of God does not make him liable to be or to do evil. On the contrary, Caputo argues that it is the very weakness of God that exonerates him from evil: "God is not to be blamed for the evils of a world God created good. God is supposed to give humankind direction, hope, and meaning . . . but not to be causally responsible for every last thing that happens."[42]

Accordingly, Caputo claims that "life has an inviolability about it, a sacredness that it is the role of the name of God to confer and confirm," whereas "the problem of evil is in part human malice, which is as old as Cain" and "in part the vagaries of disease and natural disasters."[43] Thus, while granting that the good may always be corrupted (and that the possibility of corruption is a necessary one), Caputo holds out the name of God as the name of an "unconditional love," which is "unconditionally affirmed and unconditionally promised" in the story of God's creation and in "his promise that everything he has made, *come what may*, is good."[44] The fact that what comes turns out to break the promise—"Then Cain murders Abel and the bloody course of history is launched"[45]—does not alter the fact that the *promise* of the good is primary for Caputo.

That Caputo assumes the primacy of the good is further evident from the way he construes the relation between promise and threat. On Caputo's account, the promise is a promise of the good and the threat is that the promise may be broken or betrayed (as when Cain murders Abel). Thus, even when Caputo tries to show that he has understood Derrida's notion of the promise by emphasizing that "promises are made in the face of a threat; threats threaten what we are promised,"[46] his very formulations confirm what I consider his misunderstanding, since he construes the threat as external rather than internal to the promise. For Caputo, it is axiomatic that *if the promise were kept it would be good*, so the threat is that the promise may *not* be kept. In contrast, Derrida argues that the promise is not a promise of something that is inherently good. Indeed, as I emphasize in *Radical Atheism*,

> it is precisely the axiomatic distinction between promise and threat that Derrida calls into question by aligning every act with the structure of the promise. It follows that even when I threaten to rob or kill, I am making a promise. Hence, the threat that is intrinsic to the structure of the promise does not only consist in that the promise may be broken, but can also consist in that the promise may be kept. Derrida epitomizes the interdependence of promise and threat in his claim that "the threat is not something that comes from the outside to place itself next to the promise." Rather, "the threat is the promise itself, or better, threat and promise always come together *as* the promise. This does not mean just that the promise is always already threatened; it also means that the promise is *threatening*."[47]

To break or betray a given promise may therefore be better than keeping it. Caputo disregards this logic of the promise, since the priority of the good structures not only his weak theology but also his reading of Derrida.

Let me here take a concrete example by returning to the problem of hospitality. Consistent with the general logic of his reading, Caputo links Derrida's notion of unconditional hospitality to the kingdom of God, which he glosses as "a city without walls, a nation without borders, unconditional hospitality."[48] If we wonder how such hospitality could be possible, Caputo reminds us that we are talking about the kingdom of God where the impossible is possible: "Remember that in the kingdom God rules, not the world, which means that there the human, all too human rules of entrance requirements, etiquette, and human hospitality hold no sway."[49] Caputo thereby *opposes* unconditional hospitality to conditional hospitality in a way that is at odds with Derrida's thinking. For Derrida, unconditional hospitality is not something that we are prevented from achieving because of our human limitations but rather something to which we cannot avoid being subjected. As Derrida underlines, *nothing happens* without unconditional hospitality. Unconditional hospitality is thus another name for the exposure to temporal alterity, which opens one both to what is desired and what is feared. Indeed, in a striking passage, Derrida links unconditional hospitality to the susceptibility of being "violated and raped, stolen . . . precisely where one is not ready to receive."[50] This should surely make us pause. Derrida is *not* saying that we should let ourselves be overtaken and remain unprepared for what may happen; he is saying that such passive exposure to the other, such dependence on others who may turn out to violate us, is at work in everything we do, whatever we do, and that we need to take this structural necessity into account to understand the exigencies of hospitality. If we maintain, on the contrary, that there is an axiomatic "injunction" to be unconditionally hospitable—for example, by claiming that we should "put ourselves at risk *as far as possible* in forgiveness or hospitality"[51]—we are at best operating with a pious assumption that the other is good and at worst advocating an ethics of submission, where the self should give itself over to the other even at the expense of being brutally violated or stolen.[52]

Caputo used to rely on the first alternative, claiming that the other is always "the victim, not the producer of the victim. It would never be the case that the 'other' to come would be Charles Manson, or some plunderer or rapist."[53] Responding to my critique, Caputo seems to have realized that this was an untenable argument and concedes that the other who comes can turn out to be a victimizer just as well as a victim. Given that he nevertheless wants to hold on to the imperative that we should expose ourselves as much as possible to "unknown and menacing others,"[54] the only alternative that remains is an ethics or politics of submission, where we should renounce calculation, conditions, and protection in order not to resist the open future. Indeed, for all his talk of responsibility, Caputo never seems to think of it in terms of having responsibility for a determinate other who is under threat. If he did, it would quickly become apparent that one cannot *a priori* advocate the value of exposure over the value of protection.

Caputo nevertheless tries to defend his argument by insisting that the "axiom" of deconstruction is *"always and everywhere to keep the future open."*[55] Caputo himself, however, goes on to concede that "starting out from our irreducible exposure to an unpredictable future, which is irreducibly pre-given, Derrida's next step is to ask how we are going to respond to the *claim* that is made upon us by the future."[56] For Caputo's argument to work, he would therefore have to show that there is something in the very claim made upon us by the future that "calls" us *always to be more open* rather than less, *always to expose ourselves more* rather than less. Whatever such an unequivocal call may be—and however Caputo may claim to have heard it—it would by definition deny the undecidability of the future and the responsibility of deciding whether or not one should be more or less open.[57]

That I insist on this point does not mean that I think deconstruction is a purely descriptive, value-free enterprise that does not engage in performative acts of commitment. I do not "neutralize" the coming of the other, "silence" the call of the unconditional, or deny "the unconditional *claim* of the future *upon* the moment."[58] Rather, I argue that a number of influential readers of Derrida, Caputo included, have misconstrued the relation between the unconditional and the conditional. What is "called" for by the unconditional is not something unconditional (e.g., unconditional love) but rather acts of engagement and performative commitments that are *conditional* responses to an unconditional exposure. That performative acts are conditional does not mean that they are determined in advance but that they are dependent on a context that is essentially vulnerable to change. This unconditional exposure may always alter or undermine the meaning of the performative and is therefore not reducible to it.

The relation between performative commitment and nonperformative exposure should thus be understood as *inseparable yet distinguishable*, or "heterogeneous and indissociable" to use a phrase that Derrida often employs. On the one hand, there is no unconditional and nonperformative "exposure" without a conditional being who is engaged in performative acts of commitment. On the other hand, while one cannot occur without the other, one can nevertheless make a logical distinction between the two.[59] Accordingly, Derrida insists that there is a "nonperformative exposure" to what happens, which he dissociates from the notion of an "imperative injunction (call or performative)."[60] Following Derrida's emphatic distinction, there is,

> on the one hand, a paradoxical experience of the performative of the promise (but also of the threat at the heart of the promise) that organizes every speech act, every other performative, and even every preverbal experience of the relation to the other; and, on the other hand, at the point of intersection with this threatening promise, the horizon of awaiting [attente] that informs our relationship to time—to the event, to that which happens [ce qui arrive], to the one who arrives [l'arrivant], and to the other. Involved this time, however, would be a waiting without waiting, a waiting whose horizon is, as it were, punctured by the event (which is waited for without being awaited).[61]

It is precisely this structure of the event—"what comes about in an unforeseeable and singular manner"—that Derrida describes in terms of a nonperformative exposure.[62] Derrida even provocatively emphasizes that the unconditional exposure to the event "couldn't care less about the performative."[63] The unconditional is thus the spacing of time that is not reducible to a performative commitment, since it is the condition for all performative acts, and it cannot be embraced as something good in itself, since it is the source of every chance and every threat. For the same reason, there is not another type of unconditional that is called for and that calls us to action (as Caputo claims). Rather, the unconditional exposure to time is inseparable from ("calls for") conditional, performative responses that seek to discriminate between the chance and the threat. As Derrida clearly underlines, the exposure to the event—an "exposure without horizon, and therefore an irreducible amalgamation of desire and anguish, affirmation and fear, promise and threat"—is "the condition of praxis, decision, action and responsibility."[64]

When Derrida analyzes the "unconditional" in conjunction with highly valorized terms, such as hospitality and justice, he is therefore not invoking an unconditional good. On the contrary, he seeks to demonstrate that the unconditional spacing of time is inscribed within the conditions for even the most ideal hospitality or justice. Justice and hospitality require conditional laws but at the same time they cannot be reduced to a rule for how the law should be applied. The demand for justice or hospitality is always raised in relation to singular events—for which there is no guarantee that the given laws are adequate—thereby opening the laws to being questioned, transformed, or eliminated. Derrida can thus claim that conditional laws of hospitality and justice are guided and inspired, as well as given meaning and practical rationality, by the unconditional. The point is that there would be no need for conditional laws or performative commitments without the exposure to unpredictable events. This unconditional exposure is both what gives practical rationality to conditional laws and what inspires one to defend or to challenge them, depending on the situation.

What is at stake in the distinction between the conditional and the unconditional is thus a distinction that makes explicit what is implicit in reckoning with the temporality of everything to which we are committed. As Derrida emphasizes, it is *because* one is exposed to the incalculable that it is necessary to calculate and it is *because* one is exposed to an undecidable future that it is necessary to make decisions. These conditional responses are in turn unconditionally haunted by the relation to the undecidable that remains in and through any decision. It is not only that I cannot calculate what others will do to me; I cannot finally calculate what my own decisions will do to me, since they bind me to a future that exceeds my intentions, and in this sense I am affected by my own decisions as by the decisions of an other. To insist on this condition is not to deny or neutralize the responsibility for the future, but to elucidate the inherent exigencies of such responsibility. The openness to the future is unconditional in the sense that one is necessarily open to the future, but it is not unconditional in the sense of an axiom that establishes that more openness is always better than less.[65]

The deconstructive analysis of responsibility, then, does not choose between openness and closure. Rather, it analyzes the co-implication of these apparent opposites and the autoimmunity that follows from it. As Derrida argues in *The Gift of Death*, "I cannot respond to the call, the demand, the obligation, or even the love of another without sacrificing the other other, the other others."[66] The violence of exclusion is thus inscribed *in the very act of taking responsibility* and by extension in every act of doing justice or offering hospitality. Whenever I devote myself to another, I turn away from other others and thus exercise a violent discrimination.

Derrida's argument in *The Gift of Death* thereby allows us to press home the implications of radical evil. The point is not only that what I valorize as good can turn out to be bad or that the deed I hold to be good can turn out to be evil. The point is also that *even when I do good*—even when I devote myself to someone in a loving or generous way—*I necessarily do evil*, since my very act of devotion is an act of exclusion. This notion of radical evil does not seek to justify violence or to reduce all forms of violence to the same. On the contrary, it seeks to elucidate that we are *always* negotiating violence and that our ideals of justice cannot be immune from contestation and struggle. Every ideal of justice is rather inscribed in what Derrida calls an "economy of violence."[67]

Whatever we do, then, we are inscribed in an economy of violence where matters are urgent precisely because everything we do makes a difference for better or worse. It is in this economy of violence that Derrida locates the passion for and the struggle to achieve justice. While struggles for justice are often pursued in the name of absolute justice, these claims can always be shown to be incoherent and hypocritical. There is no call for justice that does not call for the exclusion of others, which means that every call for justice can be challenged and criticized. The point of this argument is not to discredit calls for justice, but to recognize that these calls are always already inscribed in an economy of violence.

We can thus finally elucidate what Derrida means by "the messianic." More than any other term in Derrida's vocabulary, the messianic has invited the misconception that he promotes a hope for religious salvation. Such readings are due to misunderstanding Derrida's distinction between the messianic and every form of "messianism." In Derrida's vocabulary the messianic is another name for the relation to the undecidable future, which opens the chance for what is desired but at the same time threatens it from within, since it is constituted by temporal finitude. In contrast, messianism is the religious or political faith in a future that will come and put an end to time, replacing it with a perpetual peace that nothing can come to disrupt.

Consequently, Derrida emphasizes that what he calls the messianic is without messianism and without religion. Rather, Derrida seeks to unearth an "atheological heritage of the messianic," as he puts it in *Specters of Marx*.[68] The messianic is here linked to the promise of justice, which is directed both toward the past (as a promise to remember victims of injustice) and toward the future (as a promise to bring about justice). This messianic promise of justice does not express a hope for timeless peace. On the contrary, it is animated by a commitment to living on and by the exposure to a perilous future. Without the commitment to living on, one would never be motivated to keep the memory of the past or to seek justice in the future. And without the exposure to a perilous future, there would be nothing to do justice to or take responsibility for, since nothing could happen that would make justice or responsibility a matter of concern.

The commitment to survival is never innocent, however, since one always lives on at the expense of what does *not* live on. To maintain the memory and life of certain others is thus to exclude or violate other others. This necessity of discrimination is what Derrida calls the "law of finitude, law of decision and responsibility for finite existences, the only living-mortals for whom a decision, a choice, a responsibility has meaning and a meaning that will have to pass through the ordeal of the undecidable."[69]

Thus, the resistance to forgetting that is the exercise of justice is also "the place of all violences. Because if it is just to remember the future and the injunction to remember, namely the archontic injunction to guard and to gather the archive, it is no less just to remember the others, the other others and the others in oneself."[70] As a consequence, "I shall no doubt be unjust out of a concern for justice,"[71] since the memory of some entails the forgetting of others.

Hence, what Derrida analyzes as the passion for justice cannot be opposed to the violence of exclusion and the autoimmunity that opens the future cannot be opposed to the immunization that is indispensable for the formation of an identity or community. As Derrida puts it in "Faith and Knowledge," "no community is possible that would not cultivate its own autoimmunity, a principle of sacrificial self-destruction ruining the principle of self-protection (that of maintaining its self-integrity intact), and this in view of some sort of invisible and spectral survival."[72] This spectral survival can inspire both the protection and the violation of a given integrity: an integrity that one may want to defend, transform, or undermine, depending on the context. In every case, however, the survival of life depends on the sacrifice of what does *not* survive and is thereby haunted (compromised in its very integrity) by what is left behind or killed off so that something else may survive. If one survived wholly intact—unscathed by the alteration of time—one would not be surviving; one would be reposing in absolute presence. Sacrificial self-destruction in view of survival is therefore a structural necessity because it "keeps the autoimmune community alive, which is to say, open to something other and more than itself: the other, the future, death, freedom, the coming or the love of the other, the space and time of a spectralizing messianicity beyond all messianism."[73]

Now, in responding to *Radical Atheism*, Caputo claims that he too reads Derrida in terms of a passion for the life-death of survival. Yet if Caputo were to draw the consequences of such passion, he would have to abandon not only the opposition between openness and closure that underpins his notion of responsibility but also the messianic notion of peace that underpins his reading of Derrida's "religion." According to Caputo, the messianic is "where we touch upon the heart of Derrida's religion," which Caputo describes as a call for "a just one to come, a call for peace."[74] Caputo even insists that "the meaning of the messianic is, or should be, *shalom, pax*."[75] This messianic promise of peace is, according to Caputo, perverted by concrete religions insofar as they confine the messianic promise within the borders of a *people* and thereby excludes others. In contrast, Caputo promotes "a dream of justice for *all* of God's children—that is the religion that emerges from an hour on the couch with deconstruction. That religion is good news, for the oppressed and everybody else."[76] For Caputo, Derrida's notion of the messianic thus avoids the violence of determinate religion in favor of the indeterminacy of a messianic promise that opens the kingdom of God to everyone. In this kingdom, Caputo tells us, "everyone is welcomed with a jubilant divine indiscriminacy," since no one is excluded.[77]

Such a reading of the messianic is incompatible with Derrida's understanding of the term. It is true that Derrida describes the messianic as a "universal" structure of experience, but it has nothing to do with welcoming everyone in universal openness. On the contrary, the universal structure of the messianic is the exposure to an undecidable future, which entails that "the other and death—and radical evil—can come as a surprise at any moment."[78] Accordingly, Derrida maintains that the messianic may be "a fear, an unbearable terror—hence the hatred of what is thus awaited."[79] Far from promising peace, the messianic is the opening to a future that is the source of all hope but also of all fear and hatred, since it entails that the desired other can always be or become a menace. As Derrida argues, one cannot desire the coming of the future "without simultaneously fearing it," since it can "bring nothing but threat and chance at the same time."[80]

Derrida thus undermines the common denominator for religious notions of the messianic, namely, the idea that someone could come who would be immune from becoming evil. Derrida's argument is not only that such absolute immunity is impossible to actualize but also that it is not desirable, since it would cancel out the chance of the good in canceling out the threat of evil. Furthermore, without the threat that is intrinsic to the chance, one would not care about the chance in the first place. If things were fully present in themselves—if they were not haunted by alteration and loss—there would be no reason to care about them, since nothing could happen to them. The messianic is therefore *not* an endless waiting for something that never comes but *the structure of faith in the here and now*. It is *because* everything we value is threatened from within that we care about it and seek to make it come or to make it stay after it has arrived. It follows that faith is not only predicated on but also animated and sustained by the autoimmunity of survival. In order to care and to commit ourselves, we have to believe in the future not only as a chance but also as a threat.

Derrida's notion of the messianic thus articulates the logic of what I call radical atheism. A radical atheism does not simply denounce messianic hope as an illusion. Rather, it seeks to show that messianic hope does not stem from a hope for the absolute immunity of salvation but rather from a hope for autoimmune survival. Derrida himself outlined the basic premise for this argument in a talk ("Penser ce qui vient") that was presented in 1994 but not published until 2007, when *Radical Atheism* was in press. Derrida here maintains that he, "like everyone else" ("comme tout le monde"), is radically atheist ("radicalement athée"). Such radical atheism is not a matter of "personal convictions, opinions, or ideologies that could be shared by some and not by others"; it is rather a "structural atheism" that "characterizes a priori every relation to whoever comes or whatever happens."[81] Derrida thus suggests, most provocatively, a research program that runs counter to the post-secular approaches that have dominated the reception of his work on religion. Rather than reading secular concepts and secular experiences as secularized versions of theological origins, the task would be to read theological concepts and theological experiences as theologized versions of an originary and irreducible atheism.

The logic of radical atheism, then, allows not only for a critique of religion but also for a critique of traditional critiques of religion. Rather than a priori dismissing political struggles that are fought in the name of religious ideals as deluded, the logic of radical atheism allows us to see that these struggles, too, depend on a faith in and hope for survival. Thus, radical atheism does not simply renounce struggles for health or denounce hopes for safety, even if they are religiously coded. Rather, radical atheism seeks to demonstrate that these struggles and hopes are not concerned with the absolute immunity that is promoted as the religious ideal. The struggle for health and the hope for safety are not motivated by a commitment to the unscathed but by a commitment to living on.

Given the autoimmunity of survival such commitments may generate all forms of violence, and there are certainly good reasons to analyze the ways in which religious practices are complicit with forms of violence that one may want to transform or seek to eliminate. To assume that a secular struggle is always preferable over one pursued in the name of religion, however, is to adopt a form of paternalism that depoliticizes religion and the question of religion. There are any number of situations where the given structure of a society may make religious discourse the most powerful tool for mobilizing a struggle against injustice. Moreover, if we seek to show the extent to which social struggles are concerned with material injustice rather than with the religious ends to which they may profess allegiance—that is, if we seek to politicize social struggles—we presuppose the radical atheist conception of desire, according to which struggles for justice are animated and sustained by a hope for living on rather than by an aspiration toward the absolute immunity of the unscathed. Whether a given struggle should be supported or resisted is a different question, which cannot be answered through deconstructive analysis and requires concrete political engagement. Indeed, it is precisely by *not* providing an ethical or political principle that deconstruction politicizes our actions and insists on a responsibility from which one cannot be absolved.

Derrida and Messianic Atheism

RICHARD KEARNEY

Derrida has famously declared that he "rightly passes for an atheist." But what kind of atheism is he talking about? Anti-theistic? Pre-theistic? Post-theistic? Ana-theistic? Agnostic? Mystical? Messianic? This is a question I will explore here with particular, if not exclusive, emphasis on the last of these options—the *messianic*.

The specter of messianic atheism was first raised by the Jewish philosopher, Emmanuel Levinas, in *Totality and Infinity* (1961). Derrida's critical reckoning with Levinas in his essay "Violence and Metaphysics" (1964) did not prevent him from acknowledging a profound debt to his mentor in a number of subsequent works but especially in his obituary homage, *Adieu à Emmanuel Levinas* (1997). While Derrida does not privilege a specifically Jewish reading of Abrahamic messianism (he prefers, as we shall see, the quasi-transcendental term "messianicity"), with the publication of his autobiographical *Circumfession* in 1991 Derrida speaks increasingly of this aspect of his thought. He describes himself here as "*le dernier des juifs*" and recalls how he was expelled from school in Algiers because of the anti-Semitic laws of the Vichy government. He also admits that when he laments de profundis, in quasi-Augustinian "prayers and tears," he does so in the language of his religious "tradition." And he further reflects on the radical implications of the Jewish Holocaust in essays such as *Cendres* (1991) and *Shibboleth: For Paul Celan* (1986).

But none of this, let us be clear at the outset, amounts to a suggestion that Derrida is confessing any form of theism (Jewish or otherwise). One can pray in the dark without believing there is anyone to pray to. One can call without believing there is anyone listening. But in spite of his candid statement that he "passes for an atheist," Derrida's confessional gestures, captured in the ambidextrous title of *Circumfession*, betray some indelible mark of Jewish circumcision on his flesh. And this, I suspect, is not irrelevant when it comes to his later discussions of messianicity and messianism.[1]

Before proceeding to a more detailed analysis of what Derrida means by atheism, let me say a few more words about how his teacher, Levinas, addressed the relationship between atheism and messianism in *Totality and Infinity* (1961). In the wake of the Holocaust, when he lost members of his family, Levinas spoke of the necessity to reject the triumphal God of power who could allow these horrors.[2] Against all forms of theodicy, Levinas spoke of atheism as a salutary distancing from idolatrous fusion with the Totality of Being, a separation whereby each person discovers his or her own radical interiority as a self, an "I." This is the basis of autonomy and responsibility:

> One can call atheism this separation so complete that the separated being maintains itself in existence all by itself, without participating in the Being from which it is separated. . . . The break with participation is implied in this capability. One lives outside of God, at home with oneself; one is an I.[3]

And he goes on:

> The soul, the dimension of the psychic, being an accomplishment of separation, is naturally atheist. By atheism we thus understand a position prior to both the negation and the affirmation of the divine, the breaking with participation by which the I posits itself as the same and as I.[4]

Without this movement of atheistic separateness, the other as irreducibly alien could not be recognized as *other*. And that, for Levinas, would rule out the possibility of a genuinely religious relationship with God understood as absolute Other. We must, Levinas concludes accordingly, be *contre-dieu* before we can be *à-dieu*—in the double sense of taking leave from the old God (*ab-deo*) as we turn toward a God "always still to come" (*ad-deum*). By means of this double A (*ab* of away and *ad* of toward), we reopen our "home" to the radically alien. This we may call ana-theism, though Levinas himself does not use the term. A twofold movement that moves from a first a-theist moment of selfhood to a second ana-theist moment of exposure to the exteriority of the stranger: "Only if it starts from me as a separated being and goes as a host to the Other, welcoming the Other as guest, only in this manner can an eternal return within the interiority of the circle of being be escaped. For when I turn to the Other, interiority turns into exteriority."[5] It is in this context that Levinas holds that one of the greatest gifts of Judaism to humanity is atheism—namely, separation from the God of Totality so as to encounter the other as absolutely Other.

This reading of atheism is not lost on Derrida, even if he does not take Levinas's further step to an eschatological God of vertical transcendence beyond traditional theism. Let us now try to see why.

One of Derrida's most arresting contributions to the theism/atheism debate comes, in my view, in a late essay, "Sauf le Nom" (1993). Here he speaks of how we may save the divine "name" by *refusing* to determine its content. This abstentionist gesture, this discretion about naming the divine, borders on a certain style of atheism, a way of saving the name of God by not naming God at all. But we are not dealing here with antitheism, that is, with militant anti-God talk, anymore than we are dealing with subtle apologetics for apophatic theology (namely, what we *cannot* say about God while believing in God). Derrida seems, in fact, to be excavating a space for what might be called "mystical atheism." And, while he does not, to my knowledge, actually use the term, he does point to a curious reversibility between mysticism and atheism. He calls our attention to a moment of radical receptivity that he terms messianic—a moment when one abandons all inherited certainties, assumptions, and expectations (including religious ones) in order to open oneself to the radical surprise, and trauma, of the incoming Other.

In "Sauf le Nom"—meaning both "saving and exempting the divine name"—Derrida goes so far as to suggest that a genuine desire for God presupposes a certain vacillation between atheism and theism. "The desire of God, God as the other name of desire," he writes, "deals in the desert with radical atheism." And he adds:

> The most consequent forms of declared atheism will have always testified to the most intense desire for God. . . . Like mysticism, apophatic discourse has always been suspected of atheism. . . . If atheism, like apophatic theology, testifies to the desire of God . . . in the presence of *whom* does it do so?[6]

Indeed, we may echo Derrida's question: Who *is* this *whom*? While still passing for an atheist, Derrida has been said by some to be offering a post-Holocaust translation of Meister Eckhart's prayer to God to rid him of

God. Unless we let go of God as property and possession, we cannot experience that "desire beyond desire" for the Other as radical stranger. The felt absence of the old God of metaphysical sovereignty ushers in a gap, a rent, a sense of emptiness that may provoke a new desire, an unquenchable longing for the advent of the Other—the uninvited divine guest to come. But while Derrida allows for a messianicity of endless *différance*—deferral and waiting, vigilance and desire—he does not himself take a second step beyond the dichotomy of theism and atheism to a third option—what I call the ana-theist wager:[7] The retrieval of God "after" God. But I will return to this in my concluding remarks.

Derrida's deconstructive ascesis of traditional religions ultimately calls for a "religion without religion," a faith without faith that can scarce give a name to God at all. More precisely, he embraces a notion of "messianicity" beyond the concrete, historical "messianisms" of the Abrahamic (and other) traditions. Such messianicity serves less as a sacred, incarnate presence in the world than as a quasi-transcendental structure for the condition of possibility (impossibility) of religion in general. This messianicity involves an endless waiting with no sense of what kind of Other might arrive. It is an unconditional "yes" to what is always still to come.

In *Of Hospitality* (1997), Derrida defines pure hospitality in terms of an undecidable openness to the incoming stranger, whoever it may be. "I say 'come,' 'enter' whoever you are, and whatever your name, your language, your sex, your species may be, be you human, animal or divine."[8] And Derrida goes further in his 1998 Dublin dialogue, "Hospitality, Justice and Responsibility"; here he speaks, perhaps hyperbolically, of absolute hospitality as a radical welcome to the absolute other without name or face. For pure hospitality to occur, he says, "there must be absolute surprise . . . an opening without horizon of expectation . . . to the newcomer whoever that may be."[9] And he continues, reopening the question of the unpredictable stranger, the uninvited guest, the unnamable Other—"The newcomer may be good or evil, but if you exclude the possibility that the newcomer is coming to destroy your house, if you want to control this and exclude this terrible possibility in advance, there is no hospitality." The absolute stranger, he concludes, "like the Messiah, must arrive wherever he or she wants."[10] (John Caputo glosses this radical messianicity by describing it as an "impossible, unimaginable, un-foreseeable, un-believable, ab-solute surprise."[11] I would suggest that the most operative term for our present discussion is "un-believable," at least insofar as it refers to a suspension of traditional "theistic" belief.)

Derrida's atheism reaches here, I think, a critical limit. We have no way of reading the face of the incoming stranger as either messiah or murderer because we can only read *in the dark*. There is little or no room for a discernment of spirits. There is, in short, no hermeneutic discrimination possible between holy and unholy ghosts. For deconstruction all messianic "gods" are ghosts (if we are to follow Derrida's logic in *Specters of Marx* [1994]). And Derrida even concedes that we have no way of telling if any newcomer is more than pure hallucination.[12] In other words, there would seem to be no possibility of a *critical hermeneutic reading* of the mystical name as signal of justice or injustice, of love or hate, of peace or war. There is no face behind the name.

We might recall here Dionysius the Areopagite's influential book on mystical theology, *The Divine Names*. The mystical writings of Dionysius and Silesius clearly fascinate Derrida but he does not subscribe to them.[13] These Christian mystics deploy the apophatic ways of "negative theology" to point to a divine transcendence beyond all names. Derrida does not follow them but he does not deny *all* forms of faith. *Some* kind of faith, he insists, is the very structure of human experience—*il faut croire!* Why? Because "there is no such thing as perception" per se, and all readings of the world—of persons, things, works, writings—are readings "in the dark." So it is because we are all blind, in the sense outlined in *Memoirs of the Blind* (1993), that we have no choice but to *believe* in what we cannot *see*. But, I repeat, this inevitable condition of faith does not require theistic faith. By no means. It allows for it, but in no way necessitates it. In short, messianicity, for Derrida, precedes and exceeds all specific religious beliefs as such. It is an a-theistic faith that abstains from any historical instantiation of the divine—a faith devoid of specific names and revelations, narratives and prophecies, liturgies and scriptures.

There are some telling suggestions in Derrida's work of a certain communication—or "contagion"—between a messianic precondition of faith and a messianist religious faith as such; but these suggestions remain tentative and incomplete. For example, in his "Post-Scriptum" to the volume *Derrida and Negative Theology*, entitled "Aporias, Ways and Voices," Derrida seems to acknowledge the possibility of certain crossings between what he terms the abyssal "khora" of deconstruction and the abyssal "God" of mysticism.[14] With regard to khora, he develops the radically deconstructive potency of the term, first intimated in Plato's *Timaeus*, to signal an indefinable, indistinct matrix that precedes all metaphysical dualisms into form and matter, sensible and intelligible, divine and human, etc. His question then becomes how this a-theist khora might relate to God. Focusing particularly on the Christian mystic, Angelus Silesius, Derrida offers this sympathetic reading of the Silesius's faith: "'God' 'is' the name of this bottomless collapse, of this endless desertification of language . . . a God which is, at the same time, interpreted by Silesius, as the 'divinity of God as gift.'"[15] Derrida goes on to explore Silesius's notion of God's gift as a form of play and letting go, expressed in Silesius's verse—"God plays with creation / All that is play that the deity gives itself."[16] But Derrida's fascination with Silesius does not mean he identifies this divine play of Creation with the deconstructive play of khora. The latter—khora—seems to be prior and privileged for Derrida. But he can still ask of Silesius if the place (*Ort*) opened by the word (*Wort*) of God is part of divine play, God himself, or what precedes both God and his play and makes both possible. In other words, he can still question whether the invisible, inaudible, nonsensible place invoked by Silesius is "opened by God or is 'older' than the time of creation, than time itself, than history, narrative, word, etc."[17] This is where khora seems to trump God for Derrida, even if he puts the difference between them in the form of an undecidable hypothesis: "It remains to be known (beyond knowing) if the place is opened by appeal (response, the event that calls for the response, revelation, history, etc.) or if it remains impassibly foreign, like khora, to everything that takes its place and re-places itself and plays within this place, including what is named God."[18]

But if it remains unknowable is it still possible to choose between the two? On the face of it, Khora and God appear to exclude each other: "these two experiences of place, these two ways, are no doubt of an absolute heterogeneity. One place excludes the other, one (sur)passes the other, one does without the other, one is, absolutely, *without the other*."[19] On this reading, the antithesis between the two ways of God and Khora are construed as two abysses facing off against each other. On the one hand we have the biblical abyss of God (the divine abyss calling and being called by the human abyss in Psalm 41; or as Silesius glosses it, "The abyss of my spirit always invokes with cries / The abyss of God").[20] On the other hand, we have the bottomless, timeless, impassive abyss of Khora. This is how Derrida formulates the alternative:

> *On one side* . . . a profound and abyssal eternity, fundamental but accessible to the teleo-eschatological narrative and to a certain experience of historical (or historial) revelation; *on the other way*, the nontemporality of an abyss without bottom or surface, an absolute impassibility (neither life nor death) that gives rise to everything that it is not. In fact two abysses.[21]

In the end, and in spite of all his vacillating alternativism (reminiscent of a Kierkegaardian aesthete swinging between either and or), I believe that Derrida chooses a-theistic khora over theistic divinity. Khora is deconstruction, or as Derrida himself puts it: "indestructible khora . . . the very spacing of de-construction."[22]

My question, however, is this: Is there a third way between theistic divinity and atheistic khora—namely, an ana-theistic God after God? Not *theos*, not *a-theos*, but *ana-theos*? In such a wager, God would be the name of what we hope for (as Augustine once put it), a promissory note, a maybe (*posse*) that can only be (*esse*) if one responds to its solicitation or seduction. That is, if one responds ethically to the call of the good, or poetically to the call of desire. Such a third ana-theist disposition would involve a messianicity that is not a mere structural abstraction—an anonymous indifferent hold-all of spacing—but a messianicity that invites an endless multiplicity of concrete and committed messianisms: embodyings of flesh and blood, of bread and water, of singularity and thisness, of sacred times and places, calendars and carnalities, pilgrimages and practices.

This is where I have real differences with Derrida (and the deconstructors—John Caputo, Mark Taylor, J. Hillis-Miller, etc.). In the name of unconditional openness to any other at all (*tout autre est tout autre*), deconstruction's "religion without religion" seems to have no visage to speak of, no carnal or narrative presence in the here and now. "Ascesis strips the messianic hope of all biblical forms," Derrida says, "and even all determinable figures of the wait or expectation; it thus denudes itself in view of responding to that which must be absolute hospitality, the 'yes' to the 'arrivant(e),' the 'come' to the future that cannot be anticipated. . . . This hospitality is absolute only if it keeps watch over its own universality."[23] In other words, the messianic universality so dear to deconstruction is only guaranteed, it seems, at the cost of particularity; it forfeits the incarnate singularity of everyday epiphanies. "If one could 'count' on what is coming," says Derrida, "hope would be but the calculation of a program."[24] The messianic is a waiting without any horizon of expectation, and an ascesis without anchorage, image, or anticipation. Here there is no anamnesis or anaphora—no repetition forward, no "anticipatory memory" as understood by Marcuse and Benjamin as a commitment to this or that promise. There is no ground to take one's stand on for there is no ground. The A of the absconded *Autre* is so absolute as to absolve itself from all carnal experience—with no possibility for a second A of advent into history. *Absconditus* not *adventurus*. *Adieu* of departure without *adieu* of return. No double AA of "ana" but rather pure abstention of an absentee

Other that does not count and that cannot be counted on. An absencing without covenant or care. Derrida refers to this unconditional abstaining as an epoché (bracketing) of the content of faith; so much so that faith becomes a waiting without hope of any resurrection, revelation, or return (I use all three terms, advisedly, in the lower case, for they may happen at any moment of time). This hopeless absconding, espoused by Derrida, is what he himself calls the "*formality* of a *structural* messianism, a messianism without religion, even a messianic without messianism."[25]

In sum, faith serves here as a quasi-transcendental "structure of promise." It does not call for realization or incarnation in the world of particular beliefs. Its ascesis—the "epoché of the content"—remains radically atheistic. It never poses as a provisional moment before a return to the world of everyday faith and service, of eucharist or epiphany. The difference between Silesius's mystical theism and Derrida's deconstructive atheism is, therefore, it seems to me, the choice between a sacred promise of peace and healing, and an option for khora as undecidable void. And this is where Derrida's atheism contrasts with ana-theism understood as a disposition between, before, and beyond the division into theism and atheism. Where messianic atheism involves a religion "without" religion, messianic ana-theism involves a religion "before" or "after" religion.[26]

Otherwise put, we might say that Derrida's atheistic concept of *messianicity* is unconditional in its impossibility in contrast to all actual practices of *messianism*, which are conditional in their possibility. If messianism inscribes messianicity into particular religious traditions of revelation or eschatology, Derrida's messianicity without messianism risks taking the possibility out of im-possibility altogether. And by virtue of such radical excarnation, Derrida's messianicity risks becoming so devoid of any incarnate narrative, scripture, person, or presence (human or divine) that it forfeits any purchase in the world of suffering or action. The Other dissolves into the undecidability of hallucination.[27] Which leaves me with this summary question: Does deconstructive "faith" not run the danger of becoming so empty that it loses faith in *thisness* altogether? So "blind" that it cannot *see* or *touch* the supplicant face of the widow, orphan, and stranger before us?[28]

I think this is something that could never be said of Levinas's notion of "Messianic peace" or Walter Benjamin's "weak messianism" of the mystical stranger—the one who may break open the continuum of history at any moment. Benjamin spoke of the irruption of a mystical "now" (*Jetztzeit*), suggesting that each and every instant is a portal through which the Messiah might enter. Likewise, regardless of Derrida's profound debt to his mentor Levinas, his purely formal messianicity prevents him from embracing Levinas's ethical commitment to the *visage d'autrui* as the trace of God. Unlike Benjamin and Levinas, therefore, Derrida's approach to the messianic hovers in the antechamber of messianism. He does not signal a return to a God (or whatever homonym, synonym, or pseudonym one might prefer) after the death of God. He explores rather than embraces the anatheist option. His saving the Name is not a return to the Named. At best, it is an "endless waiting in the desert."[29] A waiting for Godot—one always to come who never comes.

One might note here that in Derrida's waiting in the desert, as opposed to Beckett's waiting on the road, there is no child who comes with daily messages to keep the vagrants going. Beckett confessed that the "key word of my work is Perhaps";[30] and if anatheism reads this to mean "perhaps Godot will come," deconstructive atheism is more likely to respond, "perhaps Godot won't come." The important thing is, however, that both dispositions of vigilance are open to dialogue. Interminable conversation between believers and non-believers is possible in the space of this Perhaps. We will return to this below.

Three Dialogues with Derrida

In light of all the above, I would suggest that Derrida's messianic atheism has something invaluable to contribute to a radical rethinking of the question of God. In the remainder of this essay, I revisit three conversations I conducted with Derrida on this question between 1981 and 2001. I do so in the hope that these summary exchanges may shed a little further clarification on this task of rethinking religion.

In the first of our dialogues, "Deconstruction and the Other," conducted in Paris in 1981, Derrida addresses what he calls certain messianic "effects" of deconstruction. While stating that the "Judaic dimension" of Levinas's thinking remained for him a "discreet . . . reference," he acknowledges that deconstructive openness to a radical Other (beyond philosophy) brings it into relation with a certain "effect" of prophecy.[31]

This is slippery terrain, and Derrida moves with great caution:

> [I do not] dismiss all forms of Messianic or prophetic eschatology. I think that all genuine questioning is summoned by a certain type of eschatology, though it is impossible to define this eschatology in philosophical terms. The search for objective or absolute criteria is, to be sure, an essentially philosophical gesture. Prophecy differs

from philosophy in so far as it dispenses with such criteria. The prophetic word is its own criterion and refuses to submit to an external tribunal which would judge or evaluate it in any objective or neutral fashion. The prophetic word is its own eschatology and finds its index of truthfulness in its own inspiration and not in some transcendental or philosophical criteriology.[32]

When I asked Derrida if he considered his attempts to deconstruct philosophy to have any such "prophetic" character, he gave this characteristically circuitous response: "Unfortunately, I do not feel inspired by any sort of hope which would permit me to presume that my work of deconstruction has a prophetic function. But I concede that the style of my questioning as an exodus and dissemination in the desert might produce certain prophetic resonances."[33] It is possible, he says,

> [to see] deconstruction as being produced in a space where the prophets are not far away. But the prophetic resonances of my questioning reside at the level of a certain rhetorical discourse which is also shared by several other contemporary thinkers. The fact that I declare it "unfortunate" that I do not personally feel inspired, may be a signal that deep down I still hope. It means that I am in fact still looking for something. So perhaps it is no mere accident of rhetoric that the search itself, the search without hope for hope, assumes a certain prophetic allure.[34]

He concludes with this typically two-step locution, one foot forward, one foot back: "Perhaps my search is a twentieth century brand of prophecy? But it is difficult for me to believe it."[35]

Derrida's intriguing oscillations here on the themes of hope and belief are, I think, telling. We have to believe, Derrida says, but not necessarily in God. Messianicity is a necessary structure of all experience qua faith but it does not necessitate a faith in a Messiah or Messianism as such. Messianicity simply means that "deconstruction is not an enclosure in nothingness, but an openness towards the other."[36] So, if messianism is theistic, messianicity is a-theistic, but in a sense that—in this dialogue— rules nothing out, including the possibility of different kinds of theism. And as such it comes very close at times to what I am calling ana-theism.

In our discussion entitled "Desire of God," chaired by Jack Caputo at Villanova University in 1997, Derrida expanded on several of these initial remarks about the Messianic. The vexed question of hermeneutic discernment between true or false prophets again arose. Questioning Derrida on how—given his reading of messianicity as a waiting in the desert—we might distinguish between a "desertification" of God and a "desertion" of God, he candidly replied: "as soon as you look for a clear line between desertification and desertion, between an authentic God and a false God or prophet . . . as soon as you think you have found this criterion, that is the end of faith. You can be sure that God has left."[37] So far so clear. And yet Derrida does not deny here the "terrifying" implications of such a radically non-hermeneutic messianicity: "You have to resist the resistance to [the] openness to a possible monstrosity and to [this] evil."[38] Which means, if I understand him correctly, that if "every other is every other" (Derrida's "axiom of messianicity"), then *any* other—animal, human, or divine—is "infinitely, absolutely other."[39] More pointedly still, there is no critical hermeneutic to help us tell whether messianicity means war or peace.[40]

This *is*, indeed, Derrida confesses, a "terrible moment." And he is the first to admit that when it comes to political and ethical decisions about acting justly, we are compelled to move from "absolute non-knowledge and indeterminacy" to "the necessity of criteria" for negotiation and discrimination.[41] Hence the need, where belief is concerned, to move from messianicity to messianism, for if the two are indeed heterogeneous, one cannot deny a certain "contamination" between them. What is *translation* for hermeneutics is *contamination* for deconstruction. And contamination is not a derogatory term for Derrida; it represents a mutual subversion of binary meanings in contrast to the hermeneutic principle of translation from one meaning to another: foreign to familiar, old to new, upper to lower, spiritual to carnal, or vice versa.

Derrida admits that he personally (by birth and history) shares with Caputo and myself a belonging to a specific tradition of Abrahamic messianism (whether one is atheistic or not). "If I make reference to the Messiah," he explains, "to the tradition of messianisms in our (western) culture, in order to name messianicity, it is in order to keep this memory. Even if messianicity is totally heterogeneous to messianism, there is this belonging to a tradition and language, which is mine as well as yours."[42] But my question remains: How do we *transit* from unconditional messianicity to conditional messianism, from the absolute to the practical, from the impossible to the possible? How do we account for a hermeneutics of *translation* between these two orders? How do we provide an ethics of everyday agency and action? How answer the question: What is to be done?[43]

Finally, in our third and last dialogue, conducted in New York City in 2001, Derrida returned to the question of messianicity. Here we had our most explicit conversation—more of a critical encounter (*Auseinanderset-zung*) than an intellectual exercise. And, as always, "a loving struggle." Our meeting took place on October 16, just one month after 9/11. Returning from a visit to Ground Zero together with the stench of destruction still in our lungs, the stakes seemed more relevant than ever. We cut straight to the chase. Derrida located the difference between his deconstructive take on the *messianic-to-come* and my hermeneutic take on the *God-who-may-be* by focusing on the question of hope:

> Perhaps the difference between us [is this]: the indeterminacy of the messianic leaves you unsatisfied. To speak roughly, you, Richard, would not give up the hope of some redemption, resurrection, and so forth. I would not either. But I would argue that when one is not ready to suspend the *determination* of hope, then our relation with the other becomes economical (namely political, ethical).[44]

He goes on to explain: "when I am political, juridical, and perhaps ethical, I am with you—[but] when I try to think the most rigorous relation with the other I must be ready to give up the hope for a return to salvation, the hope for resurrection, or even reconciliation. In the pure act of giving and forgiving we should be free from any hope of reconciliation."[45]

Perhaps there is a faint echo here of Levinas's claim that to get to the kingdom we must give up the Kingdom. I, for one, would have no hesitation in embracing such an idea of letting go so as to receive a gift from the absolute Other. So understood, might not the passage through the radical atheism of Derrida's "khora"—that absolutely indeterminate, nameless space—be construed as an opening to the grace of the impossible becoming possible? What is impossible to khora is possible to God. In this way, deconstructive khora might be said, as hinted above, to enter into an "exemplary" relationship of disjunction-conjunction with the work of mystics like Angelus Silesius; and Derrida does seem to leave open a sense that khora and God may somehow supplement, even as they exclude, each other. If this be so, my own reading of such mutual supplementarity would be this: If God without khora risks dogmatism, khora without God risks desolation. Perhaps khora could thus be reinterpreted as the aboriginal matrix that God would need to become flesh? And perhaps then the dark night of khora could be construed as a mystical kenosis on a return journey to a God *after* God? Perhaps, in other words, the deconstructive work of Khora might serve as an indispensable and integral prelude to ana-theism? The key word of both Khora and Kingdom is "perhaps." All this would seem to throw a bridge between us. Yes. Both of us ultimately agree that we can never *know* the Absolute Stranger for sure and that all we can do is "desire" something beyond the impossible. But, once again, where I place the emphasis on Perhaps construed as *Posse* (the God-who-may-be), Derrida tends to read it more often as *Im-Posse* (the God-who-may-not-be). What Derrida calls the *impossible* possible is what I call the *possible* impossible. It is a matter of emphasis. The difference between deconstruction and hermeneutics. A hairline. But a line nonetheless.[46]

Our New York conversation concluded by our returning to the unresolved question of the Perhaps. Defining Khora as the "only possible groundless ground for a universal [politics]," Derrida insisted that he is "not excluding anything."[47] He spoke of the "thinnest difference" existing between his own position and the anatheist "God who may be," understood as a powerless hovering between divine names and nameless khora. Reminded of his own avowal (at the Villanova conference in 1997) that "if he were interested in God, it would be a God of the powerless,"[48] Derrida endeavored to clarify the difference between our respective notions of the powerless Maybe (*Peut-être*). While he admitted sharing the "dream" of reconciliation/resurrection, he explained that as someone who "thinks deconstructively" he himself felt a "responsibility" to "obey the necessity of the possibility that there is khora *rather than* a relationship with an anthropotheologic God of Revelation."[49] Instead of translating faith into something determinable, which obliges one to keep the "name" of the resurrection, deconstructive faith, by contrast, means giving up any "determined hope." For if one says that resurrection is the horizon of one's hope, then one knows what one names when one says "resurrection"—and then "faith is not faith. It is already knowledge."[50] So, returning to the classic claim that he rightly passes for an atheist, Derrida added this revealing phrase: "Sometimes . . . you have to be an atheist *of this sort* if one is to be true to faith, to *pure* faith. . . . It is a very *complicated* logic."[51]

Complicated indeed, but no less subtle and vigilant for all that. There are, I think, some telling inflections in this last sentence. Derrida refers 1) to atheism of a specific *sort* (complicated); 2) to faith of a particularly *pure* kind (blind and unconditional); and 3) to a special, unpredictable time for this obligation (namely, "*sometimes* you have to be an atheist . . ."). These micrological qualifiers are tantalizing and intriguing. And the intrigue is heightened when Derrida reweaves the messianic woof back into the khoral warp. Any form of prayer to a Messianic Other still-to-come is, he insists, only made possible by Khora. For khora is that "neutral, indifferent, impassible spacing—that enables me to pray."[52] So "without Khora there would be no prayer"; but more dramatically, "without khora there would be no God, no *other*."[53] Khora, it now appears, is that impassable spacing of the "there is" before and "beyond being" without which there could be no prayer, reconciliation, redemption, etc. But *once you actually pray* you have left the messianic no-place of khora and embraced a messianism of determinate belief: "you can address a prayer only to some*thing* or some*one*, not to khora."[54]

To sum up: If the ana-theist God-who-may-be is, as Derrida acknowledges, "a powerless God . . . beyond sovereignty," a powerlessness to which "justice and love are precisely oriented," his own notion of khora is, by contrast, an abyssal powerlessness *prior* to love and justice. In other words, if the divine Maybe is powerless in the sense of "poor or vulnerable," khora, by Derrida's candid admission, is "powerlessness as simply no-power. No power at all."[55] Khora does not care and we cannot care for Khora. Khora is not another name for God. Khora is not a Messiah in drag, a pseudonym for divine grace. No. Khora rightly passes for atheism. Albeit a specifically deconstructive atheism: an a-theism separated, if only by the "thinnest of differences" (Derrida's phrase), from the ana-theist God who may be.[56]

Khora and messianicity are the two faces of Derrida's atheism. Khora looks before the beginning while messianicity looks beyond the end. But the Janus face is always blind and always a little mad. Because of khora, our prayers are tears. Because of messianicity, our prayers are dreams.

Notes

Introduction

1. The first conference that treated these questions directly was Deconstruction and Theology, organized by Thomas Altizer, which was published in 1982 as *Deconstruction and Theology* (New York: Crossroad, 1982).

2. In this sense, this book is not like previous volumes on Derrida and religion that speak predominantly to an audience interested in religious studies. The volume edited by Yvonne Sherwood and Kevin Hart, *Derrida and Religion: Other Testaments* (New York: Routledge, 2005), for instance, grew out from a conference at the joint annual meeting of the American Academy of Religion and the Society of Biblical Literature and its contributors are predominantly scholars of religion.

3. We would like to thank the Minda de Gunzburg Center for European Studies, the Harvard Humanities Center, the Committee on the Study of Religion, the Department of Philosophy, and the Department of Romance Languages and Literatures for their support.

4. For this see François Cusset, *French Theory: How Foucault, Derrida, Deleuze & Co. Transformed the Intellectual Life of the United States*, trans. Jeff Fort (Minneapolis: University of Minnesota Press, 2008).

5. For Derrida's most important essays concerning religion, including "Faith and Knowledge," see Gil Anidjar, ed. *Acts of Religion* (New York: Routledge, 2002). Michael Naas's recent book *Miracle and Machine* (New York: Fordham University Press, 2012) gives a particularly rich reading of this essay.

6. See among others Derrida, *Voice and Phenomena: Introduction to the Problem of the Sign in Husserl's Phenomenology*, trans. Leonard Lawlor (Evanston, IL: Northwestern University Press, 2011).

7. See Jacques Derrida, *Specters of Marx: The State of the Debt, the Work of Mourning, and the New International*, trans. Peggy Kamuf (New York: Routledge, 1994).

8. Derrida's argument was focused by the privilege to the spoken word that he identified in Ferdinand de Saussure, one of the main influences on the then-dominant school of structuralism.

9. See, for example, Jacques Derrida, *De la Grammatologie* (Paris: Editions de Minuit, 1967), 23, 117, 146.

10. Derrida, *De la Grammatologie*, 25.

11. Jacques Derrida, *Positions* (Paris: Editions de Minuit, 1967), 38.

12. Derrida, *De la Grammatologie*, 69.

13. Thus, even as Rodolphe Gasché notes the importance of religious themes, in his essay "God, for Example," he still sees the trace as being prior to God. See *Inventions of Difference* (Cambridge, MA: Harvard University Press, 1994), 161.

14. Jacques Derrida, "Circumfession," in Geoffrey Bennington, *Jacques Derrida* (Chicago: University of Chicago Press, 1993), 155.

15. See Thomas Alitzer, ed. *Deconstruction and Theology* (1982). And Taylor's work, especially *Erring* (Chicago: University of Chicago Press, 1984). Taylor draws on the "atheistic" aspects of deconstruction—he even calls deconstruction "the 'hermeneutic' of the death of God"—in order to develop his "postmodern a/theology" and to create "a new opening for the religious imagination" (6, 11).

16. The critical discussion of the relationship between Derrida's work and negative theology can be seen in some of the earliest conferences that highlight this aspect of his work. See Harold Coward and Toby Foshay, eds., *Deconstruction and Negative Theology* (Albany: State University of New York Press, 1991), and the work by Kevin Hart, especially his *The Trespass of the Sign: Deconstruction, Theology, and Philosophy* (Cambridge: Cambridge University Press, 1989).

17. See Derrida's discussion of this resemblance in *Margins of Philosophy*, trans. Alan Bass (Chicago: University of Chicago Press, 1982), 6. See also his more extended treatment of negative theology in "How to Avoid Speaking: Denials," in *Derrida and Negative Theology*, and Jacques Derrida, *On the Name*, trans. Thomas Dutoit (Stanford, CA: Stanford University Press, 1995).

18. See John Llewelyn, *Margins of Religion: Between Kierkegaard and Levinas* (Bloomington: Indiana University Press, 2009). For a recent approach to using deconstructive ideas to renew evangelical Christianity, see Ronald T. Michener, *Engaging Deconstructive Theology* (Burlington, VT: Ashgate, 2007). See also Derrida's account of tolerance in "Faith and Knowledge," in *Acts of Religion*, 59–60.

19. See John Milbank, *Theology and Social Theory* (Oxford: Oxford University Press, 1991). A similar argument is visible in some theologians who emphasize the destructive element of Derrida's thought and cast any residual religious aspects of his thought as excessively negative and abstract. Steven Shakespeare highlights the affirmative aspect of Derrida's thought, when treating those scholars such as David Klemm, Robert Magliola, and John Milbank, who protest against what they see as an excessive negativity and abstraction in Derrida's God.

See his *Derrida and Theology* (New York: T & T Clark, 2009), 183–88. Shakespeare also provides a good account of the Christian reception of Derrida's thought.

20. Though, as Derrida remarks elsewhere, it is not entirely clear whether one can define such a "classic" negative theology. See Derrida, *On the Name*, 41. The text "Sauf le nom" is a lengthy meditation on negative theology.

21. See Derrida, *Voice and Phenomenon*.

22. As we shall see, it is here that the debate between Martin Hägglund and John Caputo lies. While Caputo thinks one can have a "passion for the impossible," Hägglund denies this.

23. See Derrida, *L'Écriture et la différence* (Paris: Seuil, 1967), especially his essay on Georges Bataille, 398n1, and his essay on Emmanuel Levinas, 170–71.

24. Derrida, *L'Écriture et la différence*, 217. See also John Caputo's criticism of negative theology in *The Prayers and Tears of Jacques Derrida* (Bloomington: Indiana University Press, 1997), 11.

25. Derrida, *De la Grammatologie*, 106, 117, 201.

26. See Derrida's discussion of this question in *Derrida and Religion: Other Testaments*, 37.

27. Derrida discusses the close connections between ethics and religion, especially as found in the concept of "responsibility," which can be found in Derrida's later essays such as *The Gift of Death* and *On the Name*.

28. Derrida, *Writing and Difference*, 68. Translation amended.

29. This reading of Derrida has led to dramatic attempts to recast the traditional God of metaphysics in modern theology.

30. The use of Derrida's work and appeal to différance to destabilize the name of God has allowed many scholars, including John Caputo, to maintain religion while rejecting forms of dogmatism. Such is also Mark Taylor's goal when he draws on the idea of Christ to suggest parallels between divine incarnation in Christian theology and the recuperation of writing in Derrida's work. Similarly, Hent de Vries has suggested that God would perhaps be the best name for the trace in *Philosophy and the Return to Religion* (Baltimore, MD: Johns Hopkins University Press, 1999), 357. See also Hugh Rayment-Pickard, *The Impossible God: Derrida's Theology* (Burlington, VT: Ashgate, 2003).

31. Jacques Derrida, *L'Origine de la géometrie* (Paris: Presses universitaires de France, 1962), 163–71.

32. Derrida, *L'Écriture et la différence*, 23.

33. Indeed, Derrida suggests as much. "If you insist only on difference that is without presence or that is prior to presence, you would have to erase a lot of things in the Christian corpus." *Derrida and Religion: Other Testaments*, 48.

34. Derrida, "Circumfession," 38, see also page 9. And Caputo, *The Prayers and Tears of Jacques Derrida*.

35. See especially the interview with Elisabeth Weber in *Questioning Judaism*, trans. R. Bowlby (Stanford, CA: Stanford University Press, 2004), 40–58.

36. See for an analysis of Derrida's relationship to Judaism and Jewishness, Jürgen Habermas, *Philosophical Discourse of Modernity*, trans. Frederick Laurence (Cambridge, MA: MIT Press, 1990); Gideon Ofrat, *The Jewish Derrida*, trans. Peretz Kidron (Syracuse, NY: Syracuse University Press, 2001); Martin Srajek, *In the Margins of Deconstruction*; or Andrew König, *Splitterflüsse* (Stuttgart, Germany: Merz & Solitude, 2006); and with greater sophistication Joseph Cohen, ed., *Judéités: Questions pour Jacques Derrida* (Paris: Galilée, 2003); Hélène Cixous, *Un Portrait de Jacques Derrida en jeune saint juif* (Paris: Galilée, 2001); Dana Hollander, *Exemplarity and Chosenness* (Stanford, CA: Stanford University Press, 2008).

37. A similar exclusion of Islam was discussed in Derrida's 1994 conference in Capri, and in works on Derrida and religion ever since.

38. As Derrida mentioned in a 2002 interview, "there *is* a Christian heritage, a Judeo-Christian heritage, to deconstruction." *Derrida and Religion: Other Testaments*, 32.

39. On the ways in which Derrida's thought helps us understand both the "explosive" nature of the Abrahamic religions and "the promise of peaceful reconciliation," see Gil Anidjar's introduction to Derrida, *Acts of Religion*.

40. Indeed, the importance of Derrida for biblical studies, foregrounded in the edited volume *Derrida and Religion: Other Testaments*, has allowed the field to open up in new ways to concerns from ethnic and gender studies. As the editors wrote of the contributions, "just as several papers gather around what might be called a deconstruction of Christianity from the direction of 'the Jew,' so others exert pressure on the homo-fraternal and filial structure of religion from the direction of 'woman.'" Catherine Keller has shown how Derrida's thought can be deployed in process theology to open new feminist and ecological readings of scripture; see in particular Catherine Keller, *The Face of the Deep: A Theology of Becoming* (New York: Routledge, 2003).

41. See above all de Vries, ed., *Political Theologies: Public Religions in a Post-Secular World* (New York: Fordham University Press, 2006).

42. See Derrida, *Specters of Marx*, 73.

43. See Jacques Derrida, *Rogues: Two Essays on Reason*, trans. Pascale-Anne Brault and Michael Naas (Stanford, CA: Stanford University Press, 2005).

44. See Derrida's "Parti Pris pour l'Algérie," in *Les Temps Modernes* 580 (Jan.–Feb. 1995): 233–41.

45. See his "Force of Law: The 'Mystical Foundation of Authority,'" collected in Anidjar, ed., *Acts of Religion*, 228–98.

46. See especially Jacques Derrida, *On Cosmopolitanism and Forgiveness*, trans. Mark Dooley and Michael Hughes (New York: Routledge, 2001).

47. For a classic treatment of the relationship between Derrida and Levinas, and the possibilities this opens for an ethical reading of deconstruction, see Simon Critchley's *The Ethics of Deconstruction: Derrida and Levinas* (London: Blackwell, 1992).

48. In his *Philosophy and the Turn to Religion*, Hent de Vries asserts that Derrida's texts on religion will "distinguish Derrida's 'unwritten' ethics and politics from the textualism, the transcendental lingualism, not to mention the textual

'free play,' with which his thought was so unfortunately—and surrepticiously—associated in the earliest phases of its reception" (23).

"Et Iterum de Deo": Jacques Derrida and the Tradition of Divine Names
Hent de Vries

1. I would like to thank the organizers and conveners of the Harvard Conference, Edward Baring, Peter Gordon, and Homi Bhabha, for their kind invitation to speak on this occasion.

2. See Hent de Vries, *Philosophy and the Turn to Religion* (Baltimore, MD: Johns Hopkins University Press, 1999) and Ward Blanton and Hent de Vries, eds., *Paul and the Philosophers* (New York: Fordham University Press, 2013).

3. The question does not only arise with respect to names, especially proper names; it also has its place in Derrida's seminars on "The Nationality of Philosophy." For a discussion, see Dana Hollander, *Exemplarity and Chosenness: Rosenzweig and Derrida on the Nation of Philosophy* (Stanford, CA: Stanford University Press, 2008).

4. See Paola Marrati, *Genesis and Trace: Derrida Reading Husserl and Heidegger* (Stanford, CA: Stanford University Press, 2005), and Edward Baring, *The Young Derrida and French Philosophy, 1945–1968* (Cambridge: Cambridge University Press, 2011).

5. Derrida says of "justice" and of the Platonic "chôra" that they are "indeconstructable." I have discussed this motif and its difficulty extensively in Hent de Vries, *Philosophy and the Turn to Religion*, and *Religion and Violence: Philosophical Reflections from Kant to Derrida* (Baltimore, MD: Johns Hopkins University Press, 2002).

6. Jacques Derrida, "Faith and Knowledge: The Two Sources of 'Religion' at the Limits of Reason Alone," in *Religion*, eds. Jacques Derrida and Gianni Vattimo, trans. David Webb (Stanford, CA: Stanford University Press, 1998), 46.

7. The conference on "Deconstruction and the Possibility of Justice" took place at the Cardozo Law School at Yeshiva University, in New York, in 1989.

8. De Vries, *Philosophy and the Turn to Religion*; de Vries, *Religion and Violence*; Hent de Vries, *Minimal Theologies: Critiques of Secular Reason in Theodor W. Adorno and Emmanuel Levinas*, trans. Geoffrey Hale (Baltimore, MD: Johns Hopkins University Press, 2005).

9. I am thinking in particular of Derrida "Aporias," which draws the full consequences of readings begun in "Ousia and Gramme," in *Margins of Philosophy*, and *Of Spirit*.

10. See my, "Must We (NOT) Mean What We Say? Seriousness and Sincerity in J. L. Austin and Stanley Cavell," in *The Rhetoric of Sincerity*, ed. Ernst van Alphen, Mieke Bal, and Carel Smits (Stanford, CA: Stanford University Press, 2009), 90–118.

11. Among many editions, see René Descartes, *Meditations on First Philosophy / Meditationes de prima philosophia* (a bilingual edition), ed. and trans. George Heffernan (Notre Dame, IN: Notre Dame University Press, 1990).

12. Jacques Derrida, *Limited Inc* (Evanston, IL: Northwestern University Press, 1988), 82–83. On the different meanings of the Latin verb *iterare* and the adverb *iterum*, see the *Oxford Latin Dictionary*, ed. P. G. W. Glare (Oxford: Oxford University Press, 2005). This work reminds us that the verb *itero* also means "to perform again," "to repeat (an action)," "to repeat (another's words)," "to renew, revive (an event, situation, etc.)," etc.

13. Derrida, *Limited Inc*, 83.

14. Ibid.

15. Ibid.

16. Ibid.

17. Jacques Derrida, *Speech and Phenomena: And Other Essays on Husserl's Theory of Signs*, trans. David B. Allison (Evanston, IL: Northwestern University Press, 1973), 6.

18. Ibid.

19. Ibid., cf. also ibid., 9–10: "Ideality is the preservation or mastery of presence in repetition. In its pure form, this presence is the presence of nothing *existing* in the world; it is a correlation with the acts of repetition, themselves ideal." And this affirmation almost by itself leads to a conclusion that *Speech and Phenomena* and much of Derrida's subsequent work will seek to ascertain: "what opens the repetition to the infinite, or what is opened up when the movement of idealization is assured, is a certain relation of an 'existent' to his death . . ." (ibid., 10). Or also:

> ideality, which is but another name for the permanence of the same and the possibility of repetition, *does not exist* in the world, and it does not come from another world; it depends entirely on the possibility of acts of repetition. It is constituted by this possibility. Its "being" is proportionate to the power of repetition; absolutely ideality is the correlate of a possibility of indefinite repetition. It could therefore be said that being is determined by Husserl as ideality, that is, as repetition. For Husserl, historical progress always has as its essential form the constitution of idealities whose repetition, and thus tradition, would be assured *ad infinitum*, where repetition and tradition are the transmission and reactivation of origins. And this determination of ideality is properly a *valuation*, an ethico-theoretical act that revives the decision that founded philosophy in its Platonic form. (Ibid., 52–53)

20. Ibid., 6, 7. For Husserl, Derrida writes:

> the sole nucleus of the concept of *psyche* is life as self-relationship, whether or not it takes place in the form of consciousness. "Living" is thus the name of that which precedes the reduction and finally escapes all the divisions which the latter gives rise to. But this is precisely because it is its own division and its own opposition to its other. In determining "living" in this way, we come to designate the origin of the insecurity of discourse . . . This concept of *life* is then grasped in an instance which is no longer that

of pretranscendental naïveté, the language of the day-to-day life or biological science. But if this ultratranscendental concept of life enables us to conceive life (in the ordinary or the biological sense), and if it has never been inscribed in language, it requires *another name*. (Ibid., 14–15)

The predicament of predication, indeed, of all naming, whether of "life" and its philosophical-transcendental concept or of God, the Divine, is, I would suggest, roughly—no, exactly—the same.

21. Ibid., 7.

22. Ibid., 7, 8.

23. Ibid., 8.

24. Ibid.

25. Jacques Derrida, "Form and Meaning: A Note on the Phenomenology of Language," in *Speech and Phenomena*, 128.

26. Derrida, *Speech and Phenomena*, 11, 12, 14.

27. Jacques Derrida, *Of Grammatology*, trans. Gayatri Spivak (Baltimore, MD: Johns Hopkins University Press, 1976), 47.

28. See my "The Theology of the Sign and the Sign of Theology: The Aphophatics of Deconstruction," in *Minimal Theologies*, 631–57. See also Ferdinand de Saussure, *Course in General Linguistics*, trans. Wade Baskin, ed. Perry Meisel and Haun Saussy (New York: Columbia University Press, 2011).

29. For a more extensive discussion, see my *Religion and Violence*, 256.

30. See Stanley Cavell, "Performative and Passionate Utterance," in *Philosophy the Day after Tomorrow* (Cambridge, MA: The Belknap Press of Harvard University Press, 2005), 155–91.

31. Derrida, *Limited Inc*, 83.

32. Ibid.

33. Ibid.

34. Ibid.

35. See my "Les deux sources de la 'machine théologique': Une note sur Derrida et Bergson," *Cahiers de l'Herne* (Paris: Galilée, 2004), 255–60.

36. Derrida, *Limited Inc*, 84.

37. Martin Hägglund, *Radical Atheism: Derrida and the Time of Life* (Stanford, CA: Stanford University Press, 2008), 143.

38. See the epigraph to "Cogito and the History of Madness," in Jacques Derrida, *Writing and Difference*, trans. with an introduction and additional notes by Alan Bass (London: Routledge, 2002), 36. And, lest we forget, Derrida's reading of Foucault as of Descartes (Kierkegaard and Pascal) here is as much a matter or "repetition" as the reference to Descartes in *Limited Inc* is:

if it is true, as Foucault says, as he admits by citing Pascal, that one cannot speak of madness except in relation to that "other form of madness" that allows men "not to be mad," that is, except in relation to reason, it will perhaps be possible not to add anything whatsoever to what Foucault has said, but perhaps only to *repeat* once more, on the site of this *division* between reason and madness of which Foucault speaks so well, the meaning, a meaning of the Cogito or (plural) Cogitos (for the Cogito of the Cartesian variety is neither the first not the last form of Cogito); and also to determine that what is in question here is an experience which, at its furthest reaches, is perhaps no less adventurous, perilous, nocturnal, and pathetic than the experience of madness, and is, I believe, much less adverse to and accusatory of madness, that is, accusative and objectifying of it, than Foucault seems to think. (Derrida, *Writing and Difference*, 39)

Mutatis mutandis, everything that is said in this early essay of madness and reason translates into the relationship of "faith" and "knowledge" that Derrida's later work investigates more frontally.

39. Jacques Derrida, *Rogues: Two Essays on Reason*, trans. Pascale-Anne Brault and Michael Naas (Stanford, CA: Stanford University Press, 2005), 28.

40. Ibid., xiv.

41. Ibid.

42. Ibid.

43. Derrida, "Faith and Knowledge," 83.

44. Jacques Derrida, *Learning to Live Finally: An Interview With Jean Birnbaum*, trans. Pascale-Anne Brault and Michael Naas (Hoboken, NJ: Melville House Publishing, 2007), 36.

Not Yet Marrano: Levinas, Derrida, and the Ontology of Being Jewish
Ethan Kleinberg

1. Sartre's work was originally published in 1946 as *Réflexions sur la question juive* and translated into English in 1948 with the title *Anti-Semite and Jew*. For the purpose of this article and argument I will conserve the sense of the French title and refer to the work as *Reflections on the Jewish Question*.

2. See Anne Marie Lescouret, *Emmanuel Levinas* (Paris: Flammarion, 1994), 110–46.

3. Gabrielle Spiegel, "Revising the Past/Revisiting the Present: How Change Happens in Historiography," *History and Theory* Theme Issue 46 (December 2007): 10–11.

4. Emmanuel Levinas, "Being-Jewish," trans. Mary Beth Mader, *Continental Philosophy Review* 40 (2007): 205. This article originally published as *"Être-Juif"* in *Confluences* 7 (1947): 253–56. Jacques Derrida, "Abraham, the Other," in *Judeities: Questions for Jacques Derrida*, ed. Bettina Bergo, Joseph Cohen, and Raphael Zagury-Orly (New York: Fordham University Press, 2007).

5. Sarah Hammerschlag, "Another, Other Abraham", *Shofar* 26, no. 4 (Summer 2008): 74–96.

6. Jonathan Judaken, *Jean-Paul Sartre and the Jewish Question* (Lincoln: University of Nebraska Press, 2006), 7.

7. On the faults see Pierre Birnbaum, "Sorry Afterthoughts on *Anti-Semite and Jew*," trans. Carol Marks, *October* 87 (Winter 1999): 89–106; on addressing anti-Semitism and the Holocaust see Hammerschlag, "Another, Other Abraham," 69, and Judaken, *Jean-Paul Sartre and the Jewish Question*, 127.

8. For a succinct presentation see Michel Rybalka, "Publication and Reception of *Anti-Semite and Jew*," *October* 87 (Winter 1999): 161–82.

9. The only remaining evidence of the actual lecture is a review by Françoise Derins published in *La Nef* and subsequently translated for the special issue of *October* on Jean-Paul Sartre's *Anti-Semite and Jew*, *October* 87 (Winter 1999): 24–26.

10. Françoise Derins, "A Lecture by Jean-Paul Sartre," trans. Denis Hollier and Rosalind Krauss, *October* 87 (Winter 1999): 25. It is pure speculation that Derrida would have known about this lecture and it is certainly the case that Sartre makes reference to Kafka in his *Réflexions sur la question juive*. But it is also the case that the special issue of *October* appeared in the winter of 1999, gathering together multiple reflections on Sartre, including a text by Levinas, approximately one year before Derrida's own engagement with Sartre at the conference dedicated to the topic of "Judeities: Questions for Jacques Derrida."

11. Sartre, "Reflections on the Jewish Question, A Lecture," trans. Rosalind Krauss and Denis Hollier, *October* 87 (Winter 1999): 32–36. This issue also contains a translation of the introduction by Levinas. As a preface to the Sartre lecture, Pierre Birnbaum provides some thoughts on the written piece, our limited knowledge of its origin and or completeness, and the conspicuous absence of mention of this lecture in most works on Sartre.

12. Levinas, "Being-Jewish," 205.

13. See Ethan Kleinberg, *Generation Existential: Heidegger's Philosophy in France, 1927–1961* (Ithaca, NY: Cornell University Press, 2005), 168–83.

14. Jean-Paul Sartre, *Anti-Semite and Jew*, trans. George J. Becker (New York: Schocken Books, 1976), 69.

15. Sartre, *Anti-Semite and Jew*, 90.

16. Jean-Paul Sartre, *L'être et le néant* (Paris: NRF Gallimard, 1943), 134. See Judaken, *Jean-Paul Sartre and the Jewish Question*, 135–37.

17. Peter E. Gordon, "Out from *Huis Clos*: Sartre, Levinas and the Debate over Jewish Authenticity," *Journal of Romance Studies* 6, no. 1 and 2 (Spring 2006): 158–62.

18. See Kleinberg, *Generation Existential*, Chapter 4, "Jean-Paul Sartre."

19. Emmanuel Levinas, "Existentialism and Anti-Semitism," trans. Denis Hollier and Rosalind Krauss, *October* 87 (Winter 1999): 28.

20. Levinas, "Being-Jewish," 205.

21. Levinas, "Being-Jewish," 206.

22. Levinas, "Being-Jewish," 206.

23. Levinas, "Being-Jewish," 206.

24. Levinas, "Being-Jewish," 206.

25. Levinas, "Being-Jewish," 206–7.

26. Levinas, "Being-Jewish," 207.

27. Levinas, "Being-Jewish," 207.

28. Levinas, "Being-Jewish," 208.

29. Levinas, "Being-Jewish," 207.

30. Levinas, "Being-Jewish," 208.

31. Martin Heidegger, *Being and Time*, trans. John Macquarrie and Edward Robinson (New York: Harper and Row, 1962).

32. Emmanuel Levinas, "Reflections on the Philosophy of Hitlerism," trans. Sean Hand, *Critical Inquiry* 17, no. 1 (Autumn 1990): 63–71. This article was originally published as *"Quelques réflexions sur la philosophie de l'Hitlérisme,"* in *Esprit* 26 (November 1934): 199–208. See also, Samuel Moyn, "Judaism against Paganism: Emmanuel Levinas's Response to Heidegger and Nazism in the 1930s," *History and Memory* 10, no. 1 (Spring/Summer 1998): 25–58.

33. Emmanuel Levinas, *"De l'évasion," Recherches Philosophiques* 5 (1935/1936): 373–92; trans. Bettina Bergo as *On Escape* (Stanford, CA: Stanford University Press, 2003).

34. Levinas, "Reflections on the Philosophy of Hitlerism," 56.

35. Levinas was mobilized to serve in the French army but was captured in June 1940. See Anne Marie Lescouret, *Emmanuel Levinas* (Paris: Flammarion, 1994), 119–28; Kleinberg, *Generation Existential*, 246–48; Ethan Kleinberg, "Myth of Emmanuel Levinas," in *After the Deluge: New Perspectives on the Intellectual and Cultural History of Postwar France*, ed. Julian Bourg (Lanham, MD: Lexington Books, 2004), 212–13.

36. Recently published as Emmanuel Levinas, *Carnets de la captivité*, collected and annotated by Rodolphe Calin and Catherine Chalier (Paris: Bernard Grasset/IMEC, 2009).

37. Levinas, *Carnets de la captivité*, 75.

38. It is clear that Levinas completed the groundwork for what would become *De l'existence à l'existant* in these notebooks, but what is fascinating is the way that the category of "Judaism" is so readily apparent in the notebooks but obscured in the philosophical piece. Catherine Chalier and Robert Calin go so far as to suggest that the *être-juif* or *je suis juif* of the *Carnets de la captivité* are akin to the departure from the *je suis* articulated in *De l'existence à l'existant* (see the preface in *Carnets de la captivité*, 22–23). For Levinas's postwar philosophical break with Heidegger, see Emmanuel Levinas, *De l'existence à l'existant* (Paris: Vrin, 1993), and Kleinberg, *Generation Existential*, 248–58.

39. Levinas, *Carnets de la captivité*, 134.

40. Levinas, *Carnets de la captivité*, 186.

41. Levinas provides the Hebrew and the French, which reads *"la joie d'avoir la Thora"* (Levinas, *Carnets de la captivité*, 186).

42. Levinas, "Being-Jewish," 209.

43. Emmanuel Levinas, *Nine Talmudic Readings*, trans. Annette Aronowicz (Bloomington: Indiana University Press), 30.

44. Levinas, *Carnets de la captivité*, 188.

45. Kleinberg, "The Myth of Emmanuel Levinas," 210–13, 219–21.

46. Levinas, *Nine Talmudic Readings*, 36.

47. Levinas, *Nine Talmudic Readings*, 37.

48. Levinas, "Being-Jewish," 209.

49. Levinas, "Being-Jewish," 209.

50. Levinas, "Being-Jewish," 209.

51. Levinas, *Nine Talmudic Readings*, 36.

52. Levinas, "Being-Jewish," 208.

53. Levinas, *Carnets de la captivité*, 179–80.

54. Levinas, *Carnets de la captivité*, 210, 213. This is from the transcript of Levinas's 1945 radio broadcast "*L'expérience juive du prisonnier.*"

55. Heidegger, *Being and Time*, 286.

56. Heidegger, *Being and Time*, 294.

57. Levinas, *Carnets de la captivité*, 211. Transcript of Levinas's 1945 radio broadcast "*L'expérience juive du prisonnier.*"

58. Levinas, "Being-Jewish," 208; *Carnets de la captivité*, 173, 176.

59. Levinas, "Being-Jewish," 209.

60. In *De l'existence à l'existant*, Levinas makes the argument in philosophical terms by arguing that Heidegger's description of anxiety (angst) in the face of death is a misconception. Individual beings encounter anxiety, but after death they are returned to the realm of anonymous being, which does not. Therefore, the cause of anxiety, according to Levinas, is not the finitude of death, which is the limit of our self, but instead the infinity of anonymous being that continues long after we have shed our mortal coil. Unlike death, being never stops but is always there in its anonymity. The question for Levinas is: "Anxiety before Being—the horror of Being—is this not more original than anxiety before death?" (*De l'existence à l'existant*, 20, 98–100). Thus, for Levinas, what is frightening in death is not one's finitude but the realization that being continues infinitely after one dies—the realization that being has no need for any individual existent. But what is frightening at one level also proves to be the opening to the Other for Levinas via the category of Infinity. On this see Emmanuel Levinas, *Totality and Infinity*, trans. Alphonso Lingis (Pittsburgh, PA: Duquesne University Press, 1980), 48–49.

61. Jacques Derrida, "Abraham, the Other," 2–3.

62. Derrida, "Abraham, the Other," 3.

63. Derrida, "Abraham, the Other," 3.

64. Jacques Derrida, *Adieu to Emmanuel Levinas*, trans. Pascale-Anne Brault and Michael Naas (Stanford, CA: Stanford University Press, 1999), 3.

65. Derrida, *Adieu to Emmanuel Levinas*, 3.

66. Derrida, "Abraham, the Other," 3.

67. Derrida, "Abraham, the Other," 4.

68. Derrida, "Abraham, the Other," 12. Derrida links his mistrust of the "*exemplarist* temptation" to that of the "even more difficult and problematical language of *election*" (16). While not coterminous, the two go hand in glove throughout this essay.

69. Derrida, "Abraham, the Other," 12.

70. Derrida, "Abraham, the Other," 28.

71. Derrida, "Abraham, the Other," 29.

72. Derrida, "Abraham, the Other," 29.

73. Derrida, "Abraham, the Other," 23.

74. Derrida, "Abraham, the Other," 23.

75. Derrida, "Abraham, the Other," 23.

76. Levinas, *Nine Talmudic Readings*, 41. On Derrida and "messianicity," see "Abraham, the Other," 21; Jacques Derrida, *Archive Fever*, trans. Eric Prenowitz (Chicago: University of Chicago Press, 1996), 72.

77. Derrida, "Abraham, the Other," 34–35.

78. Derrida, "Abraham, the Other," 31.

79. Sigmund Freud, *Der Mann Moses und die monotheistische Religion: Drei Abhandlungen* (Amsterdam: Verlag Albert de Lange, 1939); *Moses and Monotheism*, trans. Katherine Jones (New York: Vintage Books, 1967). Derrida, *Archive Fever*, 67.

80. Derrida, "Abraham, the Other," 31.

81. Derrida, "Abraham, the Other," 29.

82. Jacques Derrida, *Aporias*, trans. Thomas Dutoit (Stanford, CA: Stanford University Press, 1993), 38–39. Emphasis added.

83. Derrida, *Aporias*, 74, 77.

84. Derrida, *Aporias*, 69.

85. Derrida, *Archive Fever*, 44. In this quote, Derrida is referring to Yosef Yerushalmi, but I am turning it back on Derrida as though he were speaking of himself.

86. Derrida, "Abraham, the Other," 13.

87. Exodus 2:11, 3:11, 4:13.

88. On page 109 of *Specters of Marx* (trans. Peggy Kamuf [New York: Routledge, 2006]), Derrida articulates the ways that an inheritor will "even annihilate, by watching (over) its ancestors rather than (over) certain others."

89. Derrida, *Adieu to Emmanuel Levinas*, 6.

Poetics of the Broken Tablet

Sarah Hammerschlag

1. Derrida, "Avouer—l'impossible," *1998 Comment Vivre ensemble: Acts du xxxviie Colloque des Intellectuels juifs de langue Francaise* (Paris: Presses Universitaire de France, 2001), 197. Emphasis added.

2. Jacques Derrida, *Donner la mort* (Paris: Galilée, 1999), 196, and *Gift of Death*, trans. David Wills (Chicago: University of Chicago Press, 2008), 148.

3. Jacques Rancière, "Who Is the Subject of the Rights of Man," *South Atlantic Quarterly* 103, no. 2/3 (2004): 309.

4. Ibid.

5. Jacques Rancière, "Should Politics Come? Ethics and Politics in Derrida," in *Derrida and the Time of the Political*, ed. Peng Cheah and Suzanne Guerlac (Durham, NC: Duke University Press, 2009), 274–88.

6. Elisabeth Weber, *Questions au judaisme* (Paris: Desclée de Brouwer, 1996), 80, and *Questioning Judaism*, trans. Rachel Bowlby (Stanford, CA: Stanford University Press, 2004), 43. The full line from Tsvétaeva's poem, "Poem of the End," is "In this most Christian of worlds, all poets are Jews," in Marina Tsvétaeva, *Selected Poems* (New York: Penguin, 1994), 67.

7. Jacques Derrida, *L'Écriture et la différence* (Paris: Seuil, 1967), 100, and Derrida, *Writing and Difference*, trans. Alan Bass (Chicago: University of Chicago Press, 1978), 65.

8. Derrida, *L'Écriture et la difference*, 112, and *Writing and Difference*, 75.

9. Jacques Derrida, *Schibboleth* (Paris: Galilée, 1986), 108, and Derrida, *Sovereignties in Question: The Poetics of Paul Celan*, ed. Thomas Dutoit and Outi Pasanan (New York: Fordham University Press, 2005), 61.

10. Derrida, *L'écriture et la différence*, 112, and *Writing and Difference*, 75.

11. In referring to the date in Celan's work he is referring both to Celan's meditation on the date in *Meridian* and also to the dates that appear within the poem, such as the thirteenth of February in "In Eins." Derrida, *Schibboleth*, 42, and *Sovereignties in Question*, 36.

12. Derrida, *Schibboleth*, 21, and *Sovereignties in Question*, 22.

13. Derrida, "'This Strange Institution Called Literature': An Interview with Jacques Derrida," in Jacques Derrida, *Acts of Literature*, ed. Derek Attridge (New York: Routledge, 1992), 45.

14. Derrida, *L'écriture et la différence*, 102, and *Writing and Difference*, 67.

15. Judah Loew ben Bezalel (1520–1609) was both a very real figure whose teachings strongly influenced later generations and the subject of myth. The legend of how the rabbi fashioned an anthropomorphic figure from clay and brought it to life to protect the Jews of his city circulated orally for centuries. In 1909 Yudl Rosenberg published the book *The Golem and the Wondrous Deeds of the Maharal of Prague*, in which he recounted the story of the Golem's creation and its adventures, thus making the Maharal a well-known figure of Jewish heroism even outside of religious communities.

16. Derrida, *Schibboleth*, 102, and *Sovereignties in Question*, 57.

17. Derrida, *L'écriture et la différence*, 430, and *Writing and Difference*, 295.

18. Derrida, "Avouer—l'impossible," 197, citing Emmanuel Levinas, *Quatre lectures talmudiques* (Paris: Minuit, 1968), 61, and *Nine Talmudic Readings*, trans. and with introduction by Annette Aronowicz (Bloomington: Indiana University Press, 1990), 28.

19. Levinas, *Quatre lectures talmudiques*, 61 and *Nine Talmudic Readings*, 28.

20. See in particular *Adieu to Emmanuel Levinas*, trans. Pascale-Anne Brault (Stanford, CA: Stanford University Press, 1999), and Sarah Hammerschlag, *The Figural Jew: Politics and Identity in Postwar French Thought* (Chicago: University of Chicago Press, 2010), 247–52.

21. Derrida, *Donner la mort*, 177, and *Gift of Death*, 132.

22. Ibid.

23. Derrida, *Donner la mort*, 196, and *Gift of Death*, 148.

24. Derrida, *Donner la mort*, 179, and *Gift of Death*, 134.

25. Derrida, "Abraham, l'autre," *Judéités: Questions pour Jacques Derrida*, ed. Joseph Cohen and Raphael Zagury-Orly (Paris: Galilée, 2003), 17, and "Abraham, the Other," in *Judeities: Questions for Jacques Derrida*, ed. Bettina Bergo, Joseph Cohen, and Raphael Zagury-Orly, trans. Bettina Bergo and Michael B. Smith (New York: Fordham University Press, 2007), 7.

26. Derrida, *Donner le mort*, 179, and *Gift of Death*, 134.

27. Rancière, "Should Politics Come?," 278.

28. Derrida, *Judéités*, 12, and *Judeities*, 13.

29. Rancière, "Should Politics Come?," 278.

30. See Kristin Ross, *May '68 and Its Afterlives* (Chicago: University of Chicago Press, 2002), 56, and Jacques Rancière, *Aux bords du politique* (Paris: La fabrique, 1998), 157.

31. Jacques Rancière, *Disagreement, Politics and Philosophy*, trans. Julie Rose (Minneapolis: University of Minnesota Press, 1999), 127. Alain Finkielkraut, *Le juif imaginaire* (Paris: Seuil, 1980), 26, and *The Imaginary Jew* (Lincoln: University of Nebraska Press, 1994), 18. For more on their differing interpretations of the May '68 chant, see Sarah Hammerschlag, *The Figural Jew*, 1–6.

32. Derrida, *Judéités*, 13, and *Judeities*, 14.

33. Emmanuel Levinas, *Difficile liberté* (Paris: Albin Michel, 1976), 247, and *Difficult Freedom*, trans. Sean Hand (Baltimore, MD: Johns Hopkins University Press, 1990), 176–77.

34. Derrida, *Judéités*, 13, and *Judeities*, 14.

Theism and Atheism at Play: Jacques Derrida and Christian Heideggerianism
Edward Baring

1. As I will suggest at the end of this essay, Derrida's early unpublished writings are less equivocal in their treatment of religious questions than the later, better-known texts.

2. See especially section 11 of Jacques Derrida, *Introduction to Husserl's Origin of Geometry*, trans. J. Leavey (Lincoln: University of Nebraska Press, 1978).

3. See Ethan Kleinberg, *Generation Existential* (Ithaca, NY: Cornell University Press, 2005), and Stefanos Geroulanos, *An Atheism That Is Not a Humanism Emerges in French Thought* (Stanford, CA: Stanford University Press, 2010).

4. Martin Heidegger, *Lettre sur l'humanisme*, trans. Roger Munier (Paris: Aubier, 1957), and Martin Heidegger, "Lettre à Jean Beaufret," trans. Joseph Rovan, in *Fontaine* 58 (July 1946): 786–804, and *Fontaine* 63 (November 1947): 786–804.

5. See, for example, Tom Rockmore, *Heidegger and French Philosophy: Humanism, Anti-Humanism, and Being* (London: Routledge, 1995), 86–87.

6. See Jacques Derrida, *L'Écriture et la différence* (Paris: Seuil, 1967), 207.

7. See, for example, Jacques Derrida, "Histoire et vérité," University of California, Irvine, Archives and Special Collections, Jacques Derrida Papers (MS-001) 8:9–10 (hereafter: Irvine Box: Folder).

8. Henri Birault, "Heidegger et la pensée de la finitude," reprinted in Birault, *De l'être, du divin, et des dieux* (Paris: Cerf, 2005), 486–87.

9. Birault, "Heidegger et la pensée de la finitude," 487.

10. See Plato, *The Sophist*, 259e.

11. Birault, "Heidegger et la pensée de la finitude," 488.

12. Birault, "Heidegger et la pensée de la finitude," 488. As Birault continued, this meant that "discourse [*discours*] is the true beginning of atheism" because it inserted negativity into the heart of the "old Absolute": "every speech [*parole*] is blasphemy and to speak is always to speak against God."

13. Birault, "Heidegger et la pensée de la finitude," 490. Here Birault cited Malebranche's *Entretien d'un philosophe chrétien et d'un philosophe chinois*. The reference makes it clear that by naming this form of the finite "Judaic," Birault was not making any rigorous theological or confessional argument.

14. Birault, "Heidegger et la pensée de la finitude," 490.

15. Birault, "Heidegger et la pensée de la finitude," 492.

16. Birault, "Heidegger et la pensée de la finitude," 494.

17. Birault, "Heidegger et la pensée de la finitude," 495.

18. Birault, "Heidegger et la pensée de la finitude," 496.

19. Birault, "Heidegger et la pensée de la finitude," 496.

20. Birault, "Heidegger et la pensée de la finitude," 496. Birault argued that this was assumed by all of Leibniz, Kant, Hegel, and Sartre.

21. Birault, "Heidegger et la pensée de la finitude," 499.

22. Birault, "Heidegger et la pensée de la finitude," 497.

23. Birault, "Heidegger et la pensée de la finitude," 503.

24. Birault, "Heidegger et la pensée de la finitude," 506–7.

25. Birault, "Heidegger et la pensée de la finitude," 485.

26. Birault, "Heidegger et la pensée de la finitude," 506.

27. Birault, "Heidegger et la pensée de la finitude," 507.

28. Martin Heidegger, *Über den Humanismus,* 11th ed. (Frankfurt: Vittorio Klostermann, 2010), 52.

29. Birault, "Heidegger et la pensée de la finitude," 509. Compare with Derrida, *L'Écriture et la différence*, 212–13.

30. Birault, "Heidegger et la pensée de la finitude," 510.

31. Though Birault does not mention the ontological difference in this article, it is a mainstay of his other work. See Birault, "Heidegger et la pensée de la finitude," 540, among others. Further, the ontological difference was a leitmotif of much Christian Heideggerianism of the period, see my article "Humanist Pretensions: Catholics, Communists, and Sartre's Struggle for Humanism in Post-War France," *Modern Intellectual History* 7, no. 3 (November 2010): 581–609.

32. Henri Birault, "De l'être, du divin, et des dieux," originally published in *Cahiers de l'actualité religieuse*, 16 (1961), 49–76, reprinted in Birault, *De l'être, du divin, et des dieux*, 513–50.

33. Birault, "De l'être, du divin, et des dieux," 514. Birault also suggested that this might require the putting aside of claims of God's singularity and "asking oneself if the precipitation of the Divine in the simultaneously metaphysical and Christian idea of a single God does not drive [*enfonce*] our world even further into the forgetting of Being and the Sacred [*Sacré*]," 515.

34. Birault, "De l'être, du divin, et des dieux," 518. As Birault explained later, Kierkegaard's idea of God was unable to escape the conceptual terms of Hegel's absolute religion.

35. Birault opposed *christianité* to *christianisme*: the primordial experience of faith to the form of Christianity that participates in the *Entgötterung* of human thought. Birault, "De l'être, du divin, et des dieux," 521.

36. Birault, "De l'être, du divin, et des dieux," 516.

37. Birault, "Heidegger et la pensée de la finitude," 489. We can see in this understanding the attraction that Derrida must have felt toward linguistic philosophy and how this might have articulated with his religion-oriented thought.

38. The course begins with a meditation on Birault's article. Derrida, "Peut on dire oui à la finitude?" Irvine 7:9, sheet 19.

39. Derrida, "Peut-on dire oui à la finitude?" Irvine 7:9, sheet 21.

40. Derrida, "Peut-on dire oui à la finitude?" 7:9, sheet 40. In an earlier course, *Penser, c'est dire non*, Derrida argued that Husserl's phenomenology was similarly structured, the "no" of the reduction was dependent on a "yes" to immediate intuition. Irvine 4:16, sheet 40–41.

41. Derrida, "Peut-on dire oui à la finitude?" 7:9, sheet 47.

42. Derrida, "Peut-on dire oui à la finitude?" 7:9, sheet 48–49. See also sheet 65. See a similar aporia of the irresponsibility of ethics in his later work, Jacques Derrida, *The Gift of Death*, trans. David Wills (Chicago: University of Chicago Press, 2008).

43. Derrida, "Peut-on dire oui à la finitude?" 7:9, sheet 48. Cf. Derrida, introduction to *L'Origine de la géométrie*, by Edmund Husserl (Paris: Presses Universitaires de France, 1962), 170. It is important to recognize that "speech" did not yet have the place in Derrida's writing that it would assume after the publication of the "Of Grammatology" essays in 1965–1966.

44. Derrida, "Peut-on dire oui à la finitude?" 7:9, sheet 49. See also, Derrida "Méthode et métaphysique," Irvine 7:7, sheet 64, and Derrida, *L'Écriture et la différence*, 103, which develops a similar argument.

45. Derrida discussed at length the Nietzschean "Dionysiac yes" as a possibility. This was the "affirmation of the finite by the finite," and rejected the God of the classical philosophers. But in being beyond Man, the "yes" of the Overman manifested a self-overcoming not essentially different from that described in the classical sense of finitude. Derrida, "Peut on dire oui à la finitude?" 7:9, sheets 50–52.

46. Derrida, "Peut-on dire oui à la finitude?" 7:9, sheet 66. The pages Derrida read were 154, 156–57, and 161 (page numbers from original version).

47. Derrida, "Peut-on dire oui à la finitude?" 7:9, sheet 67. Derrida's discussion of Heidegger is quite brief here. For a fuller treatment, which guides my reading, see Derrida, "Méthode et métaphysique," 7:6, sheet 28.

48. See Jacques Derrida, De la Grammatologie (Paris: Éditions de Minuit, 1967), 33–38, 206. In the course, however, Derrida did suggest that the choice of the word Endlichkeit implied that Heidegger had not fully liberated himself from classical onto-theology. Derrida, "Peut-on dire oui à la finitude?" 7:9, sheet 67.

49. Birault, "Heidegger et la pensée de la finitude," 513.

50. See Jean Beaufret, Dialogue avec Heidegger: Le Chemin de Heidegger (Paris: Éditions de Minuit, 1975), 49.

51. Derrida, "Ontologie et théologie," Irvine 8:12. See also Derrida's treatment of Jules Lagneau in his 1960–1961 "Cours sur Dieu," Irvine 7:4.

52. Derrida, "Ontologie et théologie," Irvine 8:12, sheets 3 and 5. See also Derrida, "Violence et métaphysique," in L'Écriture et la différence, 215.

53. Derrida, "Ontologie et théologie," Irvine 8:12, sheet 4.

54. Derrida, "Ontologie et théologie," Irvine 8:12, sheet 4. Compare with Derrida's discussion of Offenbarung and Offenbarkeit in "Faith and Knowledge," in Acts of Religion, ed. Gil Anidjar (New York: Routledge, 2002), 48–55.

55. Derrida, "Ontologie et théologie," 7:9, sheet 7. See Derrida, L'Écriture et la différence, 220.

56. See Derrida, L'Écriture et la différence, 222. Derrida suggests that this argument derives from Levinas.

57. Derrida, "Ontologie et théologie," Irvine 8:12, sheet 8.

58. Derrida, L'Écriture et la différence, 47–48, 105, 285, 358, 389; Derrida, De la grammatologie, 31–32, 73; and Derrida, Marges de la philosophie (Paris: Éditions de Minuit, 1972), 163.

59. Derrida, L'Écriture et la différence, 203–4, and "Peut-on dire oui a la finitude?" Irvine 7:9, sheets 26 and 48, where Derrida relates Nietzschean philosophy to the traditional conception of finitude, and in Derrida, "Heidegger et la question de l'être et de l'histoire," Irvine 9:1, sheet 13, where Derrida reiterates the Heideggerian criticism of Nietzsche's philosophy as an onto-theology of the will-to-power. In De la Grammatologie Derrida recuperates this aspect of Nietzsche, tying his rejection of Being to the denial of a transcendental signified. Derrida, De la Grammatologie, 31–32.

60. Birault, "De l'être, du divin, et des dieux," 539–40. Birault, "Démystication de la pensée et démythisation de la foi: la critique de la théologie chez Nietzsche," in De l'être, du divin, et des dieux, 174.

61. Birault, "De l'être, du divin, et des dieux," 540. See also Birault "Démystication de la pensée," 174–76.

62. In Heidegger's language, it was the "Differenter der Differenz." Birault, "De l'être, du divin, et des dieux," 540–41. Birault used this analysis to criticize the French translations of Verfallen and Geworfenheit as déchéance and déréliction,

and thus compounded his attack on the Sartrian and humanist reading of Heidegger.

63. Birault, "De l'être, du divin, et des dieux," 548.

64. Birault, "De l'être, du divin, et des dieux," 549.

65. Birault, "De l'être, du divin, et des dieux," 549. See Derrida, *L'Écriture et la différence*, 47, 428.

66. Henri Birault, "Nietzsche et le pari de Pascal," in Birault, *De l'être, du divin, et des dieux*, 19. Originally published as "Pascal e Nietzsche," in *Archivio di filosofia* 3 (1962): 67–90.

67. Birault, "Nietzsche et le pari de Pascal," 30.

68. See Birault, "Science et métaphysique chez Descartes," in Birault, *De l'être, du divin, et des dieux*, 78, where he argues through Pascal that though the God of philosophers may eventually seem ridiculous [*ridicule*], it is not thereby false [*fallacieux*].

69. Birault, "Nietzsche et le pari de Pascal," 28.

70. Birault, "Nietzsche et le pari de Pascal," 32.

71. Birault, "Nietzsche et le pari de Pascal," 30–33. We should note, however, that according to Birault, Pascal's conception of God, which finds its place in this opening, remained caught in the dogmatic scholastic tradition. See, among others, Birault, *De l'être, du divin, et des dieux*, 64, 108.

72. Derrida, *L'Écriture et la différence*, 428.

73. Although it should be noted that Derrida regarded the "death of God" as a peculiarly Christian invention, which is resisted by Judaism and Islam. See "Sauf le nom," in Jacques Derrida, *On the Name*, 63, or "Faith and Knowledge," in *Acts of Religion*, 51.

74. Henri Birault, "Existence et vérité d'après Heidegger," in *De l'être, du divin, et des dieux*, 355, and "La Foi et la pensée d'après Heidegger," though in the later texts, and particularly the works we have discussed most here, Birault seems to be moving away from this position.

75. As Derrida remarked in a later interview, "on or about 'grace given by God,' deconstruction, as such, has nothing to say or do," in Yvonne Sherwood, ed., *Derrida and Religion: Other Testaments* (New York: Routledge, 2005), 39.

76. It would be worth reading Birault here alongside Derrida's discussion of the "two sources" of religion, in Derrida, "Faith and Knowledge," *Acts of Religion*.

77. Derrida, "Violence et Metaphysique," 221. And in this sense Derrida leans toward Levinas rather than Birault.

78. See Jacques Derrida, *Positions* (Paris: Éditions de Minuit, 1972), 4. For an analysis of this shift, see my *The Young Derrida and French Philosophy 1945–1968* (Cambridge: Cambridge University Press, 2011), part 2.

79. One might suggest that these traces are clearest in the vexed question of the ethics of deconstruction. The reference to God gives a clear reason for why we should deconstruct philosophical systems: they do violence to the divine. But in Derrida's later work, onto-theology is presented as the trace of the trace, and

so is itself constituted by différance. It remains unclear why we should deconstruct this manifestation of différance in favor of others. The ethical value attributed to deconstruction might then be considered as a residue of the earlier, more religious period in Derrida's thought.

80. Jacques Derrida, "Circumfession," in Geoffrey Bennington, *Jacques Derrida* (Chicago: University of Chicago Press, 1993), 155.

Called to Bear Witness: Derrida, Muslims, and Islam
Anne Norton

1. The phrase comes from Gaston Bachelard, *Poetics of Space* (Boston: Beacon Press, 1994).

2. Jacques Derrida, *Acts of Religion*, ed. Gil Anidjar (New York: Routledge, 2002), 47. See also 58–59.

3. Jacques Derrida, *Rogues: Two Essays on Reason*, trans. Pascale-Anne Brault and Michael Naas (Stanford, CA: Stanford University Press, 2005), 28.

4. Derrida, *Rogues*, 28. See also Derrida, *Acts of Religion*, 46. Derrida's argument in *Rogues* is surprisingly close to Samuel Huntington's argument for a "clash of civilizations," albeit with a slightly different cast of characters. Derrida's division of the world, like Huntington's, starts as a dubious taxonomy and narrows to a single suspect binary: Islam and the West.

5. Iran is not "Arabic and Islamic," though Derrida may regard it as included in his reference to "the Arabic literality of the language of the Koran." *Rogues*, 28. It is, however, the most plausible candidate for the term "theocracy" in the set Derrida defines. Most other regimes in Arab and Muslim states, however authoritarian, have (like their counterparts in the West and East) pretended to the names of "republic" and "democracy."

6. Ruhollah Khomeini, *Islam and Revolution*, ed. and trans. Hamid Algar (Berkeley, CA: Mizan Press, 1981), 31, 58, 130.

7. One of the most interesting political features of Khomeini's constitutional theory is the subordination of the legislative to the judicial power. This sociologically unsurprising feature of the theory is a reversal of the position, canonical in Western political thought, that the legislative power has primacy. It is worth noting that most Western theorists regard legislative power as a problem to be managed, not as a virtue, a position that reflects their general anxiety about democracy.

8. Derrida, *Rogues*, 28.

9. The problem of taking secularism as a supplement to democracy is the risk that this supplement would operate in a Derridian sense—adding only to replace. That risk is evident in "Faith and Knowledge." Derrida, *Acts of Religion*, 47.

10. Carl Schmitt, *Political Theology* (Chicago: University of Chicago Press, 2006), 36. See also chapter 3.

11. Carl Schmitt, *Concept of the Political*, trans. George Schwab (Chicago: University of Chicago Press, 2007), 5.

12. I discuss this model in "Pentecost: Democratic Sovereignty in Carl Schmitt," *Constellations* 18, no. 3 (Sept. 2011): 389–402.

13. Carl Schmitt, *Roman Catholicism and Political Form*, trans. G. L. Ulmen (Westport, CT: Greenwood Press, 1996).

14. Leo Strauss, "Why We Remain Jews," in *Leo Strauss: Political Philosopher and Jewish Thinker*, ed. Kenneth Deutsch and Walter Nicgorski (New York: Rowman and Littlefield, 1994), 43–79. I discuss this essay and its relation to Islam in our time in "Why We Remain Jews," in *The Legacy of Leo Strauss*, ed. Tony Burns and James Connolly (Exeter, UK: Imprint Academic, 2010).

15. Schmitt, *Political Theology*, 49.

16. There is much more to be said about Derrida's treatment of sovereignty in *Rogues*, but it lies outside the purview of this essay. Wendy Brown provides a discerning analysis of Derrida's treatment of sovereignty in *Rogues* in "Sovereign Hesitations," in *Derrida and the Time of the Political*, ed. Pheng Cheah and Suzanne Guerlac (Durham, NC: Duke University Press, 2009), 114–32.

17. Derrida, *Rogues*, 30. For more on Derrida's (though not only Derrida's) attempt to justify this position, see "Taking a Stand for Algeria," in *Acts of Religion*, 301–8.

18. Derrida, *Rogues*, 33.

19. Martin Hägglund, *Radical Atheism: Derrida and the Time of Life* (Stanford, CA: Stanford University Press, 2008), 13.

20. Derrida, *Rogues*, 30.

21. Derrida, *Rogues*, 33.

22. Derrida, *Rogues*, 33.

23. Derrida, *Rogues*, 30.

24. Derrida, *Rogues*, 32.

25. Derrida, *Rogues*, 31.

26. Al Farabi argues that multiple human beings with diverse talents and resources can be adequate to the rule of a divinely inspired prophet. See, for example, Aphorism 58 in *Al Farabi, The Political Writings: Selected Aphorisms and Other Texts*, trans. Charles Butterworth (Ithaca, NY: Cornell University Press, 2001).

27. John Locke, *Second Treatise, Two Treatises on Government*, ed. Peter Laslett (Cambridge: Cambridge University Press, 1988), 279–80 (chapter 3:18); Anne Norton, "Zeit und Begehren," in *Die Wiederentdeckung der Zeit*, ed. Antje Gimmler, Mike Sandbothe, and Walter Chr. Zimmerli (Darmstadt, Germany: Primus Verlag, 1997).

28. Derrida, *Rogues*, 36.

29. Derrida, *Rogues*, 63.

30. Derrida, *Rogues*, 68.

31. Derrida, *Rogues*, 64.

32. Jacques Derrida, *Aporias*, trans. Thomas Dutoit (Stanford, CA: Stanford University Press, 1993), 81.

33. John Caputo, *The Prayers and Tears of Jacques Derrida: Religion without Religion* (Bloomington: Indiana University Press, 1997), 304–5.

34. Gil Anidjar, *The Jew, the Arab: A History of the Enemy* (Stanford, CA: Stanford University Press, 2003). See also *Semites: Race, Religion, Literature* (Stanford, CA: Stanford University Press, 2007). Anidjar's nevertheless brilliant reading of the Arab, the Jew, tends to collapse the Arab in the Jew, concealing once again the presence of the Muslim. Perhaps heritage and genealogy fall before the imperative to bear witness.

35. *Qu'ran*, Sura 17, "The children of Israel," *Al-Quran*, trans. Ahmed Ali (Princeton, NJ: Princeton University Press, 1984).

36. Roxanne Euben, *Journeys to the Other Shore: Muslim and Western Travelers in Search of Knowledge* (Princeton, NJ: Princeton University Press, 2006), 21.

37. *Pieds noirs*, black feet, is the name the French give to Algerian settler colonists. They were associated, during and after the war, with right-wing politics and the attempted coup against de Gaulle. The *harkis* were Algerian soldiers, usually Muslim, who fought with the French. Some of them were resettled en masse in France after Algeria won its independence. They are regarded as traitors by most Algerians but were not welcomed by the French.

38. Paul Silverstein, *Algeria in France: Transpolitics, Race and Nation* (Indianapolis: Indiana University Press, 2004).

39. As good *Maghrebis*, Westerners, the Derridas looked West to Hegel's *Abendland*, the land of the ever-opening and uncertain future, in naming their son for Jackie Coogan. The late modern West would serve Derrida well.

40. *Maghreb* means "West" in Arabic. It is also the name of Morocco, and a term for North Africans more generally.

41. An interview broadcast in the program prepared by Didier Cahen over France-Culture, "Le bon plaisir de Jacques Derrida," on March 22, 1986, and published with the title "Entretien avec Jacques Derrida," in *Digraphe* 42 (December 1987): 14–27. This translation appeared as "There Is No 'One' Narcissism," in *Points:. . . Interviews 1974–1994*, by Jacques Derrida, trans. Elisabeth Weber (Stanford, CA: Stanford University Press, 1995), 196–216.

42. Gayatri Spivak, introduction to *Of Grammatology*, by Jacques Derrida (Baltimore, MD: Johns Hopkins University Press, 1997), lxxxv.

43. Geoffrey Bennington and Jacques Derrida, *Jacques Derrida*, trans. Geoffrey Bennington (Chicago: University of Chicago Press, 1993).

44. Jacques Lacan, *The Seminar, Book XI, The Four Fundamental Concepts of Psychoanalysis*, ed. Jacques-Alain Miller, trans. Alan Sheridan (New York: W. W. Norton, 1998), 197.

45. Geoffrey Bennington and Jacques Derrida, *Jacques Derrida*, 8.

46. Hélène Cixous, *Portrait of Jacques Derrida as a Young Jewish Saint*, trans. Beverley Bie Brahic (New York: Columbia University Press, 2005), 1, 69, 123.

47. Cixous's hostility to the Muslim, the Arab, in her own past informs her reading of Derrida. See Anne Norton, "The Red Shoes: Islam and the Limits of Solidarity in Cixous's *Mon Algériance*," *Theory and Event* 14, no. 1 (2011).

48. On the Abrahamic see Gil Anidjar's introduction to Derrida, *Acts of Religion*, 9.

49. Jacques Derrida, *The Gift of Death*, trans. David Wills (Chicago: University of Chicago Press, 1995), 64, 72.

50. With regard to Derrida's writings—and silences—on Islam, one does well to know the questions that surround the sacrifice of Abraham. Is one son sacrificed or two? Are Isaac and Ishmael confounded for Derrida? Is Ishmael the friend or the enemy? Is Ishmael outside the covenant or does the divine covenant with him as well?

51. Carl Schmitt, *Political Theology*, trans. George Schwab (Chicago: University of Chicago Press, 2005), 5.

52. Derrida, *The Gift of Death*, 69. Frantz Fanon offers a still darker reading, I believe. I discuss this in Anne Norton, *Bloodrites of the Poststructuralists: Word, Flesh and Revolution* (New York: Routledge, 2002), 129–37.

53. Derrida, *The Gift of Death*, 68–69.

54. Derrida, *The Gift of Death*, 70.

55. The Qu'ran is ambiguous saying only "a son." "Those Who Stand in Rows," 37:102–7.

56. The figure of the *Muselmann*, the one reduced to bare life, unites two forms of the alien, the other, who is nevertheless one's own. On the question of the *Muselmann*, see Anidjar, *The Jew, The Arab*.

57. French law does not permit official identification of ethnic or religious populations within the French citizenry. Nevertheless, the police are widely thought to direct suspicion, violence, and the machinery of the law against people of color, especially those thought to be Muslim.

58. See Joan Wallach Scott, *The Politics of the Veil* (Princeton, NJ: Princeton University Press, 2007), for a brilliant account of the debate over the veil in France. Scott's work provides insight into the context of Muslim politics in France during the last years of Derrida's life.

59. Derrida, *The Gift of Death*, 69–70.

60. Anidjar, *The Jew, The Arab*, 54.

61. The most famous is Rabbi Akiba's martyrdom by the Romans, in which he died under torture while reciting the *Shema*, and with the last word on his lips as he died. The *Shema* also figures iconically in contemporary accounts of death by terrorism characterized as martyrdom. Faisal Devji observes in *Landscapes of Jihad* (Ithaca, NY: Cornell University Press, 2005) that the innocent victims of suicide bombing and other martyrdom operations are also regarded as martyrs. In Islam, as in Derrida, the link between death and bearing witness is entangled with an uncertain, iridescent subject: friend and enemy.

62. Derrida, *Acts of Religion*, 9.

63. Genesis 15:13.

64. Jacques Derrida, *The Politics of Friendship*, trans. Gorge Collins (New York: Verso, 2005), 75.

65. Derrida, *Politics of Friendship*, 152.

66. Derrida, *Politics of Friendship*, 5.

67. As Derrida argued in "Hostipitality," the word *hospitality* "allows itself to be parasitized into its opposite." Jacques Derrida, "Hostipitality," trans. Barry Stocker with Forbes Morlock, *Angelaki: Journal of the Theoretical Humanities* 5, no. 3 (December 2000): 3.

68. Derrida, *Politics of Friendship*, 148.

69. Derrida, *Politics of Friendship*, 306.

70. Derrida, *Politics of Friendship*, 232.

71. Derrida, *Politics of Friendship*, 89.

72. Tariq Ramadan, *Western Muslims and the Future of Islam* (New York: Oxford University Press, 2003).

73. Friedrich Nietzsche, *The Gay Science*, trans. Walter Kaufmann (New York: Vintage, 1974), 203.

74. Jacques Derrida, *Of Grammatology*, trans. Gayatri Chakravorty Spivak (Baltimore, MD: Johns Hopkins University Press, 1976).

75. Ramadan, *Western Muslims and the Future of Islam*, 65–78.

76. Jacques Derrida, "Sauf le nom," in *On the Name*, trans. David Wood, ed. Thomas Dutoit (Stanford, CA: Stanford University Press, 1995), 56.

77. Martin Heidegger, *Building Dwelling Thinking*, trans. Albert Hofstadter (New York: Harper Colophon Books, 1971).

78. Derrida, *On the Name*, 93.

79. Derrida, *On the Name*, 93. See also, 56, 76, 83 (the conflict between maintaining a specific secret and inclusion), and 104, where Derrida points to the importance of politics in this question.

80. Jacques Derrida, *The Ear of the Other: Otobiography, Transference, Translation*, trans. Peggy Kamuf (New York: Schocken Books, 1985).

81. Many people throughout the Francophone world know this fable by heart, word for word. Jean de la Fontaine, "Le loup et l'agneau," *La Fontaine Fables*, ed. Jean-Pierre Collinet (Paris: Galliard, 1991).

82. Derrida, "Faith and Knowledge," in *Acts of Religion*, 57.

83. Derrida, "Faith and Knowledge," in *Acts of Religion*, 58. It is worth noting that throughout this essay "we" are opposed to Islam. No presumptive "we" should be swallowed easily, but in this case there are powerful reasons, no less scholarly than political, for rejecting inclusion in this "we." For more on the stakes, see *Acts of Religion*, 90–91. Wendy Brown takes up an important aspect of this question in her essay "Sovereign Hesitations," in *Derrida and the Time of the Political*, ed. Pheng Cheah and Suzanne Guerlac (Durham, NC: Duke University Press, 2009) 114–32.

84. Hans Wehr, *A Dictionary of Modern Standard Arabic* (London: MacDonald and Evans and Librairie du Liban, 1980).

85. Derrida, *Aporias*, ix–x. In reading this passage in this way I am only following Derrida in "twisting a little" an expression in which "I hear accord."

1. Originally published in French as *Judéités: Questions pour Jacques Derrida*, ed. Joseph Cohen and Raphael Zagury-Orly (Paris: Galilée, 2003); translated into English as *Judeities: Questions for Jacques Derrida*, ed. Joseph Cohen, Raphael Zagury-Orly, and Bettina Bergo, trans. Bettina Bergo and Michael B. Smith (New York: Fordham University Press, 2007).

2. Pierre Bouretz, *D'un ton guerrier en philosophie: Habermas, Derrida & Co.* (Paris: Gallimard, 2011).

3. Jürgen Habermas, *The Philosophical Discourse of Modernity: Twelve Lectures*, trans. Frederick Lawrence (Cambridge, MA: MIT Press, 1990); originally *Die philosophische Diskurs der Moderne: Zwölf Vorlesungen* (Frankfurt: Suhrkamp, 1985), hereafter PDM.

4. PDM, 181.

5. PDM, 181.

6. PDM, 181.

7. PDM, 165. Emphasis added.

8. PDM, 182.

9. PDM, 182.

10. PDM, 182, quoting Jacques Derrida, *Of Grammatology*.

11. PDM, 183.

12. PDM, 183.

13. PDM, 183.

14. PDM, 184.

15. PDM, 183.

16. PDM, 192.

17. PDM, "Excursus," 186.

18. PDM, 210.

19. PDM, 210.

20. On Habermas and the *Historikerstreit*, see Charles S. Maier, *The Unmasterable Past: History, Holocaust, and German National Identity* (Cambridge, MA: Harvard University Press, 1998).

21. Walter Benjamin, "The Work of Art in the Age of Its Technological Reproducibility," in *Walter Benjamin: Selected Writings*, ed. Michael W. Jennings and Howard Eiland, vol. 4, *1938–1940* (Cambridge, MA: Harvard University Press, 2003), 251–83, esp. 283.

22. Jürgen Habermas, "Public Space and the Political Public Sphere," in *Between Naturalism and Religion*, (Cambridge: Polity Press, 2008), 19.

23. Why fundamental ontology had to run off into the blind alley of the philosophy of the subject it was supposed to be steering clear of is easy to see. Ontology with a transcendental twist is guilty of the same mistake that it attributes to classical epistemology: Whether one gives primacy to the Being-question or to the knowledge-question, in either case the cognitive relation

to the world and fact-stating discourse—theory and propositional truth—hold a monopoly as what is genuinely human and in need of clarification. (PDM, 151)

24. For an intellectual history of the entire reception, see Ethan Kleinberg, *Generation Existential: Heidegger's Philosophy in France, 1927–1961* (Ithaca, NY: Cornell University Press, 2005).

25. See, for example, the synthetic treatment by Alphonse De Waelhens, *La Philosophie de Martin Heidegger* (Louvain, Belgium: Éditions de l'Institut supérieur de philosophie, 1942); and his many translations: Martin Heidegger, *De l'essence de la vérité* (Louvain, Belgium: Nauwelaerts, 1948); Martin Heidegger, *Kant et le problème de la métaphysique* (Paris: Gallimard, 1953); Martin Heidegger, *L'Être et le temps*, trans. §§ 1–44, R. Boehm (Paris: Gallimard, 1964).

26. It is worth remembering that in the early 1970s, Derrida's own French contemporaries charged him with a crypto-Heideggerian irrationalism that would import ideological elements of the old German right into the French New Left. For a summary of these debates, see Peter E. Gordon, "Hammer without a Master: French Phenomenology and the Origins of Deconstruction (or, How Derrida read Heidegger)," in *Histories of Postmodernism*, ed. Mark Bevir, Jill Hargis, and Sara Rushing (New York: Routledge, 2007).

27. Martin Heidegger, *Introduction to Metaphysics*, ed. Gregory Fried and Richard Polt (New Haven, CT: Yale University Press, 2000), 213.

28. Jürgen Habermas, "Mit Heidegger gegen Heidegger denken: Zur Veröffentlichung von Vorlesungen aus dem Jahre 1935," *Frankfurter Allgemeine Zeitung*, 25 July, 1953; republished in English as Jürgen Habermas, "Martin Heidegger: On the Publication of the Lecture of 1935," in *The Heidegger Controversy*, ed. Richard Wolin (Cambridge, MA: MIT Press, 1993), 186–197.

29. As evidence Habermas cited only a single essay by Derrida, "The Ends of Man." See PDM, 162.

30. PDM, 167.

31. "February 15, or What Binds Europeans Together: A Plea for a Common Foreign Policy, Beginning at the Core of Europe," reprinted in *The Derrida-Habermas Reader*, ed. Lasse Thomassen (Chicago: University of Chicago Press, 2006), 270–77.

32. It is interesting to note that Hent de Vries himself resists the strong narrative structure that would divide Derrida's work into "early" and "late" and he does not emphasize a *shift* in Derrida's religion. See Hent de Vries, *Philosophy and the Turn to Religion* (Baltimore, MD: Johns Hopkins University Press, 1999); Jacques Derrida, *De l'Esprit: Heidegger et la question* (Paris: Galilée, 1987); in English as Jacques Derrida, *Of Spirit: Heidegger and the Question*, trans. Geoffrey Bennington and Rachel Bowlby (Chicago: University of Chicago Press, 1991); Jacques Derrida, "Adieu á Emmanuel Lévinas," in *Libération* 28, no. 12 (1995): 4; later in book form as Jacques Derrida, *Adieu - à Emmanuel Lévinas* (Paris: Galilée, 1997).

33. Jacques Derrida, "Violence et métaphysique. Essai sur la pensée d'Emmanuel Lévinas," originally in *Revue de Métaphysique et de Morale* 69, no. 3 (July–September):

322–54, and 69, no. 4 (October–December): 425–73; reprinted in Jacques Derrida, *L'écriture et la différence* (Paris: Seuil, 1967).

34. Jacques Derrida, "Violence and Metaphysics," in *Writing and Difference* (Chicago: University of Chicago Press, 1980), 111.

35. Derrida, "Violence and Metaphysics," 111.

36. Nor should we neglect to mention that Derrida typically maintained only the most complicated and conflicted relation to his own Jewish identity. The very notion of "identity," with all its proprietary significance, aroused his philosophical discomfort, magnified perhaps by a biographical and intellectual heritage of sometimes contesting identifications, North African, Jewish, French—and, indeed, Christian. As Edward Baring has explained, Derrida's philosophical formation brought him into the close orbit of Christian existentialists. See Edward Baring, *The Young Derrida and French Philosophy, 1945–1968* (Cambridge: Cambridge University Press, 2011), 18.

37. Derrida, "Violence and Metaphysics," 111.

38. Derrida, "Violence and Metaphysics," 152.

39. Derrida, "Violence and Metaphysics," 153.

40. Derrida, "Violence and Metaphysics," 153.

41. Jacques Derrida, *Adieu to Emmanuel Levinas*, trans. Pascale-Anne Brault and Michael Naas (Stanford, CA: Stanford University Press, 1999), 2–13. The lines that immediately follow the passage quoted above also bear consideration:

> The regret, my regret, is not having said this to him enough, not having shown him this enough in the course of these thirty years, during which, in the modesty of silences, through brief or discreet conversations, writings too indirect or reserved, we often addressed to one another what I would call neither questions nor answers but, perhaps, to use another of his words, a sort of "question, prayer," a question-prayer that, as he says, would be anterior to all dialogue." (Derrida, *Adieu*, 12–13)

42. Paul Celan, untitled poem, in *Paul Celan: Poems*, trans. Michael Hamburger (New York: Persea Books, 1980), 240–42. On Celan's relations with Heidegger, see James K. Lyon, *Paul Celan and Martin Heidegger: An Unresolved Conversation, 1951–1970* (Baltimore, MD: Johns Hopkins University Press, 2006). Lyon does not discuss Celan's untitled "addition" to the poem "Todtnauberg," from which I have quoted above.

43. Victor Farías, *Heidegger et le nazisme. Traduit de l'espagnol et de l'allemand par Myriam Benarroch et Jean-Baptiste Grasset* (Lagrasse, France: Verdier, 1987); Emmanuel Faye, *Heidegger: The Introduction of Nazism into Philosophy in Light of the Unpublished Seminars of 1933–1935*, trans. Michael B. Smith (New Haven, CT: Yale University Press, 2009).

44. Jürgen Habermas, "How to Answer the Ethical Question," in *Judeities* (New York: Fordham University Press, 2007), 142–54.

45. Habermas, "How to Answer the Ethical Question," 142.

46. Jacques Derrida, "The Future of the Profession," reprinted as "The University without Condition," in Jacques Derrida, *Without Alibi*, trans. and ed. Peggy Kamuf (Stanford, CA: Stanford University Press, 2002), 202–37.

47. Habermas, "How to Answer the Ethical Question," 144.

48. Habermas, "How to Answer the Ethical Question," 154.

49. Significantly, Habermas evades Levinas's attempt to distance himself from Kierkegaard; instead he seems to agree with Derrida that the gap between Kierkegaardian religion and Levinasian ethics is less dramatic than Levinas supposed.

50. Habermas, "How to Answer the Ethical Question," 149.

51. Habermas, "How to Answer the Ethical Question," 150–51.

52. Habermas, "How to Answer the Ethical Question," 151. Emphasis added.

53. Habermas, "How to Answer the Ethical Question," 124; Habermas is quoting from Theodor W. Adorno, *Minima Moralia* (London: Verso, 1984), 247.

54. Habermas, "How to Answer the Ethical Question," 154.

55. Habermas, "How to Answer the Ethical Question," 154.

56. Jacques Derrida, *Of Grammatology*, trans. Gayatri Chakravorty Spivak (Baltimore, MD: Johns Hopkins University Press, 1998), 47.

57. Jacques Derrida, *Specters of Marx: The State of the Debt, the Work of Mourning, and the New International* (New York: Routledge, 1994), 73.

58. Habermas also recalled the comparison between Adorno and Derrida as philosophers affiliated by Jewish thought. The relevant passage is worth quoting at great length:

> Derrida never met Adorno. But when he was awarded the Adorno Prize he gave a speech in the Paulskirche in Frankfurt, which in its train of thought could not have been closer to Adorno's spirit, right down to the secret twists of Romantic dream motifs. Their Jewish roots are the common factor that links them. While Gershom Scholem remained a challenge for Adorno, Emmanuel Levinas became an authority for Derrida. So it is that his oeuvre can also have an enlightening impact in Germany, because Derrida appropriated the themes of the later Heidegger without committing any neo-pagan betrayal of his own Mosaic roots.

The German reads thus:

> Gershom Scholem blieb für Adorno eine Herausforderung, Emmanuel Levinas ist für Derrida zu einem Lehrer geworden. Derridas Werk kann in Deutschland auch deshalb eine klärende Wirkung entfalten, weil es sich den späten Heidegger aneignet, ohne an den mosaischen Anfängen neuheidnisch Verrat zu üben.

Originally published as Jürgen Habermas, "Ein letzter Gruß. Derridas klärende Wirkung," *Frankfurter Rundschau* (October 11, 2004); and published two days later in French: "Présence de Derrida," *Liberation* (October 13, 2004); translation in *The Derrida-Habermas Reader*, 307–8; quote from 308.

59. There is a small but intriguing discrepancy between the version of the question as phrased in the English text (included in the volume from Fordham University Press) and the French version as published in *Judéités*. The French version corresponds closely to the German text Habermas published some years later. The French version reads thus: "*Et, pour le cas où serait satisfaite l'exigence de rendre plus explicites ces connotations*—qui, et ce n'est pas un accident, nous rappellent une tradition religieuse spécifique—, quelle serait la 'colonne vertébrale' des justifications qui s'ensuivrait alors?" The German text corresponds to the French as follows: "Kann Derrida die normativen Konnotationen der ungewissen Ankunft eines unbestimmten Ereignisses so undefiniert lassen wie Heidegger? Wenn nicht, welche Beweislasten ergäben sich dann aus der Bereitschaft, *diese Konnotationen, die sich nicht zufällig aus einer bestimmten religiösen Überlieferung ergeben*, explizit zu machen?" We can translate the original passage thus: "Can Derrida leave the normative connotations of an uncertain arrival of an indeterminate event as undefined as Heidegger does? If not, what burdens of proof would then be on offer, if we were prepared to make explicit these connotations, *connotations which do not accidentally derive from a determinate religious inheritance?*" The relevant passage, italicized here for emphasis, dramatizes the "specific" religious import of Derrida's language, and is presumably a reference to Derrida's recourse to the language of *Judaism*. The difference between the two versions is suggestive, as it implies Habermas may have wished to press the question as to whether a *particular* religious tradition could be expected to bear normative contents of a non-particularist application. German text quoted from Jürgen Habermas, "Wie die Ethische Frage zu Beantworten Ist: Derrida und die Religion," in Jürgen Habermas, *Ach, Europa: kleine politische Schriften, XI* (Frankfurt, Germany: Suhrkamp Verlag, 2008), 40–60; quote from 60.

60. For Habermas's theory of translation as the bridge between substantive religious norms and the public sphere, see the excellent summary of the current debate in Hugh Baxter, *Habermas: The Discourse Theory of Law and Democracy*, especially chapter 5, "After *Between Facts and Norms*: Religion in the Public Square, Multiculturalism, and the 'Postnational Constellation'" (Stanford, CA: Stanford Law Books, 2011). Also see Peter E. Gordon, "What Hope Remains?" review of *An Awareness of What Is Missing: Faith and Reason in a Post-Secular Age*, by Jürgen Habermas (Polity Press, 2010); and Judith Butler, Jürgen Habermas, Charles Taylor, and Cornel West, *The Power of Religion in the Public Sphere*, ed. Eduardo Mendieta and Jonathan Vanantwerpen (New York: Columbia University Press, 2011); in *The New Republic* (December 14, 2012).

61. Jürgen Habermas, *Post-Metaphysical Thinking: Philosophical Essays*, trans. William Mark Hohengarten (Cambridge, MA: MIT Press, 1994).

62. Jacques Derrida, "The Ends of Man," *Philosophy and Phenomenological Research* 30, no. 1 (September 1969): 31–57.

Abraham, the Settling Foreigner
Joseph Cohen and Raphael Zagury-Orly

1. In reference to the "multiplicity" of the Abrahamic figure in the Bible, we ought here to refer to the important article by Thomas Römer, "Qui est Abraham? Les différentes figures du patriarche dans la Bible hébraïque," in *Abraham. Nouvelle jeunesse d'un ancêtre*, ed. Thomas Römer (Geneva: Labor et Fides, 1997), 13–43. In this article, Römer proposes a highly original reading of the Abrahamic figure, stressing the "quasi-structural" impossibility of categorizing this figure by inscribing it into a fixed identity or static concept.

2. Genesis 15:13.

3. On the question of revelation and its difference with the meaning of truth as *a-letheia* and its deployment through the rapport between *Offenbarung* and *Offenbarkeit*, see Jacques Derrida, "Faith and Knowledge: The Two Sources of 'Religion' at the Limits of Reason Alone," in *Religion*, ed. Jacques Derrida and Gianni Vattimo (Stanford, CA: Stanford University Press, 1998), and Raphael Zagury-Orly, "Apories de la révélation. Pour une nouvelle structure de l'expérience," in *Questionner encore* (Paris: Galilée, 2011).

4. By deploying the question of "European cultural identity" and by revealing the inherent "aporias" involved in this very questioning, Derrida reflects, in this text, on the impossible-possible duty (*devoir*) to think, without relinquishing the "logic" by which Europe has constituted and signified itself, toward another heading for Europe:

> It is a logic, logic itself, that I do not wish to criticize here. I would even be ready to subscribe to it, but with one hand only, for I keep another to write or look for something else, perhaps outside Europe. Not only in order to look—in the way of research, analysis, knowledge, and philosophy—for what is already found outside of Europe, but not to close off in advance a border to the future, to the to-come [*à-venir*] of the *event*, to that which *comes* [*vient*], which comes perhaps and perhaps comes from a completely other shore. (Jacques Derrida, *The Other Heading: Reflections on Today's Europe* [Bloomington: Indiana University Press, 1992], 69)

5. We are, of course, referring here to Derrida's opening address, entitled "Abraham, l'autre," at the Judéités: Questions pour Jacques Derrida conference held in December 2000. Derrida's address was published in the proceedings of the conference: *Judéités. Questions pour Jacques Derrida*, ed. Joseph Cohen and Raphael Zagury-Orly (Paris: Galilée, 2003). The proceedings were translated in English under the title *Judeities: Questions for Jacques Derrida*, ed. Bettina Bergo, Joseph Cohen, Michael B. Smith, and Raphael Zagury-Orly (New York: Fordham University Press, 2007).

6. The final version of "The Spirit of Christianity and Its Fate" can be found in English language translation in the selection of Hegel's early theological writings (selection of writings from both the Bern [1795–1797] and Frankfurt [1797–1800]

periods) edited by T. M. Knox and collected in the volume entitled *Early Theological Writings* (Philadelphia: University of Pennsylvania Press, 1975). The complete German edition of Hegel's early writings was edited by H. Nohl under the title *Hegels theologische Jugendschriften* (Tübingen, Germany: Mohr, 1907). For the present essay, all quotations from *The Spirit of Christianity and Its Fate* are referenced in the English language edition.

7. There are numerous scholarly studies of Hegel's interpretation of Judaism in his early theological writings. Let us here refer to the most important published: Bernard Bourgeois, *Hegel à Francfort. Judaïsme, Christianisme, Hellénisme* (Paris: J. Vrin, 1971); Joseph Cohen, *Le spectre juif de Hegel* (Paris: Galilée, 2005); Jacques Derrida, *Glas* (Paris: Galilée, 1973); Emil Fackenheim, *The Religious Dimension in Hegel's Thought* (Bloomington: Indiana University Press, 1971); Otto Pöggeler, "L'interprétation hégélienne du judaïsme," in *Etudes hégéliennes* (Paris: J. Vrin, 1985); Yirmiyahu Yovel, *Dark Riddle: Hegel, Nietzsche and the Jews* (Philadelphia: Pennsylvania State University Press, 1988).

8. Hegel, "The Spirit of Christianity and Its Fate," 205.

9. Hegel, "The Spirit of Christianity and Its Fate," 182. In the opening paragraph, Hegel marks it clearly: "With Abraham, the true progenitor of the Jews, the history of this people begins, i.e., his spirit is the unity, the soul, regulating the entire fate of his posterity."

10. Hegel, "The Spirit of Christianity and Its Fate," 187.

11. On the question of sacrifice in Hegel's philosophy, and most particularly in the *Phenomenology of Spirit*, see Joseph Cohen, *Le sacrifice de Hegel* (Paris: Galilée, 2007).

12. We are, of course, referring here to Kierkegaard's *Fear and Trembling*. Derrida interpreted this work, and most particularly Kierkegaard's reading of the sacrifice of Isaac, in Jacques Derrida, *The Gift of Death* (Chicago: Chicago University Press, 1995).

13. Matthew 6:4.

14. Jacques Derrida, "Abraham, the Other," in *Judeities: Questions for Jacques Derrida*, 1–35.

Unprotected Religion: Radical Theology, Radical Atheism, and the Return of Anti-Religion
John D. Caputo

1. The present study appeared in a longer and more fully elaborated form in "The Return of Anti-Religion: From Radical Atheism to Radical Theology," *The Journal of Cultural and Religious Theory* 11, no. 2 (Spring 2011): 32–125. http://www.jcrt.org/archives/11.2/caputo.pdf.

2. Martin Hägglund, *Radical Atheism: Derrida and the Time of Life* (Stanford, CA: Stanford University Press, 2008). Hereafter referred to as RA.

3. Quentin Meillassoux, *After Finitude: An Essay on the Necessity of Contingency*, trans. Ray Brassier (London: Continuum, 2008), 18. For robust rebuttals

of Meillassoux, see Adrian Johnston, "Hume's Revenge: À Dieu, Meillassoux," and Martin Hägglund, "Radical Atheist Materialism: A Critique of Meillassoux," in *The Speculative Turn: Continental Materialism and Realism*, ed. Levi Bryant, Nick Srnicek, and Graham Harman (Melbourne: re.press, 2011), 92–113 and 114–29, respectively.

4. Michael Naas, *Derrida From Now On* (New York: Fordham University Press, 2008), 62–80; see especially 239n5, in which Naas succinctly states my views on Derrida and religion with a judiciousness absent from RA.

5. Christopher Watkin, *Difficult Atheism: Post-Theological Thinking in Alain Badiou, Jean-Luc Nancy and Quentin Meillassoux* (Edinburgh: Edinburgh University Press, 2011), 3–11.

6. Jacques Derrida, "Circumfession: Fifty-Nine Periods and Periphrases," in *Jacques Derrida*, Geoffrey Bennington and Jacques Derrida (Chicago: University of Chicago Press, 1993), 58.

7. Clayton Crockett, "Surviving Christianity," *Derrida Today* 6, no.1 (2013): 29–33.

8. "STD," I cannot resist adding, is not far from "S.T.D.," the abbreviation for *sacrae theologiae doctor*.

9. As Derrida once pointed out, he first found the paradigm of phenomena constituted by their impossibility in Husserl's fifth *Cartesian Meditation*, where the alter ego is internally constituted by the impossibility of experiencing the experiences of the other person. Were that impossibility not possible, the phenomenon would be ruined. Jacques Derrida, "Hospitality, Justice and Responsibility," in *Questioning Ethics: Contemporary Debates in Philosophy*, ed. Mark Dooley and Richard Kearney (London: Routledge, 1999), 71.

10. John D. Caputo, *Radical Hermeneutics: Repetition, Deconstruction and the Hermeneutic Project* (Bloomington: Indiana University Press, 1987), 1–7.

11. In making Derrida's atheism into a "position," a "thesis," Hägglund undoes everything that is interesting about Derrida's atheism, all the undecidability and the faith embedded in it. Derrida says that while he "rightly passes" as an atheist, he cannot say he *is* an atheist. "I can't say, myself, 'I am an atheist.' It's not a *position*. I wouldn't say, 'I am an atheist' and I wouldn't say, 'I am a believer' either. I find the statement absolutely ridiculous. . . . Who *knows* that? . . . And who can say, 'I am an atheist?'" Jacques Derrida, "Epoche and Faith: An Interview with Jacques Derrida," in *Derrida and Religion: Other Testaments*, ed. Yvonne Sherwood and Kevin Hart (New York: Routledge, 2005), 47.

12. Jacques Derrida, *On the Name*, ed. Thomas Dutoit (Stanford, CA: Stanford University Press, 1995), 64.

13. Jacques Derrida, *Paper Machine*, trans. Rachel Bowlby (Stanford, CA: Stanford University Press, 2005), 96.

14. John D. Caputo, *The Weakness of God: A Theology of the Event* (Bloomington: Indiana University Press, 2004), 113. Hereafter referred to as WG.

15. Catherine Malabou, *What Should We Do with Our Brain?*, trans. Sebastian Rand (New York: Fordham University Press, 2008), 69.

16. Derrida, *Paper Machine*, 79.

17. Jacques Derrida, *Rogues: Two Essays on Reason*, trans. Pascale-Anne Brault and Michael Naas (Stanford, CA: Stanford University Press, 2005), 90.

18. Derrida, *Rogues*, 135, 142, 151, respectively.

19. Jacques Derrida, *The Beast and the Sovereign*, vol. 1, trans. Geoffrey Bennington (Chicago: University of Chicago Press, 2009), 110.

20. Jacques Derrida, *Without Alibi*, ed. and trans. Peggy Kamuf (Stanford, CA: Stanford University Press, 2002), 202.

21. Derrida, *Without Alibi*, 204–5.

22. Derrida, *Without Alibi*, 206.

23. Jacques Derrida, "The Force of Law," in *Acts of Religion*, ed. Gil Anidjar (New York: Routledge, 2002), 243.

24. Nor is the undeconstructible an "essential meaning" clothed in the materiality of a word, which is Žižek's misunderstanding of my view of the event. Slavoj Žižek and John Milbank, *The Monstrosity of Christ: Paradox or Dialectic*, ed. Creston Davis (Cambridge, MA: MIT Press, 2009), 256–60. This is a debate about whether Christianity or atheism is the true materialism!

25. Jacques Derrida, *Given Time: I. Counterfeit Money*, trans. Peggy Kamuf (Chicago: University of Chicago Press, 1991), 30.

26. The "desire" of Madame de Maintenon would be to "give what she cannot give"; "that is the whole of her desire. Desire and the desire to give would be the same thing, a sort of tautology. But maybe as well the tautological designation of the impossible." Derrida, *Given Time*, 4–5.

> For finally, if the gift is another name of the impossible, we still think it, we name it, we desire it . . . . In this sense one can think, desire, and say only the impossible, according to the measureless measure of the impossible . . . .
> If one wants to recapture the proper element of thinking, naming, desiring, it is perhaps according to the measureless measure of this limit that it is possible, possible as relation *without* relation to the impossible. (29)

27. Derrida, *Acts of Religion*, 254.

28. Derrida, *Rogues*, 74.

29. Derrida, *Given Time*, 29. Emphasis added.

30. Derrida, *Given Time*, 6.

31. Derrida, *Given Time*, 29.

32. Derrida, *Given Time*, 29. Emphasis added.

33. Derrida, *Given Time*, 30.

34. Allow me to note in passing the evolution of Derrida's use of "experience" from *Given Time* to *Psyché*. In *Given Time* he consigns "experience" to the order of presence in order to affirm the impossible beyond presence and experience. In *Psyché* he defines deconstruction as the "experience of the impossible" beyond presence. From the impossibility of experience to the experience of the impossible. See Derrida, *Acts of Religion*, 244, and *Psyche: Inventions of the Other*, vol. 1, trans. Peggy Kamuf and Elizabeth Rottenberg (Stanford, CA: Stanford University Press, 2007), 15.

35. Derrida, *Given Time*, 30.

36. Jacques Derrida, *Of Grammatology*, corrected edition, trans. Gayatri Spivak (Baltimore, MD: Johns Hopkins University Press, 1997), 60.

37. Derrida, *Of Grammatology*, 60–62.

38. Jacques Derrida, *Glas*, trans. Richard Rand and John Leavey (Lincoln: University of Nebraska, 1986), 151–62a, where the word "quasi-transcendental," which largely replaces "ultra-transcendental," is introduced at the end of a sentence split by an eleven-page break. See my *More Radical Hermeneutics* (Bloomington: Indiana University Press, 2000), 95–101.

39. The merit of Hägglund's book is to show that *différance* is not an immaterial being or a transcendental form. It can "take place" only in a material substance, only by spatially inscribing time and temporally inscribing space (RA, 27), taking off from Derrida's reference to a new transcendental aesthetics, beyond Kant's and Husserl's (Derrida, *Of Grammatology*, 290). We see such an "aesthetics" already when Derrida argued that by calling upon the "danger" of "writing" to explain the "origin of geometry" Husserl implied that the constitution of "ideal" objects requires a material-technological substance; this does not undermine ideal objects but explains how they are constituted. *Différance* is formally indifferent to the distinction between phonic and graphic or any other material substance, but it is not indifferent to the material substance in general. Its (quasi-)formality is "found," as it were, only in the "materiality" of spacetime, of "spacing-timing," which is what *différance* "is," if it is. But of itself, *différance* neither is nor is not, is neither ideal nor real, is neither a form nor a material substance, is "not more sensible than intelligible," is no more a matter of materialism than of formalism or idealism, just because it supplies the quasi-condition, "before all determination of the content," under which all such differences are constituted. The constitutive force of *différance* lies in the invisible (or inaudible) play of differences between visible (or audible) things, the "pure movement which produces difference," like the spacing between "ring, king, sing," the interval, the space, the slash between them (Derrida, *Of Grammatology*, 62). It "is" the between "itself," *s'il y en a*. It is, as such, the difference as such, which as such does not exist. So it is as inadequate to say Derrida is a materialist or a realist as to say he is an idealist; the less confusing thing to say is that he is not an anti-materialist, an anti-realist, or an anti-idealist.

40. Derrida, *Of Grammatology*, 61.

41. See "The Becoming Possible of the Impossible: An Interview with Jacques Derrida," in *A Passion for the Impossible: John D. Caputo in Focus*, ed. Mark Dooley (Albany: State University of New York Press, 2003), 26–27. This is an interview of Derrida by Mark Dooley about *The Prayers and Tears of Jacques Derrida*, followed by my reply to Derrida, "A Game of Jacks," 34–49. On the question of the religious turn, see Edward Baring's contribution to this volume.

42. Hägglund thinks that Levinas, who spent a good deal of World War II in a Nazi work camp, is defeated by this question (RA, 89)—without ever discussing Levinas's own reply. Hägglund does his best to distance Derrida from Levinas

(RA, 94–100), even on this point, their common notion that our obligation to the singular other is always divided by the other others (the "third"). Hägglund labors under the misunderstanding that Levinas is some kind of Neoplatonist who thinks that when you die you enjoy eternal happiness outside of time, whereas that was Levinas's critique of Kierkegaard's Christian eudaemonism. Quoting Levinas saying that the dream of "happy eternity" (meaning eternal happiness in Kierkegaard's Christianity) needs to be demythologized into fecundity (children) and the endless time it takes to do good (more time, either a new idea of time or a time of messianic vigilance), Hägglund mistakes Levinas's reference to "the eternal" as a Neoplatonic absolute *outside* time (RA, 133), also missing Levinas's opening for a distinctively Jewish "death of God" theology. Interestingly, both François Laruelle and Ray Brassier single out Levinas for having identified the very *structure* of the "real," even if it is restricted to the reality of the other person. Levinas reduces "religion" (other-worldly) to ethics (time) more radically than does Kant's *Religionbuch*, with assumptions as merciless as Nietzsche's about the myth of the *Hinterwelt*. Levinas thinks that when you die you rot, that you sur-vive only by living-on in more time (he is one of Derrida's sources on this point!), or in your children, and that life is postponing death. Hägglund notes this last point, but simply laments that Levinas should have been more consistent about it (RA, 91)!

43. In RA, 85, Hägglund conflates this point with the "non-ethical opening of ethics." But these are two different matters. The nonethical opening of ethics is archi-writing, *différance*, opening the space in which one can constitute ethical and legal categories, like good and bad, legal and illegal; that pre-ethical "violence" or archi-writing is what Levi-Strauss missed in his Rousseauizing of the Nambikwara (Derrida, *Of Grammatology*, 139–40). Archi-violence (= archi-writing) is to be distinguished from "the common concept of violence" (112). From this Hägglund concludes that the relation to the other cannot be "ethical" as such, which does not follow.

44. Derrida, *Of Grammatology*, 61–62.

45. Jacques Derrida, *The Gift of Death*, trans. David Wills (Chicago: Chicago University Press, 1995), 71; Derrida, *Acts of Religion*, 248.

46. Derrida, *The Beast and the Sovereign*, 108.

47. Jacques Derrida, *Negotiations: Interventions and Interviews: 1971–2001*, trans. Elizabeth Rottenberg (Stanford, CA: Stanford University Press, 2002), 105; cf. 182.

48. Derrida, *Negotiations*, 94.

49. Jacques Derrida, "An Apocalyptic Tone That Has Recently Been Adopted in Philosophy," in *Raising the Tone of Philosophy*, ed. Peter Fenves (Baltimore, MD: Johns Hopkins University Press, 1993), 164. Cf. Derrida, *Psyche*, 45.

50. Derrida, *Negotiations*, 94, adding: "One must think the event from the 'Come [*viens*]' and not the reverse."

51. John D. Caputo, *The Prayers and Tears of Jacques Derrida: Religion without Religion* (Bloomington: Indiana University Press, 1997).

52. Derrida, "An Apocalyptic Tone," 162. In the middle of the account of citationality, Derrida says the *singularity* of the "come" is "absolute," that is, each usage (John of Patmos's, his, etc.) is unique, and "divisible," that is, repeatable (not absolutely singular) (165). Hägglund cites this text and effectively undermines it with his gloss. Omitting the reference to "singularity," he says the "come" is "absolute because it is the condition of everything," but that is reduced to meaning that events can only be events by succeeding one another (RA, 46). So for Hägglund the text announces (quite *un*apocalyptically!) the absolute being of space and time. Never a word about the prayer, the injunction, the call, the appeal, which is "beyond being" (Derrida, "An Apocalyptic Tone," 166). The text is simply deposited in the bank accounts of radical atheism, despite the fact that it undermines the central premise of *Radical Atheism*, that events have a purely descriptive status in deconstruction.

53. Derrida, "An Apocalyptic Tone," 165.

54. Derrida, "An Apocalyptic Tone," 165.

55. Derrida, "An Apocalyptic Tone," 166.

56. Derrida, "An Apocalyptic Tone," 166.

57. Derrida, "An Apocalyptic Tone," 167.

58. Jacques Derrida, *Margins of Philosophy*, trans. Alan Bass (Chicago: University of Chicago Press, 1982), 12.

59. Derrida, *Of Grammatology*, 323n3.

60. As Jacques Derrida said to Kevin Hart when asked about "supernatural" grace (as opposed to the grace of the event), "deconstruction, as such, has nothing to say or to do . . . . deconstruction has no lever on this. And it should not have any lever." "Epoche and Faith: An Interview with Jacques Derrida," in *Derrida and Religion: Other Testaments*, ed. Yvonne Sherwood and Kevin Hart (New York: Routledge, 2005), 39.

61. Jacques Derrida, "Roundtable," in *Augustine and Postmodernism*, ed. John D. Caputo and Michael Scanlon (Bloomington: Indiana University Press, 2005), 38–39.

62. Mark Taylor, *Erring: A Postmodern A/Theology* (Chicago: University of Chicago Press, 1985).

63. Caputo, *The Prayers and Tears of Jacques Derrida*, 14.

64. Derrida, *Margins of Philosophy*, 6.

65. Caputo, *The Prayers and Tears of Jacques Derrida*, § 1.

66. John D. Caputo, *The Mystical Element in Heidegger's Thought* (New York: Fordham University Press, 1982), 222–40.

67. Jacques Derrida, "Afterw.rds: Or, at Least, Less than a Letter about a Letter Less," trans. Geoffrey Bennington, in *Afterwords*, ed. Nicholas Royle (Tampere, Finland: Outside Books, 1992), 200.

68. "The Becoming Possible of the Impossible: An Interview with Jacques Derrida," 28.

69. Derrida, *On the Name*, 76.

70. I am chided for misunderstanding Derrida on this point (RA, 116), but when the "correct" understanding is set forth, it simply repeats what I have said

for thirty years and is the basis of my disagreement with Jean-Luc Marion. See Caputo, *The Prayers and Tears of Jacques Derrida*, §§3–4, especially pages 45–48; and Caputo, *More Radical Hermeneutics*, ch. 10.

71. Before I published *The Prayers and Tears of Jacques Derrida* I sent the typescript to Derrida, who responded by saying, "vous me lisez comme j'aime être lu, là où les choses restent le plus risquées, le plus obscures, le plus instables, le plus hyperboliques," and added, "Je vous en remercie du fond du coeur, et je sais, à vous lire, que vous comprenez mieux que quiconque ce que je veux dire par là . . . ." (Personal Correspondence, February 24, 1996). In his interview with Mark Dooley, Derrida expresses his interest in seeing theology opened up in a deconstructive mode ("The Becoming Possible of the Impossible," 23–24), as he does also in "The Force of Law," in Derrida, *Acts of Religion*, 236; "Epoche and Faith: An Interview with Jacques Derrida," 27–50. The latter was an interview that Sherwood, Hart, and I conducted with Derrida at a memorable plenary session of the American Academy of Religion in 2002. I introduce all this not as an *auctoritas*, which would only return the gift to the donor. Indeed, in both the "Edifying Divertissements" of *The Prayers and Tears of Jacques Derrida* and in *Weakness of God* I take deconstruction where Jackie, "a little black and Arab Jew," cannot go—into a deconstruction of Christian theology, which gives "God" and theology some time (remembering that *donner* also includes *donner un coup*). My point is to show that Derrida and I share a common interest in letting deconstruction reopen and reinvent theology, a project close to the heart of deconstruction, not least because deconstruction has a heart, but quite foreign to *Radical Atheism*.

72. Jacques Derrida, *Learning to Live Finally: The Last Interview*, trans. Pascale-Anne Brault and Michael Naas (Hoboken, NJ: Melville House, 2007), 31; Derrida, *Rogues*, 158.

73. John D. Caputo, *Against Ethics* (Bloomington: Indiana University Press, 1993), 15–19.

74. Derrida, "Circumfession," 154.

75. Hägglund is mistaken to say that I gloss the "rightly pass for an atheist" passage (Derrida, "Circumfession," 155) by claiming that for me Derrida is merely an atheist about a Hellenistic God, which is a "finite creature," but not about the Biblical God, which is not a finite creature (RA, 227n61). I have consistently maintained that the name of God is an effect of the play of traces, that every "God" is a finite creature. What interests me in this passage is the *play* in the name to which Derrida confesses when he says "rightly pass." That is what they say about me and they are right, but there are so many other voices in me that cannot be arrested by this intimidating word, which is what Hägglund undertakes to do by trying to freeze dry the a/theological effect of deconstruction as "radical atheism." In the passage Hägglund cites (Caputo, *The Prayers and Tears of Jacques Derrida*, 334–36), and in *The Prayers and Tears of Jacques Derrida* generally, I am arguing that to approach Derrida by way of "negative theology" is to overemphasize Christianity and Neoplatonism and to have no ear for Der-

rida's Jewish side, which is tuned to the sensuous and strange images of God in the Tanach. Derrida is not an orthodox Jew, still less a Christian. He is even a bit of an Arab. When Hägglund goes on to sketch the mortal God in the rest of that note, he joins me in the project of constructing a weak theology.

76. "For there are those who say that what I am doing is really a hidden or cryptic religious faith, or that it is just skepticism, nihilism or atheism. He [Caputo] has never shared these prejudices." Dooley, "The Becoming Possible of the Impossible," 23.

77. Caputo, "A Game of Jacks," 36.

78. Derrida's work both shocks and emancipates confessional believers by showing that their faith is co-constituted by a non-faith, that they can only "rightly pass" for Christians (or anything else), an exquisite formula paralleling Johannes Climacus's refusal of the compliment of "Christian" as he is only trying to become one. On Augustine's use of *facere veritatem*, see *Confessions*, X, 1; cf. Derrida, "Circumfession," 47–48.

79. François Laruelle, in *Future Christ: A Lesson in Heresy* (trans. Anthony Paul Smith [London: Continuum, 2011]), uses the "future Christ" as a figure of immanence rather than of a transcendent being come down to earth to authorize the Inquisition and burn heretics.

80. Derrida, "Circumfession," 3.

81. Derrida, *Rogues*, 157; cf. xiv–xv, 114; "Epoche and Faith," 42: "If it is as weak and vulnerable that Jesus Christ represents or incarnates God, then the consequence would be that God is not absolutely powerful."

82. When Schelling says that God is not a being but a life, and hence subject to suffering and death (see Slavoj Žižek, *The Parallax View* [Cambridge, MA: MIT Press, 2006], 184–85), the radical atheism of *Radical Atheism* becomes a prolegomenon to radical theology. When invited once to replace *khora* with the God of love, I declined because that would load the dice and remove the risk. See James H. Olthuis, "Testing the Heart of Khora: Anonymous or Amorous," and my response, "The Chance of Love," in *Cross and Khora: Deconstruction and Christianity in the Work of John D. Caputo*, ed. Neal Deroo and Marko Zlomsic (Eugene, OR: Pickwick Publications, 2010), 174–96.

83. It is this "dangerous memory" of suffering and of the dead that I see inscribed in Derrida's gloss on Luke 9:60 about letting the dead bury the dead. Caputo, *The Prayers and Tears of Jacques Derrida*, 147. Glossing this text I do not side with Jesus, who is saying something very sassy, especially to Jews (it meant: seek the Kingdom of God first and put everything else second), but with Derrida, that this would be injustice. Absolute life, I say, "constitutes, for Derrida, the very definition of 'absolute evil,'" which is, alas, always possible. When I mark the difference between the impossible that we love and the impossible we may end up with, like the difference between the democracy to come and the National Socialism to come, Hägglund complains (RA, 141–42) that I am denying that the promise of justice is haunted by the threat of injustice, denying that as a structural matter laws that do justice to some sell others short, or the memory

of some is the forgetting of others. Those are things I point out clearly in other contexts and the complaint is simply groundless. Caputo, *The Prayers and Tears of Jacques Derrida*, 202–5.

84. Derrida says that he writes with a mixture of tragedy and laughter and that "Jack [Caputo] understood that he had to do the same with me. He understood that he had to make serious jokes." Derrida, "The Becoming Possible of the Impossible," 25–26.

85. "For me, God is precisely the one who would share my desire for the impossible, even if he doesn't respond to, or satisfy that desire. This is a dream." Derrida, "The Becoming Possible of the Impossible," 29. See Derrida's remarks on the endless fluctuation between God and the impossible (Ibid., 28) and my commentary on this passage in Caputo, "A Game of Jacks," 38–39. One of the many things sold short in *Radical Atheism*, chapter 4, is Hent de Vries's important argument that for Derrida the name of God is paradigmatic of every name, of the name itself, as that which is always already written under erasure, under the logic of the *sans*.

86. John D. Caputo, *The Insistence of God: A Theology of Perhaps* (Bloomington: Indiana University Press, 2013).

87. When my gloss on the New Testament sayings on the "Kingdom of God" are cited (RA, 121), the text I am glossing is confused with my point.

88. "Creation is quite an 'event,' which means it opens up a long chain of subsequent and unforeseeable events, both destructive and re-creative ones, and the creator is just going to have to live with that undecidability that is inscribed in things." WG, 72.

89. "The whole drama of creation follows a simple but bracing law: without the elements, there is no chance in creation, and without chance, there is no risk, and without risk and uncertainty, our conception of existence is an illusion or fantasy." WG, 74. "The two narratives have a kind of good news/bad news structure: 'Good, yes, yes, but.'" WG, 75.

90. As Derrida said to Dooley, "Don't forget that Jack Caputo speaks of religion *without* religion." Derrida, "The Becoming Possible of the Impossible," 22.

91. Derrida, *The Gift of Death*, 49.

92. Derrida, *On the Name*, 69.

93. Caputo, *The Prayers and Tears of Jacques Derrida*, 6–12, and Caputo, *Radical Hermeneutics*, ch. 10.

94. Derrida, *Learning to Live Finally*, 24.

95. Jean-Louis Chrétien, "The Wounded Word: The Phenomenology of Prayer," trans. Jeff Kosky, in *Phenomenology and the "Theological Turn:" The French Debate* (New York: Fordham University Press, 2001).

96. Jacques Derrida, *H.C. for Life, That Is to Say . . .* , trans. Laurent Melesi and Stefan Herbrechter (Stanford, CA: Stanford University Press, 2006), 2; cf. 36. See Hélène Cixous, *Insister of Jacques Derrida*, trans. Peggy Kamuf (Stanford, CA: Stanford University Press, 2007), 179; "Promised Belief," in *Feminism,*

Sexuality and Religion, ed. Linda Alcoff and John D. Caputo (Bloomington: Indiana University Press, 2011), 146.

The Autoimmunity of Religion
Martin Hägglund

1. Jacques Derrida, "Faith and Knowledge," trans. Samuel Weber, in *Acts of Religion*, ed. Gil Anidjar (London: Routledge, 2002), 100. The first sentence reads with untranslatable economy in French: "Il se fait violence et se garde de l'autre," Jacques Derrida, *Foi et savoir* (Paris: Seuil, 2000), 100.

2. A first version of this text was written for the Derrida and Religion conference at Harvard. I am grateful to the organizers, Edward Baring and Peter Gordon, as well as to all the participants, in particular John Caputo, Hent de Vries, and Richard Kearney. I also want to thank Sean D. Kelly for his insightful response to my paper at the conference. For valuable comments on an earlier draft of this chapter I thank Joshua Andresen, Edward Baring, Peter Gordon, Samir Haddad, David E. Johnson, and Rocío Zambrana.

3. Richard Kearney, *Anatheism: Returning to God after God* (New York: Columbia University Press, 2009), 73.

4. Richard Kearney, *Debates in Continental Philosophy* (New York: Fordham University Press, 2004), 290.

5. John D. Caputo, *The Weakness of God* (Bloomington: Indiana University Press), 33.

6. Caputo, *The Weakness of God*, 15.

7. John D. Caputo, *Deconstruction in a Nutshell* (New York: Fordham University Press, 1996), 159.

8. John D. Caputo, *The Prayers and Tears of Jacques Derrida* (Bloomington: Indiana University Press, 1997), xxi.

9. See Martin Hägglund, *Radical Atheism: Derrida and the Time of Life* (Palo Alto, CA: Stanford University Press, 2008).

10. John D. Caputo, "Unprotected Religion: Radical Theology, Radical Atheism, and the Return of Anti-Religion," 173, in this volume. In a few places, I will also refer to a longer version of Caputo's response to my work, published under the same title in the *Journal for Cultural and Religious Theory* 11, no. 2 (2011): 32–125.

11. Thus, my critique of Caputo's reading of the relation between deconstruction and negative theology takes issue with his argument that "'deconstruction desires what negative theology desires and it shares the passion of negative theology'" (see Hägglund, *Radical Atheism*, 116, 120–21). Instead of responding to this critique, Caputo claims that I am charging him with a theological argument à la Jean-Luc Marion, which is not the case.

12. Derrida, "Faith and Knowledge," 84n30.

13. Derrida, "Perhaps or Maybe," *PLI: Warwick Journal of Philosophy* (Summer 1997): 9.

14. Ibid.

15. Ibid.

16. Ibid.

17. Derrida, "Faith and Knowledge," 82.

18. Ibid.

19. Ibid., 83.

20. Jacques Derrida, *Politics of Friendship*, trans. George Collins (London: Verso, 1997), 16.

21. Jacques Derrida, *Rogues: Two Essays on Reason*, trans. Michael Naas and Pascale-Anne Brault (Stanford, CA: Stanford University Press, 2005), 153.

22. Derrida, *Rogues*, 153.

23. See, for example, *Limited Inc*, where Derrida addresses the status of his argument concerning the "necessary possibility of repetition/alteration" (iterability). Derrida first seems to describe such iterability exclusively in terms of a "structural possibility" and thus limit himself to the claim that the possibility of iteration is necessary, whereas something can occur only once without in fact being iterated. However, Derrida goes on to problematize the status of this "in fact" and explicitly emphasizes that it only *seems* as if something can occur "only once:"

> I say *seems*, because this one time is in itself divided and multiplied in advance by its structure of repeatability. This obtains *in fact*, at once, from its inception on; and it is here that the graphics of iterability undercuts the classical opposition of fact and principle, the factual and the possible (or the virtual), necessity and possibility. In undercutting these classical oppositions, however, it introduces a more powerful "logic." (Jacques Derrida, *Limited Inc*, trans. Samuel Weber [Evanston, IL: Northwestern University Press, 1988], 48)

As Derrida goes on to specify, this logic of iterability hinges on the fact that any "moment is constituted—i.e. divided—by the very iterability of what produces itself *momentarily*" (49), thereby requiring a deconstruction of the very concept of presence and hence of actuality.

24. Derrida, *Rogues*, 127.

25. Consequently, in elucidating the notion of spacing I do *not* appeal to "a materialist metaphysics of becoming" or a "materialistic metaphysics of absolute being," as Caputo claims in his response ("Unprotected Religion," 167). In the essay where I do address the question of materialism (and to which Caputo refers) I explicitly emphasize that the trace is not an ontological stipulation about being as such. Rather, the trace is a logical structure that spells out the minimal conditions for the constitution of time. Furthermore, I certainly do not hold that "the universe itself" has "a vision of its future" or is "surprised by what happens" (Caputo, "The Return of Anti-Religion" *JCRT*, 117). On the contrary, I develop a distinction between the living and the nonliving, where the possibility of having a vision of or being surprised by the future (or, more generally, the possibility of caring about the future at all) is dependent on the contingent advent of life and not a feature of the material universe as such. See Martin Hägglund, "Radical

Atheist Materialism: A Critique of Meillassoux," in *The Speculative Turn: Continental Materialism and Realism*, ed. Levi Bryant, Nick Srnicek, and Graham Harman (Melbourne: re-press, 2011), 114–29.

26. Derrida, *Rogues*, 152; see also, 143–44.

27. See, for example, Jacques Derrida, *Specters of Marx* (trans. Peggy Kamuf [London: Routledge, 1994]), where "absolute life, fully present life" is described as "absolute evil" (175). See also the analysis in Hägglund, *Radical Atheism*, 28–30, 140–41.

28. Caputo, "The Return of Anti-Religion," 168.

29. John D. Caputo, "Love among the Deconstructibles," *Journal for Cultural and Religious Theory* 5, no. 2 (2004): 38.

30. See Caputo, "Love among the Deconstructibles," 38.

31. John D. Caputo, "Without Sovereignty, Without Being," *Journal for Cultural and Religious Theory* 4, no. 3 (2003): 14.

32. Derrida, "Faith and Knowledge," 58–59.

33. Caputo, *The Weakness of God*, 89.

34. Jacques Derrida, "Nietzsche and the Machine," in *Negotiations: Interventions and Interviews, 1971–2001*, ed. Elizabeth Rottenberg (Palo Alto, CA: Stanford University Press, 2002), 248.

35. Caputo, *Prayers and Tears*, xx, and Caputo, *The Weakness of God*, 104.

36. Jacques Derrida, "Autoimmunity: Real and Symbolic Suicides," trans. Michael Naas and Pascale-Anne Brault, in *Philosophy in a Time of Terror* (Chicago: University of Chicago Press, 2003), 120.

37. Jacques Derrida, "As If It Were Possible, 'Within Such Limits,' " trans. Benjamin Elwood and Elizabeth Rottenberg, in *Negotiations*, 361.

38. Caputo, *The Weakness of God*, 102; see also 87–88.

39. Caputo, *The Weakness of God*, 112.

40. Caputo, "The Return of Anti-Religion," *JCRT*, 44.

41. Caputo, *The Weakness of God*, 178, 88.

42. Caputo, *The Weakness of God*, 77.

43. Caputo, *The Weakness of God*, 192.

44. Caputo, *The Weakness of God*, 88, 92–93.

45. Caputo, *The Weakness of God*, 178.

46. Caputo, "The Return of Anti-Religion," *JCRT*, 44n31.

47. Hägglund, *Radical Atheism*, 138.

48. Caputo, *The Weakness of God*, 278.

49. Caputo, *The Weakness of God*, 259.

50. Jacques Derrida, "Hostipitality," trans. Gil Anidjar, in *Acts of Religion*, 361.

51. Caputo, "The Return of Anti-Religion," *JCRT*, 89.

52. The oscillation between these two conceptions of an "ethics of alterity" (one assuming that the other is good or at least helplessly in need, the other suspending the question of goodness but nevertheless advocating an ethics of submission) is precisely what I criticize in Levinas. Rather than engaging this critique,

Caputo claims that "Hägglund labors under the misunderstanding that Levinas is some kind of Neoplatonist who thinks that when you die you enjoy eternal happiness outside of time" ("Unprotected Religion," 246). In fact, my critique of Levinas has nothing to do with the question of the afterlife or eternal happiness. Rather, I provide a detailed account of why and how Levinas fails to think through the undecidability of alterity and its consequences for ethics.

53. John D. Caputo, "Discussion with Richard Kearney," in *God, the Gift, and Postmodernism*, ed. John D. Caputo and Michael J. Scanlon (Bloomington: Indiana University Press, 1999), 131. See also Caputo's claim in *Prayers and Tears*: "The *tout autre* always means the one who is left out, the one whose suffering and exclusion lay claim to us and interrupt our self-possession" (248).

54. Caputo, "The Return of Anti-Religion," *JCRT*, 88–89.

55. Caputo, "The Return of Anti-Religion," *JCRT*, 40. In his contribution to this volume, Caputo does not provide any criteria for what it would mean to keep the future open rather than close it down. For a critique of the criteria he has provided elsewhere, see Martin Hägglund, "The Radical Evil of Deconstruction: A Reply to John Caputo," *Journal for Cultural and Religious Theory* 11, no. 1 (2011): 144–45.

56. Caputo, "The Return of Anti-Religion" *JCRT*, 83–84.

57. Caputo tries to draw support for his argument by appealing to an interview where Derrida claims that "one should only ever oppose events that one thinks will block the future or that bring death with them: events that would put an end to the possibility of the event" (quoted in "Unprotected Religion," 164). The meaning of Derrida's remark, however, depends on the overall logic of the passage in which it appears. If we were to take the remark literally it would mean that we should not oppose any political events (e.g., racism, sexism, colonial oppression, and so on) as long as they do not put an end to the possibility of the event, which according to Derrida's own analysis is impossible except through an absolute violence that would eliminate the possibility for anything to happen. Derrida's remark would thus mean that we should not oppose any political events that fall short of being absolutely violent, which includes all forms of political violence that actually take place. What Derrida is arguing in the interview, however, is that the coming of the event is *not* good in itself and that we should *not* "give up trying to prevent certain things from coming to pass (without which there would be no decision, no responsibility, ethics or politics)" (quoted in "Unprotected Religion," 164). Consequently, Derrida's argument does not support the view that it is better to be more open rather than less open to the future. To be sure, "even when we block things from happening, that is a way to keep the future open" (as Caputo points out in "Unprotected Religion," 164), but it does not follow from this argument that we should block less rather than more in a given case. Furthermore, Caputo does not provide any reason for why we should make this inference; he merely assumes it.

58. Caputo, "The Return of Anti-Religion" *JCRT*, 66.

59. For a further discussion of Derrida's distinction between performative commitment and nonperformative exposure—as well as an elaboration of the political stakes of the distinction—see Martin Hägglund, "Beyond the Performative and the Constative," *Research in Phenomenology* 43, no. 1: 100–7.

60. Derrida, *Rogues*, 91.

61. Jacques Derrida, "Marx & Sons," in *Ghostly Demarcations: A Symposium on Jacques Derrida's* Specters of Marx, ed. Michael Sprinker, (London: Verso, 2008), 250–51.

62. Jacques Derrida, "Typewriter Ribbon," trans. Peggy Kamuf, in *Without Alibi* (Stanford, CA: Stanford University Press, 2002), 146.

63. Derrida, "Typewriter Ribbon," 146.

64. Derrida, "Marx & Sons," 249.

65. See, for example, Derrida's succinct account in *Rogues* of the relation between the conditional and the unconditional, the calculable and the incalculable: "According to a transaction that is each time novel, each time without precedent, reason goes through and goes between, on the one side, the reasoned exigency of calculation or conditionality and, on the other, the intransigent, nonnegotiable exigency of unconditional incalculability. This intractable exigency wins out [*a raison de*] and *must* win out over everything. On both sides, then, whether it is a question of singularity or universality, and each time both at once, *both* calculation *and* the incalculable *are necessary*" (150). Accordingly, there is always an "autoimmune aporia of this impossible transaction between the conditional and the unconditional, calculation and the incalculable. A transaction without any rule given in advance, without any absolute assurance. For there is no reliable prophylaxis against the autoimmune. By definition. An always perilous transaction must thus invent, each time, in a singular situation, its own law and norm, that is, a maxim that welcomes each time the event to come. There can be responsibility and decision, if there are any, only at this price" (151).

66. Jacques Derrida, *The Gift of Death*, trans. David Wills (Chicago: University of Chicago Press, 1995), 68.

67. See Jacques Derrida, "Violence and Metaphysics," in *Writing and Difference*, trans. Alan Bass (Chicago: University of Chicago Press, 1978), 128–33. See also Hägglund, *Radical Atheism*, 82–84, 170–71.

68. Derrida, *Specters of Marx*, 168.

69. Derrida, *Specters of Marx*, 87.

70. Jacques Derrida, *Archive Fever: A Freudian Impression*, trans. Eric Prenowitz (Chicago: University of Chicago Press, 1995), 77.

71. Ibid., 63.

72. Derrida, "Faith and Knowledge," 87.

73. Ibid.

74. Caputo, *Prayers and Tears*, xxviii.

75. Caputo, *Prayers and Tears*, 190.

76. Caputo, *Deconstruction in a Nutshell*, 160.

77. Caputo, *Weakness of God*, 278.

78. Derrida, "Faith and Knowledge," 56.

79. Derrida, *Politics of Friendship*, 173.

80. Derrida, *Politics of Friendship*, 174.

81. Derrida, "Penser ce qui vient," in *Derrida pour les temps à venir*, ed. René Major (Paris: Éditions Stock, 2007), 21.

Derrida and Messianic Atheism
Richard Kearney

1. Jacques Derrida and Geoffrey Bennington, *Circumfession* (Chicago: University of Chicago Press, 1999). On the question of confessing circumcision, I recall Paul Ricoeur, another of Derrida's mentors, saying to me having just read a copy of *Circumfession* that Derrida had sent him: "I would never dare to write a philosophy of my penis!"

2. Emmanuel Levinas, "Useless Suffering," in *Between Us* (London: Athlone Press, 1997).

3. Emmanuel Levinas, *Totality and Infinity*, trans. Alfonso Lingis (Pittsburgh, PA: Duquesne University Press, 1969), 58.

4. Ibid.

5. John Llewelyn, *Emmanuel Levinas: The Genealogy of Ethics* (London: Routledge, 1995), 67.

6. Jacques Derrida, "Sauf le Nom (Post-Scriptum)," in *On the Name*, ed. Thomas Dutoit, trans. John Leavey Jr. (Stanford, CA: Stanford University Press, 1995), 82.

7. I try to explore further the crucial difference between Derrida's atheism and my own notion of ana-theism in chapter 3 of *Anatheism: Returning to God after God* (New York: Columbia University Press, 2009).

8. Jacques Derrida, *Of Hospitality*, trans. Rachel Bowlby (Stanford, CA: Stanford University Press, 2000), 138–39. The original French text, *De l'hospitalité*, was published by Calmann-Levy (Paris, 1997).

9. Jacques Derrida, "Hospitality, Justice and Responsibility" (1998 Conversation at University College Dublin), in *Questioning Ethics: Contemporary Debates in Continental Philosophy*, ed. Richard Kearney and Mark Dooley (London: Routledge, 1998), 77–78.

10. Ibid., 66.

11. John Caputo, *The Prayers and Tears of Jacques Derrida: Religion without Religion* (Bloomington: Indiana University Press, 1997), 73. Caputo offers, in my view, the most persuasive and profound reading available of Derrida's thinking on God, religion, theology, and mysticism. I am indebted to our ongoing creative and critical conversations on these subjects.

12. Jacques Derrida, "Hospitality, Justice and Responsibility," 77. On the question of deconstruction as a blind "reading in the dark," see Derrida's admission: "We always read in the dark, we always write in the dark. . . . this is a general law." "Desire of God: An Exchange," a conversation between Jacques Derrida, Richard Kearney, and John Caputo at Villanova University, 1997, published in

After God: Richard Kearney and the Religious Turn in Continental Philosophy, ed. John Manoussakis (New York: Fordham University Press, 2006), 304.

13. See, for example, Jacques Derrida, "Post-Scriptum: Aporias, Ways and Voices," in *Derrida and Negative Theology*, ed. Harold Coward and Toby Foshay (Albany: State University of New York Press, 1992).

14. Ibid. See here Derrida's crucial essay, "Khora," in *On the Name*, 89–130, and my own critical engagement with Derrida and Caputo on this subject in Richard Kearney, "God or Khora?" in *Strangers, Gods and Monsters* (London: Routledge, 2003), 191–212.

15. Derrida, "Post-Scriptum: Aporias, Ways and Voices," 300–1.

16. Ibid., 301.

17. Ibid., 314.

18. Ibid., 314.

19. Ibid., 315.

20. Ibid., 315.

21. Ibid., 315.

22. Ibid., 318.

23. Jacques Derrida, *Specters of Marx*, trans. Peggy Kamuf (London: Routledge, 1994), 166. I am grateful to my friend and colleague Neal Deroo for bringing my attention to several relevant passages in this text.

24. Ibid., 168–69.

25. Ibid., 59. See Martin Hägglund's challenging reading of Derrida's "religion without religion" as rigorously and uncompromisingly anti-theistic, *Radical Atheism: Derrida and the Time of Life* (Stanford, CA: Stanford University Press, 2008).

26. On this possibility of something or someone called "God" beyond both theistic Godness and atheistic Godlessness (what Heidegger called *Gottlosigkheit*), see my exploration of the notion of a "God after God" (*ana-theos*) in *Anatheism: Returning to God after God*.

27. See Derrida on deconstruction and the hallucination of the Other in the 1998 Dublin dialogue, "Hospitality, Justice and Responsibility."

28. See my essays on a carnal/diacritical hermeneutics of the sacred: Richard Kearney, "Eros, Diacritical Hermeneutics and the Maybe," in *Philosophical Thresholds: Crossings of Life and World*, Selected Studies in Phenomenology and Existential Philosophy, vol. 36, ed. Cynthia Willett and Leonard Lawlor, *Philosophy Today*, SPEP Supplement, 2011; Richard Kearney, "What is Diacritical Hermeneutics?," in *The Journal of Applied Hermeneutics* 1, no. 1 (2011): 1–14; and Richard Kearney, "Diacritical Hermeneutics," in *Hermeneutic Rationality/ La rationalité herméneutique*, ed. Maria Luisa Portocarrero, Luis Umbelino, and Andrzej Wiercinski (Münster, Germany: LIT Verlag, 2011), 177–96. The difficulty with deconstructive analysis, as I see it, is that it is often less concerned with concrete existential examples than with quasi-transcendental allusions. See, for instance, Derrida's brilliant but quintessentially non-committal readings of Mount Moriah, Blanchot's "L'Instant," Celan's *Shibboleth*, etc., where Derrida's

texts are always texts reading other texts—philosophical, poetic, religious—but rarely or ever texts reading human experiences, carnalities, or testimonies. No Holocaust witnesses, no political narratives (Gandhi, Martin Luther King, Dorothy Day), no lives of the Saints, no phenomenologies of the incarnate life-world. Deconstruction, in the first and last analysis, is the end of phenomenology. It is literary, not lived. Unlike the tradition of philosophy as healing—from Socrates and the Stoics to Wittgenstein, Freud, and Foucault—deconstruction flirts with literariness to the point of excarnation; even though Derrida does so with extraordinary scholarship, genius, and style. Deconstruction reads and writes but rarely speaks or acts. It risks the elision of the real. And that, perhaps, is what Derrida meant.

29. Jacques Derrida, "Deconstruction and the Other: Dialogue with Richard Kearney," in Richard Kearney, *Debates in Continental Philosophy: Conversations with Contemporary Thinkers* (New York: Fordham University Press, 2004), 139. See in particular where Derrida describes his own philosophical position as that of a wandering *émigré* committed to a "politics of exodus" (151).

30. Samuel Beckett interview with Tom Driver, "Beckett by the Madeleine," in Lawrence Graver and Raymond Federman, eds., *Samuel Beckett: The Critical Heritage* (London: Routledge, 1979), 220.

31. Ibid., 141. Derrida goes on to spell out some of the radical consequences of this claim: "Deconstruction is in itself a positive response to an alterity which necessarily calls, summons, or motivates it. The other, as the other than self, the other that opposes self-identity, is not something that can be detected and disclosed within a philosophical space. . . . [it] precedes philosophy and necessarily invokes and provokes the subject before any genuine questioning can begin" (141). Then, referring explicitly to prophecy, Derrida intimates that a possible non-biblical sense of this term might obtain for certain "effects" of deconstruction. "When deconstructive themes begin to dominate the scene, as they do today, one is sure to find a proliferation of prophecies. And this proliferation is precisely a reason why we should be all the more wary and prudent, all the more discriminating" (149). But how can we be discriminating if we can only read in the dark, as he insisted to me in the Villanova exchange "Desire of God" (1997, see note 12 above), and have no way of telling the difference between messiahs or hallucinations?

32. Ibid., 150.

33. Ibid., 150.

34. Ibid., 150.

35. Ibid., 150.

36. Ibid., 155.

37. Derrida, "Desire of God," 304–5.

38. Ibid., 305.

39. Ibid., 307.

40. Ibid., 307.

41. Ibid., 307–8.

42. Ibid., 307.

43. Jacques Derrida, "Hospitality, Justice and Responsibility," 67. In this Dublin Dialogue Derrida seems to me to deepen the dilemma by affirming that it is not a personal self or subject who decides or discerns in these matters but the other:

> Not only should I not be certain that I made a good decision; I should not even be certain that I made a decision. A decision *may* have happened. . . . "I" never decide. . . . I am passive in a decision, because as soon as I am active, as soon as I know that "I" am the master of my decision, I am claiming that I know what to do. (67)

In short, the event of decision is a matter of the other (in me), not me. Once again, the question of ethical agency and responsibility arises. In saying this, however, I am speaking of the limits of deconstruction as I see it, and not of Derrida's own courageous personal commitment to political and social causes from educational reform and emigration rights to apartheid and justice for prisoners (see, for example, his unstinting support for the *sans papiers* and death row prisoners like Abu Jamal).

44. Jacques Derrida, "Terror, Religion and the New Politics," in Kearney, *Debates in Continental Philosophy*, 5.

45. Ibid.

46. On my contrasting hermeneutic reading of khora see Kearney, "God or Khora?," 211; and in particular the appendix entitled "Derrida and the Double Abyss," 208–11. I develop this discussion of my differences with the deconstructive readings of khora in Derrida and Caputo in an alternative interpretation of khora as womb of natality, as it relates both to the Abrahamic-Christian mother (the womb of Sarah and Mary as *khora akhoraton*: containers of the uncontainable) and the eschatological image of *perichoresis*, namely the three strangers/persons circling the *khora* at the midst of the divine-human eschaton (see Kearney, *Anatheism*, chapter 1, and "Eros, Diacritical Hermeneutics and the Maybe," part 3). For a more detailed account of my critical reading of Derrida's notion of *le peut-être* see my *The God Who May Be* (Bloomington: Indiana University Press, 2001), 93–100. In my analysis of Derrida's philosophy of religion in chapter 3 of *Anatheism* I suggest he may be read as an *ana-theist atheist* rather than an *ana-theist* theist like Levinas, Ricoeur, Bonhoeffer, and myself. But I am not sure Derrida would have accepted the term. For an opposing reading of Derrida as an *anti*-theistic atheist, see the very clear and cogent arguments of Martin Hägglund, *Radical Atheism: Derrida and the Time of Life*. I am also grateful to my Boston College colleagues, Kevin Newmark and Kalpana Sheshandri, for their challenging and helpful comments on this theme.

47. Derrida, "Terror, Religion and the New Politics," 12.

48. Ibid., 13.

49. Ibid., 12.

50. Ibid., 12.

51. Ibid., 12–13. Emphasis added.

52. Ibid., 13.

53. Ibid., 13.

54. Ibid., 14.

55. Ibid., 13. In our New York dialogue, "Terror, Religion and the New Politics," Derrida and I discussed this critical relationship between his deconstructive "Maybe" (mentioned in numerous of his later works) and my own eschatological "God-who-May-Be" as explored in *Poétique du Possible* (Paris: Beauchesne, 1984) and later in *The God Who May Be* (Bloomington: Indiana University Press, 2001). Derrida's essay on the Perhaps, "Comme si c'était possible, 'within such limits'. . . ." (*Revue Internationale de Philosophie* 3, no. 205 [1998]), was written, as he acknowledges, in part as a response to my hermeneutics of the *Peut-Etre* in *Poétique du Possible*. My response to his response is contained in chapter 5 of *The God Who May Be*, entitled "Possibilising God," 93–100. As always, I am grateful to Derrida for the honor and the provocation that makes such exchanges possible— this current essay being another modest example.

56. Derrida, "Terror, Religion and the New Politics," 13, and Kearney, *Anatheism*, 62–65, 106–7. By way of epilogue, let me summarize what I see as some of the most important differences that distinguish our respective positions. First and most obviously there is the difference of faith—my anatheist theism as opposed to what I call Derrida's anatheist atheism. Both of us share an anatheist openness to wagering for or against faith in a religious God, but the difference expresses itself in our distinct, and often opposing, readings of specific events, images, persons, and narratives. I have already referred to our contrasting interpretations of khora and Christian revelation, but it might be helpful to add here our respective readings of the Abrahamic story. For Derrida this begins on Mount Moriah with the impossible sacrifice of Isaac—as signaled in Derrida's title *Donner la mort: The Gift of Death*. For me it begins under the tree at Mamre with Abraham's impossible hospitality to the strangers—*donner la vie: the gift of birth* (as presented in the opening chapter of *Anatheism*). In the first instance we have the sacrifice of a child, in the second the conception of a child—the same child, Isaac (meaning "laughter" in Hebrew because the barren Sarah laughs when she hears the strangers announce the arrival of an impossible son when they will return the following year). In Mount Moriah, as read by Derrida after Kierkegaard, Abraham is full of "fear and trembling": That is what the deconstructive Other does to one. In Mamre, by contrast, Abraham turns from fear to trust as he treats the incoming stranger (*ger/xenos/hostis*) as guest rather than enemy (the word *hostis* can mean both guest and enemy in most languages). Here Abraham becomes a host who turns his guest into God—a sacred stranger—by turning hostility (his initial fear and trembling before the arrival of the desert vagrants) into hospitality (he and Sarah offer them food and drink). The Genesis text describes the three aliens becoming divine in the sharing of the food—a moment celebrated in Andrei Rublev's famous icon of the *perichoresis*: a trinity of divine strangers seated around the chalice/bowl/womb/khora. But in the Moriah

narrative, Abraham is suddenly prepared to abandon his role as host to the stranger's gift—namely, the impossible birth of Isaac—and turn his original act of hospitality into one of hostility: the command of the Absolute to kill his son. Now I am not suggesting for a moment that Derrida's atheism leads to death while my anatheism leads to life—God forbid! I am simply pointing to a different emphasis of election and interpretation when it comes to God stories. If Derrida reads through the deconstructive lens of Kierkegaard—who, he confessed, was a more important philosophical influence than the three Hs (Hegel/Husserl/Heidegger)—I am more inclined to read through the hermeneutic lens of Ricoeur and Gadamer, where a wager on community, dialogue, and translation trumps the terror of the solitary Knight of Faith, alone on the hill, out of his mind, obsessed and violated by the Absolute. For me, the Derridian-Kierkegaardian option is *too* impossible, irrational, "mad," and "blind." There is too much fear and too much trembling for any workable ethics of action or poetics of saying. Derrida agrees with Kierkegaard that the only adequate human response to this impossible, horrible, command of death is silence. (Either total speech or total muteness; either total knowledge or blind faith.) But Abraham, Kierkegaard, and Derrida all ended up speaking. They let the word out. And we have endless writings and readings to prove it—hermeneutics in spite of itself. Language that dares not speak its name. Hence, as a result, the fortunate possibility of ongoing interpretation and discussion. (Even though I must confess that struggling with Derrida's elusive style is sometimes like trying to have a fistfight with the fog.) Where deconstruction speaks of "contagion" and "contamination" between guest and host languages, hermeneutics speaks of conversation and translation (defined by Ricoeur as "linguistic hospitality" in *On Translation*). Once again, the thinnest of differences but differences nonetheless. So while a deconstructive response to the voice or face of the other is, as noted, always a matter of reading in the dark, a hermeneutic response reads in half-light, twilight, wagering on some form of practical wisdom (*phronesis*), however tentative, inspired by a mix of carnal savvy, narrative understanding, moral reckoning, and discernment of spirits. Where deconstruction reads the khora of alterity as a gaping unspeakable abyss, hermeneutics reads it as a matrix of possible sensings, mappings, journeyings, storyings, hopes. Deconstruction and hermeneutics: two different approaches to the absolute Other, that perhaps need each other in other to be fully answerable to the stranger in every other.

Contributors

Edward Baring is Assistant Professor in Modern European Intellectual and Cultural History at Drew University. He is the author of *The Young Derrida and French Philosophy, 1945–1968* (Cambridge University Press, 2011), which won the Morris D. Forkosch Prize from the *Journal of the History of Ideas* for Best Book in Intellectual History. He has written articles on Derrida and Sartre, which have appeared in *Critical Inquiry, Modern Intellectual History,* and elsewhere. He is currently working on a Europe-wide history of phenomenology in the period before 1950.

John D. Caputo is Thomas J. Watson Professor Emeritus of Religion at Syracuse University and the David R. Cook Professor Emeritus of Philosophy at Villanova University. His most recent books are *The Insistence of God: A Theology of Perhaps* (Indiana University Press, 2013) and *Truth* (Penguin, 2013). He is best known for *Radical Hermeneutics* (Indiana University Press, 1986), *The Prayers and Tears of Jacques Derrida* (Indiana University Press, 1997), and *The Weakness of God: A Theology of the Event* (Indiana University Press, 2004), which received the American Academy of Religion award for work in constructive theology. He has addressed wider-than-academic audiences in *On Religion* (Routledge, 2001) and *What Would Jesus Deconstruct?* (Baker Academic, 2007). Three books have appeared about his work: *Cross and Chora: Deconstruction and Christianity in the Work of John D. Caputo* (Wipf and Stock Publishers, 2010), *A Passion for the Impossible: John D. Caputo in Focus* (SUNY Press, 2002), and *Religion With/Out Religion: The Prayers and Tears of John D. Caputo* (Routledge, 2002).

Joseph Cohen is Lecturer of Philosophy at University College Dublin (Ireland). He has written *Le spectre juif de Hegel* (Galilée, 2005), *Le sacrifice de Hegel* (Galilée, 2007) and *Alternances de la métaphysique: Essais sur E. Levinas* (Galilée, 2009). In collaboration with Dermot Moran, he coauthored *The Husserl Dictionary* (Continuum, 2012). He also edited, in collaboration with Raphael Zagury-Orly, the volume *Judeities—Questions for Jacques Derrida* (Fordham University Press, 2007) and, in collaboration with Gérard Bensussan, *Heidegger—le danger et la promesse* (Kimé, 2006). He is, since 2008, a permanent member of the editorial committee for the journals *Les Temps Modernes* (Gallimard) and *Cités* (Presses Universitaires de France). His domains of research are German idealism, phenomenology and contemporary French and German philosophy.

Peter E. Gordon is Amabel B. James Professor of History and Harvard College Professor at Harvard University, where he teaches modern European intellectual history from the late eighteenth to the late twentieth century, focusing chiefly on themes in continental philosophy and social thought in Germany and France since the 1920s. His books include: *Rosenzweig and Heidegger: Between Judaism and German Philosophy* (University of California Press, 2003), which received three separate awards: the Salo W. Baron Prize from the Academy for Jewish Research, the Goldstein-Goren Prize for Best Book in Jewish Philosophy, and the Morris D. Forkosch Prize from the *Journal of the History of Ideas* for Best Book in Intellectual History. He has coedited several scholarly volumes, including *The Modernist Imagination: Essays in Intellectual History and Critical Theory in Honor of Martin Jay* (Berghahn, 2008); *The Cambridge Companion to Modern Jewish Philosophy* (Cambridge University Press, 2007); and *Weimar Thought: A Contested Legacy* (Princeton University Press, 2013). His most recent book was *Continental Divide: Heidegger, Cassirer, Davos* (Harvard University Press, 2010), which received the Jacques Barzun Prize from the American Philosophical Society. Gordon is founder and co-chair of the Harvard Colloquium for Intellectual History.

Martin Hägglund is a tenured Associate Professor of Comparative Literature and Humanities at Yale University. He is the author of three books: *Dying for Time: Proust, Woolf, Nabokov* (Harvard University Press, 2012), *Radical Atheism: Derrida and the Time of Life* (Stanford University Press, 2008), and *Kronofobi: Essäer om tid och ändlighet* (Östlings Bokförlag Symposion, 2002). His work is the subject of a special issue of *CR: The New Centennial Review, Living On: Of Martin Hägglund*.

Sarah Hammerschlag is Assistant Professor of Religion and Literature at the University of Chicago Divinity School. She is the author of *The Figural Jew: Politics and Identity in Postwar French Thought* (University of Chicago Press, 2010) and numerous articles on Maurice Blanchot, Emmanuel Levinas, Jacques Derrida, and others. Currently she is editing an anthology of French-Jewish writing and is at work on two manuscripts, one on the renaissance of Jewish thought in postwar Paris and the other on Derrida, Levinas, and Literature.

Richard Kearney holds the Charles B. Seelig Chair of Philosophy at Boston College and has served as a Visiting Professor at University College Dublin, the University of Paris (Sorbonne), the University of Nice, and the Catholic University of Australia. He is the author of over twenty books on European philosophy and literature (including two novels and a volume of poetry) and has edited or coedited eighteen more. His publications include a trilogy entitled *Philosophy at the Limit*. The three volumes are *On Stories* (Routledge, 2002), *The God Who May Be* (Indiana University Press, 2001), and *Strangers, Gods, and Monsters* (Routledge, 2003). More recently, Richard Kearney has published *Debates in Continental Philosophy* (Fordham University Press, 2004), *The Owl of Minerva* (Ashgate, 2005), *Navigations* (Syracuse University Press, 2007), and *Anatheism: Returning to God after God* (Columbia University Press, 2009).

Ethan Kleinberg is Professor of History and Letters and Director of the Center for the Humanities at Wesleyan University as well as Executive Editor of *History and Theory*. He is the author of *Generation Existential: Heidegger's Philosophy in France, 1927–1961* (Cornell University Press, 2005) and coeditor of *Presence: Philosophy, History, and Cultural Theory for the Twenty-First Century* (Cornell University Press, 2013). His research focuses on modern intellectual history and philosophy and theory of history. He is finishing a book-length manuscript on Emmanuel Levinas's Talmudic lectures in Paris after World War II and a book about deconstruction and the writing of history.

Anne Norton is Edmund and Louise Kahn Term Professor of Political Science and Comparative Literature at the University of Pennsylvania. She is the author of a number of books, including *Bloodrites of the Poststructuralists: Word, Flesh and Revolution* (Routledge, 2002), *Leo Strauss and the Politics of American Empire* (Yale University Press, 2004), and the recent *On The Muslim Question: Politics, Philosophy and the Western Street* (Princeton University Press, 2013). She has written articles on a variety of subjects, including Schmitt on democratic sovereignty and Hélène Cixous's "Mon Algériance." Her present research concerns democracy and the problem of property.

Hent de Vries is Professor in the Humanities Center and the Department of Philosophy at the Johns Hopkins University, where he holds Russ Family Chair and serves as the Director of the Humanities Center. He is currently also a Distinguished Visiting Professor of Comparative Religion at the Hebrew University, Jerusalem, and, from 2014 to 2018, he will serve as the next Director of the School of Criticism and Theory, at Cornell University. His principal publications include: *Philosophy and the Turn to Religion* (Johns Hopkins University Press, 1999, 2000), *Religion and Violence: Philosophical Perspectives from Kant to Derrida* (Johns

Hopkins University Press, 2002, 2006), and *Minimal Theologies: Critiques of Secular Reason in Theodor W. Adorno and Emmanuel Levinas* (Johns Hopkins University Press, 2005). He was the coeditor, with Samuel Weber, of *Religion and Media* (Stanford University Press, 2001); the coeditor, with Lawrence Sullivan, of *Political Theologies: Public Religions in a Post-Secular World* (Fordham University Press, 2006); and the coeditor, with Ward Blanton, of *Paul and the Philosophers* (Fordham University Press, 2013). In addition, he was the General Editor of the five-volume miniseries entitled *The Future of the Religious Past*, as well as of its first title, *Religion Beyond a Concept* (Fordham University Press, 2008). Currently, he is completing two book-length studies, entitled *Of Miracles, Events, and Special Effects: Global Religion in an Age of New Media* and *Spiritual Exercises: Concepts and Practices*.

Raphael Zagury-Orly teaches philosophy at the Bezalel Academy of Fine Arts in Jerusalem and at the Cohn Institute of the University of Tel Aviv. He is the Head of the MFA Program at the Bezalel Academy of Fine Arts. He has authored *Questionner encore* (Galilée, 2010). He has also coedited, with Joseph Cohen and Bettina Bergo, *Judeities—Questions for Jacques Derrida* (Fordham University Press, 2007). As a permanent member of the editorial committee of the French journal *Les Temps Modernes*, he has coordinated, in collaboration with Joseph Cohen, *Heidegger: Qu'appelle-t-on le lieu?* (July–October 2008, no. 650), and *Derrida: L'événement déconstruction* (July–October 2012, no. 669–670). He is also Scientific Editor at the Resling Editions in Tel-Aviv (Israel) where he has directed Hebrew translations of Derrida, Deleuze, and Bataille.

Index

Abraham, 132–50; Abraham-Isaac story, 58, 66–67, 99, 100–3, 125–27, 140–42, 145–49, 234n50, 260n56; Abrahamic messianism, 199, 209; Christ contrasted with, 141–42; in Europe, 149–50; as exilic, 139; fixed identity resisted by, 133; gaze of, 149; Hegel on, 134, 138–43, 144, 149, 242n9; Kierkegaard on, 66, 100, 134, 143–47, 149, 162; language of, 145; more than one, 133; name transformed from *Avram* to *Abraham,* 132, 133; as other, 134, 136; philosophical thought's relation to figure of, 132–36; precedence of, 135; revelation of, 133, 241n1; as "settling foreigner," 133, 136, 149, 150; and site of Holocaust, 100, 101; solitude of, 143, 145, 147; as translatable unthought, 134

"Abraham, the Other" (Derrida), 40, 49–50, 53, 55, 56, 68, 135

adhan, 97–98

Adieu to Emmanuel Levinas (Derrida), 49, 120, 122–23, 199, 238n41

Adorno, Theodor, 112, 116, 127, 239n58

Against Ethics (Caputo), 172

Agamben, Giorgio, 101, 102

Ahlan wa sahlan, 108–9

Akiba, Rabbi, 234n61

"À la pointe acérée" (Celan), 64

Algerian elections of 1991–1992, 91–94

alterity. *See* Other, the

Althusser, Louis, 81

ana-theism: ana-theistic God, 205, 211, 212; atheistic messianicity comes close to, 208;

Derrida does not take step to, 202, 207; Derrida's atheism contrasted with, 206; Derrida's influence on, 10; Levinas and, 200–1; question of Derrida's as moot, 29–30

Anatheism: Returning to God after God (Kearney), 178

Anidjar, Gil, 95, 102, 216n39, 233n34

Anselm of Canterbury, Saint, 168

"Anti-Semitism and Existentialism" (Levinas), 41, 221n11

apocalyptic time, 165–66

"Aporias, Ways and Voices" (Derrida), 203

aporias: Derrida's employment of, 4, 72; of the gift, 160; openness associated with, 108; of philosophical modernity for Habermas, 115; philosophy as consisting of, 130; Socrates on, 110; three aporetic places, 88

Aporias (Derrida), 54, 55, 95, 217n9

Aristotle, 93, 101, 105

assimilation, 42–43, 57, 58

atheism: absolute immunity denied by traditional, 186–87; ana-theism contrasted with Derrida's, 206; ascetic, 152; binary of theism and, 153, 172, 180; Birault on, 79, 227n12; classical, 168–69; deconstructive, 206, 207; Derrida and messianic, 199–212; Derrida's attitude toward religion contrasted with, 13; Derrida's "passing as an atheist," 5–7, 87, 169, 172–73, 199–200, 211, 212, 243n11, 248n75; of early Heidegger, 77, 78; on finitude as originary, 76, 77; as

atheism (*cont.*)
interwoven in religion, 5–6; *khora* as
atheistic, 205; Levinas on messianism
and, 200–1; Marranos associated with,
95; mystical, 201; new, 178; question
of Derrida's as moot, 29–30; religion
without religion and Derrida's, 176; of
Sartre, 73, 79, 81. *See also* radical atheism
Augustine, Saint: *Confessions*, 154, 172, 173,
249n78; Derrida's engagement with, 5;
on desire for perishable things, 168, 169;
dualism of, 12, 153, 154, 161, 167, 173,
174, 180; on God as the name of what we
hope for, 205; immaterialism of, 155; on
problem of evil, 181
Austin, J. L., 20
authenticity: Hegel on Abraham's, 139;
Heidegger on, 44, 47, 51; for Jews, 41,
51, 55, 57; of work of art, 116
autoimmunity, 178–98; autoimmune
community, 195; and co-implication
of openness and closure, 193; and
deconstruction, 154–55; democratic,
92, 93, 105; Derrida on, 184; Hägglund
employs in name of radical atheism,
169; and logic of time, 152, 183–84; no
reliable prophylaxis against, 255n65;
radical atheism associated with, 153; and
radical evil, 182, 183; in reinvention of
religion, 154; relation between conditional
and unconditional as autoimmune, 186;
of survival, 184, 196, 197
l'à venir (to-come), 165–67, 247n52
"Avowing" (Derrida), 59

Bachelard, Suzanne, 2
Badiou, Alain, 60
Baring, Edward, 10, 238n36
Beaufret, Jean, 73, 74, 82
Beckett, Samuel, 207
"Becoming Possible of the Impossible, The"
(Dooley), 248n71, 249n76, 250n84,
250n85
Being and Nothingness (Sartre), 41
Being and Time (Heidegger), 16, 19, 44, 51,
77, 118
"Being, the Divine, and the Gods in
Heidegger" (Birault), 82
Beiträge zur Philosophie: Vom Ereignis
(Heidegger), 125
Benjamin, Walter, 118, 205, 206, 207
Bennington, Geoffrey, 98, 172
Bergson, Henri, 13, 31
"Beschneide das Wort" (Celan), 66
Birault, Henri: on atheism, 79, 227n12; on
Being and God, 83–85; "Being, the
Divine, and the Gods in Heidegger,"
78, 82; *christianité* and *christianisme*
contrasted by, 228n35; on continuity of

early and later Heidegger, 77; Derrida
influenced by, 74, 80, 81, 83; on error, 76;
on faith, 86; on finitude, 74, 75, 83; on
God's singularity, 228n33; "Heidegger
and the Thought of Finitude," 74, 78, 79;
on Heidegger on *Endlichkeit*, 77–78, 79;
in introduction of Heidegger into France,
73–74; on Kierkegaard's idea of God, 78,
228n34; negative theology in texts of, 87;
"Nietzsche et le pari de Pascal," 85; on
Nietzsche on Being and God, 83–84, 85,
86; on non-Being, 74–75; on ontological
difference, 78, 227n31; as resistant to
dogmatism, 86; on the sacred, 78
Birnbaum, Pierre, 221n11
Blanchot, Maurice, 19, 27
Boehme, Jakob, 173
Book of Questions, The (Jabès), 62, 64–65
Bouretz, Pierre, 111
Brandom, Robert, 129
Brassier, Ray, 172, 246n42
Brown, Wendy, 232n16, 235n83
Brunschvicg, Léon, 21

Caputo, John: *Against Ethics*, 172; on
deconstruction, 179, 188, 191, 251n11;
Hägglund responds to, 179–80, 185–92,
195–96, 252n25; Kearney on, 205; on
Marrano, 95; *The Prayers and Tears of
Jacques Derrida*, 9, 165–66, 169, 170,
172–73, 174, 248n71, 248n75, 249n83,
254n53; *Radical Hermeneutics*, 172; on
radical messianicity, 202; on religion
without dogmatism, 215n30; on religion
without religion, 6; on unprotected
religion, 12; at Villanova discussion of
1997, 208, 209; on violence of religion,
178, 179; on weak God, 8, 171, 173–76,
179, 188, 189; *The Weakness of God: A
Theology of the Event*, 157, 173–76, 188,
248n71
Cartesian Meditations (Husserl), 243n9
Cavell, Stanley, 20, 26, 34
Celan, Paul, 62–63; "À la pointe acérée," 64;
analogy between rabbi and poet in work
of, 61; "Beschneide das Wort," 66; "Einem,
der vor der Tür Stand," 64; and Heidegger,
124; messianic speech of poetry of, 66;
Die Niemandsrose, 61
Celestial Hierarchy (Pseudo-Dionysius), 26
Cendres (Derrida), 199
Certeau, Michel de, 19
Cherubinic Wanderer, The (Silesius), 26
Chrétien, Jean-Louis, 176
Christianity: Abraham and Christ contrasted,
141–42; Birault contrasts *christianité* and
christianisme, 228n35; circumcision sets
Jews and Muslims apart from, 98, 102;
democracy linked to, 90; Derrida and

Christian Heideggerianism, 10, 72–87; the event of Christ, 149; Hegel on, 148–49; incarnate God in, 91; Kierkegaard on, 148–49; Kierkegaard on Abraham and, 146; Levinas on modern world as essentially Christian, 43

circumcision, 61, 62, 63–64, 67, 98–100, 102

"Circumfession" (Derrida), 9, 98–100, 104, 154, 176, 199, 200, 249n78

Cixous, Hélène, 100, 177, 233n47

"Cogito and the History of Madness" (Derrida), 219n38

Cohen, Joseph, 11

Cohn-Bendit, Daniel, 69

Colloque des Intellectuels Juifs de langue Française, 59

Confessions (Augustine), 154, 172, 173, 249n78

Corbin, Henry, 119

covenant, 66, 67

Crockett, Clayton, 154, 155

Damian, Peter, 171

Dawkins, Richard, 178

"Death of God": Altizer's interest in Derrida, 6; anatheism versus, 207; Derrida on Christianity and, 230n73; finitude and, 76; Nietzsche on, 84, 112; radical theology versus, 170, 171; Taylor on deconstruction and, 214n15

decision, 259n43

deconstruction: in American literary studies, 3; and a priori arguments against, 168, 247n60; as at odds with religion, 5, 153; and autoimmunity, 154–55; being-Jewish is the experience of, 54; as blind reading in the dark, 256n12; for breaking down exclusionary walls, 10; Caputo on, 179, 188, 191, 251n11; criticism of, 12; "Deconstruction and the Possibility of Justice" conference, 18, 217n7; in Derrida's *Of Grammatology*, 2, 4; descriptive versus prescriptive views of, 161–65, 191; for de-sedimenting our most sedimented concepts, 153; as disciplinarily nomadic, 3; early formulations of, 72; ethics of, 11, 230n79; as experience of the impossible, 167, 170; as forever haunted by metaphysics, 130; and grace of God, 230n75; Habermas on, 113, 114–15, 116, 118; Hägglund's abridgments and alterations of, 156–69; and Heidegger's *Destruktion*, 116; hermeneutics distinguished from, 209, 211; as hyper-realism, 156; Jewishness associated with, 9–10, 60; Judeo-Christian heritage in, 216n38; Kearney on, 257n28; of literature and philosophy,

4, 118; logic in, 176; messianic effects of, 207–8; negative theology associated with, 6–7, 8, 170, 251n11; "openness of the future is worth more" as axiom of, 164, 191; as openness to the other, 207, 208, 258n31; opens structure of experience, 172; radical atheism associated with, 152–53, 155, 179–80; realism of, 155–56; and/or religion, 17–18; reopens and reinvents religion, 155; resistance to antithesis of genuine and false, 6–7; saves us from being saved, 176; secularization distinguished from, 35; skepticism of, 87; slippage into apophatic-kataphatic discourse, 27; in sphere of future active participle, 165; as structured like a prayer, 165, 170; Taylor's use of, 169–70; as theory of responsibility, 163, 198; the undeconstructible, 15, 157–58; of Western metaphysics, 4. See also *khora*

Deleuze, Gilles, 13, 172, 173

De l'existence à l'existant (Levinas), 222n38, 223n60

democracy: in Algeria, 91–94, 106, 108; as deferred, 93, 94, 104; democratic autoimmunity, 92, 93, 105; democratic desire, 158; democratic rogues, 94, 95; democratic sovereignty, 91, 92; Derrida on "democracy to come," 11, 60, 69, 109; European commitment to, 90; al Farabi and, 93; friendship associated with, 104; Islam seen as Other of, 88, 89–95; liberalism versus, 94; secularization associated with, 90, 92, 93, 231n9; universalism associated with, 108

Derrida, Jacques

atheism of: ana-theism contrasted with, 206; and messianic atheism, 199–212; as moot question, 29–30; as "passing as an atheist," 5–7, 87, 169, 172–73, 187, 199–200, 211, 212, 243n11, 248n75; and radical atheism, 29, 34, 82, 169, 184–85, 196–97; and religion without religion, 176; religious atheism attributed to, 6; as strategic, 87

biography: background of, 2, 10, 39; Cambridge University honorary degree controversy, 3; circumcision of, 98–100; death of, 89; early life in Algeria, 97; education, 2, 39; expulsion from school, 39, 199; French citizenship revoked in 1940, 9; teaching career of, 2; as traveler, 96

and Islam and Arab world, 88–109; on Algerian elections of 1991–1992, 91–94; Algerian immigrants compared with, 97; denial of his Arab heritage, 97–98; Ishmael in works of, 104; Islam disavowed by, 10, 89, 95, 105–6, 109

Derrida, Jacques (*cont.*)
and Judaism: on being Jewish, 48–58; born
into Jewish family, 2, 10, 39; at Colloque
des Intellectuels Juifs de langue Française,
59; on constitutive dissymmetry in Jewish
identity, 51–52, 53, 56, 57–58;
engagement with Jewish textual tradition,
12, 130, 238n36, 240n59; on Jewish
election, 50–51, 53, 54, 62, 69, 71;
Judéités: Questions pour Jacques Derrida
conference, 111, 124, 241n5; as "last of
the Jews," 8–10, 19, 56, 71, 199; in second
generation of post-Holocaust world, 39;
sees himself as a Marrano, 95, 96, 98
and other thinkers: Adorno, 116, 239n58;
Birault, 74, 80, 81, 83; Cixous, 100, 177;
Habermas, 110–31; Heidegger, 10, 73, 81,
119; Husserl, 4, 73, 119; Levinas as cited
by, 59–60; Levinas contrasted with,
39–40; Levinas as influence on, 10, 49,
52, 54–56, 57–58, 61; Levinas in
"Violence and Metaphysics," 7, 27,
120–21, 199; Marx, 4; Nietzsche, 5, 50,
52, 83; Rancière misreads his relation to
Levinas, 60–61; Schmitt, 90, 92, 101
philosophical views of: aporia in method of,
4; on "as if" and political identity, 61, 69;
on autoimmunity, 184; on *l'à venir*
(to-come), 165–67, 247n52; closings as
preoccupation of, 108; on contamination
of transcendental and empirical, 15;
criticism of, 3; on democracy to come,
11, 60, 69, 109; on desire, 158–60, 180,
187–88; destructive element of thought
of, 214n19; on economy of violence,
193–94; ethics of, 162; and existentialism,
81, 238n36; on finitude, 79–81, 194;
grafts poetry onto philosophy, 171–72;
"grammatological opening" in thought of,
87; irrationalism attributed to, 237n26;
on iteration, 20–24, 27–29, 33, 37, 153,
218n19; and linguistic philosophy,
228n37; on living on, 152, 174; logic of
time of, 152, 183–84; as materialist, 151,
155, 156; open-ended critical practice of,
115–16; on the Other, 121–22, 125; on
the otobiographical, 107; philosophy and
literature distinguished, 116–18; on the
poet, 61–62; on the promise, 189, 192;
on radical evil, 180–83; on Rousseauian
nostalgia versus Nietzschean forgetting,
85–86; on salutations, 108; seen as
French Nietzschean, 83; on sovereignty,
90–91, 232n16; on speech privileged over
writing, 4; strategies for reading texts as
emphasis of, 3–4; "turns" in philosophy,
3, 11, 14, 72, 120, 123, 124, 153, 162,
179, 237n32; on the ultra-transcendental,
160–61, 162, 163, 164, 166; on

unconditionals, 156–57, 184, 186, 190,
191–93; on the undeconstructible, 15,
157–58
religious views of: on Being and God, 82,
87; and Christian Heideggerianism, 10,
72–87; on "death of God," 230n73;
diversity of texts treating religion, 11;
draws on resources from several religions,
2; on faith, 86, 182–83, 203; God effaced
in philosophy of, 87; on God and the
impossible, 250n85; God as understood
by, 7–8; on idea of the unscathed and
religion, 180, 182, 184; indeterminacy
of his relation to religion, 2; as infinitely
close to and at infinite remove from
religion, 13; on literary transformation of
religious figure, 66–68, 69; on Luke 9:60,
249n83; as "man of prayers and tears,"
9; meaning of "and" in "Derrida and
Religion," 14–20; messianism as
conceived by, 129, 130–31, 194, 196, 201,
202; on moving from messianicity to
messianism, 208–9; and negative
theology, 6–7, 19, 170, 176, 203, 214n16,
248n75; and Nietzschean antireligious
tradition, 5; philosophy and religion
cohabit in writings of, 15; on prophecy,
207–8; provocation of his engagement
with religion, 1; as radical theist, 32;
religion without religion of, 6, 86, 153,
154, 170, 173, 176, 179, 202, 205, 206,
257n25; stance of belonging without
belonging to a tradition, 14; on two
sources of religion, 171; two ways of
thinking about religion and, 169–70;
writing insists on deep significance of
theological archive, 22
works: "Abraham, the Other," 40, 49–50,
53, 55, 56, 68, 135; *Adieu to Emmanuel
Levinas*, 49, 120, 122–23, 199, 238n41;
"Aporias, Ways and Voices," 203; *Aporias*,
54, 55, 95, 217n9; "Avowing," 59;
Cendres, 199; "Circumfession," 9, 98–100,
104, 154, 176, 199, 200, 249n78;
"Différance," 21, 27; "Edmond Jabès and
the Question of the Book," 62, 64–65,
81; "The Ends of Man," 83; "Force and
Signification," 8, 83; "The Force of Law,"
157, 248n71; *Given Time I: Counterfeit
Money*, 244n26; *Given Time to Psyché*,
244n34; *Glas*, 161, 245n38; "Hospitality,
Justice and Responsibility," 202; "How to
Avoid Speaking: Denials," 26, 27, 72;
introduction to Husserl's *Origin of
Geometry*, 8, 80, 82, 245n39; "Khora,"
257n14; *Learning to Live Finally*, 37;
Literature in Secret, 59, 66–67, 68;
Margins of Philosophy, 20, 21, 118, 217n9;
Memoirs of the Blind, 203; *Monolingualism*

Judaism (*cont.*)
central themes of, 138; circumcision,
61, 62, 63–64, 67, 98–100, 102;
deconstruction associated with
Jewishness, 9–10, 60; Derrida as "last
of the Jews," 9, 19, 56, 71, 199; Derrida
on being Jewish, 48–58; Derrida's
identification with, 2, 8–10, 12, 39,
238n36; exemplarism, 50, 51, 52–55, 57,
223n68; as faith and ethnicity, 95; figure
of the Jew in Derrida's political model, 61;
finitude in, 75–76, 227n13; Habermas on
Derrida's religious inheritance, 130,
240n59; Hegel's *The Spirit of Judaism*,
136–38; incarnate God rejected by, 91;
the Jew as the Other, 41, 60; Judéités:
Questions pour Jacques Derrida
conference, 111, 124, 241n5; Kabbalah,
26, 36; Levinas on being-Jewish, 42–48,
70; Marranos, 55–58, 70–71, 95–96, 97,
98; May 1968 demonstrators as all
German Jews, 69, 71; and modernity, 40,
42, 43; ontology of being Jewish, 39–58;
philosophical thought reappropriates
Hebraism, 135–36; poets and Jews
compared, 61–62; rabbis, 61, 62–65, 71;
Shema, 102, 103, 234n61; travel as central
to experience of, 96; Wandering Jew, 96.
See also Abraham; election; Holocaust
Judaken, Jonathan, 41
Judéités: Questions pour Jacques Derrida
(conference), 111, 124, 241n5
justice: calls for laws, 159; in economy of
violence, 193, 194; and the good,
188; passion for, 194, 195–96; as
unconditional, 192; as undeconstructible,
157–58

Kabbalah, 26, 36
Kafka, Franz, 40–41, 68, 80
"Kafka, a Jewish Writer" (Sartre), 40–41,
221n9, 221n10
Kant, Immanuel: on antinomies of reason,
169; on enlightened age versus age of
enlightenment, 131; on ideals, 157;
Meillassoux's correlationism on, 151;
on radical evil, 180–81; *Religionbuch*,
246n42; *Religion within the Limits of
Reason Alone*, 36, 181; on space and time,
161; on the sublime, 136; on thinking
versus knowledge, 159; on transcendental
illusion, 160
Kearney, Richard, 8, 10–11, 178–79
Keller, Catherine, 216n40
Kepel, Gilles, 94
Khomeini, Ayatollah Ruhollah, 89, 231n7
khora, 106–8; belongs to the desert, 98, 108;
deconstruction and, 18; God and, 203–5,
210–12, 259n46; messianic faith without

messianism and, 36; *qara'a* compared
with, 106, 107; radical atheism of, 210
"Khora" (Derrida), 257n14
Kierkegaard, Søren: on Abraham, 66, 100,
134, 143–47, 149, 162, 260n56; on
Christianity, 148–49; on decision, 34;
and Derrida, 5, 129; either/or, 205; on
ethics, 121, 143–44; existentialism of,
118, 121; *Fear and Trembling*, 146; God
for, 78, 228n34; Hegel distinguished
from, 147–50; humor of, 174; Levinas's
critique of, 246n42; on messianism, 147;
on the Other, 121, 125–28; on sacrifice,
143–44, 147; and suspension of the
ethical, 164
Kleinberg, Ethan, 10
Klemm, David, 214n19

laïklik, 92
language: event of, 28, 29; failure to secure
stable meaning, 6; idea of stable reality
independent of, 5; metaphysics and, 19,
23; as never fully ours, 9; Nietzsche on,
83; performatives, 166, 191–93; poet's
relation to, 61; proper names and system
of, 16; Saussure's *langue–parole*
distinction, 25. *See also* logocentrism;
metaphor; names; speech; writing
langue–parole distinction, 25
Laruelle, François, 172, 246n42, 249n79
"Last Farewell" (Habermas), 130–31
Lavalle, Louis, 73
Learning to Live Finally (Derrida), 37
Le Senne, René, 73
Letter on Humanism (Heidegger), 77, 78, 125
Levinas, Emmanuel: on Abraham, 133; on *à
Dieu/adieu*, 19; "Anti-Semitism and
Existentialism," 41, 221n11; on asking
forgiveness to speak of God, 59, 68; on
atheism, 200–1; background of, 39; on
being Jewish, 42–48, 70; at Colloque des
Intellectuels Juifs de langue Française, 59;
death of, 49, 120; in debate on Derrida
and religion, 11; *De l'existence à l'existant*,
222n38, 223n60; Derrida absorbs themes
from thought of, 122; and Derrida on
Jewishness, 10, 49, 52, 54–56, 57–58,
61; Derrida's "Abraham, the Other" as
engagement with, 40; Derrida's *Adieu to
Emmanuel Levinas*, 49, 120, 122–23, 199,
238n41; Derrida's citation of, 59–60;
Derrida's *Literature in Secret* and, 66–67;
in Derrida's "Violence and Metaphysics,"
7, 27, 120–21, 199; empiricism of, 122;
ethical commitment to *visage d'autrui* as
trace of God, 206–7; ethics of submission
and, 253n52; *Être-Juif*, 39, 40, 41, 42–45,
47; in first generation of post-Holocaust
world, 39; geographical and cultural gulf

between Derrida and, 39–40; on giving up the kingdom to get the kingdom, 210; Habermas on his influence on Derrida, 239n58; in Habermas's earlier assessment of Derrida, 114; in Habermas's later assessment of Derrida, 123–29; Heidegger and, 19, 44–45, 123; on Heidegger's ontology as totalizing, 120–21, 123; on Hitlerian anti-Semitism, 47; on the Infinite, 26, 121; on irrecusability, 164; on Jewish election, 10, 43, 44, 45–47, 50, 52–53, 56, 61, 67, 68, 69, 70; Judaism becomes central to philosophy of, 45–46; Kierkegaard critiqued by, 246n42; on literature, 65–66; on messianism, 199, 200–1; on modern world as essentially Christian, 43; "On Escape," 44; on the Other, 45, 120–22, 123, 200–1; prison notebooks of, 44–45, 46, 221n38; as prisoner of war, 44, 48, 221n35, 245n42; question of *tout autre*, 245n42; Rancière misreads Derrida's relation to, 60–61; "Reflections on the Philosophy of Hitlerism," 44; "The Temptation of Temptation," 45–46, 49, 52; *Totality and Infinity*, 16, 26, 199, 200, 223n60; "To the Other," 65; on trace, 27; Western philosophical tradition reevaluated by, 45

Lévi-Strauss, Claude, 7, 86, 246n43

Limited Inc (Derrida): on graphematic drift, 25–26; on the *iterum*, 14, 20–24, 27–29, 252n23; on substituting writing for God, 28–34

literature: Derrida on literary transformation of religious figure, 66–68, 69; Levinas on, 65–66; philosophy distinguished from, 116–18; and religion, 65–68. *See also* poetry

Literature in Secret (Derrida), 59, 66–67, 68

Logical Investigations (Husserl), 22

logocentrism: Habermas on critique of, 118; of Hägglund's *Radical Atheism*, 176; negative theology associated with, 7; Western metaphysics associated with, 4

Luke 9:60, 249n83

Magliola, Robert, 214n19

maieutics, 110

Malabou, Catherine, 156

Mallarmé, Stéphane, 161

Marcuse, Herbert, 205

Margins of Philosophy (Derrida), 20, 21, 118, 217n9

Marion, Jean-Luc, 20, 154, 171, 248n70

Marranos, 55–58, 70–71, 95–96, 97, 98

martyrdom, 103, 234n61

Marx, Karl, 4, 28

McDowell, John, 16

Meditations (Descartes), 14, 20–21, 27–29, 31, 32

Meillassoux, Quentin, 151, 161, 172

Memoirs of the Blind (Derrida), 203

Merleau-Ponty, Maurice, 172

messianism: Abrahamic, 199, 209; ana-theist disposition involves, 205; Celan's messianic speech, 66; deconstruction's messianic effects, 207–8; Derrida absorbs from Levinas's thought, 122, 123; and Derrida on being Jewish, 52; Derrida and messianic atheism, 199–212; Derrida's conception of, 129, 130–31, 194, 196, 201, 202; of the event, 146, 147, 148; Habermas on, 129, 131; Hegel on, 147; Kierkegaard on, 147; Levinas on atheism and, 200–1; in Levinas's account of being Jewish, 48; martyrdom associated with, 103; messianic faith, 36, 203; messianic peace, 186, 195–96, 206; messianic time, 165–66; "messianic without messianism," 11, 36, 101, 127, 131, 195, 206; moving from messianicity to, 208–9; no to-come without messianic memory, 37; of presence, 147–48; radical messianicity, 202; weak, 206; without religion, 194, 206

metaphor: Derrida on translating traditional concepts into metaphorical concepts, 23; in Heidegger, 119; and philosophical thinking, 4, 118; subordination to reason, 116

Metz, Johann Baptist, 173

Milbank, John, 6, 214n19

Miller, J. Hillis, 205

Mind and World (McDowell), 16

Minimal Theologies (de Vries), 19

modernist art, 116

Mohel, 63–64

Monolingualism of the Other (Derrida), 9, 61

monotheism: clears path to the Enlightenment, 115; Derrida's ethical loyalty to, 125; Derrida's monotheism of the "event," 129; Heidegger goes back beyond beginnings of, 114; Heidegger's notion of the event and, 127; three Abrahamic religions, 100, 102

Montaigne, Michel de, 99

Moses, 53, 56

Moses and Monotheism (Freud), 53

Munier, Roger, 73

Mustafa, Farouk, 108

Mystical Theology (Pseudo-Dionysius), 26

mysticism. *See* negative theology

Naas, Michael, 151

names: Derrida's "Faith and Knowledge" on, 16, 24; divine, 17, 19, 21–38, 201; insufficiency of, 31; negative theology on divine transcendence beyond, 203; speaking the unspeakable, 37

Perspectives in Continental Philosophy
John D. Caputo, series editor

Karl Jaspers, *The Question of German Guilt*. Introduction by Joseph W. Koterski, S.J.

Jean-Luc Marion, *The Idol and Distance: Five Studies*. Translated with an introduction by Thomas A. Carlson.

Jeffrey Dudiak, *The Intrigue of Ethics: A Reading of the Idea of Discourse in the Thought of Emmanuel Levinas*.

Robyn Horner, *Rethinking God as Gift: Marion, Derrida, and the Limits of Phenomenology*.

Mark Dooley, *The Politics of Exodus: Søren Kierkegaard's Ethics of Responsibility*.

Merold Westphal, *Overcoming Onto-Theology: Toward a Postmodern Christian Faith*.

Edith Wyschogrod, Jean-Joseph Goux, and Eric Boynton, eds., *The Enigma of Gift and Sacrifice*.

Stanislas Breton, *The Word and the Cross*. Translated with an introduction by Jacquelyn Porter.

Jean-Luc Marion, *Prolegomena to Charity*. Translated by Stephen E. Lewis.

Peter H. Spader, *Scheler's Ethical Personalism: Its Logic, Development, and Promise*.

Jean-Louis Chrétien, *The Unforgettable and the Unhoped For*. Translated by Jeffrey Bloechl.

Don Cupitt, *Is Nothing Sacred? The Non-Realist Philosophy of Religion: Selected Essays*.

Jean-Luc Marion, *In Excess: Studies of Saturated Phenomena*. Translated by Robyn Horner and Vincent Berraud.

Phillip Goodchild, *Rethinking Philosophy of Religion: Approaches from Continental Philosophy*.

William J. Richardson, S.J., *Heidegger: Through Phenomenology to Thought*.

Jeffrey Andrew Barash, *Martin Heidegger and the Problem of Historical Meaning*.

Jean-Louis Chrétien, *Hand to Hand: Listening to the Work of Art*. Translated by Stephen E. Lewis.

Jean-Louis Chrétien, *The Call and the Response*. Translated with an introduction by Anne Davenport.

D. C. Schindler, *Han Urs von Balthasar and the Dramatic Structure of Truth: A Philosophical Investigation*.

Julian Wolfreys, ed., *Thinking Difference: Critics in Conversation*.

Allen Scult, *Being Jewish/Reading Heidegger: An Ontological Encounter*.

Richard Kearney, *Debates in Continental Philosophy: Conversations with Contemporary Thinkers*.

Jennifer Anna Gosetti-Ferencei, *Heidegger, Hölderlin, and the Subject of Poetic Language: Toward a New Poetics of Dasein*.

Jolita Pons, *Stealing a Gift: Kierkegaard's Pseudonyms and the Bible*.

Jean-Yves Lacoste, *Experience and the Absolute: Disputed Questions on the Humanity of Man*. Translated by Mark Raftery-Skehan.

Charles P. Bigger, *Between* Chora *and the Good: Metaphor's Metaphysical Neighborhood*.

Dominique Janicaud, *Phenomenology "Wide Open": After the French Debate.* Translated by Charles N. Cabral.

Ian Leask and Eoin Cassidy, eds., *Givenness and God: Questions of Jean-Luc Marion.*

Jacques Derrida, *Sovereignties in Question: The Poetics of Paul Celan.* Edited by Thomas Dutoit and Outi Pasanen.

William Desmond, *Is There a Sabbath for Thought? Between Religion and Philosophy.*

Bruce Ellis Benson and Norman Wirzba, eds., *The Phenomenology of Prayer.*

S. Clark Buckner and Matthew Statler, eds., *Styles of Piety: Practicing Philosophy after the Death of God.*

Kevin Hart and Barbara Wall, eds., *The Experience of God: A Postmodern Response.*

John Panteleimon Manoussakis, *After God: Richard Kearney and the Religious Turn in Continental Philosophy.*

John Martis, *Philippe Lacoue-Labarthe: Representation and the Loss of the Subject.*

Jean-Luc Nancy, *The Ground of the Image.*

Edith Wyschogrod, *Crossover Queries: Dwelling with Negatives, Embodying Philosophy's Others.*

Gerald Bruns, *On the Anarchy of Poetry and Philosophy: A Guide for the Unruly.*

Brian Treanor, *Aspects of Alterity: Levinas, Marcel, and the Contemporary Debate.*

Simon Morgan Wortham, *Counter-Institutions: Jacques Derrida and the Question of the University.*

Leonard Lawlor, *The Implications of Immanence: Toward a New Concept of Life.*

Clayton Crockett, *Interstices of the Sublime: Theology and Psychoanalytic Theory.*

Bettina Bergo, Joseph Cohen, and Raphael Zagury-Orly, eds., *Judeities: Questions for Jacques Derrida.* Translated by Bettina Bergo and Michael B. Smith.

Jean-Luc Marion, *On the Ego and on God: Further Cartesian Questions.* Translated by Christina M. Gschwandtner.

Jean-Luc Nancy, *Philosophical Chronicles.* Translated by Franson Manjali.

Jean-Luc Nancy, *Dis-Enclosure: The Deconstruction of Christianity.* Translated by Bettina Bergo, Gabriel Malenfant, and Michael B. Smith.

Andrea Hurst, *Derrida Vis-à-vis Lacan: Interweaving Deconstruction and Psychoanalysis.*

Jean-Luc Nancy, *Noli me tangere: On the Raising of the Body.* Translated by Sarah Clift, Pascale-Anne Brault, and Michael Naas.

Jacques Derrida, *The Animal That Therefore I Am.* Edited by Marie-Louise Mallet, translated by David Wills.

Jean-Luc Marion, *The Visible and the Revealed.* Translated by Christina M. Gschwandtner and others.

Michel Henry, *Material Phenomenology.* Translated by Scott Davidson.

Jean-Luc Nancy, *Corpus.* Translated by Richard A. Rand.

Joshua Kates, *Fielding Derrida.*

Sarah LaChance Adams and Caroline R. Lundquist, eds., *Coming to Life: Philosophies of Pregnancy, Childbirth, and Mothering.*

Thomas Claviez, ed., *The Conditions of Hospitality: Ethics, Politics, and Aesthetics on the Threshold of the Possible.*

Roland Faber and Jeremy Fackenthal, eds., *Theopoetic Folds: Philosophizing Multifariousness.*

Jean-Luc Marion, *The Essential Writings.* Edited by Kevin Hart.

Adam S. Miller, *Speculative Grace: Bruno Latour and Object-Oriented Theology.* Foreword by Levi R. Bryant.

Jean-Luc Nancy, *Corpus II: Writings on Sexuality.*

David Nowell Smith, *Sounding/Silence: Martin Heidegger at the Limits of Poetics.*

Gregory C. Stallings, Manuel Asensi, and Carl Good, eds., *Material Spirit: Religion and Literature Intranscendent.*

Claude Romano, *Event and Time.* Translated by Stephen E. Lewis.

Frank Chouraqui, *Ambiguity and the Absolute: Nietzsche and Merleau-Ponty on the Question of Truth.*

Noëlle Vahanian, *The Rebellious No: Variations on a Secular Theology of Language.*

Michael Naas, *The End of the World and Other Teachable Moments: Jacques Derrida's Final Seminar.*

Jean-Louis Chrétien, *Under the Gaze of the Bible.* Translated by John Marson Dunaway.

Edward Baring and Peter E. Gordon, eds., *The Trace of God: Derrida and Religion.*

Vanessa Lemm, ed., *Nietzsche and the Becoming of Life.*

Aaron T. Looney, *Vladimir Jankélévitch: The Time of Forgiveness.*

Robert Mugerauer, *Responding to Loss: Heideggerian Reflections on Literature, Architecture, and Film.*